Drawing for Science Education

Drawing for Science Education

An International Perspective

Edited by

Phyllis Katz
University of Maryland, USA

SENSE PUBLISHERS
ROTTERDAM/BOSTON/TAIPEI

A C.I.P. record for this book is available from the Library of Congress.

ISBN: 978-94-6300-873-0 (paperback)
ISBN: 978-94-6300-874-7 (hardback)
ISBN: 978-94-6300-875-4 (e-book)

Published by: Sense Publishers,
P.O. Box 21858,
3001 AW Rotterdam,
The Netherlands
https://www.sensepublishers.com/

Printed on acid-free paper

All Rights Reserved © 2017 Sense Publishers

No part of this work may be reproduced, stored in a retrieval system, or transmitted in any form or by any means, electronic, mechanical, photocopying, microfilming, recording or otherwise, without written permission from the Publisher, with the exception of any material supplied specifically for the purpose of being entered and executed on a computer system, for exclusive use by the purchaser of the work.

TABLE OF CONTENTS

Preface and Acknowledgements — vii

1. Introduction: Drawing and Science Are Inseparable: Drawing is a Human Expression for Teaching/Learning — 1
Phyllis Katz

Section One: Drawing a Single Image

2. Draw Your Physics Homework? Art as a Path to Understanding and Assessment in Undergraduate Science Education — 11
Jatila van der Veen

3. Reflective Drawings as Means for Depicting ICTs Roles in Science and Engineering Learning in the 21st Century — 31
Miri Barak

4. Can I Get Directions to My Kidneys Please? Social Interactions as a Source of Knowledge of Internal Anatomy — 41
Patricia Patrick

5. Development of Biological Literacy through Drawing Organisms — 55
Amauri Betini Bartoszeck and Sue Dale Tunnicliffe

6. Anatomic Drawing for Medical Education — 67
Gary Wind

7. Learning from Children's Drawings of Nature — 73
Amy Dai

8. The Understanding of Human Anatomy Elicited from Drawings of Some Bangladeshi Village Women and Children — 87
Sue Dale Tunnicliffe and Angshuman Sarker

Section Two: Drawings in a Series to Examine Change

9. Drawing Experiences in Marine Conservation — 97
Jill Cainey, Lauren Humphrey and Rob Bowker

10. Discovering Children's Science Associations Utilizing Drawings — 111
Susanne Neumann and Martin Hopf

11. Using Drawings to Demonstrate Informal Science Learning Experiences through the Contextual Model of Learning — 123
Katrina Roseler and Michael Dentzau

12. Appropriate Integration of Children's Drawings in the Acquisition of Science Concepts — 135
Ni Chang

13. Changes in Children's Knowledge about Their Internal Anatomy between First and Ninth Grades — 147
Michèle Stears and Edith Roslyn Dempster

14. Learning Physics at Science Centers: Use of Visitors' Drawings to Investigate Learning at an Interactive Sound Exhibit — 155
Terrence McClafferty and Léonie Rennie

Section Three: Drawings That Illustrate the Perceived Culture of Science (Who and What)

15. The Evolution of the Analysis of the Draw-a-Scientist Test: What Children's Illustrations of Scientists Tell Us and Why Educators Should Listen — 171
Donna Farland-Smith

16. Using Drawing to Reveal Science Teachers' Beliefs about Science Teaching — 179
Sulaiman Al-Balushi and Abdullah Ambusaidi

TABLE OF CONTENTS

17. Primary School Students' Views on Science and Scientists 191
Sinan Özgelen

18. Understanding the Meanings Secondary Biology Students Construct Around Science through Drawings 205
Jeremy F. Price

Section Four: Drawings to Consider the Illustrator's Identity Development as a Science Teacher

19. Drawings as Identity Data in Elementary Science Teacher Education 219
Felicia Moore Mensah and Robin Fleshman

20. Drawings to Improve Inclusive Science Teaching: A Teacher's Action Research Narrative 227
Shiellah Keletso

21. Using Drawings to Examine Prospective Elementary Teachers' Moral Reasoning about Climate Change 235
J. Randy McGinnis and Emily Hestness

22. Preservice High School Science Teacher Identity: Using Drawing Enhanced Learning Monographs 247
David Winter and Chris Astall

About the Contributors 263

Index 269

PREFACE AND ACKNOWLEDGEMENTS

I began to think about a book on the use of drawing in science education when I gave a presentation at a conference about how I used drawings for research in the science enrichment program I headed. It elicited heated criticism about the degree of inference in interpretation. Having majored in English during my first round of higher education, I knew I had spent many hours interpreting words and their implications. With fellow students I argued the meanings of phrases by Shakespeare, Milton and James Joyce interpreting the word images. I also developed a healthy respect for punctuation (we could say, graphical clues) as more than linguistic rules from tormenting grammarians. Those small commas could certainly help clarify meanings. One humorous example is the difference between, "Let's eat Grandma," or "Let's eat, Grandma." As a consequence of my language studies, I found these challenges about excessive inference in the use of drawing data curious. I understood all human communication as inferential in its interpretations, colored by context, gesture and tone. Meanings come from an interaction between the observer and a phenomenon interacting within a culture. Reviewing the literature on the historic use of drawings in teaching and learning science I was struck by how pervasive and important this method of information sharing has been. And yet there was a disconnection between modern science education and the use or study of drawing. There has been some renaissance with the influence of graphical interfaces from computers, but there was little evidence that drawing was valued, taught, or encouraged among the skills of science or science education research. The increased use of verbal/literary communication had taken center stage. When science education developed in the late 19th century drawing skills were a part of the school curricula. Students were expected to be able to illustrate their observations. Drawing faded as the 20th century progressed. Cameras became readily available and affordable. Standardized short answer testing was an efficient way to compare results for individuals and across countries. Curricula became crowded with new study areas. However drawing, with its eye-mind-hand coordination continues to offer us opportunities for science learning and teaching. It is one of multiple tools that we can use to teach and investigate what people are thinking.

The original call for this book was about drawings as data—learning evidence that teachers and researchers could use in science education. However as the chapters were submitted, I had the opportunity to think more deeply about the illustrators' perspective and what the act of creating a drawing could mean to them. There are other books on the use of visual data. Pedersen and Finson (2009) edited a collection of examples of visual data for research in the general field of education. Later, they assembled a volume more specific to science education (Finson & Pedersen, 2013). Neither volume focused solely on drawings and their physical, mental, emotional and contextual effects, as well as contribution to both the creators and other interpreters. This book has gathered authors from around the globe working with drawing as one of their instruments. Some of their experiences coincide and some present us with alternate ways to use this tool.

As we have learned in social science research, a variety of methods can take us closer to consensus on what our students (or the public) is observing or retaining in the context of our work. I wanted to gather and provide evidence for what drawings have meant in science education. Furthermore, it is not at all clear to me that we can separate the learning of science from the act of drawing, whether by pen and pencil or, more recently, electronics. And that is part of the point in this book—that science and drawing have been intimately bound together. Drawing has been used to record (e.g. Audubon) to envision (e.g. Leonardo daVinci), and to invent (e.g. Alexander Graham Bell). In science education research, drawing has been used to gain insights into the illustrator's content information, attitudes, values, beliefs and motivations.

In my own work, I had found drawing a non-threatening way to obtain information in the afterschool science program I developed and which grew to a national scope with NSF funding. In encouraging children and their families to engage in afterschool science, we explained how it would be different from most science programs in school. We offered more freedom to express the children's own thinking of the world, smaller groups than the usual classroom, and lots of material manipulation. We also described the opportunity as one in which there would be no tests. That is one of the complementarities of out-of-school science education, or what I term *continual science learning* (CSL). Schools need to have data to show status and answer to their tax-paying or tuition paying public in terms of standards and goals. CSL settings concentrate on keeping excitement up, on developing identities as continually interested science learners, and in providing resources (places, materials, approaches) that may not be readily available anywhere else. And yet, we, too, had grant funders who wanted to know just what was being gained by being in our CSL science enrichment program. I turned to drawing because children do not associate it with testing. I was able to obtain thousands of drawings with no protest. Those of us who reviewed them were able to see trends of what made an impression on the children in terms of content and affect. I learned that this was a very limited use of drawing as a science skill.

I was intrigued by how White and Gunstone (1992) used drawings to better understand how their students represented connections and processes. I had followed the use of drawings in the 1980's that were employed to develop evidence about gender bias and other conceptions about who did science (Chambers, 1983; Schibeci & Sorenson, 1983; Kahle, 1985). Working with Dr. Randy McGinnis at the University of Maryland on Project Nexus, we used drawings over the course of years to observe how the answers to "Please draw yourself teaching science," and "Please draw you students learning science," changed during and after the teacher preparation program (Katz et al., 2011, 2013). As I read the developing literature on the subject, I came to see that drawing continues to be an essential tool for science work and science education. Coincidentally, I had recently read Noah Gordon's book *The Physician* (1986), set in the eleventh

PREFACE AND ACKNOWLEDGEMENTS

century. It tells the tale of an English orphan who is driven by his interest in medicine to travel to Isfahan in Persia to study with the famous Avicenna. In this novel, the dedicated protagonist is nearly executed for his efforts to draw (from post mortem dissection) the physiology of a man who has given his permission for others to learn from him upon his death. Religion forbid it. Medicine suffered. How important drawing was before photography and electronic imaging. The physician in this book on science drawing is also a medical illustrator. Gary Wind is a surgeon who helps put the combat-wounded back together. He tells you in his own words (Chapter 4) how he melded his interests in drawing and healing. His textbook on the vascular system is a beautiful and finely detailed teaching tool (Wind & Valentine, 2013). Medicine needs drawings just as contractors need blueprints. All of science needs drawing. There was no one book that brought a variety of these rich multiple drawing uses together. This book had its start as a result of my accumulated experiences.

I read about work being done by my colleagues around the globe. Some have invented ways to interpret the communication of drawings. Some have asked questions that are new to the use of drawings in science education. Some are replicating studies and comparing results across cultures. I find it exciting.

ACKNOWLEDGEMENTS

I have been fortunate to be able to work in science education and to contribute to the field. I thank Michel Lokhorst and his team at Sense Publishers for bringing to fruition the vision within my original book proposal. While I had personal contact with many of the authors, I approached others because of their work within our journals. I thank all of them, both those who knew me and those who trusted me sight-unseen, for sharing their use of drawings in our field.

I would like to acknowledge the late David J. Lockard. He encouraged me to become a researcher as well as a practitioner. David was a world expert on mushrooms, as well as science teaching. I think of him every time I make my stuffed mushroom recipe and of his wonderful course in medicinal and poisonous plants. I drew many times in that course. There was an added pleasure to his mentorship. My father had given me a copy of the UNESCO book, *700 Science Experiments* (1958) when I was a child. It was exciting to know that my graduate mentor was an editor of this childhood treasure. Randy McGinnis was my next advisor and mentor. I used drawing data in my dissertation on mothers as science teachers, revisited recently as a chapter on science teacher identity development (Avraamidou, 2015). Dr. McGinnis encouraged me to foster my own identity as a science education researcher as I led the team at the organization that was developing and delivering afterschool science options. Those were challenging years and it is a pleasure to see how our work has now coincided once again in this book. Randy has continued to use drawing as a data collection technique (Chapter 21). Most importantly, I have also been fortunate to have my husband, Victor, as a scholarly partner. We spend many hours discussing our work and its implications. For this book, in addition to collegial talks, he made time to input my edits, as he is a much speedier typist than I am. Together, we have been tolerant of how our work impacts on a quirky lifestyle of suppers and bedtimes that vary by how intense our projects and grandparent demands are.

There are several people who fostered this book in small but meaningful ways. When I exchanged emails with Kevin Finson, who has the two books cited above on visual learning in science education, his response to my wanting to produce another volume was to offer assistance, if needed,—a gentleman and a scholar. Julie Thomas and Donna Farland-Smith, likewise had preceded me in publishing about the use of drawings and were gracious in sharing their thinking.

There are people who have facilitated my work in pervasive ways. George Tressel was my first program officer at the National Science Foundation. After he left the Foundation we developed a friendship. He has been my guru in many ways and I have always appreciated his blend of philosophy and practical knowledge. We discussed this book's material among our many science education conversations. My children have always been a cheering team and are each teaching now in different ways. Sharon Katz Cooper is responsible for science education dissemination for one of our ocean exploration vessels. She and I have talked about the use of images in our work. My son, Ari, is generous with his thoughts on international teacher education, global needs, and technology. Our talks have included visual evaluation. Naomi teaches through art. A costume designer by training, she has studied the ways in which art communicates, making me more aware of intentional techniques. This has given me clues to consider in the unintentional—that is, what people draw to communicate science learning without an artistic product as a conscious result.

Most of the chapters in this book are research reports. There are, however, two essays that don't conform to that genre. One is the chapter mentioned above by Gary Wind (Chapter 4). The second is by a middle school teacher in Botswana. Shiellah Keletso tells us of an action research project in which she utilized drawings after finding Project Nexus' *DrawnToScience* website through an internet search. She was seeking a way to improve her teaching so that she could become a more inclusive teacher (Chapter 20). Both of these chapters bring to the reader a different perspective from that of a professional science education researcher. They enrich this book, meant to provide examples for both science education researchers and teachers, whether in classrooms or other learning settings.

REFERENCES

Chambers, D. W. (1983). Stereotypic images of the scientists: The draw-a-scientist test. *Science Education, 67*, 255–265.
Finson, K. D., & Pederson, J. E. (2013). *Visual data and their use in science education.* Charlotte, NC: Information Age Publishing, Inc.
Gordon, N. (1986). *The physician.* New York, NY: Simon & Shuster.
Kahle, J. B. (1985). *Women in science*, a report from the field. Philadelphia, PA: Falmer Press.

Katz, P., McGinnis, R., Hestness, E., Riedinger, K., Marbach-Ad, G., Dai, A., & Pease, R. (2011). Professional identity development of teacher candidates participating in an informal science education internship: A focus on drawings as evidence. *International Journal of Science Education, 33*(9), 1169–1197.

Katz, P., McGinnis, R., Riedinger, K., Marbach-Ad, G., & Dai, A. (2013). The influence of informal science education experiences on the development of two beginning teachers' science classroom teaching identity. *Journal of Science Teacher Education, 24*(8),1357–1379.

Pederson, J. E., & Finson, K. D. (2009). *Visual data.* Rotterdam: Sense Publishers.

Schibeci, R. A., & Sorenson, I. (1983). Elementary school children's perceptions of scientists. *School Science and Mathematics, 83,* 14–19.

UNESCO. (1958). *700 science experiments.* New York, NY: Doubleday.

White, R., & Gunstone, R. (1992). *Probing understanding.* New York, NY: The Falmer Press.

Wind, G., & Valentine, J. (2013). *Anatomic exposures in vascular surgery* (3rd ed.). Philadelphia, PA: Wolters Kluwer/Lippincott, Williams & Willkins.

PHYLLIS KATZ

1. INTRODUCTION: DRAWING AND SCIENCE ARE INSEPARABLE

Drawing is a Human Expression for Teaching/Learning

The act of drawing is an act of recording. Science requires the recording of data to seek insights and patterns. The mind that contemplates recording in a place and with a medium that will be seen by others at a future time implies a mind that can conceive of a future and also believes in teaching/learning through communication. Some researchers believe that it is likely that this cognitive ability—in this case, provided by drawing data—marks the distinction between our species and other hominids (Suddendorf & Corballis, 2007). We humans could plan for a future we could imagine. We could record, build knowledge, and convey it to others we would never know. Long before the technologies of printing, photography, and digital imaging, drawing was the only way to create a representation of features, construction, orientation, or pattern. We see this in portraits, maps, and paintings of historic events. Children begin early in their lives to make marks in mud, sand or snow as well as with intentional crayons and other art materials (Anning, 1999). Where to present or leave drawings and how to create a medium with which to draw are themselves evidence of early consideration of the characteristics of materials—what we could choose to call nascent technology. The alphabets and numerals that were developed later are drawn symbols for already standardized language. In mathematics, the symbols combine as visual shortcuts of communication to describe relationships and patterns. Drawing has been essential to our intellectual development. Where would science be without the drawings of Copernicus, Da Vinci, Audubon, Darwin, Bohr, Watson, Crick and Franklin, in depicting models, processes, and possibilities? Many other examples of science illustration have been collected for examination (e.g. http://hyperallergic.com/97027/when-art-was-the-scientists-eye-400-years-of-natural-history-illustrations/ or http://digitalcollections.nypl.org/collections/pictures-of-science-700-years-of-scientific-and-medical-illustration#/?tab=about).

As you will see in this book, drawing continues to have communication benefits that are different from those of writing. One of these benefits is accessibility. Creating drawings on rocks and other surfaces for information has been possible for many people in many places since pre-history (Chippindale & Nash, 2004). Recording verbal and literary data came relatively late in human history and began with immediate limits. We could not use writing as a communication tool before we had those standardized alphabetic symbols. Teaching these symbols for reading and writing was a guarded process before such education was considered a universal right. Scribes who could copy accurately were sought after and had years of training. In some cases scribes had a place among those with sacred talents. Calligraphers crossed the boundaries of science and art by applying their talents to embellished alphabets and illustrations. These were done frequently to enhance spiritual life with instruction and beauty. These products were commissioned by the wealthy. Availability of writing materials was a technological limitation. The opportunity to record and learn from data was thus limited to those relatively few in control of the power and wealth to obtain these writing materials and writing teachers. According to the critical theorists in our field, control of records is always bound up in the power structure of cultures (Treagust, Won, & Duit, 2014). I would agree that by limiting participation and viewpoint, we limit the development of science. Consider that for thousands of years, drawings were perhaps more democratic in science observations as pre or non-literate people picked up charcoal, sticks, ink, and pencils to draw out what they saw for others. From Dewey (1920), through Rutherford and Ahlgren (1989) to a recent report published for UNESCO (Tibbetts, 2015) educators state an interest in universal, quality education to empower democratic participation and personal, knowledgeable choice. Could more use of drawing advance this goal for students, teachers and researchers?

Writing has its communication difficulties, especially when unaccompanied by illustration. Lengthy word descriptions run the risk of the reader's losing track of the whole argument for a pattern description. Such descriptions in Indian and Arabic mathematics not only reduced participants to those who could read, but also ran the risk of copy replication errors—not to mention the loss of student attention! Euclid's illustrations endure, however. The introduction of mathematical symbols facilitated the comprehension of the flow of ideas in compact images and standardized communications among mathematicians (Katz & Parshall, 2014). Drawing can make learning accessible, can provide clarity, and may be more efficient than verbal descriptions in certain circumstances. In this book, for example, you will find data from young children and non-literate adults for whom descriptive writing is not an option.

We use drawings today when there is critical information to be conveyed quickly. This is especially true when it is important for speakers and readers of multiple languages to understand the message. For example, we have international road signs for drivers, as in Figure 1 and 2. Another example is air travel. When we sit down in an airplane seat, the signs above tell us when to fasten our seat belts and that we must not smoke. Words, even in two languages, are apparently not considered sufficient. In several of the chapters in this book, the authors reference the advantage of drawings where there are multiple languages among a group (Chapter 13, Stears & Dempster; Chapter 9, Caney, Humphrey & Bowker) or where children are too young to write their thoughts (Chapter 7, Dai, Chapter 12, Chang), or where schooling has not been available (Chapter 8, Tunnicliffe & Angshuman; Chapter 9, Caney, Humphrey & Bowker).

P. Katz (Ed.), Drawing for Science Education, 1–8.
© 2017 Sense Publishers. All rights reserved.

Figure 1. International road sign for "no U-turn allowed here"   *Figure 2. International road sign for road work ahead*

In human history, early illustrators provided us with data about their surroundings. They told us what animals they encountered. Evidence of the drawing impulse is widespread. We can see mammoths in the Chauvet cave in France, rhinos in the Coliboaia cave in Romania, kangaroos in Australia, cow figures in Namibia and India, or a jaguar in Brazil (Marchant, 2016). Scientists have found decorated tools in South Africa dated to tens of thousands of years ago. These convey, "I have put my mark on this tool as an individual who creates." We drew before we could write. Recent evidence of ochre production in South Africa suggests that creating images made with ochre paint dates back 100,000 years (Henshilwood et al., 2011). The newer dating techniques are good examples of the leapfrog nature of technology and data availability in research. Carbon dating has been limited to organic materials. New techniques with inorganic materials allow for a broader range of exploration which can now include ochre, an extensively used early human drawing medium. Just as we find the earliest hominid remains in Africa, we are finding and dating the earliest drawings there. Our African roots are not only physical, they are intellectual and artistic as we should expect in defining "human" as an emerging species in paleontology.

The intent of those who drew so many years ago is unknown. While we find many animal pictures on cave walls, we do not know why they were put there. Are they records of successful hunts to sustain the human need for nourishment? Are they desires of the same? Are they pleas to spirits for appreciation or supplication? Are they the artistic impulse of random illustrators or purposeful records of dedicated scribes? We cannot yet answer these questions but we do know that the existence of the drawings is a visible activity—a record of humans who wanted to express their thoughts for themselves and others to see as in Figures 3 and 4 below. What was the purpose of the hand prints found recently in Indonesia, dated to 35,000 years ago? At the very least, they record that someone wanted to note a human presence. Inference continues to be a question in interpreting these visual data. I consider this issue in a later section of this introduction. Recently, a pictographic calendar supported the intent of Lakota Indians (Wyoming) to keep seasonal records confirming this particular communication process through images among people without a literature (Momaday, 2015). It is important to recognize that drawing is an early and continued form of communication across time and about the world into which drawing for science education is a subset.

Figure 3. Male figures. rock art, Kakadu National Park, Australia. Photo by Phyllis Katz, 1995   *Figure 4. Animal figure. Rock art, Kakadu National Park, Australia. Photo by Phyllis Katz, 1995*

INTRODUCTION: DRAWING AND SCIENCE ARE INSEPARABLE

THEORETICAL BACKGROUND

The primary theoretical consideration for the use of drawings is intertwined with theories of mind. We often use the language of images when we speak about our thinking: We have "viewpoints." We have "insights." We say, "picture this," or "let's focus." We talk of "illustrating a point" and of "visualizing" a situation or a concept. The theoretical framework for drawing as data begins with evidence that we use images, at least in part, to think. In arguing that "image" in its pictorial sense is limited in terms of sensory input for mental processing, Pylyshyn (1973) nevertheless stated, "Imagery is a pervasive form of experience and is clearly of utmost importance to humans. We cannot speak of consciousness without, at the same time, implicating the existence of images"(p. 2). "Visual/ spatial thinking involves purposeful use of your 'mind's eye' to develop mental pictures or images," wrote Alan J. McCormack (1988, p. 2). He continued to describe how this kind of mental imaging permeates all human thinking whether one is packing a suitcase, reading, considering chess movements, or planning global politics on a map. He notes that Frederick Kekulé visualized the benzene ring in a dream. McCormack related that many phenomena in today's science are not directly observable, but need to be visualized to be understood. As Sousa (2001), wrote about learning and the brain for teachers, he told us that visual images work to process new learning and to store information. He related that the brain processes our inner images in the same way that it does when the eyes see something in real time. He tied this into the survival value of such a system. It is crucial to be able to "run by" our minds the possibilities for selecting the safest immediate or long term benefit to our choices. By 2014, we have access to Dual Coding Theory (DCT) that provides a mental processing framework for inclusive verbal and non-verbal brain activity (Pavio). More recently, neuroscientists with brain imaging tools have explored the hexagonal geometry on which spacial data appear to be mapped and are finding that there may be similar brain maps for other stimuli, networking with each other (Constantinescu et al., 2016). As technology develops new instruments for investigation, research brings us evidence that within our brains there is an interaction between highly developed visual imagery and verbal capacities. In practical terms, the theoretical support for gaining insights into people's thinking suggests that it would be well to elicit images as well as verbal/literary information.

If we accept the theory of mind as largely image loaded, we then consider evidence for how drawing can reflect those images as one window on the mind—that what we draw is a representation of how we are thinking about our experience. Researchers and educators have concurred that drawings can provide information that may be elusive in other forms of inquiry (White & Gunstone, 1992; Bell et al., 2009). Klepsch and Logie (1982) studied Indian (North American) children using drawings as one of their data sources. They reported,

> Unwittingly, he [the illustrator] sketches in some details of his own traits, attitudes, behavior characteristics, personality strengths and weaknesses. In other words, he leaves an imprint, however incomplete, of his inner self upon his drawing. Since drawing also reflects the person, the ideas of using it as a measurement of personality, of self in relation to others, of group values, and of attitude is not out of line...Long before written language existed, man scratched drawings on cave walls to record his feelings, needs, and actions. Drawing communication, then, is elemental and basic. It is also universal. (p. 6)

In 2005, Van Meter and Garner, published a literature review of "learner-generated" drawing in a broad range of school settings, seeking to provide evidence for its effectiveness as a teaching strategy. Writing of the interplay of text and illustrations in provided teaching materials, they speculate that

> ...the selection of additional elements, in this back and forth consideration, the two internal representations act as mutual constraints during construction of the mental model...When, drawing, the internal verbal elements are organized into a coherent representation. This representation then serves as the foundation for constructing the internal nonverbal representation. (p. 317)

They are concerned that researchers were not asking " if drawing can improve observational processes, support the writing process, or improve learner affect" (p. 315). We move into the question of how we remember what we experience in our continual processing of information. Supporting theories speak to the role of drawing and memory. After conducting a series of experiments to test for memory effects of drawing as a way to recall, Wammes, Meade and Fernandes (2016) found a strong positive effect compared to writing. They conclude that "the mechanism driving the effect is that engaging in drawing promotes the seamless integration of many types of memory codes (elaboration, visual imagery, motor action, and picture memory) into one cohesive memory trace, and it is this that facilitates later retrieval of the studied words." As with other hands-on aspects of science education, the act of participating, and of being asked to pay attention to an aspect of one's thoughts engages more neural networks. Landin (2015) wrote of her choice to include illustration in her college biology classes that "Creating a high-quality scientific illustration requires a thorough understanding of biological processes, anatomy, and structural diversity...If you wish to differentiate fir and spruce trees, look carefully at how the needles attach to the twig. It's all there—if you just look closely and precisely." In developing theory, it follows that drawing, using multiple senses, would impress the experience for later recovery. Learning about the world requires paying attention and banking concepts in memory—all moderated by context, both physical and social as described, for example, by Rosseler & Dentzau (Chapter 11) or understanding students' interpretations of physics as Vander Veen has done (Chapter 2).

3

DRAWING AS DATA IN SCIENCE EDUCATION RESEARCH

I would like to be clear that while I believe that drawing is essential to science education, none of us in this volume have claimed it is to be used today as an exclusive data collection tool. Every author speaks to the need to have an illustrator's notes, interviews, or in one case, video recordings (Winter & Astall, Chapter, 22) to complement what is drawn, concurring for example, that drawing and writing elicited more information than drawing alone when English and Australian children were compared for what they knew about technology (Rennie & Jarvis, 1995) or that interviews and drawings are most fruitful in understanding children's drawings of scientists (Finson, 2002). In fact, as Winter and Astall point out, our verbal communications are so nuanced that gesture, facial expression, body posture and words increase the likelihood that what the illustrator intended to communicate is enhanced through the accompaniment of videotaped (visual) description, so readily available today. Is this not another example of the reason that science education researchers have long recommended triangulation of multiple methods and sources of data collection in order to offer the best possible interpretation of what is happening within a given context (e.g. Guba & Lincoln, 1989; LeCompte, & Preissle, 1993; Banks, 2007)?

Concerns about drawing as a data source center around the degree of inference (and therefore validity) that may be used in interpreting this data. (Di Leo, 1983; Farland & McComas, 2004). Chambers (1983), in describing his development and research with the "draw-a-scientist" procedure noted this issue. He concluded, "DAST is easier to administer than most tests; however, a number of interpretive difficulties may arise" (p. 264). Ways of addressing these issues have been to refine the drawing prompts in their specificity, to develop rubrics for coding agreement, and to have multiple coders who reach consensus among themselves for meanings, or to have multiple drawings done by the same participants to help establish the stability of mental images. I add here a personal observation as well. Having majored in English during my first round of higher education, I knew that I had spent many classes and many hours interpreting words and their meanings. It was not only poetry that brought my classes to multiple views of word images. I developed a healthy respect for punctuation as more than rules from grammarians out to torture students. Those little commas could certainly help. I find myself puzzled at this particular concern for inference in drawings used as data. All human communication is inferential in its interpretations. What is true has much to do with context, culture and the receiver's personal history. As a simple example of written inference confusion, I relate the following two examples: Driving along the PA turnpike, there was a flashing sign, "Trucks and busses right lane only." Does this mean that the right lane is exclusively for trucks and busses, or that all vehicles may use the right lane, but trucks and buses must? Convention tells us the latter, but what of foreign drivers who do not use this road regularly? What about a child's announcement, "Look, here comes mother!" Are we welcoming our maternal parent, or are we a six year-old who is warning his friend that they should get their hands out of the cookie jar? Interpretation will depend on context and tone. In using quantitative or qualitative research methods (or any combination thereof), we need to consider context, history, relationships, response energy or fatigue, timing among other activities. Social science research is as complex as people are. And we argue by our work with drawings that they are useful pieces of information toward understanding.

Researchers who collect drawing data describe the setting, participants and prompts, as well as images. Some are looking for trends and do so by collecting large numbers of drawings within an age group and about specific concepts (e.g. Bartoscek & Tunnicliffe, Chapter 5). Others look at changes before and after an experience (Stears & Dempster, Chapter 13; Keletso, Chapter 20; Caney & Bowker, Chapter 9). Researchers have sought the presence or absence of elements (Barak, Chapter 3, or McClafferty & Rennie, Chapter 14). Presenting the variety of uses is part of the purpose of this book

As recently as a hundred years ago, drawing was required as part of the school curriculum (Landin, 2015). As we teach science with a more democratic educational effort to greater numbers of people, drawing has taken a backseat to verbal/literary teaching and learning, which has developed efficient ways of scoring large amounts of data for many people. Drawing as a social science research method began in the early 20th century. There are authors in this volume who provide a detailed history but I include a synopsis here to indicate the length and development of the method. Florence Goodenough was the first to systematically correlate drawings of "a man" with the early intelligence tests that were being developed at that time (1926). Mead and Metraux mention using drawings in their landmark work on the image of scientists; however they provided no details of how they used them (1957). Chambers first utilized drawings to explore the images that children held of scientists (1983). White and Gunstone (1992) provided clear examples of how drawings brought out information that other methods had not revealed. Other researchers have investigated scientist stereotypes and also applied drawing methods to assess other attitudes, understandings, and affect (e.g. Flick, 1990; Mason, Kahle, & Gardner, 1991; Rosenthal, 1993; Schibeci & Sorensen, 1983; Thomas et al., 2001; Farland et al., 2011; Katz et al., 2013; Hillman et al., 2014). The authors in this volume carry the methods of using drawings in science education forward in the 21st century, finding a richness that words alone have not captured.

When we ask people to draw today we are asking them to engage in this act of creating a visual record. They agree to put their thoughts on paper, choosing sizes, spaces, symbols, shapes and sometimes colors. It is a different way of sharing knowledge from written language with its rules for meaningful sounds, sentence structure, syntax, spelling and other descriptive boundaries. It is just this set of rules that makes language work as cultural developments of distinctive speech. While there is evidence that drawing, as any human artifact, is also nested within a culture, we have seen that it can have the power to cross some boundaries, much as some sounds (pain, alarm, happy exclamations) transcend culture in their communication. With the increasing use of digital tools, visual imagery and graphic design (drawing, in this case) have the potential to increase democratization of observation and communication as images jump across the internet internationally. This book focuses on handmade drawings using paper, pencil, crayon or inks. The eye, mind, hand coordination that drawing requires supports science learning. As Mensah and Fleshman suggest, drawing can be used to revisit memories and consider them from a different perspective, perhaps reinforcing a positive attitude toward self in science education (Chapter 19).

It is interesting to note that drawings in the name of science have been a part of major controversies. Our very sense of who we are has changed as science tools and culture allowed for world views that were illustrated first with the earth and then with the sun as the center of our collection of planets. As Gary Wind points out in his chapter (6) on medical illustration, teachable knowledge of the human body was delayed for centuries by the prohibition against human dissection and the drawings and notes that accompanied this anatomical data when access was permitted. Thus healing methods that depended on the recording of images that could be taught to medical personnel from one generation to another could not happen. When allowed, compendiums such as Gray's Anatomy (Standring, Ed. 1858/2015) became essential medical basics, as did Dr. Wind's own work as the author of texts on the vascular system (Wind & Valentine, 2013). While this is a dramatic example of the impact of drawing (or the lack thereof) it is the drawings that our predecessors left us that provide evidence of not only the flora and fauna in recent earth history, but to varying degrees, how our ancestors thought of themselves in it.

Given that drawing was an early and continuous means of providing data in science, I found it odd that teaching and research books such as *Taking Science to School* (NRC, 2007), the *Handbook of Qualitative Research,*(2000), or the *Handbook of Research on Science Education* (2013), have no index heading for "drawing" as a method for teaching, learning and research. The latter does have a heading for "draw-a-scientist test." In this book, the authors use drawings as central evidence to gain insights into the thinking of participants in a broad range of cultures, settings, and stages of life.

There were options for how this book could be organized. Hope (2005) looked at children's design drawings and classified them as picture, single-draw, and multi-draw prior to children's use of drawings for idea development. Focusing then on the process of using drawings for design, she classified children's drawings into multi-draw, progressive and interactive, depending on how the child approached design development before construction. Ainsworth, Prain and Tytler (2011) considered the rational for drawing as a critical skill and classified these as (1) Drawing to enhance engagement; (2) Drawing to learn to represent in science; (3) Drawing to reason; (4) Drawing as a learning strategy (5) Drawing to communicate. My own choice was historical. I find that a developmental approach helps to establish the building blocks of a field, providing the same history that we seek when we do a literature review to situate new knowledge. The chapters in this book are grouped into four sections that follow the ways in which the use of drawings has evolved and can still be in practice for science education. I made this decision because I hope that the book will be useful to practitioners as well as researchers.

Drawing then, is the oldest form of intentional human communication to transcend time. People were creating drawings before alphabets or pictograms were put down on stone, clay, or papyrus to leave records for the future. Drawings were used before alphabets symbolized sounds that had combinations for meaning. Drawings were useful before, perhaps, language was standardized. Drawing is thus a communication tool that we developed early in our human history. It is important. And yet, as Anning noted (1999), "At school, children quickly learn that drawing has low status," (p. 171) and it more often concentrates on adapting to certain practices. This book then, is about how drawing complements the written and the spoken. It is about how necessary this is in the varied ways people have chosen to use the process of drawing in science teaching and research—teaching about how the world works. It relates how, across cultures, those who draw are given a way to express what they are thinking that can be more open than verbal/literary responses. It is a book of examples that others may adapt. The following are brief descriptions of the material.

SECTION ONE—A SINGLE IMAGE

In an effort to attract more women as well as those who might not register for a university introductory physics course, Jatila Vanderveen describes how she incorporates visual thinking into her curriculum for her course on Symmetry and Aesthetics in Contemporary Physics at the University of California at Santa Barbara (UCSB). She begins by asking students to draw their understanding of Einstein's 1936 essay, *Physics and Reality*. Her chapter describes her analysis of visualization styles and her measurements of accomplishment.

Miri Barak explored the role of information and communication technologies (ICT's) at the Technion in Israel by prompting a sample of science and engineering undergraduates to "draw a learning situation in higher education" and requesting written explanations as well. From the drawing evidence, she considers the difference between the instructional culture of academia and the alternative learning strategies revealed in her study, finding a considerable distance between the two.

In working with pre-service middle and secondary level teachers, Patricia Patrick sought insights into the social contexts in which these teacher candidates learned about anatomy. The drawings served as discussion objects between participants who first drew the anatomical systems in both a human and a pig (as closely related). Prior research had indicated that anatomical drawings of humans concentrate on the gastrointestinal and cardiovascular systems without investigating the source of this information. This study explored the potential for shared cultural conceptions and misconceptions as that source.

Amauri Bartoszeck and Sue Dale Tunnicliffe collected hundreds of drawings by students in four studies within this chapter. The illustrators ranged upwards from four years old and came from rural settings, towns, and suburban areas in Brazil where these researchers explored children's general levels of understanding of organisms, both plant and animal. They find that drawing is a useful tool to access mental models. This trend data confirms the ability of children to represent increasing detail in their observations and representations.

Gary Wind, a teaching physician at the U.S. Uniformed Services University of the Health Sciences, has contributed an essay on the history of medicine's reliance on drawing. He describes early anatomical illustration as it developed into a critical teaching tool for the healing arts. Dr. Wind has been an eager medical artist himself, speaking to his first interest in cartooning as it grew alongside his interest in anatomy. In high school, he became aware of Vesalius' work, setting him on the path to his own work as a microvascular practitioner and teacher.

In exploring children's concepts of nature, Amy Dai asked children entering formal schooling in Taiwan to draw their ideas about nature. Most children live in densely populated areas where the original (natural) environment has been altered for human habitation. From this study, Dr. Dai concluded that children and teachers would benefit from planned green spaces for direct observation of the interrelationship of plants, animals and humans. She also notes that children come to school with prior knowledge, both positive and negative, in their "nature" concepts.

Working in Bangladesh with rural women who had not had the opportunity to advance their formal schooling, Sue Dale Tunnicliffe and Angshuman Sarker investigated anatomical knowledge. The women were provided with a body outline to draw their internal organs. They were also asked where they had learned about their bodies. The researchers were surprised to find some well-placed knowledge of kidneys, unlike comparable Western data. Taking advantage of children's presence, drawings also revealed that schooling did yield more anatomical information.

SECTION TWO—MULTIPLE DRAWINGS TO EXPLORE CHANGE

Pre and post drawings of a marine environment enabled Jill Cainey, Lauren Humphrey and Rob Bowker to assess learning in two settings. In the UK's Plymouth Aquarium, children's drawings showed increased mastery of detailed observation. In an adult training program aimed at the connection between between reef conservation and the economy in Mauritius, the researchers found that the training program met its learning goals for low-income ESL workers. They found that using drawings enabled feedback independent of language and initial educational skills.

In considering the prior conceptions that students bring to their school science studies, Susanne Neumann and Martin Hopf discuss research on the terms "energy" and "chemistry." They also had an unusual opportunity to conduct research among Austrian students (age 9–12), about the concept of "radiation" before and two years after the Fukushima accident in Japan (2011). They suggest that among this young age group, the international media coverage and ensuing discussions resulted in a doubling of drawn motifs related to radioactivity.

Katrina Rosseler and Michael Dentzau analyzed drawings through the contextual model of learning to investigate informal science education. Pre and post drawings after a series of visits to the E.O. Wilson Biophilia Center in Florida provided data within the model's categories of personal, sociocultural and physical contexts as they combine over time. There is clear evidence that the Center visit enhanced the understanding of the longleaf pine forest for fourth graders. In other research, they asked undergraduates to draw and annotate an image of themselves participating in science outside of schools, gaining insights into informal science experiences.

Working with young children, Ni Chang argues for visual teaching and learning alongside the traditional emphasis on reading and writing. In this integrated curriculum, she finds power for children who enter a multimedia world, cautioning that teachers must state clear learning purposes for drawing. This chapter describes the findings of 70 pre-service teachers who worked with 140 children (4–7 years old) through four semesters in a Midwest American university teacher preparation program utilizing pre-post instruction drawings for comparison.

In the multi-lingual context of South Africa, Michelle Stears and Edith R. Dempster found that drawings helped to remove the distinction between affluent and poorer schools that text-based assessments highlighted. They investigated the growth of information about internal anatomy between first (7 year olds) and ninth graders (15 year olds). They concurred with other studies that children's awareness grows from what they can feel (bones and beating heart) to that of organs and systems and suggest a teaching sequence that integrates systems thinking.

At two science centers in Australia, Terence McClafferty and Leonie Rennie sought to gain insights into how visitors used interactive exhibits meant to teach the physics of sound and what they learned. To focus the visitors' illustrations, they presented partially drawn diagrams to complete and thereby convey an understanding of the exhibits' scientific concepts. They found that this method was efficient for the science center setting where visitors would find it easier to draw what they understood, rather than verbally describe it. Half of the study participants provided evidence that visitors learned something new, with females and younger visitors in the lead.

SECTION THREE—DRAWINGS THAT ILLUSTRATE THE PERCEIVED CULTURE OF SCIENCE

Donna Farland-Smith writes of her work refining the Draw-A-Scientist Test (DAST) developed by Chambers in 1983. For nearly 30 years, the test was used to make claims about stereotypical images of the who, what, and where of science. Countering the controversy surrounding this "test," in terms of its validity and reliability, she collaborated in the development of a modified protocol and rubric in 2013 to standardize data collection in her work in the USA. The modification included multiple drawings by the same illustrator. Farland-Smith asserts that these drawings reveal rich data with both cultural clues and representations of personal identities.

Noting some of the limitations of the DAST-C (Draw-A-Scientist Checklist), Sulaiman Al-Balushi and Abdullah Ambusaidi explored the beliefs of their prospective science teachers at Sultan Qaboos University in Oman. They found that their students represented a teacher-centered classroom although observations in practicum situations did include a wider variety of methods, leading to suggestions for DAST development to include analysis of practice as well as beliefs. They conclude that further research on combined drawing and interviewing would be helpful.

In Turkey, Sinan Ozgelen gave third grade students the option to draw images along with open-ended survey questions when he asked what science was, who did it, and how it was done. He was thus able to collect data on student preferences for written responses, drawn responses or a combination of both. The influence of Turkish curricular textbooks is considered and compared to other drawing data in light of recent reforms, with notable differences credited to the way in which scientists are presented in the country's newer material.

Seeking to understand the meanings that learners construct around science, Jeremy Price asked high school students from a diverse middle track class in the northeastern USA to draw a picture and reflect about (in writing and discussions) what doing science looks like to them. He repeated the procedure early and at the end of a two month period of collaboration with the teacher and class. The drawings aided analysis of the students' current concepts of where science is done, with what equipment, knowledge and concept development, who is involved and how.

SECTION FOUR—DRAWING FOR AND ABOUT SCIENCE TEACHER IDENTITY DEVELOPMENT

Felicia Moore Mensah and Robin Fleshman use drawings and narrative with their pre-service teachers in the USA to help their students revisit their past conceptions and rethink their emerging new science teacher identities. Their procedure, DESTIN (Drawing-Elementary-Science-Teacher-Not) uniquely analyzes diversity as it is examined in multicultural education. Drawings are thus not only a source of student images, but a proactive tool to construct thoughtful and positive representations as students learn during teacher preparation.

In Botswana, the term "inclusion" is evolving from a focus on disabilities, to a term that connotes the effort to teach students who are at risk of failure to reach their maximum potential. Shiellah Keletso has written a personal narrative as a teacher-researcher, using drawings to gather information of her students' perception of her teaching. She used this information to change her own teaching behaviors to better communicate with her students and provide a learning environment to encourage them to succeed. She found inspiration on the Project Nexus website at the University of Maryland.

Randy McGinnis and Emily Hestness (USA) explored prospective elementary teachers' perspectives on climate change, seeking insights into their moral reasoning on this socioscientific issue. Combined with narratives, they used drawings as a way to elicit information in a creative and non-threatening way, with a prompt that asked for all that a student knew about the causes and effects of climate change. They consider how prospective teachers must contemplate the personal and societal responsibility of issues in light of the rational emphasis that is common in science.

New Zealand teacher educators David Winter and Chris Astall extended the use of drawings through the addition of video narratives to create learning monographs among a small group of students enrolled in a postgraduate education qualification. In repeated drawing opportunities, a sample of volunteer students spoke to a video camera describing and explaining what they had drawn. Not only do the students clarify and provide additional thoughts, but this method gives them the opportunity to engage in self-reflection through observing their own work.

Taken together, these chapters present a variety of ways in which drawing helps not only teacher/researchers learn what their students or audience already know, or what they take from a teaching setting, but how the illustrators may see themselves in the process of learning science. As I read these chapters, I became more concerned that drawing, unlike reading, is not front and center in science education. Participating in constructing mental images to communicate is part of our heritage. Observing the world (and oneself in it) and expressing one's thoughts by organizing and producing images are useful to illustrator and researcher alike.

REFERENCES

Abell, S., & Lederman, N. (Eds.). (2013). *Handbook of research on science education*. Mahwah, NJ: Lawrence Erlbaum Associates.

Ainsworth, S., Prain, P., & Tytler, R. (2011). Drawing to learn in science. *Science, 333*, 1096–1097.

Anning, A. (1999). Learning to draw and drawing to learn. *International Journal of Art & Design Education, 18*(2), 163–172.

Banks, M. (2007). *Using visual data in qualitative research*. Washington, DC: Sage.

Bell, P., Lewenstein, B., Shouse, A. W., & Feder, M. A. (Eds.). (2009). *Learning science in informal environments: People, places and pursuits*. Washington, DC: The National Academies Press.

Brookes, M. (1986). *Drawing with children, a creative teaching and learning method that works for adults, too*. Los Angeles, CA: Jeremy P. Tarcher, Inc.

Chambers, D. W. (1983). Stereotypic images of the scientist: The draw-a-scientist test. *Science Education, 67*, 255–265.

Chippindale, C., & Nash, G. (2004). Pictures in place: Approaches to the figured landscapes of rock-art. In C. Chippindale & G. Nash (Eds.), *Pictures in place, the figured landscapes of rock-art*. Cambridge: Cambridge University Press.

Constantinescu, A. O., Reilly, X. O., & Behrens, T. E. J. (2016). Organizing conceptual knowledge in humans with a gridlike code. *Science, 352*(6292), 1464–1468.

Denzin, N. K., & Lincoln, Y. (Eds.). (2000). *Handbook of qualitative research* (2nd ed.). Thousands Oaks, CA: Sage Publications, Inc.

Dewey, J. (1916). *Democracy and education*. New York, NY: Macmillan.

DiLeo, J. H. (1983). *Interpreting children's drawings.* New York, NY: Brunner/Mazel Publishers.

Finson, K. (2002). Drawing a scientist: What we do and do not know after fifty years of drawings. *School Science and Mathematics, 102,* 335–345.

Flick, L. (1990). Scientist in residence program improving children's image of science and scientists. *School Science and Mathematics, 90,* 204–214.

Goodenough, F. (1926). *Measurement of intelligence by drawings.* New York, NY: Harcourt Brace.

Guba, E. G., & Lincoln, Y. S. (1989). *Fourth generation evaluation.* Newbury Park, CA: Sage Publications.

Henshilwood, C. H., d'Errico, F., van Niekerk, K. L., Coquinot, Y., Jacobs, Z., Lauritzen, S., Menu, M., & García-Moreno, R. (2011). A 100,000-year-old ochre-processing workshop at Blombos Cave, South Africa. *Science, 334,* 219.

Hillman, S. J., Bloodsworth, K. H., Tilburg, C. E., Zeeman, S. I., & List, H. E. (2014). K-12 students' perceptions of scientists: Finding a valid measurement and exploring whether exposure to scientists makes an impact. *International Journal of Science Education, 36*(15), 2580–2595.

Hope, G. (2005). The types of drawings that young children produce in response to design tasks. *Journal of Design and Technology Education, 10*(1), 43–53.

Katz, P., McGinnis, R., Hestness, E., Riedinger, K., Marbach-Ad, G., Dai, A., & Pease, R. (2011). Professional identity development of teacher candidates participating in an informal science education internship: A focus on drawings as evidence. *International Journal of Science Education, 33*(9), 1169–1197.

Katz, P., McGinnis, R., Riedinger, K., Marbach-Ad, G., & Dai, A. (2013). The influence of informal science education experiences on the development of two beginning teachers' science classroom teaching identity. *Journal of Science Teacher Education, 24*(8), 1357–1379.

Katz, V., & Parshall, K. (2014). *Taming the unknown, a history of algebra from antiquity to the early 20th century.* Princeton, NJ: Princeton University Press.

Klepsch, M., & Logie, L. (1982). *Children draw and tell, an introduction to the projective uses of children's human figure drawings.* New York, NY: Brunner/Mazel, Publishers.

Landin, J. (2015, September 4). *Rediscovering the forgotten benefits of drawing.* Retrieved from http://blogs.scientificamerican.com/symbiartic/rediscovering-the-forgottn-benefits-of-drawing

LeCompte, M. D., & Preissle, J. (1993). *Ethnography and qualitative design in educational research.* San Diego, CA: Academic Press, Inc.

Marchant, J. (2016). The awakening. *Smithsonian, 46*(9), 80–95. (Washington, DC: Smithsonian Institution.)

Mason, C., Kahle, J. G., & Gardner, A. L. (1991). Draw-a-scientist test: Future implications. *School science and mathematics, 91*(5), 193–198.

McCormack, A. J. (1988). *Visual/spatial thinking: An essential element of elementary school science* (Monograph). San Diego, CA: Council for Elementary Science International (Division affiliate of NSTA).

Mead, M., & Metreaux, R. (1957). Image of the scientist. *Science, 126*(3270), 384–390.

Medin, D. L., & Bang, M. (2014). The cultural side of science communication. *Proceedings of the National Academy of Sciences, 111*(4), 13621–13626.

Momaday, N. S. (2015). The year that the stars fell, a pictographic calendar evokes the lost world of the Lakota. *Smithsonian, 45*(9), 42–43.

NRC. (2009). *Taking science to school.* Washington, DC: National Academies Press.

Paivio, A. (2014). Intelligence, dual coding theory, and the brain. *Intelligence, 47,* 141–158.

Pedersen, J. E., & Finson, K. D. (2009). *Visual data. Understanding and applying visual data to research in education.* Rotterdam: Sense Publishers.

Pylyshyn, Z. W. (1973). What the mind's eye tells the mind's brain, a critique of mental imagery. *Psychological Bulletin, 80,* 1.

Rennie, L. J., & Jarvis, T. (1995). Children's choice of drawings to communicate their ideas about technology. *Research in Science Education, 25*(3), 239–252.

Rosenthal, D. B. (1993). Images of scientists: A comparison of biology and liberal studies majors. *School Science and Mathematics, 93,* 212–216.

Rutherford, J., & Ahlgren, S. (1989). *Science for all Americans.* New York, NY: Oxford University Press.

Schibeci, R. A., & Sorensen, I. (1983). Elementary school children's perceptions of scientists. *School Science and Mathematics, 83,* 14–20.

Schwartz, G. (1986). A note to scientists, educators, and parents. In M. Brookes (Ed.), *Drawing with children* (pp. xv–xvii). Los Angeles, CA: Jeremy P. Tarcher, Inc.

Sousa, D. A. (2001). *How the brain learns.* Thousand Oaks, CA: Corwin Press.

Standring, S. (Ed.). (2015). *Gray's Anatomy.* The Netherlands: Elsevier.

Suddendorf, T., & Corballis, M. C. (2007). The evolution of foresight: What is mental time travel, and is it unique to humans? *Behavorial and Brain Sciences, 30,* 299–351.

Tibbetts, F. (2015). *Curriculum development and review for democratic citizenship and human rights education.* France: UNESCO/Council of Europe/Office for Democratic Institutions and Human Rights of the Organization for Security and Co-operation in Europe/Organization of American States Curriculum Development.

Treagust, D. F., Won, M., & Duit, R. (2014). Paradigms in science education research. In N. G. Lederman & S. K. Abell (Eds.), *Handbook of research in science education.* New York, NY: Routledge.

Van Meter, P., & Garner, J. (2005). The promise and practice of learner-generated drawing: Literature review and synthesis. *Educational Psychology Review, 17*(4), 285–325.

Wammes, J. D., Meade, M. E., & Fernandes, M. A. (2016). The drawing effect: Evidence for reliable and robust memory benefits in free recall. *The Quarterly Journal of Experimental Psychology, 69*(9), 1752–1776.

White, R., & Gunstone, R. (1992). *Probing understanding.* New York, NY: The Falmer Press.

Wind, G., & Valentine, R. J. (2013). *Anatomic exposures in vascular surgery* (3rd ed.). Philadelphia, PA: Lippincott, Williams & Wilkins.

Phyllis Katz
University of Maryland, USA

SECTION ONE

DRAWING A SINGLE IMAGE

JATILA VAN DER VEEN

2. DRAW YOUR PHYSICS HOMEWORK?

Art as a Path to Understanding and Assessment in Undergraduate Science Education

INTRODUCTION: ARTS-BASED TEACHING- A PATH TOWARD INCREASING DIVERSITY IN PHYSICS?

In spite of government initiatives to attract a more diverse population of learners into science and technology, results of a number of studies in the United States (Hazari et al., 2010; Blickenstaff, 2005, e.g.) and Europe (Sjøberg & Schreiner, 2007, e.g.) suggest that the standard introductory physics curriculum – the gateway course for all science and technology majors – may be a deterrent for many students, particularly females. Thus, my initial motivation for incorporating arts-based teaching strategies in an introductory physics course was an attempt to redress the persistent gender bias in physics by attracting a broader population of learners *in general*, which would naturally include females. After eight years of teaching this course, I can report that, although it remains a small-sized elective, 41% of the students who have completed my course are female – slightly more than double the most recent count of the percentage of women earning bachelors degrees in physics (http://www.aps.org/ programs/education/statistics/womenstem.cfm, 2015). The evaluations remain consistently high, with many students reporting in their anonymous exit comments that they would not have taken physics in college if not for this class, and several physics majors reporting that this course renewed their interest in pursuing a physics degree.

The separation of arts and sciences has been ingrained in Western society at least since the 17th century, and has been embedded in American education since the 19th century (Eisner, 2002). Eisner attributes the cultural dominance of science over the arts to the Enlightenment in Western society, which was heavily influenced by the emergence of Newtonian physics:

Science was considered dependable; the artistic process was not. Science was cognitive; the arts were emotional. Science was teachable; the arts required talent. Science was testable; the arts were matters of preference. Science was useful; the arts were ornamental. It was clear to many then, as it is to many today, which side of the coin mattered. (Eisner, 2002, p. 6)

In spite of this separation in education, *people* are not so compartmentalized in their ways of thinking, and many scientists pursue serious recreational or semi-professional endeavors in the arts. Historically, there is a likely correlation between explorations in music and discoveries in physics (Pesic, 2014). In my own life in physics and dance, I have noticed a great many people, both men and women, whom I meet at serious amateur recreational dance events (folk dance, contra dance, and ballroom competitions) have jobs in science or technology, and I know a surprising number of other semi-professional dancers (like myself) who have Ph.D.'s in science, engineering, or medicine. An email survey I sent to three international recreational dance mailing lists revealed that no fewer than 60% of respondents who dance have jobs in physics, engineering, or computer science (van der Veen, 2006). According to the U.S. Census for the year 2000, only 27% of middle-income urban populations held jobs in STEM fields, including architecture. The recent movement towards "turning STEM to STEAM" in K-12 and colleges in many states is evidence that educators, artists, and scientists are beginning to reach across the divide.

My research on arts-based teaching strategies in introductory physics is intertwined with my work on restructuring the introductory physics curriculum. In my undergraduate seminar, *Symmetry and Aesthetics in Contemporary Physics*, we explore Symmetry as the mathematical foundation of physics as well as the conceptual link between physics and the arts. We trace the development of symmetry and group theory from their origins in pure mathematics to their various manifestations in the phenomenological universe, and investigate how contemporary ideas of spacetime evolved from the discovery of broken symmetries in the late nineteenth and early twentieth centuries in classical mechanics, electromagnetic theory, and the discovery of the speed of light. Throughout the course we use drawing and other artistic representations to explore, explain, and comment upon mathematics and contemporary physics.

Symmetry in physics refers to the concept of 'sameness within change,' and is the basis of all the laws of physics. Symmetry is the set of rules that allow us to define the invariance of a system under rotations, reflections, and translations. Historically, when physicists have confronted an apparent paradox, it has been resolved by finding the symmetry that explains away the paradox by a change of coordinates (perspective). Thus, the search for deeper symmetries in Nature propels advancements in contemporary physics. Symmetry is also an important concept in human perception, biology, evolution, neuroscience, and chemistry. Symmetry and asymmetry are central to our aesthetic experiences in the arts, and thus provide a natural foundation for an interdisciplinary physics course that incorporates arts-based teaching strategies.

I start with contemporary physics as being more interesting and relevant to the lives of 21st century youth than classical Newtonian mechanics (Levrini, 1999), and treat math and the arts as complimentary semiotic systems for interrogating the physical universe (van der Veen, 2007, 2012, 2013). Teaching beginning students about Relativity and curved spacetime brings them face to face with some

P. Katz (Ed.), Drawing for Science Education, 11–29.
© *2017 Sense Publishers. All rights reserved.*

of the ontological questions that motivate contemporary physics at the largest scales. Moreover, teaching about Relativity in its historic context provides the iconic example of how symmetry has come to play a fundamental role in the development of contemporary physics. It also brings to the fore Professor Emmy Noether, whose theorems on the relationship between continuous symmetries in nature and conservation laws in physics have played a seminal, yet little known, role in the development of new physical theories, and thus foregrounds the discrimination that women in physics have faced historically, and continue to face.

The seminal question motivating my research is: Can we use the arts to bring more people into a healthy dialog with physics, thus potentially increasing the diversity of learners who choose to study physics, whether to become scientists, engineers, teachers, or as part of a contemporary education? From this starting point, several results have emerged which have implications for physics education as well as education in general, regarding drawing and other arts-based approaches in curriculum design and assessment, including:

- Having students draw their understanding of an article, concept, or equation allows students to get in touch with their own visualization and thinking styles, and provides instructors insight into the kinds of thinkers their students are, so as to design curricula appropriately;
- Having students design their own artistic representations of science concepts at the undergraduate level allows them a form of expression through which to develop their own voices in math and physics, and thus deepen their personal connection with these often impersonal subjects;
- Having students design their own representations of math and physics concepts provides instructors with an alternate, in many ways deeper and more comprehensive, assessment of their understanding;
- Incorporating arts-based teaching strategies at the undergraduate level, especially in intimidating subjects such as physics, has the potential to increase interest in the subject for students who may otherwise have avoided physics.

DRAWING AS A MEANS FOR STUDENTS TO GET IN TOUCH WITH THEIR OWN VISUALIZATION AND THINKING STYLES

In my work with college students, I have found that drawing is a means by which a learner (artist) can get in touch with and express her or his own inner language and visualization style, and understand how he or she goes about the internal process of making sense of externally received information. Swiss educator Johann Heinrich Pestalozzi (1746–1827) was the first to propose the idea of the *Anschauung*: mental imagery developed by abstraction from phenomena that have been directly experienced (Pestalozzi, 1805/1894). Pestalozzi advocated a threefold system of interrogating the world: visualization, numeration, and description, or what he called form, number, and language. For successful education, these three aspects of making sense and creating meaning out of the physical world cannot be separated (Pestalozzi, 1805/1894). Einstein himself was trained in this method of Anschauung at the Kantonsschule at Arrau (Miller, 1989).

Mathematician Jacques Hadamard studied thinking processes among mathematicians and scientists in the first half of the 20th century, and found a widespread reliance on visual thinking. In a frequently-quoted letter to Hadamard as part of this study, Einstein wrote:

The words or the language, as they are written or spoken, do not seem to play any role in my mechanisms of thought. The physical entities which seem to serve as elements in thought are certain signs and more or less clear images which can be voluntarily reproduced or combined…. this combinatory play seems to be the essential feature in productive thought before there is any connection with logical construction in words or other kinds of signs which can be communicated to others. (Hadamard, 1945/1954, p. 142)

In training students to think like scientists, the use of drawing and other arts-based representations, both student generated original representations and the study of professional artists' representations of physics concepts, should be an integral part of our science and math curriculum. The importance of visualization in scientific thought and discovery cannot be overstated, yet most early physics training at the undergraduate level relies exclusively on problem solving and the interpretation of graphs.

Some students visualize mathematical relationships quite easily, as reported by this first-year male physics student in 2007:

I think of calculus, differentials, and many other things visually. I am so entrenched in math that I use rudimentary forms of 'visual calculus' even when I play games. To imagine a curve of a damped oscillator is as intimately connected with a spring as the word 'apple' is to holding one in your hand.

For others, visualizing and translating their mental images into a physical representation is more difficult, as reported by a female political science major in 2011:

It is definitely very difficult to translate my mental image from my mind through a pen and onto paper. Although they are formed by me in my head, I almost can't grasp exactly how it appears to me.

Nevertheless, by the end of my course all the students are able to create a representation of a concept which inspired them, through the artistic medium of their choice – drawing, painting, sculpture, computer graphics, literature, poetry, dance, music, or a combination of media. They are able to communicate their ideas through their physics works of art to each other as well as to a general public audience in a gallery showing of their final physics works of art. They leave with a sense of pride, accomplishment, and community.

To set the tone of the course, I begin by interrogating the process of physics and the role of mathematics as a language of nature. For the first art assignment I ask students to draw their visualizations of Einstein's description of the nature of physics in his article *Physics and Reality*. Although Einstein wrote this essay in 1936, it is still relevant today.

FIRST DRAWING ASSIGNMENT: REPRESENTING AN ARTICLE BY EINSTEIN ON THE NATURE OF SCIENCE

Einstein's highly visual thinking style is evident in his 1936 essay, *Physics and Reality*. I assign this article as the first reading assignment in my course, Symmetry and Aesthetics in Contemporary Physics, which I teach every year in the College of Creative Studies at the University of California, Santa Barbara. The foundational assumptions of western science as articulated by Einstein in this piece make it an excellent starting point for discussions on the Nature of Science, summarized in the following quotes:

1. "The whole of science is nothing more than a refinement of everyday thinking" (p. 23);
2. "One may say 'the eternal mystery of the world is its comprehensibility.' It is one of the great realizations of Immanuel Kant that the postulation of a real external world would be senseless without this comprehensibility" (pp. 23–24);
3. "The aim of science is, on the one hand, a comprehension, as complete as possible, of the connection between the sense experiences in their totality, and, on the other hand, the accomplishment of this aim by the use of a minimum of primary concepts and relations" (p. 24).

In Einstein's view, primary concepts are connected directly to sensory experiences but lack in "logical unity." They are then connected to each other through a secondary level of concepts, which has a higher degree of logical unity, but is removed from direct sensory experience, and which is connected through successively higher layers until

we have arrived at a system of the greatest conceivable unity, and of the greatest poverty of concepts of the logical foundations, which is still compatible with the observations made by our senses. (p. 25)

The first art project I assign each year is for students to draw their understanding of this essay by Einstein. His visual writing style, coupled with my opinion that to understand the nature of science one must read the opinions of those who create and define the field, make this article an ideal starting point for introducing drawing as a means of understanding and sense-making in physics, especially in a course that seeks to create an oppositional identity to mainstream introductory physics.

Classifying Visualization Styles through Students' Drawings

Over the eight years I have taught this course I have observed that students' drawings fall into certain rather clear categories, suggesting that visualization style is a characteristic that reveals the way in which an individual makes internal sense out of the external world – a *language of the mind* (John-Steiner, 1997).

Previous studies have looked at the binary classification of visual and verbal learners, while others have further classified visual learners either spatially-oriented or object-oriented. According to Kozhevnikov, Kosslyn, and Shepphard (2005), object-oriented visualizers process images holistically, as a unit, while spatially-oriented visualizers process images analytically, part by part. Results of their study suggest that scientists and engineers tend to be spatially-oriented visualizers who have an easier time recalling processes, while artists tend to be object-oriented visualizers who have an easier time recalling static images as a whole. Other studies have claimed that males tend to be spatial visualizers while females tend to be object-oriented visualizers. The results of Kozhevnikov et al. (2005) suggest that there is no clear correlation between biological gender and either spatial visualization strategy or ability to solve abstract mathematical problems. A number of studies suggest that males tend to perform better than females on a variety of spatial orientation and mental rotation tasks (Collins & Kimura, 1997; Geary & Soto, 2001, e.g.). Hegarty and Kozhevnikov (1999) found that visual-spatial representations used by elementary school children while solving mathematical problems can be reliably classified as primarily schematic, associated with understanding spatial relationships from multiple perspectives, or primarily pictorial and object oriented. Moreover, they found that the use of primarily schematic spatial representations was positively correlated with success in mathematical problem solving, while the use of primarily pictorial representations was negatively correlated with success in math but positively correlated with success in art (p. 51). On the other hand, studies of visual imagery by Campos, Gomez-Juncal, and Perez-Fabello (2007) suggest that it is experience, rather than gender, which dictates a student's competence at generating mental images, and that the ability to produce vivid mental images is a learned skill that can be enhanced through instruction and practice.

When I began analyzing my students' drawings, I was curious to see whether the drawing styles of physics majors, biology majors, arts majors, and humanities majors would have any distinguishing recognizable characteristics, and whether the drawing styles of biological males and females would be different. I find that elements of spatial, temporal, and part-by-part visualizations, as well as holistic, at-a-glance types of drawings described in previous studies do not follow boundaries of gender or major in college. Rather, I observe six general categories of visualization styles, which emerged after four years of collecting students' drawings of their interpretation of the Einstein article. In the spirit of Grounded Theory, in which theory emerges from data, I developed a means of coding students' drawings based on general characteristics I found in their representations from year to year:

1. the type of symbols used: abstract or pictorial;
2. the type of representation: direct mapping of concept in the article to symbol in the picture or representation of the article as a whole by a pictorial analogy or metaphor;
3. the representation of some sort of temporal progression;
4. the representation of the article as a whole with an allegory or "what if" scenario (van der Veen, 2012).

Based on these characteristics, I named six categories of visualization style: *direct-symbolic, abstract- representational, metaphoric/analogical, allegorical-creative, flow chart,* and *hybrid* (van der Veen, 2012). After eight years, these categories remain. Moreover, certain themes within the general visualization styles have begun to repeat themselves.

Direct-symbolic drawings utilize recognizable objects or symbols to represent concepts in the article in a literal, one-to-one mapping of symbol to concept, sometimes with arrows drawn to indicate correspondences, or with labels placed directly on the drawing. Some drawings depict the heirarchy of concepts with a pyramid, while others use examples of what students consider to be a hierarchical ordering of concepts (microscopes to telescopes, e.g.), but all are more-or-less literal interpretations of the article (Figures 1–4).

Abstract-representational drawings are also literal interpretations of the article, but use abstract symbols with a one-to-one correspondence between the symbol in the drawing and the concept in the article instead of recognizable objects. No labels are included directly on the drawing, but the direct, one-to-one correspondence between symbol in the drawing and concept in the article is described by the student in the written or verbal description of his/her drawing (Figures 7 and 8).

Metaphoric/analogical drawings use a metaphor or analogy to represent the article as a whole with a single vision, almost a poetic painting that captures what the student artist senses as the gestalt of the article (Figures 9–11).

Allegorical-creative drawings represent the article as a whole with a pictorial story (allegory or 'what if' scenario) that seems to begin where the article leaves off (Figure 12).

Flow charts incorporate some element of temporal progression using arrows to indicate the sequential nature of science or the flow of concepts. The drawings I have classified as flow charts utilize a range of symbols connected by arrows to represent the flow of ideas in the article, from completely pictorial to completely verbal (Figure 13).

Hybrid drawings do not appear to fit squarely into a single category, but embody elements of two or more categories, such as direct-symbolic and allegorical (Figures 5a and 5b), direct-symbolic and metaphoric-analogical (Figure 6), and flow chart and metaphoric-analogical (Figure 14).

After four years of giving the same initial drawing assignment, I noticed these patterns and named them. I searched for a theoretical model through which to build a case for a relationship between students' preferred visualization styles and their preferred learning styles, and found Felder and Silverman's (1988) model of learning preferences of engineering students (Felder & Silverman, 1988; Felder, 1993). In their original model, Felder and Silverman describe five opposing traits which, in varying proportions, describe students' learning preferences: sensory vs. intuitive, visual vs. verbal, inductive vs. deductive, active vs. reflective, and sequential vs. global. I looked for a correlation between the visualization styles I found in my students' drawings and Felder and Silverman's learning preferences model (van der Veen, 2012). However, after eight years of giving the same initial drawing assignment, I feel that it is more appropriate to interpret these visualization styles as "languages of the mind" (John-Steiner, 1997) rather than constrain them by any specific cognitive-behavioral descriptions, as students who draw the same type of visualization do not necessarily fit into similar learning patterns. Rather, students' preferred visualization styles are a kind of window into their minds, providing insights into their backgrounds, the experiences they bring to the study of physics, their prejudices and personal philosophies, as well as how they process information. In a very real sense, students' drawings in an undergraduate physics seminar reveal the literacy narratives they bring with them (Kendrick & McKay, 2010), and use to make sense out of their study of physics.

I use this first drawing assignment not only to set the tone of using drawing as a means of sense-making and communication in physics, but also to encourage students to find their individual 'visualization voices,' and understand their own internal ways of knowing and sense making. My students continue to develop their representational competence in three more arts-based assignments throughout the course, culminating in their final physics works of art. The final projects are displayed in one of the campus art galleries, with a public reception in which the students must explain the concept(s) they have chosen to represent to an audience of peers, faculty and staff, and members of the public (see, for example: http://www.news.ucsb.edu/2015/015237/art-physics).

Below I present examples of the six types of visualization categories that have emerged from the first art assignment, "Draw your understanding of Einstein's article, *Physics and Reality*."

Direct Symbolic Representations

The unifying feature of direct-symbolic drawings is the one-to-one mapping of symbol in the drawing to concept in the article, often with labels written directly on the drawing. Some students choose to represent the *process* of doing science described by Einstein as a linear progression, while others choose to represent the *hierarchy of concepts*, but in either case there is no ambiguity as to the correspondence between symbols in the drawing statements in the article. Examples of of direct-symbolic drawings by a literature major, a political science major, an art major, and a religious studies major are shown in Figures 1, 2, 3, and 4, respectively. I have chosen these examples because they are all direct symbolic drawings, but also display a range of interpretations by students who have had limited or no prior exposure to physics.

Figure 1 was drawn by a literature major, who stated that she would have been more comfortable doing a literary interpretation, such as a poem (which she did for her final project), than a drawing:

> In this essay, Einstein discusses the limits of human knowledge. He describes a subjective reality which is built on the framework of "sense perceptions" tied together by logical deductions. Einstein then describes an ontological hierarchy, a pyramid of sorts, in which primary concepts and statements of reality are narrowed down until we are left with the point of the pyramid, which is the essence of reality.

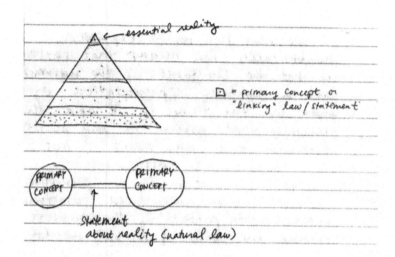

Figure 1. Direct symbolic representation. Female literature major, 2007 (Van der Veen, 2007,2012)

Figure 2, drawn by a female political science major, depicts the process of doing science as linear, starting from external events which are taken in by the senses to form an internalized concept of reality, represented by an array of mathematical and musical symbols, depicted in no particular order.

> The ability to construct a reality or external world comes from the associations we make between our sensory inputs and our concept of bodily objects. Our minds give significance to these concepts and the relations between different concepts allow us to connect sense expressions and create a "reality." This translates into comprehensibility which is the production of some sort of order among sense impressions.

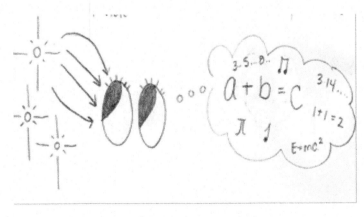

Figure 2. Direct symbolic drawing. Female political science major, 2011

Figure 3 was drawn by a third year female art major. I classify it as direct symbolic because of her use of labels on the drawing.

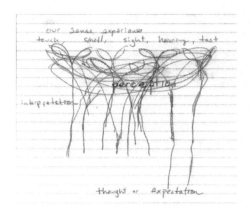

Figure 3. Direct symbolic drawing. 3rd year female art major, 2007

In her brief description she referred only to statements made by Einstein in the first two pages of the article:

Einstein is saying that a physicist must start to philosophize because the foundation of our experience is shifty. Because science is thinking, it is then natural to examine the process of thought.

Her interpretation of Einstein's culmination of the layers of sensory input and theory leading to the *"greatest conceivable unity"* of concepts as merely *"thought or expectation"* could represent the fact that she did not complete the reading assignment, but did not want to come to class empty-handed, or perhaps I should have recognized her drawing as a sign that she was going to need extra help. Throughout most of the course she expressed an intense mistrust of physics and physicists, including physicists' use of language and their emphasis on theory over sensory perception. Her frustration reached its peak expression in her literary argument with Nobel Laureate Richard Feynman's description of the surface of a cylinder as a flat space (Feynman, 1963):

…when it comes to a cylinder whose space seems to be obviously curved we find it does not have curved space because Euclidian geometry holds. My first reaction is to say that the definition that Feynman gave in the beginning must be wrong because a cylinder is obviously curved to an outside perspective despite not having intrinsic curvature.

She contined with her verbal confrontations about this issue with me, with the physics majors in the class, and after class with a post-doctoral scholar with whom I shared an office at that time. By the end of the course, though, she reversed her opinion, and wrote in her final evaluation:

I found this course to be wonderfully exciting. The instructor and the students were wonderful and passionate, which made the class a pleasure. I had to overcome and grapple with a lot of struggles with math and understanding the language of science. I wish that this class would continue and I could continue to study the math and science in such an integrated way.

Figure 4 was drawn by a third year male religious studies major. I classified his drawing as direct symbolic because he lists his legend in the upper left, and uses labels and arrows to indicate the correspondence of symbols in his drawing to his legend.

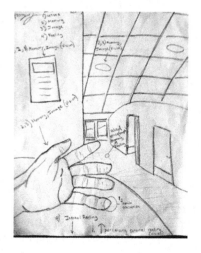

Figure 4. Direct symbolic. 3rd year male religious studies major, 2014

Like the art major who drew Figure 3, his interpretation of the article also diverges from Einstein's intention. He starts with sensory input, but ends not with "logical unity" but with *feeling*. In his drawing, "Internal Feeling" is indicated with an arrow as being outside the perimeter of the drawing, off the page (bottom) or out the door. Kendrick and McKay (2002) suggest that children's drawings reveal a great deal about the literacy narratives they bring with them to school. Referencing Vygotsky (1978), they suggest that drawings represent "a graphic speech that conceptualizes an internal representation of story".

Both Figures 3 and 4 suggest that the science-literacy narratives their creators brought to the course differ significantly from the majority opinion in the physics community. For his final project, the artist who drew Figure 4 chose to draw his interpretation of an article we read by theoretical physicist Andrei Linde about the "multiverse" – the possibility that ours is only one of an infinite number of universes – as a male being inflating a balloon. He wrote:

> The idea behind the drawing is that someone is blowing up the balloon bringing up the question of a divine being behind all of the universes [sic] activity. […] It seems that there is [sic] always new theories pertaining to the external world, and a lack of looking inwardly for explanations of physical reality.

Figures 5a, 5b, and 6, drawn by male physics majors in 2013, 2015, and 2014 respectively, are examples of what I consider hybrid drawings because they combine elements of direct symbolic mapping of the narrative of the article with allegorical and metaphoric elements.

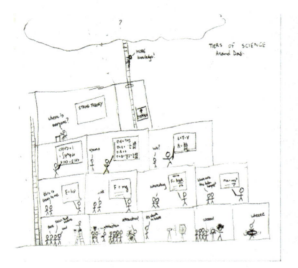 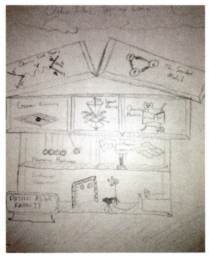

Figure 5. Hybrid: Direct symbolic/allegorical. 5a (left): Ananda Das, 3rd year physics major, 2013.
5b (right): 1st year male physics major, 2015

Figures 5a and 5b show the process of doing phyics, starting from sensory observation on the first floor, moving up through increasingly abstract levels, and ending with the unknown – represented by clouds above. As cartoon-like interpretations of Einstein's article, these drawings relate his levels of abstraction described to the artists' personal experiences. The artist who drew Figure 5a explained:

> This was my interpretation of Einstein's article. The bottom floor represents the "sense impressions", those basic observables that everyone sees and agrees with and as you go higher up, we see the scientists need to attain logical unity, creating more and more abstract formulas to describe more and more general stuff. As you go higher in the building, less people can relate as we go farther from the "sense impressions".

Figure 5b represents the first instance in 8 years that I have seen of the recurrance in a subsequent year, not just of a drawing type, but almost a repeat of the same drawing.

Hybrid

Figure 6, a water color painted by a first year physics major, is a picture at a glance of the process of physics, with a beach scene as a metaphor for the development of theories from direct observations, but also has elements of a direct symbolic drawing because of his one-to-one mapping of concept in the article to symbol in the drawing.

The artist described his work thus:

> I took the process of "doing physics" not to mean how an individual does physics, but rather how we as a people do physics. Furthermore, I see physics as the restless science, it never ceases to look for answers. Where biology and chemistry stop, physics

Figure 6. Direct symbolic/metaphoric. 1st year physics major, 2014

continues. It seeks to understand the true nature of everything. Here I have a watercolor landscape of a beach. It is a metaphor for our understanding of everything. You may notice the island out in the distance and the small rocks embedded in the surf. I used the rocks and the island to symbolize distinct points of knowledge waiting to be discovered out in the universe. We start from one, perhaps the smallest might be our realization of kinematics; it is closest to us relative to our sensory experiences. We can all observe a falling object, an object in motion. From here we may build upon our observation and form layers as Einstein described it. The next rock perhaps symbolizes the discovery of the unity of Electricity and Magnetism, and the large rocks to the left a truer glimpse of reality as we know it. They might represent Relativity, Quantum Mechanics. The island is a great distance away, but one might say reachable. As you can see the colors are typically muted. I used an assortment of grays to give the impression of a fog, in order to symbolize the obscurity in the universe and the abstraction that comes with the accumulation of layers, in this case symbolized by the distance from our rather modest start, the humble pebbles in the surf.

Abstract Representational Drawings

Abstract-representational drawings are one-to-one mappings between concept in the article and symbolic representation on the paper using abstract symbols, rather than recognizable objects. Figure 7, drawn by a first year female physics major in 2007, is my iconic example of an abstract representation of the article.

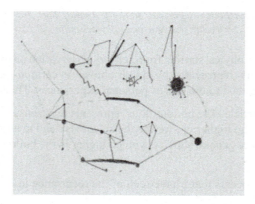

Figure 7. Abstract representational drawing. 1st year female physics major, 2007

She wrote:

In my visual representation, each dot represents a sensory perception of the nebulous reality (shaded area). The size and substance of each dot may represent the accuracy of our measurements, or the number of times the sensory perception has been repeated and confirmed by different people/methods. The lines between sensory perceptions are mental connections we have made. […] Some connections are broken, as they have been shown by substantial sensory experience to be unlikely. There are not well-defined layers, since, as Einstein stated in his article, "the layers…are not clearly separated. It is not even absolutely clear which concepts belong to the primary layer."

Figure 8 was drawn by a fourth year male physics major. He explained that the five corners with different types of abstract designs represent the five senses, each sense giving a different perception of external input.

Figure 8. Abstract representational drawing, 4th year male physics major, 2015

Metaphoric / Analogical Representations

Figures 9 through 11 are examples where the student represented Einstein's description of the process of doing physics with a single pictorial metaphor. Whereas the direct symbolic and abstract representational drawings are more or less pictorial mappings of the *processes* described by Einstein, these metaphoric drawings are a snapshot of the *gestalt* of the article *as a whole*, as experienced by these artists.

Figure 9a was drawn by a second year male math major. He explained his drawing:

Figure 9. Metaphonic/analogic drawings. Left (9a): The Reptile of Science, second year male math major, 2008.
Right (9b): (no title), first year male physics and math major, 2007

At the top, you see a fairly detailed, intricate picture of something that looks intimidating, but as the viewer's eyes progress down, the shape is simplified and simplified until it becomes an innocent, almost stickfigure-esque drawing. This symbolizes how our sense impressions of the real world, a powerful experience, is abstracted by science until it becomes something simpler and more friendly to use.

The artist who drew Figure 9b was a first year male double-major in physics and math. Rather than give his reader (in this case, the instructor) a blow-by-blow description of his drawing, he lets the symbolism speak for itself:

> Einstein proposes that the goal of science is reductionist by its very nature. To take the entirety of our sensory experiences (and now, things that are well beyond it) and congeal it, if you wish, into a form which is both elegant and complete. He suggests that we must strike a balance between seeking logical unity through "abstraction" and a direct connection with our experiences.

Figure 10 was drawn by a first year male physics major. He likened the process of doing physics to peeling back the layers of an onion:

> The way I picture the creative process of scientific discovery, especially in theoretical physics, it's quite overwhelming. The amount of theories and equations before one can find the truth, are endless and even then we can only be so sure. This contrast of beauty and struggle reminded me of an onion; on the outside it's wrapped in crunchy, dirty brown paper but as the first layer is removed it's quite shiny and pretty and as each layer is torn off the next is smoother and whiter, quite like how science is less

messy and more elegant and symmetrical at each major breakthrough. But in the process of peeling back the platinum layers of the onion there's a pungent smell and tears begin to flow this reminded me of the feeling of awe when learning about Einstein's theory relativity for the first time, how it seems wildly incompatible with the reality we experience but at a closer look it is absolutely correct. At the center of the onion I drew an eye at the point where the onion stops being layers, when there is normally just a small white bulb, to represent the final truth, as if to be looking into the eye of god at the end of the journey.

Figure 10. Metaphoric/analogical drawing by 1st year male physics major, 2015

Hybrid

Figure 11, drawn by a second year male math major, I have classified as hybrid, as I feel it combines elements of a metaphoric/analogical representation of the article as a whole with an allegorical/creative story in which the artist interprets Einstein's intentions with a scenario that goes beyond the article. He writes:

> My picture is of a man meditating inside of a particle accelerator. However the darkened, meditating man is only a symbol for Einstein's "sense experience." […] This person represents the essence of the creativity and intuition of whoever made what's being studied possible. […] The man in the middle of the accelerator is referring to this intelligent being of collective thought that has been produced alongside the information that was received by the researchers, the people that made the hardware possible, and the theorists. This seems to encourage the collaboration of mankind toward science as well as advocate intuition in physics and science. When gathering information from this particle accelerator you not only see the information you're after, but you also see the stream of intelligent thought that went into this creation in knowledge. I think in his article Einstein wants to portray the importance of intuition and creativity in the scientific method for discovery.

Figure 11. Metaphoric/analogical drawing, 2nd year male math major, 2015

Allegorical Representations

Allegorical representations take off from the article with a pictorial allegory or a 'what if?' scenario. These drawings often have a whimsical flavor reminiscent of the drawings of highly creative adolescents described in the famous study by Getzels and Jackson (1962), in which they contrasted high-I.Q. and highly creative adolescents in a Midwest suburban high school. When asked to produce drawings, the students identified as high-I.Q. depicted literal representations of the drawing prompts, whereas those identified as highly creative drew whimsical, less rule-bound interpretations (Getzels & Jackson, 1962).

Figure 12 is my iconic example of a 'what if' scenario, drawn by a second year female political science major. In her drawing she explores the possibility of a different reality that would be developed by beings in which the sense of sight is missing. She wrote on her drawing, "This is a lighted version of a world with no eyes." Above the picture she drew a sun with a circle around it, crossed by a diagonal slash, as if to indicate "No Sun here." The fingers and toes of her beings have extended pads, indicating an enhanced sense of touch. She described her drawing:

> In a world with no sight priorities for necessities in a house would change. People would maybe [be] ultra-sensitive and appreciate things like music and fuzzy walls more. Here there would be less absolutes [sic] without visual aids. The idea that the blanket is warm and fluffy is stronger than the idea of the blanket itself.

She added a few notes at the bottom of her paper: "6th sense: heat sensory? Privacy is not a term. Beauty changes."

Other examples of allegorical drawings that my students have depicted include the familiar story of Plato's Cave (see van der Veen, 2012, p. 388) and the story of the blind scientists who try to define an elephant by each investigating a small portion of the animal.

Figure 12. A world without sight. Second year female political science major, 2011

Discussion. The use of drawing for understanding has the potential to reveal highly creative students, who would probably go unrecognized in a conventional introductory physics class. Anthropologist Sheila Tobias refers to the search for talent that is "differently packaged from the norm" (Tobias, 2006) as *stalking the second tier* (Tobias, 1990). In her study of highly motivated, "A" students from non-science majors, some of whom had positive experiences with physics in high school but all of whom avoided physics in college, Tobias found that the impersonal culture of the introductory physics classroom and the lack-of-narrative, no-room-for-questions pedagogical style were some of the main reasons why a large portion of talented students avoid physics in college. From my students' weekly and end-of-term evaluations (which are supposed to be anonymous, but some students choose to sign them), it is evident that the approach taken in this course has the potential to redress some of the culture of physics issues which serve as barriers to many talented, non-traditional students:

> Thank you for one of the craziest (cool) classes I've taken my whole time being here. Not many classes care about what you think, but in your class I felt like my understanding was the whole point. (female political science major, 2011)

> The creation of the final project was important for me to be able to digest many of the concepts that we discussed in class. It gave me the ability develop an understanding and a personal reference to concepts that I found challenging. This was an invaluable part of my study of physics and I greatly appreciated the opportunity to learn in an integrated manner. (female art major, 2007)

> Thank you so much for teaching this class. I don't think I've ever been quite so stimulated by a class here as much as your class has done for me. I thought the material was awesome and the readings were great, although difficult at times. Thank you for opening up my mind more! (female biopsychology major, 2010)

Flow Charts

I define flow charts as visual representations that indicate progressive relationships between concepts, often depicted with arrows or connecting lines. Though other drawing styles may contain elements of temporal progression, in flow chart drawings the mapping of the flow of ideas is the dominant characteristic. Figure 13 was drawn by a fourth-year male physics major in 2007. On his drawing he wrote,

It is fairly easy to draw this as there is something fundamentally simple going on: using logic to refine logic.

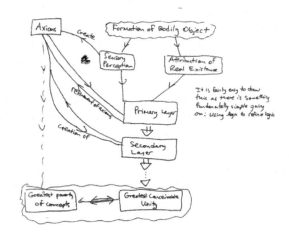

Figure 13. Flow chart, 4th year male physics major, 2007

Figure 14 is a hybrid between a metaphoric/analogical representation of the article-at-a-glance and a flow chart, in the sense that it depicts a temporal progression of the development of ideas as an equation, going from left to right across the page, but uses the metaphor of a pictorial representation of an equation to represent the hierarchy of the layers of understanding. The artist explained his drawing, "The sum, from i = 0 to infinity of all forms of existence adds up to an increasingly accurate picture of reality." The "Higher Order Terms" represent what we don't yet understand.

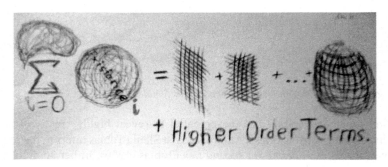

Figure 14. Hybrid: flow/chart/metaphoric-analogical, 1st year male physics major, 2010

Over eight years of teaching this course and giving this assignment, with an average of ten to twelve students in each class, only five students have drawn what I call flow charts, and only one student drew a flow chart without any accompanying pictures (Figure 13). (He also used the same drawing style in a later assignment (van der Veen, 2007, Figure. 6.13, p. 265). I cannot say whether visualizing in temporal progression is an uncommon thinking style, or whether a course called Symmetry and Aesthetics in Contemporary Physics, which advertises a physics work of art as the final project simply does not attract these kind of thinkers.

Discussion. Assigning a visual representation of Einstein's essay as the first drawing and reading assignment of the course sets the direction in terms of both content and expectations. His article describes physics as the search for deeper and more unifying theories; this sets the trajectory for the course, in which we take the point of view that symmetry provides the framework for that search. Having students draw their interpretation of his article sets the expectation of developing one's internal visualization style for the purpose of understanding and communication of ideas and opinions; and critiquing this article by one of the most idolized icons of the physics community encourages and endorses students' forming and sharing their own opinions about the practice of physics. For most students, this assignment represents their first experience with being asked to draw their understanding of a text, and being asked to give their opinion about physics. This first drawing assignment is also an opportunity for the instructor to get an idea of his or her students' visualization styles. While students' comfort levels and competence at designing representations of physics concepts is expected to improve over the duration of the course, their visualization *styles* do not change. Thus by getting an idea of how each student processes information, the instructor can use this knowledge to assess students' understanding of concepts through their visual representations throughout the course. In the next section I present examples of students' representations of concepts in theoretical physics, comparing correct representations with representations that illustrate where students are having difficulty.

UNDERGRADUATES' ARTISTIC REPRESENTATIONS OF CONCEPTS IN SPECIAL AND GENERAL RELATIVITY

Having students design their own artistic representations of science concepts at the undergraduate level allows them a form of expression so as to develop their own voices in math and science, and provides an alternate, in many ways deeper and more comprehensive, assessment of their understanding. Having students design their own representations of concepts in physics also encourages the development of *meta-representational competence* (diSessa, 2004, pp. 293–294) which includes having students invent or design new representations for concepts in science, explain and critique representations, and understand how representations function in conveying ideas (ibid.). In conventional physics classes, students are taught to interpret and reproduce standard representations (graphs, force diagrams, e.g.), but by inventing their own representations, they are actually participating in the work of scientists, who continually seek ways to artistically represent new ideas and discoveries to the public and to each other. In this section I present examples that illustrate when students' clear understanding is apparent from their artistic representations of concepts, as well as examples of how to use students' representations to understand where they need help as well as what they do know. In addition, I have included some of the same artists whose visualization styles were represented in the previous section, to highlight the consistency of students' visualization styles.

For the final physics work of art students select a topic from the course that most interested them, or one which generated questions they wish to explore beyond the scope of the course. Figures 15 and 16 show two different representations of the concept of the light cone. Figure 15a, a wire sculpture representing the intersecting light cones of two observers in relative motion at a constant velocity, was done by a third-year physics major (see also Figure 5a). In a post-course interview the artist explained his motivation to create this physics work of art:

> My motivation behind creating this piece was that Special Relativity confuses everyone, even the physics majors, and I definitely needed to see it three or four times before I really grasped it. And so I wanted to come up with a way to easily demonstrate weird three dimensional, four dimensional concepts that they talk about. And in particular, a certain paradox that I've found interesting, and easy to illustrate as well.

Figure 15. Two representations of the light cone. Left (a) Wire sculpture, depicting the relative rotation of reference frames for two observers moving at constant relative velocity that is close to the speed of light, each at the center of his own light cone. Artist is a 3rd year physics major. Right (b) Computer-generated illustration of the cross section of a light cone for a single observer. Artist is a 2nd year computer science major, 2013

Figure 15b, a computer-generated work of art, was produced by second-year computer science major. In his written explanation the artist describes the concept and his fascination with the ideas of Special Relativity, approaching a kind of awe or reverance, and he uses his work to inspire others. He writes,

> For my final project I decided to present the Einstein-Minkowski spacetime, characteristically represented by a light cone which was first conceived by Hermann Minkowski. The double cone is centered at every event in spacetime, with the upper (future) cone representing the future of a light-flash emitted at that event, and the lower (past) cone representing all the direction from which the light-flash could have come from [sic]. The slope of the cone is dependent on the speed of light. <…> For me, the light cone is a symbol that represents not only how modern physics has changed our perception of space and time, but also causality, existence and the physical limitations of what is possible for us to detect and know.

Figure 16 shows part of the illustrated explanation of the wire sculpture shown in Figure 15a. The artist writes,

> If a person in the dark emits a flash of light, he perceives himself to be at the center of an expanding sphere of light, but another person running away from the first will also perceive himself to be at the center of an expanding sphere of light. How can this be? The explanation is that motion can rotate your perception of space and time.

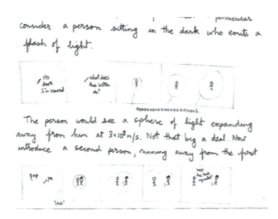

Figure 16. Portion of the explanation of the light cone show in Figure 15. Artist is a 3rd year physics major, 2013

He wrote a multi-page illustrated explanation, which he designed in the traditional physics way of posing a question, confronting an apparent paradox, and then removing the apparent contradiction with a change of reference frame in which the paradox vanishes. His visualization and representational style is consistent, from his first assignment (Figure 5a) to the final project, as is his incorporation of humor.

The top row of the cartoon depicts a single person, who is apparently in the dark ("It's dark. I'm scared.") and who turns on a light ("what does this button do?"). From that 'event' in spacetime (i.e., turning on the light) we then see a cross section of the expanding light cone. In the bottom row we see a second observer appear, whose motivation to run in a different direction is the fact that he stole the first person's wallet ("Hey, he stole my wallet!"). I would also include my write-up as part of the art project, because I enjoyed doing it, and I definitely think that humor and simplicity are very important in communicating a deep concept, because I definitely found a lot of people just switch their brains off when someone talks ab out their physics to them. And it's important to kind of trick them into learning something new.

Figures 17a and 17b contrast two students: the first, a physics major, who has a solid command of the topic of length contraction and time dilation for two observers in relative motion at constant velocity close to the speed of light; and the second, a non-physics major who is struggling with the concepts, has understood some of them, but has missed some of the key elements. Both were drawn in response to reading a short section about the Lorentz Transformation from Einstein's short book entitled *Relativity – The Special and the General Theory – A Clear Explanation that Anyone Can Understand*, which he intended for a general audience. Prior to assigning this reading, students had a lecture-presentation on the historic development of Special Relativity. The class was then given the reading by Einstein for homework, with the assignment to draw the way they each visualized what he was describing through his equations and discussion. The goal of this assignment was to see whether, after having had some practice with visualizations of Einstein's writing and some of the math of symmetry, students could read a new text and apply their visualization strategies to a new concept.

Figure 17a (drawn by a fourth year physics major) is an allegorical representation illustrating the apparent paradox of two reference frames – the frame of the snake and that of the platform – in relative motion at speeds close to the speed of light ("c"). The caption says:

Snake moving at .99c: In its reference frame, the cutters appear to be closer together, and will easily cut the snake in 3. But, in the cutters' reference frame, the snake seems shorter, short enough not to be cut. Which happens?

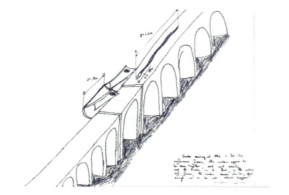 

Figure 17. Representations of the apparent paradox of relative motion of two observers at a constant velocity, when their relative speed is close to the speed of light. Left (a), Will the snake get cut? 4th year male physics major, 2011. Right (b). Observer in two reference frames, K and K'. Second year female political science major, 2011

His drawing of the snake was also in part a criticism of my choice of the reading assignment, which he felt fell short because it lacked an explanation of the consequence of a relative motion, namely the lack of simultaneity of events. In his reading reflection on the text, he writes:

[Einstein] doesn't explain the consequences of the Lorentz transformation very much: time dilation and length contraction. There are real-world consequences that elevate this beyond a purely mathematical exercise – I would like to see a discussion of them, and in particular their consequences for near-c travel. Also, I would like to see a discussion of how all this destroys the notion of simultaneity, which leads me into my Einstein drawing.

The destrction of the notion of simultaneity inherent in his drawing is that if the front and back blades descend simultaneously from the viewpoint of an observer on the cutters (at rest with respect to the platform, represented by the eyes drawn on the cutters), from the viewpoint of the snake the front blade will descend before the back blade does. (I leave the gruesome consequences to the imagination of the reader.) This drawing depicts a story, a what-if scenario, so that I would categorize his visualization style as allegorical/creative.

Figure 16b was drawn by the same student who drew the World without Sight (Figure 12). In her description of her drawing she wrote:

Disclaimer: I had a lot of trouble understanding any of this, but this is what I do understand. K is a reference frame…for example if I was on a train and I threw a ball, to me the ball goes up and down, but from the earth perspective the ball moves horizontally. Einstein looked at a light pulse in both reference frames <…>. X is the distance traveled, c is the speed of light and t is the time. The assumption, that if you look at ct light in one reference frame, time and distance change. The only thing that stays the same is c…I think that's the idea.

Note that even though she struggled with the concepts in this assignment, her characteristic allegorical/creative visualization style still comes through in her drawings of the two observers in relative motion (Einstein and a dragon).

I chose the examples in Figures 17a and 17b to contrast the representation drawn by a student who clearly understands the material with that of a less experienced student. To be able to assess students' comprehension through their drawings requires that an instructor be completely familiar with the concepts, so as to be able to differentiate the nuances of understanding demonstrated by students' representations. Any physics instructor can recognize the problem correctly posed by the drawing of the snake, and assess that this student understands the material. The drawing is sparse and to the point, including only relevant details (the eyes on the cutters represent the observer on the platform). The drawing of Einstein and the dragon contains many irrelevant and unconventional details, but on closer inspection it is clear that this student does understand some of the important points that are brought out by the Lorentz Transformation: namely, that the speed of light is constant for all observers, and that relative motion at high speeds rotates the reference frames of two observers.

Students' Representation of Concepts in General Relativity

Professor Andrea DiSessa (U.C. Berkeley) coined the term conceptual homomorphism to indicate a description that is less detailed than the full (mathematical) description of a concept, but preserves the relevant structural relationships (2013, pers. comm.). The piece shown in Figure 18 is an example of a conceptual homomorphism, a representation of the concept of General Covariance, the dynamical symmetry of General Relativity which describes the deformation of 4-dimensional space-time due the presence of mass-energy. Created by a first-year art major, it is a booklet of transparencies which represent 2-dimensional slices through 4-dimensional space-time demonstrating distortion of an image in regions of space-time that are distorted by the presence of mass (gravity). The drawings are accomplished by understanding the rule that maps one image into the next through consecutive slices of distorted space-time. In her description she wrote:

This piece was inspired by the concept of general covariance. Nine drawings were drawn on nine unique grids. The image of the man and woman is distorted and layered one on top of the other. Each drawing is warped, as spacetime will do, yet still preserves a system and basic foundation.

This physics work of art is an excellent artistic rendition of the conceptual meaning behind Einstein's field equations of General Relativity, which are the set of rules that tell you how spacetime is curved in a particular region due to the particular local configuration of mass and energy contained within that volume of spacetime. Mona's nine grids, layered on top of one another, are the set of rules that tell her how to distort the image of the man and woman drawn on the top transparency. She has represented curved geometry as we experience it, by representing slices through it (think of a contour map). Quoting Professor Andrea diSessa, " [A] "curved" shape is actually (typically) a slice of space that is up/down symmetric, and which would look like a "flat plane" from the side, e.g., the plane of an orbit" (diSessa, 2013, pers. comm.).

Compare the correct conceptual homomorphism shown in Figure 18 with the representation shown in Figure 18, in which the artist, a third-year art major (Figure 3) attempted to represent the way mass curves spacetime with her hanging installation of dried beans deforming knitted squares which are suspended from all four corners by string. This representation is really an *embedding diagram* – a two-dimensional analog of four-dimensional spacetime curvature – and, although it is commonly used in text books, it is actually not a correct conceptual homomorphism of true spacetime curvature.

Figure 18a. Booklet of transparencies illustrating the principle of General Covariance. Artist, a 1st year art major, 2013

Figure 18b. One of the transparencies from the booklet above

Figure 19 Gravity-inspired installation, 3rd year female art major, 2007

As with Figures 17a and 17b, Figures 18 and 19 contrast a student who demonstrates a more complete understanding of a concept with one who has a partial or incomplete understanding. The drawings of Figure 16 were in-progress assignments during the course, while those of Figures 17 and 18 were final projects. Through the students' drawings, a discerning instructor can see which students understand the concepts fully, and where some students need help with incomplete understanding. The artist who drew Figure 16b understands that a Lorentz boost rotates spacetime axes, but because of her lack of familiarity with physics, needs help seeing that such a rotation goes through "complex" space, so that rotated axes appear flattened from our perspective (as in the light cones of Figure 15a). The artist who created the installation shown in Figure 19 understands that mass deforms spacetime, but needs help to visualize this as taking place in three dimensions (for example, with the analogy of the gravitational field of the Earth, where the notions of "up" and "down" vary from the northern to southern hemispheres).

DISCUSSION

I started teaching *Symmetry & Aesthetics in Contemporary Physics* as an experiment to develop an alternative to the standard introductory physics curriculum which was designed to make physics more appealing and accessible to a broad spectrum of learners, including students who might be curious about physics but avoid the traditional large introductory classes. Over the eight years I have taught the class, I have continued to refine the curriculum and improve my own understanding of how to use what I have called *arts-based teaching strategies* to help students visualize abstract concepts, as well as use students' creative representations to assess their understanding of the concepts. The progression of assignments through the course is designed to have students first understand their personal visualization styles, and then to use their visualization strategies to develop effective ways of communicating their understanding of concepts to others.

Other studies have emphasized the importance of having students develop their own visualizations and creative representations of concepts as an important strand of science education. The term *meta-representational competence* (MRC) coined by Professor of Physics and Education Andrea diSessa (2004) is described as "the ability to choose the optimal external representation for a task, use novel external representations productively, and invent new representations as necessary" (Heggarty, 2011, p. 1240). DiSessa (2004) suggests that "learning may implicate developing one's own personally effective representations for dealing with a conceptual domain" (p. 299), while Heggarty recommends that "more attention should be paid to teaching people to use, design, and critique external spatial representations, in addition to training their internal visualization abilities" (p. 1241). Psycholinguistics professor Vera John-Steiner defines thinking as "to hold an idea long enough to unlock and shape its power in the varied contexts of shared human knowledge" (John-Steiner, 1997, p. 9).

Overall, students' reactions to the curriculum and methodology have been quite positive in all years, as indicated by their final evaluations. In 2007, I administered the Maryland Physics Expectation Survey (MPEX) (Redish, Saul, & Steinberg, 1998). The students in my class demonstrated significant gains in attitudes toward physics as compared with students in the original survey of 1500 undergraduates, whose attitudes towards physics declined after a one-year introductory course (van der Veen, 2007). I have not administered the MPEX again; rather, students' weekly exit cards and end-of-course evaluations indicate their positive reactions, and the course scores well above the standard undergraduate physics courses in the end-of-quarter numeric evaluations. Since we started displaying the final physics works of art in the college's art gallery and holding a public reception, the course has been attracting additional attention, so that this year I had students who enrolled in the class because they have seen the gallery show and wanted the opportunity to participate. At the time of this writing, in response to an article written about the recent gallery show (March, 2015), my students have been invited to exhibit their work in a prominent place in the university library for three months.

CONCLUSION: THE IMPORTANCE OF DRAWING AND OTHER ARTISTIC REPRESENTATIONS IN SCIENCE EDUCATION

Incorporating arts-based teaching strategies at the undergraduate level, especially in intimidating subjects such as physics and math, can increase interest in the subject for majors and non-majors alike. Thus by providing alternate mental pathways to access these subjects we may actually be able to increase diversity in physics, math, and engineering by allowing students the opportunity to express their own voice and creating hybrid spaces within classrooms (Hazari et al., 2010, p. 19). Having students get in touch with their inner visualization strategies and creatively use them to communicate their ideas and opinions should be an important part of science education, both for science majors and non-science majors. Students' comments support this recommendation:

> This course has been my favorite course that I have taken thus far at UCSB. I am so glad I got the opportunity to interact with you and my fellow classmates and to engage in discussions that dig deeper than most classes. Every project was challenging but left me more interested in the material. (Anonymous final evaluation, 2014)

> This was a really awesome course, truly interdisciplinary. I think using an artistic perspective to learn/interpret physics is really beneficial, and I learned and was way more driven than I would be in a regular physics or art course. The course is more than a sum of its parts. Keep it up! (Anonymous final evaluation, 2013)

> Thank you so much for teaching this class. I don't think I've ever been quite so stimulated by a class here as much as your class has done for me. (Anonymous final evaluation, 2011)

> It is really refreshing to see an unconventional approach to physics and view the world around us from both points of view. My mind was opened up to so much this quarter. <...> These ideas really apply to art but nowhere does art teach it or explore the questions that one might have. I was really glad to make my final project, it helped me develop my view of the interconnectedness of things. (female art major, 2011)

> I'm really glad that I got to take this class & that classes like this exist. I feel like I learned a lot & that I will retain it because I enjoyed learning it, and I think it is useful & really interesting information. It was awesome to learn about something so unlike what I normally study, and from so many different perspectives. (anonymous student, 2012)

> I feel doubtful that I will ever "click" with the math. I'm just very glad that my not-understanding does not make me feel desperate, as this seems sort of a "safe environment" where it is good thinking that counts, which I am capable of. (February 9, 2007, reported in vander Veen, 2007)

> I think – I was – I was very, kind of disillusioned from my other physics classes, and I'm glad I had this class to take, and remind me that physics is cool, and that there's lots of – there's broad concepts out there that we *should* get excited about. To me, if

you add physics and creativity to it, that's the part of physics that I love … instead of the…Oh, I can solve an integral which is really hard. 'Yay!' – 'h-h'. Yeah. As a physics major in my senior year, I've felt that our curriculum, though very demanding and informative, lacks the history of how the laws came to be, as well as the thought process that was taken to get to that point. Your class seems to be one that will fill those holes, and I am truly excited to learn more about it. (anonymous exit card comment, 2013)

In conclusion, I suggest that:

- Having students design their own representations of abstract concepts in physics, and explain their representations to non-experts, helps them develop meta-representational competence;
- Teaching physics in an interdisciplinary setting in which high importance is placed on students designing their own representations improves self-confidence regarding the study of physics for arts and humanities students who might otherwise avoid a traditional introductory physics course;
- Students' drawings, along with students' written and verbal explanations, can serve as an alternative form of assessment to traditional tests and problem sets, that give deeper insight into students' understanding of concepts as well as the way students process information;
- Students' drawings, along with students' written explanations provide valuable feedback to the instructor as to the effectiveness of his/her instruction, which the instructor can use in refining the course and assignments;
- The use of arts-based teaching strategies and open-ended assignments that encourage students' creativity has the potential to increase access to physics, and thus attract a broader population of learners to study physics.

The work reported on in this chapter has been supported by NASA grant 1388406 from the Planck Mission, Jet Propulsion Laboratory, in Pasadena, California.

REFERENCES

Blickenstaff, J. C. (2005). Women and science careers: Leaky pipeline or gender filter? *Gender and Education, 17*(4), 369–386.

Collins, D. W., & Kimura, D. (1997). A large sex difference on a two-dimensional mental rotation task. *Behavioral Neuroscience, 111*, 845–849.

Compos, A., Gomez-Juncal, R., & Perez-Fabello, M. J. (2007–2008). Experience in imagery and imagery vividness. *Imagination, Cognition, & Personality, 27*(4), 337–348.

diSessa, A. A. (2004). Metarepresentation: Native competence and targets for instruction. *Cognition and Instruction, 22*(3), 293–331.

Einstein, A. (2003). Physics and reality. *Daedalus, 132*(4), 22–25. (Original work published 1936)

Eisner, E. W. (2002). What can education learn from the arts about the practice of education? *Journal of Curriculum and Supervision, 18*, 4–16.

Feynman, R. (1963). Curved space, Chapter 42 of *The Feynman Lectures on Physics*, Vol.1.

Felder, R. (1993). Reaching the second tier: Learning and teaching styles in college science education. *Journal of College Science Teaching, 23*(5), 286–290.

Felder, R. M., & Silverman, L. K. (1988). Learning and teaching styles in engineering education. *Engineering Education, 78*(7), 674–681.

Geary, D. C., & Soto, M. C. (2001). Sex differences in spatial abilities among adults from the United States and China: Implications for evolutionary theory. *Evolution and Cognition, 7*(2), 172–177.

Getzels, J. W., & Jackson, P. W. (1962). *Creativity and intelligence: Explorations with gifted students*. London: Wiley & Sons.

Greene, M. (2001). *Variations on a blue guitar* (Lincoln Center Institute Lectures on Aesthetic Education). New York, NY: Teachers College Press.

Hadamard, J. (1945/1954). *The psychology of invention in the mathematical field*. Princeton, NJ: Princeton University Press, 1945; New York, NY: Dover Publications, Inc., 1954.

Hazari, Z., Sonnert, G., Sadler, P. M., & Shanahan, M. C. (2010). Connecting high school physics experiences, outcome expectations, physics identity, and physics career choice: A gender study. *Journal of Research in Science Teaching, 47*, 978–1003.

Hegarty, M. (2011). The cognitive science of visual–spatial displays: Implications for design. *Topics in Cognitive Science, 3*(3), 446–474.

Hegarty, M., & Kozhevnikov, M. (1999). Types of visual–spatial representations and mathematical problem solving. *Journal of Educational Psychology, 91*, 684–689.

John-Steiner, V. (1997). *Notebooks of the mind: Explorations of thinking* (Rev. Ed., pp. 1–294). New York, NY: Oxford University Press.

Kendrick, M., & McKay, R. (2002). Uncovering literacy narratives through children's drawings. *Canadian Journal of Education, 27*(1), 45–60.

Kozhevnikov, M., Kosslyn, S., & Shephard, J. (2005). Spatial vs. object visualizers: A new characterization of visual cognitive style. *Memory & Cognition, 33*(4), 710–726.

Levrini, O. (1999). *Teaching modern physics on the basis of a content knowledge reconstruction*. Retrieved from http://www.ipn.uni-kiel.de/projekte/esera/ book/118-lev.pdf

Livio, M. (2005). *The equation that couldn't be solved*: Chapter 1 (Symmetry) and Chapter 2 (eyE s'dniM eth ni yrtemmyS). New York, NY: Simon and Schuster.

Miller, A. I. (1989). Imagery and intuition in creative scientific thinking: Albert Einstein's invention of the special theory of relativity. In D. Wallace & H. Gruber (Eds.), *Creative people at work* (pp. 171–185). New York, NY: Oxford University Press.

Osborne, J. (1990). Sacred cows in physics—Towards a redefinition of physics education. *Physics Education, 25*, 189–195.

Pesic, P. (2014). *Music and the making of modern science*. London: MIT Press.

Pestalozzi, J. (1805/1894). *How gertrude teaches her children an attempt to help mothers to teach their children and an account of the method* (L. Holland & F. Turner, Trans., pp. 1–256). London; Syracuse: Swann Sonnenschein

Redish, E. F., Saul, J. M., & Steinberg, R. N. (1998). Student expectations in introductory physics. *American Journal of Physics, 66*(3), 212–224.

Sjøberg, S., & Schreiner, C. (2007). Science education and youth's identity construction—Two incompatible projects? In D. Corrigan, J. Dillon, & R. Gunstone (Eds.), *The re-emergence of values in the science curriculum*. Rotterdam: Sense Publishers.

Sjøberg, S., & Schreiner, C. (2010). *The ROSE project: An overview and key findings*. Retrieved from http://roseproject.no/network/countries/norway/eng/nor- Sjoberg-Schreiner-overview-2010.pdf

Tobias, S. (1990). *They're not dumb, they're different: Stalking the second tier*. Tucson, AZ: Research Corporation.

Tobias, S. (2006). Letter to the editor. *Physics Today, 59*(7), 10.

van der Veen, J. (2006). *Ethnic dance and physics: Correlations and possible implications for physics education* (preprint). Retrieved December 15, 2014, from web.physics.ucsb.edu/~jatila/papers/Dance-and-Physics_Results.pdf van der Veen, J. (2007, September). *Symmetry and aesthetics in introductory physics: An experiment in interdisciplinary physics and fine arts education* (Ph.D. Dissertation). University of California, Santa Barbara, CA.

van der Veen, J. (2012). Draw your physics homework? Art as a path to understanding in physics teaching. *American Educational Research Journal, 49*(2), 356–407.

van der Veen, J. (2013). Symmetry as a thematic approach to physics education. *Symmetry: Culture and Science, 24*(1–4), 463–484.

Vygotsky, L. (1978). *Mind in society: The development of higher psychological processes.* Cambridge, MA: Harvard University Press.

Zee, A. (1986, 1999, 2007). *Fearful symmetry: The search for beauty in modern physics.* New York, NY: Macmillan Publishing Company.

Jatila van der Veen
University of California
Santa Barbara, USA

MIRI BARAK

3. REFLECTIVE DRAWINGS AS MEANS FOR DEPICTING ICTS ROLES IN SCIENCE AND ENGINEERING LEARNING IN THE 21ST CENTURY

LEARNING IN THE 21ST CENTURY

Learning in the 21st century necessitates the mastery of a broad set of competencies that are important to success in today's global and changing world. The special capabilities of advanced information and communication technologies (ICTs), in the form of mobile devices and cloud applications, generate learning environments that are not only ubiquitous – anytime and anywhere, but also omnipresent – anywhere at once (Barak & Levenberg, 2014). Economic changes, shifts in workforce demands, scientific innovations, and technological advancement are redefining the skills that students need in order to be prepared for today's globalized society. Several international consortiums of educational experts, industry leaders, and government representatives, assembled to specify key skills required for working and learning in the 21st century (NRC, 2012; OECD, 2013; P21, 2006, 2008). Two broad domains of skills were identified: cognitive (i.e. critical thinking, problem solving, reasoning and argumentation, information literacy) and non-cognitive (i.e. flexibility, responsibility, initiative, communication, conflict resolution, collaboration). Among the many competencies, ICT literacy is prominent.

The Partnership for 21st Century Skills (P21, 2006, 2008) was one of the first consortiums to point out an articulated list of skills. This list included four domains: learning and innovation skills; information, media and technology skills; life and career skills; core subjects and interdisciplinary themes. Shortly afterwards, the Organization for Economic Cooperation and Development (Ananiadou & Claro, 2009; OECD, 2013) published a report on a set of desired skills, dividing them into three dimensions: information, communication, and ethics and social impact. This was followed by the Assessment and Teaching of 21st Century Skills Project that identified and organized ten skills into four groupings: ways of thinking, ways of working, tools for working, and living in the world (Griffin, McGaw, & Care, 2012). In the same year, the National Research Council listed three main domains: cognitive, interpersonal, and intrapersonal, presenting different facets of human thinking (NRC, 2012). Some reports use the term 'skills' when referring to the working and learning requirements in the 21st century (Griffin, McGaw, & Care, 2012; P21, 2008). Others use the term 'competency' to emphasize that skills and knowledge are intertwined (NRC, 2012; Ananiadou & Claro, 2009; OECD, 2013). In these reports, competency is conceptualized as the ability to adequately apply learning outcomes in a defined context, such as education, work, personal, or professional development (Ananiadou & Claro, 2009).

Although specifically related to the 21st century, some skills are not new. Collaboration, critical thinking, problem solving, creativity, and other skills were widely discussed and examined in the previous century. However, their nature has changed since the emergence of advanced ICTs. For example, collaboration in the workplace was the focal point of many organizations and educational studies in the 20th century, but its importance has increased in this century because of new technologies that facilitate global communication without limitations of time and place. While there are disagreements among policy makers about the best way to classify 21st century skills, they all agree that ICT literacy is an essential skill needed for work, citizenship, and self-actualization.

ICT literacy is one of the 21st century skills that are new and constantly evolving. ICT literacy is conceptualized as the ability to efficiently use advanced technologies for study, research, creation, and communication, while sharing knowledge in schools, workplaces, and the World Wide Web community (NRC, 2012). Due to the fact the ICTs are constantly advancing, ICT literacy is a skill that is frequently challenged.

ICTS AND NET GENERS

ICT innovations (devices, software, and applications) provide tools for science and engineering education, including gathering and analyzing data, representing information, solving problems, and communicating results. Increased computing capacity enables large-scale data analysis, wide-array instrumentation, remote sensing, and advanced scientific modeling (NSTA, 2009). Science education studies indicate that ICTs can serve as facilitators of collaborative learning (Barak & Dori, 2009; Selwyn, 2010) and reform-based teaching (Bell, Maeng, & Binns, 2013). They can enhance conceptual understanding (Barak & Dori, 2005), visualization (Barak, 2013), and higher order thinking skills (Barak & Dori, 2009). Although ICTs can facilitate cognitive operations essential for learning science and engineering, their potential is not fully tapped.

Today's higher education students are part of what is called 'Net Geners' (Net Generation) or 'Generation Y' (Dede, 2004; Tapscott, 2008). Net Geners students are considered as those who were born in the 1980s–1990s. They grew up with technology and rely on it to perform all their life tasks (Dede, 2004). Based on interviews of 6,000 people from around the world, Tapscott (2008) found characteristics that describe the typical Net Gener, differentiating them from their parents. His findings indicated that Net Geners prize

P. Katz (Ed.), Drawing for Science Education, 31–40.
© 2017 Sense Publishers. All rights reserved.

freedom of choice and are inclined to customize and personalize things. They are natural collaborators, preferring a conversation than a lecture. They expect to have fun, even at work or school. They are accustomed to speedy changes, and they tend to think innovatively as part of their life (Tapscott, 2008). Similarly, other studies indicated that the 21st century learner is expected to be able to adapt to frequent changes and explore new venues, to collaborate and communicate in digital environments, and to manage information and generate innovative ideas (Barak & Levenberg, 2014; Barak, Morad, & Ragonis, 2013).

Net Geners are todays' undergraduate and graduate students. Their characteristics demonstrate the need for rethinking the way higher education is perceived and provided. They demonstrate the need for extending the educational reforms that started in schools by applying student-cantered and active learning in universities (Barak et al., 2007). Armed with smart phones, laptops, tablets, and other gadgets, Net Geners preferences and abilities to use technologies are obvious. However, it is still not clear whether and how they perceive the use of ICTs in academic learning. In light of the aforesaid, this study applied the reflective drawing analysis method to examine the way Net Geners depict academic learning in the 21st century.

REFLECTIVE DRAWINGS AS TOOLS FOR DATA COLLECTION AND ANALYSIS

The use of drawings as a research tool is unique because it enables the researcher to collect information that might not be obtained by other tools (see for example: Barak, 2014; Furth, 1988; Katz et al., 2011). Drawings can be used to uncover hidden thoughts, ideas, and feelings that are sometimes difficult to express in words (Hammer, 1980; Orland-Barak & Klein, 2005). Studies indicated that forgotten memories and subconscious thoughts are more likely to be uncovered in drawings than any other qualitative method, such as interviews or observations (Hammer, 1980; Weber & Mitchell, 1996). A large part of what we see, know, think, remember, and/or repress in our minds 'drain' into the drawing page, uncovering dilemmas, contradictions, and unsolved issues. Following their study, Weber and Mitchell concluded that "Writing paints pictures with words, while drawings speak with lines and colors" (Weber & Mitchell, 1996, p. 304).

Drawings provide people with a good opportunity to reflect their feelings and perceptions toward other people and situations they experience. They can serve as a direct route to emotions and unconscious responses underlying behaviors during change (Kearney & Hyle, 2003). Their analysis can reveal social, cultural, and personal aspects of knowledge and beliefs. Issues that have been suppressed in speech or writing may be exposed in drawings. In 1990 Nossiter and Biberman conducted a study specifically for the purpose of examining the usefulness of drawings as a research methodology. They concluded that drawings focus a person's response and lead to respondent honesty. Similarly, Kearney and Hyle (2003) found that using drawings as a qualitative-naturalist research tool enables a thorough representation of the participant's experiences and helps to understand their feelings and thoughts. It enables the establishment of research trustworthiness by triangulating data gathered by other tools. In light of the aforesaid, this study used drawings as a research tool to gain a better understanding on perceptions about ICTs of undergraduate students in science and engineering. The following paragraphs describe relevant studies in the field of education with relation to adult drawings and drawings in science education and ICT research.

In the context of adult drawings and educational research, Weber and Mitchell (1996) used drawings in order to research student-teachers perceptions about the teacher's image. In their research, student-teachers were asked to draw an image of a teacher. Analysis of the students' drawings showed that only a small group of the teachers drew "modern" teachers and innovative learning environments (Weber & Mittchell, 1996). Orland-Barak and Klein (2005) used drawing analysis as a research tool for examining mentors' representations of a mentoring conversation and its realization in practice. The participants were asked to draw their concept of a mentoring conversation. The study revealed that relationship between 'the expressed' and 'the realized' in mentoring conversations is complex and multifaceted.

In the context of science education, the Draw-A-Scientist Test (DAST), originally developed by Chambers (1983), is the most recognized and practiced. By using drawing tests, Chambers was able to show that children began to develop stereotypical views of scientists from a very early age. Katz and colleagues (2011) asked teacher candidates to respond to two prompts: 'Draw yourself teaching science' and 'Draw your students learning science'. These two prompts allowed the researchers to analyze the similarities and differences between the teacher candidates' illustrations of their teaching actions and their students' learning actions. The researchers provided evidence that the infusion of an informal science education internship in a formal science teacher education program influenced positively participants' professional identity development as science teachers (Katz et al., 2011).

In the context of ICT research, the use of drawings for data analysis is in its initial stages. Barak and colleagues (2013) examined the way undergraduate students express innovative ideas when asked to illustrate the ideal learning environment. The analysis of students' drawings indicated that only few illustrated innovative learning scenarios. Findings showed that although most of the students made a shift from desktops to mobile computers, their drawings did not reflect the added value of ubiquitous learning. Another study examined pre-service science teachers' attitudes and perceptions about the effectiveness of various learning methods and, in specific, the use of information and communication technologies (ICTs) as a means for enhancing progressive education (Barak, 2014). Findings indicated a conflict between participants' attitudes, stated via closed-ended questionnaires, and their perceptions, depicted in the drawings. This conflict signified a gap between the science teachers' inclination to coincide with educational trends, and their actual views about the use of ICTs in the classrooms.

In summary, the literature review on reflective drawings as research tools in education indicated that studies in the educational field used drawings as a research tool focused on teacher's self-image and beliefs (see for example: Katz et al., 2011; Weber & Mittchell, 1996), mentor-mentee relations (Orland-Barak & Klein, 2005), and students' perceptions about scientists (Chambers, 1983). Studies that utilize drawings for examining ICT-enhanced learning are in initial stages and should be further expanded, especially due to the rapid changes in the way Net Geners acquire information and construct knowledge (Barak, 2014).

GOAL AND PARTICIPANTS

Following the changes in the way information is obtained and communication is conducted in the 21st century, this study was set to examine undergraduate students' perceptions about the role of ICTs in academic learning. The research goal raised the following two questions:

1. How do Net Geners depict ICTs in academic learning?
2. What are the Net Geners perceptions about learning in the 21st century?

The research was conducted among science and engineering undergraduate students who voluntarily participated in the study. The participants were recruited from one university through personal invitations – announcements in lecture halls, and online messages via a learning management system. In some cases, students stayed after lecture time to participate in the study, and in other cases, students came to the research lab. From 98 drawings that were collected, six were removed since they were blurry; and 46 (every second drawing) were randomly selected for deep qualitative analysis. The participants' demographics (gender and age) reflected that of the general students' population. More than half (60%) were males studying in engineering faculties, and their age ranged from 21-to-28 years old.

METHODOLOGY AND RESEARCH TOOLS

The current study applied the *Reflective Drawing Analysis* (RDA) approach which corresponds with qualitative-naturalist approaches to research (Barak, 2014). It is based on the findings of a previous study the premise that drawings are a form of text, and as such they can be 'read' and analyzed. In this study, the word 'drawing' is used to describe pen or pencil sketches on a white paper. The undergraduate students were asked to draw a situation that depicts contemporary academic learning and explain it in writing. They were also asked to write their perceptions about learning in the 21st century. The analysis of both the drawings and students' assertions provided data for answering the two research questions.

The *Reflective Drawing Analysis* (RDA) includes three main steps. First, we study each drawing separately by describing it textually according to six indicators (described below). Second, we apply content analysis methods (inductive and deductive) for identifying specific conceptual categories that are central to the study's goal and research questions. Third, we use written explanations to corroborate our findings. Data triangulation is achieved by the use of drawings, their description, and participants' written explanations. Investigator triangulation is achieved by involving two or three researchers in various stages of the RDA process (Barak, 2014).

The six indicators were generated in a previous study (Barak, 2014), inspired by the work of Hammer (1980). They help researchers to notice all the details that are important for understanding the drawing. Therefore, while analyzing a drawing, researchers should look at:

1. The surrounding in which the drawing is located.
2. The type and number of images that appear in the drawing.
3. The location of each image on the page and its relative size.
4. The details presented in each image.
5. The images' facial expressions.
6. The interactions among images and movement.

By describing each indicator separately, the researcher's attention is drawn to various aspects of the drawing, allowing a deep and detailed understanding of the participant's thoughts, feelings, and views (Barak, 2014; Barak, Morad, & Ragonis, 2013). The six indicators provide points of reference for examining each drawing separately, according to specific constructs that are the focal points of the study.

In this study, both the researchers' description of the drawings and the textual explanations were analyzed by applying the direct/ deductive content analysis approach (Hsieh & Shannon, 2005). The 21st century learning attributes that were identified by Barak and Levenberg (2014) represented one facet of our analysis. This included four pre-defined categories: (1) Adapting to frequent changes (2) Exploring new venues, (3) Communicating in digital environments, and (4) Managing information. The second facet of our analysis examined aspects of progressive strategies (Barak, 2014) in order to determine ICT's role in advancing constructivist learning in higher education. This included the following four categories: (a) student-centered learning, (b) learning by doing, (c) providing and receiving feedback, and (d) enjoying the learning process.

Below is an example of a reflective drawing analysis (RDA) process. The square brackets include the identified categories of both learning attributes and constructivism. The pre-defined categories are denoted by numbers or letters, according to the two lists above.

An Example of a Reflective Drawing Analysis (RDA) Process

Uri (pseudonym), a sophomore civil engineering student, drew a learning situation that depicts individual learning while solving engineering problems (Figure 1).

Figure 1. Uri's drawing of a learning situation

The six drawing indicators, which served as an analysis guide, are outlined below. Identified ICT roles are indicated in square brackets.

1. *Drawing surrounding* – Uri drew a room, an indoor surrounding, and a student sitting near a desk, facing the computer, with his back to the viewers.

   Uri wrote in his explanations: *I drew a situation in which the student is sitting in his room, working on an exercise sheet, solving authentic engineering problems* [b. learning by doing]. *In our university, we are expected to work individually in solving engineering problems, sometime I feels quite lonely.*

2. *Type and number of images* – The drawing includes seven single images: a student, an exercise sheet, a smart phone, a laptop, a chair, a desk, and a carpet.

   Uri: *When I work on problem solving assignments, I use the laptop to look for information and a smartphone for calculations* [4. managing information]. *I want to know immediately if my answers are correct, so in some cases, I use my smart phone to send messages to our WhatsApp group* [c. receiving immediate feedback].

3. *Location and relative size of each image* – The laptop computer is the relatively largest image in the drawing, whereas the student is proportionally smaller. This may suggest that Uri ascribes great importance to the laptop with relation to his learning process.

   Uri: *My laptop is my entire learning environment. I use it for writing all my notes, I download lecture materials, I save annotated papers and book chapters* [4. managing information], *I listen to video lectures, I search the web for relevant material, try new platforms for computing* [2. exploring new venues], *I send messages to my colleagues* [3. communicating in digital environments] *and receive their input* [c. receiving feedback]. *I can add my comments and remarks and I can arrange the learning materials in an efficient way, according to my personal preferences* [4. managing information].

4. *The details presented in each image* – Uri drew the laptop in detail, showing a screenshot of Wolfram Alpha, a sophisticated search engine that assists in computing the answers to scientific and engineering problems.

   Uri: *When I am not sure if my answer is correct, I use Wolfram Alpha* [c. receiving feedback]. *I heard about Wolfram Alpha from one of my friends and decided to see how it works* [2. exploring new venues]. *I used to work with another system, but this is much faster and accurate* [1. adapting to frequent changes].

5. *Facial expressions* – The drawing does not show the students' face. It is not clear whether the student is happy, sad, or frustrated related to the learning process.

   Uri: *I did not draw the student's face since it doesn't seem to be important... receiving a correct answer to a complicated problem makes me happy and I get a feeling of accomplishment* [d. enjoying the learning process].

6. *Interactions and movement* – There is an indication of interactions between the student and the mobile devices, reaching his hands toward both the laptop and smartphone. There is also an indication of a cognitive process: the cloud callout with the mathematical equation. The question mark indicates confusion and uncertainty.

> Uri: *Sometimes I sit for hours struggling to answer a complex problem. This can be very frustrating. With the use of online technologies, I can look for more information or send queries to my friends* [3. communicating in digital environments].

FINDINGS

This section is divided into two parts. The first part describes how science and engineering undergraduate students depict ICTs in academic learning. The second part describes their perceptions about learning in the 21st century.

The Way Net Geners Depict ICTs in Academic Learning

The analysis of the participants' drawings indicated that Net Geners depict ICTs as necessary tools for learning in higher education. The ICTs were depicted as cognitively inseparable from the learning process and physically inseparable from the students' palms; Most of the drawings depicted ICTs in a positive way; however a few drawings presented criticism related to students' dependence on technology, superficial learning, and unethical behavior. The following paragraphs present the analysis of the drawings' contents, according to the six RDA indicators. Each figure was summarized by two constructs: Learning attributes and Constructivism that included categories relevant to the drawing and written explanations. The collection of all categories from all the drawings assisted in understanding the way Net Geners depict ICTs in academic learning.

1. *Drawing surrounding* All the drawings that were analyzed (n = 46) included the use of ICTs, whether they were laptops or smartphones, indoor or outdoor settings. Only a third of the drawings (33%) outlined the surroundings of a lecture hall or a classroom; the rest outlined at home learning (42%) or outdoors/natural surroundings (25%). More than half of the drawings (58%) indicated some modes of communication and collaborative learning; from providing or receiving online feedback, through working on a joint problem. Individual learning was portrayed as working on homework assignments (32%) or learning from a distance (10%). In general, the drawings' surroundings indicated that Net Geners welcome new ways of learning (Figure 2).

Figure 2. Learning attributes: exploring new venues; Constructivist strategies: learning by doing

2. *Type and number of images* The drawings outlined images of 136 university students (males and females equally). Surprisingly, only 15 drawings (less than a third) outlined an image of a lecturer in a classroom setting. Four drawings indicated an image of a lecturer in an online learning situation. Little indication was found for traditional teaching and learning tools or props, such as: regular whiteboard (in three drawings), notebooks and books (in two drawings). Surprisingly, there were no images of calculators, an essential learning aid for science and engineering students for many years. The drawings included 112 images of ICT devices: laptops (46%), smart phones (31%), tablets (13%), desktops (10%); an average of 1.2 devices for each student image. In some drawings students held both a laptop and a smartphone. This suggests that mobile devices are dominant in their learning environment. Some drawings detailed the use of specific online platforms or social networks, such as: Facebook, Google, Wikipedia, WhatsApp, Instagram, etc. This suggests that Net Geners use diverse ICTs for communication and collaboration. Figure 3 provides an example of such ICT usage. The picture shows a big computer screen (standing on a table). It depicts a learning situation in which two students, one from China (on the screen) and one from Israel, communicating from distance while working on a joint project.

Figure 3 Learning attributes: communicating and collaborating in digital environments; Constructivist strategies: student-centered learning

3. *Location and relative size of each image* In most drawings (67%), the students and the digital devices were placed in the center of the frame. The drawings that outlined a traditional lecture hall or a classroom (28%) placed the lecturer in the center of the drawing. In other drawings (5%), the digital device was in the center of the framework. These results may indicate the decreasing role of the lecturer in a traditional lecture hall and the increasing role of ICTs in science and technology students' learning process.

4. *The details presented in each image* In more than half of the drawings (54%) the images of the students and the ICT devices were drawn in detail, whereas the lecturers' images were detailed in only five drawings. The students' images included eyes, mouth, hair, body, hands, fingers, etc. However, in about a third of the drawings (34%) the images of the ICT devices were more detailed than the student's image, including keyboards, microphones, screens, and Wifi. These results may suggest the importance that students place on ICTs as facilitators of learning (Figure 4).

Figure 4. Learning attributes: generating data and managing information; Constructivist strategies: providing and receiving feedback

5. *Facial expressions* Most of the students' images (81%) included a smiling face, indicating satisfaction from the way the learning is conducted in the outlined situation. The unhappy faces were noted in drawings that depicted large lecture halls, where students were asleep or showed signs of boredom. There were two indications of 'surprised faces' depicted in situation in which students were asked by the lecturer to read a book instead of using their laptop computers. In half of the drawings that included a lecturer image, the facial expressions indicated frustration. These results may suggest that Net Geners enjoy the learning process that involves open access to information and free choice to pursue diverse ways for acquiring knowledge.

*Figure 5. Learning attributes: Adapting to frequent changes in ways of acquiring knowledge;
Constructivist strategies: enjoying the learning process*

6. *Interactions and movement* Among the 46 drawings, ten indicated 'interactions' or 'movements' using dashed lines, exclamation marks, arrows, or written comments (cloud callouts). The drawings indicated interactions between students and their digital devices, for typing answers, searching the web, and conducting online discussions. Only four drawings indicated interactions between students in a classroom, depicting them having a conversation.

Overall, the reflective drawing analysis (RDA) indicated that most drawings and written explanations (78%) illustrated ICTs in a positive way. They indicated the important role of ICTs in realizing constructivist strategies and enhancing contemporary learning. However, some drawings and written explanations illustrated the downsides of ICTs, indicating factors that may impede on students' learning. The upsides and downsides of ICTs in academic learning are presented in Table 1.

Table 1. Summary of the upsides and downsides of ICTs

Learning attributes	Upside: ICTs may serve as	Downside: ICTs could cause
1. Adapting to frequent changes	Flexible tools that facilitate changes in the way learning is conducted	Superficial and shallow learning
2. Exploring new venues	Promoters of freedom to choose what, how, when, where, and with whom to learn	Confusion related to learning goals and direction
3. Collaborating with a global mindset	Efficient tools for communicating and collaborating with peers	Dependency on receiving immediate answers or feedback
4. Generating data and managing information	Organizing tools for managing contents and the learning process	Dependency on digital applications instead of memorization methods

Net Geners Perceptions about Academic Learning in the 21st Century

Content analysis of students' assertions indicated that Net Geners depend on mobile devices for everyday life as well as for learning. Net Geners feel that they are one step (or more) ahead of the lecturers in ways of acquiring and managing knowledge. Data indicated four main characteristics of learning in the 21st century, as detailed in the following (all names are pseudonyms).

1. *Learning in the 21st century is flexible, ubiquitous, and autonomous* According to the students' assertions, their learning occurs anytime and anyplace via mobile devices such as laptops, tablets and smart phones; they use desktops only on campus. There is no separation between learning and leisure, information is always accessible. Learning can be conducted anywhere, even during break; but there are many distractions that obstruct learning. The lectures in the lecture halls are only one of many resources of information that they can choose from.

John: *It doesn't really matter in what situation I am in; if I am in a lecture hall, at home, or outside with friends, whenever I am curious about something, I use Google or other search engines to learn about a topic. However, many times I find myself distracted; I tend to read interesting articles or news that are not in the center of my studies.*

Sarah: *In many cases I look for diverse resources. I read e-books, interesting articles, or see videos of other lecturers…because I use my laptop, I can be connected anywhere, as long as there is Wi-Fi. It is good that we have many options for learning, but sometime it is too crazy, and I need to take a break and keep a distance from my laptop.*

Sam: *I often use search engines to find answers… especially during the lecture. In many cases the lecturer does not provide an immediate answer to my question, either because he doesn't know or because it is not directly linked to the topic of the lecture. In such a case, I look for the answer myself.*

2. *Learning in the 21st century dismisses memorization and rote learning* According to the students' assertions, rote learning and memorizing information should not be part of academic learning, since all the necessary data are at their fingertips, a push of a button away. Accordingly, they expect to receive immediate answers to their questions. If their curiosity is not met in the classroom, they will immediately search the web for answers and sometimes challenge the lecturers.

Liz: *There is so much information… trying to learn everything by heart is not realistic. More emphasis should be placed on how to use smart search engines, to retrieve relevant and accurate data, and how to manage it in an organized way.*

Barry: *I learn about things whenever I search them on the web… When I need information about complex concepts, I look at several websites to have a wide viewpoint and better understanding. I usually remember the main ideas, but if I forget the details, I know where to find them.*

Rachel: *During the lectures I have many questions. I use Wikipedia to look for additional information and sometimes to see if the lecturer is correct. If I find discrepancies, I ask for explanations. Once I found that the lecturer's explanations were incorrect, and once I found a mistake in a mathematical equation that was written on the white board.*

3. *Learning in the 21st century prioritizes technology over pens, papers, and books* Students asserted that during the lectures, they type into their laptop the summary or download PDF files and use digital annotations. They also use their tablets or smart phones to take snapshots of the whiteboard instead of hand-copying it.

Tami: *I stopped brining pens or pencils, everything is in the computer; even the books can be downloaded as PDF. This way I can mark important sentences, add annotations, and add my remarks.*

Mark: *Whenever the lecturer is asking us to write down equations that he developed on the whiteboard, I use my smartphone to take a picture and then I save it in my laptop. I rarely open a notebook or write down things.*

Barry: *Instead of printing out articles, I read them on my computer and use the comments tool to write annotation... I hardly ever go to the library or use books or binders.*

4. *Learning in the 21st century is broadwise rather than deepwise* Students are overwhelmed with masses of information from various sources. They use a cognitive mechanism that allows them to glance over a lot of data and filter the most relevant information at a certain time and situation. They would rather view short and concise videos than read long manuscripts. They use the 'fast forward' button to speed things up.

Debby: *There is a lot of information that I need to know as an engineer and there is a lot of information that I find interesting... I have no choice but to glance over things and stop to learn deeper only the things that I need 'now and here'.*

Mark: *I read a lot of materials and see a lot of lecture videos, some more relevant than others... The videos are a great solution since I can always fast forward boring parts or run it slower when more complicated issues are explained. I do not remember all of it, but I know where to find it when I need it again.*

Ziv: *When I study, I rather see a video with visualizations than listen to a long lecture. Even when the lecturer is doing his best to solve equations in an interesting way, he is still boring compared to digital technologies and colorful simulations.*

In addition to the four main characteristics of learning in the 21st century, mentioned above, five students asserted that ICTs can be misused for unethical behavior. Two students referred to the use of smartphones for cheating in a test. Two students mentioned the use of special programs that mechanically solve complex equations that are given as homework assignments. One student indicated the use of 'copy' and 'paste' operations for writing an essay without really understanding the learning material.

SUMMARY AND DISCUSSION

This study was designed to examine how science and engineering undergraduates, at the ages of 21-to-28 (Net Geners), depict the role of ICTs in academic learning in the 21st century. With the use of the *reflective drawings analysis* (RDA), our findings literally portray ICTs as critical players in contemporary learning. All the drawings depicted ICTs as physically inseparable from the students' hand or palm. Only a third of the drawings outlined the surroundings of a lecture hall or a classroom; suggesting that traditional lecture-based academic learning is sidelined by mobile devices, social networks, and online videos. Books, notebooks, and pens were scarcely depicted; suggesting a shift in the way students acquire and construct knowledge. These findings indicate a gap between how Net Geners are accustomed to acquiring knowledge and the way higher education is designed and delivered.

Most of the drawings and assertions indicated that Net Geners who participated in the study manage their learning digitally in online, cloud-based environments. They are natural collaborators in the learning process, and they build their learning on immediate answers and feedback. They are accustomed to exploring new learning venues and tend to personalize the learning materials. They expect the learning materials to be easily accessible and the learning process to be fun. These findings are in line with previous studies that examined hundreds of participants born in the 1980s and 1990s (Tapscott, 2008; Martin, 2005). People who were born into the digital era recognize the Internet as the main (or even the only) resource of multiple sources of information (Tapscott, 2008). This induces new modes of learning, based on seeking, sieving, and synthesizing information; rather than on assimilating a single 'validated' source of knowledge as from a professor lecturing or books (Dede, 2004).

Most of the drawings depicted ICTs in a positive way; however a few drawings indicated negative aspects and pointed out threats related to superficial learning, complete dependence on technology, and unethical behavior. These findings are in line with other studies that indicated that ICTs might serve as promoters of superficial and shallow learning (Oppenheimer, 2003). Recent studies on the integration of ICTs for educational purposes criticize their simplistic and tokenistic inclusion, emphasizing the roles of the lecturers or teachers (Barak, 2014; Jimoyiannis, 2010); however, our study provides an additional explanation for this phenomenon that lies upon the downsides of students' use of ICTs as summarized in Table 1.

The special capabilities of ICTs and cloud applications can be harnessed to generate learning environments that are not only ubiquitous (anytime and anywhere) but also omnipresent (anywhere at once), while promoting students' interactivity through a variety of modalities. However, many universities still adhere to traditional models of teaching and learning. In higher education, ICTs are typically used for presenting slides in lecture halls and organizing the learning materials via online management systems. In many cases they are used to augment teacher-centered practices, instead of being used to facilitate reform-based instruction (Barak, 2014; Barak et al., 2007). Their capabilities for enhancing 21st century skills are not effectively realized. In order to do this, ICTs should be used for projects and inquiry-based learning, authentic outdoor learning, and connecting contents to everyday life (Barak & Ziv, 2013; NRC, 2012). They should be used for enhancing a universal mindset, providing the skills needed for lifelong learning and for working in the global market (OECD, 2013).

This study metaphorically portrays one of the biggest problems facing higher education today: the gap between Net Geners' contemporary learning and the instructional culture in universities. Net Geners who acquire their knowledge in online environments are taught by lecturers who use pre-digital and outdated methods. Our study shows that these two 'parallel educational worlds' can meet by integrating constructivist instructional strategies into academic learning. The drawings, together with the students' written assertions, indicated that Net Geners, who are accustomed to speedy changes, freedom of choice, digital communication, and personalization, use ICTs intuitively for integrating constructivist learning processes into academic education in the 21st century. This idea is portrayed in a pyramid model, showing that Net Geners characteristics are the baseline that supports current learning attributes. The model also shows how learning attributes scaffolds constructivist learning, which in return can foster innovative academic learning (Figure 6).

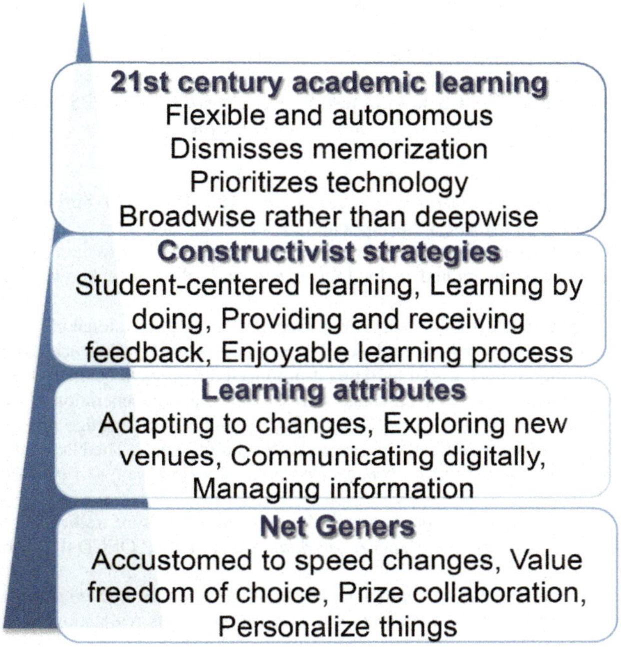

21st century academic learning
Flexible and autonomous
Dismisses memorization
Prioritizes technology
Broadwise rather than deepwise

Constructivist strategies
Student-centered learning, Learning by doing, Providing and receiving feedback, Enjoyable learning process

Learning attributes
Adapting to changes, Exploring new venues, Communicating digitally, Managing information

Net Geners
Accustomed to speed changes, Value freedom of choice, Prize collaboration, Personalize things

Figure 6. A pyramid model indicating the potential of integrating constructivist learning into academic education when learning attributes are positively realized

Through their metaphorical power, the reflective drawings, analyzed in this study, provided a direct route to the way participants' perceive and use ICTs. Building upon the work of similar studies (Barak, 2014, Orland-Barak & Klein 2005; Katz et al., 2011), we suggest Reflective Drawing Analysis as a method for understanding students' learning and thinking in the 21st century. In many studies that use drawings as research tools, the participants are young children. In this study, our participants were undergraduate students who were asked to express their thoughts and ideas in drawings. This study suggests the use of drawings as a catalyst for reflective thinking, not only about what we learn, but also about how we go about it. This is in line with studies that suggest drawings as an effective cognitive tool for obtaining direct and honest answers (Backett-Milburn & McKie, 1999; Nossiter & Biberman, 1990). Following a long line of studies based on subjects' drawings (Barak, 2014; Banks, 2001; Katz et al., 2011; Theron et al., 2011), this study shows how they can be used as a trigger for expressing perceptions that, in some cases, the participants were not aware of before.

Alongside the benefits mentioned above, the use of drawings among adult subjects is challenging. Most of the participants in this study were uncomfortable with the idea of expressing their thoughts or feelings in drawing. They complained about not having the necessary skills to draw. Some mentioned that they had not drawn since elementary school. They considered drawing as a childish act, and some refused to cooperate. However, through all the difficulties, drawings as a research tool have much potential and should be further implemented and examined in additional studies.

REFERENCES

Ananiadou, K., & Claro, M. (2009). *21st Century skills and competencies for new millennium learners in OECD countries* (OECD Education Working Papers, No. 41). Paris: OECD Publishing. doi:10.1787/218525261154

Backett-Milburn, K., & McKie, L. (1999). A critical appraisal of the draw and write technique. *Health Education Research, 14*(3), 387–398. doi:10.1093/her/14.3.387

Banks, M. (2001). *Visual methods in social research*. London, England: Sage.

Barak, M. (2013). Making the unseen seen: Integrating 3D molecular visualizations in elementary, high school, and higher education. In J. Suits & M. Sanger (Eds.), *Pedagogic roles of animations and simulations in chemistry courses*. Washington, DC: ACS Books Pub. doi:10.1021/bk-2013-1142.ch011

Barak, M. (2014). Closing the gap between attitudes and perceptions about ICT-enhanced learning among pre-service STEM teachers. *The Journal of Science Education and Technology, 23*(1), 1–14. doi:10.1007/s10956-013-9446-8

Barak, M., & Dori, Y. J. (2005). Enhancing undergraduate students' chemistry understanding through project-based learning in an IT environment. *Science Education, 89*(1), 117–139. doi:10.1002/sce.20027

Barak, M., & Dori, Y. J. (2009). Enhancing higher order thinking skills among in-service science education teachers via embedded assessment. *Journal of Science Teacher Education, 20*(5), 459–474.

Barak, M., & Levenberg, A. (2014, April). *Harnessing cloud applications for promoting progressive education principles among science teacher trainees*. National Association for Research in Science Teaching (NARST), Pittsburgh, PA, USA.

Barak, M., & Ziv, S. (2013). Wandering: A Web-based platform for the creation of location-based interactive learning objects. *Computers & Education, 62*, 159–170.

Barak, M., Harward, J., Kocur, G., & Lerman, S. (2007). Transforming an introductory programming course: From lectures to active learning via wireless laptops. *Journal of Science Education and Technology, 16*(4), 325–336. doi:10.1007/s10956-007-9055-5

Barak, M., Morad, S., & Ragonis, N. (2013, September). *Students' innovative thinking and their perceptions about the ideal learning environment* (pp. 111–125). The 8th International Conference on Knowledge Management in Organizations, Kaohsiung, Taiwan.

Bell, R. L., Maeng, J. L, & Binns, I. C. (2013). Learning in context: Technology integration in a teacher preparation program informed by situated learning theory. *Journal of Research in Science Teaching, 50*(3), 348–379.

Chambers, D. W. (1983). Stereotypic images of the scientist: Draw-a-scientist test. *Science Education, 67*(2), 255–265.

Dede, C. (2004). *Planning for "Neomillenia" learning styles: Implications for investments in technology and faculty*. Cambridge, MA: Harvard Graduate School of Education.

Furth, G. M. (1988). *The secret world of drawings: Healing through art*. Boston, MA: Sigo Press.

Griffin, P., McGaw, B., & Care, E. (Eds.). (2012). *Assessment and teaching of 21st century skills*. Dordrecht: Springer.

Hammer, E. F. (1980). *The clinical application of projective drawings*. Springfield, IL: Charles C. Thomas.

Hsieh, H., & Shannon, S. E. (2005). Three approaches to qualitative content analysis. *Qualitative Health Research, 15*(9), 1277–1288. doi:10.1177/1049732305276687

Jimoyiannis, A. (2010). Designing and implementing an integrated technological pedagogical science knowledge framework for science teachers' professional development. *Computers & Education, 55*, 1259–1269.

Katz, P., McGinnis, J. R., Hestness, E., Riedinger, K., Marbach-Ad, G., Dai, A., & Pease, R. (2011). Professional identity development of teacher candidates participating in an informal science education internship: A focus on drawings as evidence. *International Journal of Science Education, 33*(9), 1169–1197.

Kearney, K. S., & Hyle, A. E. (2003). Drawing out emotions: The use of participant-produced drawings in qualitative inquiry. *Qualitative Research, 4*(3), 361–382.

Martin, C. A. (2005). From high maintenance to high productivity: What managers need to know about Generation Y. *Industrial and Commercial Training, 37*(1), 39–44.

National Research Council (NRC). (2012). Education for life and work: Developing transferable knowledge and skills in the 21st century. In J. W. Pellegrino & M. L. Hilton (Eds.), *Committee on defining deeper learning and 21st century skills*. Washington, DC: The National Academies Press.

National Science Teachers Association (NSTA). (2009). *21st century skills map. Task force report to the NSTA board of directors*. Retrieved from http://www.p21.org/storage/documents/21stcskillsmap_science.pdf

Nossiter, V., & Biberman, G. (1990). Projective drawings and metaphor: Analysis of organizational culture. *Journal of Managerial Psychology, 5*(3), 13–16.

OECD. (2013). *OECD skills outlook 2013: First results from the survey of adult skills*. Paris: OECD Publishing. Retrieved from http://dx.doi.org/10.1787/9789264204256-en

Oppenheimer, T. (2003). *The flickering mind: The false promise of technology in the classroom and how learning can be saved*. New York, NY: Random House.

Orland-Barak, L., & Klein, S. (2005). The expressed and the realized: Mentors' conversation and its realization in practice. *Teaching and Teacher Education, 21*(4), 379–402.

Partnership for 21st Century Skills (P21). (2006). *A state leader's action guide to 21st century skills: A new vision for education*. Tucson, AZ: Partnership for 21st Century Skills. Retrieved from http://www.p21.org/storage/documents/stateleaders071906.pdf

Partnership for 21st Century Skills (P21). (2008). *21st century skills, education & Competitiveness*. Tucson, AZ: Partnership for 21st Century Skills. Retrieved from http://www.p21.org

Selwyn, N. (2010). Web 2.0 and the school of the future, today. In OECD (Ed.), *Inspired by technology, driven by pedagogy*. Paris: OECD report.

Tapscott, D. (2008). *Grown up digital: How the net generation is changing your world*. New York, NY: McGraw-Hill.

Theron, L., Mitchell, C., Smith, A., & Stuart, J. (Eds.). (2011). *Picturing research: Drawing as visual methodology*. Rotterdam: Sense Publishers.

Weber, S. J., & Mitchell, C. (1996). Drawing ourselves into teaching: Studying the images that shape and distort teacher education. *Teaching and Teacher Education, 12*(3), 303–313.

Miri Barak

Technion – Israel Institute of Technology, Israel

PATRICIA PATRICK

4. CAN I GET DIRECTIONS TO MY KIDNEYS PLEASE?

Social Interactions as a Source of Knowledge of Internal Anatomy

A drawing is a translation. That is to say each mark on the paper is consciously related, not only to the real or imagined "model", but also to every mark and space already set out on the paper…Every time a figuration is evoked in a drawing, everything about it has been mediated by consciousness, either intuitively or systematically.

(Berger, 1982, p. 93)

INTRODUCTION

Isabel (To protect the identity of participants all names are pseudonyms.): "Tell me about your drawing."

Mary: "Well, this is the digestive system. This is the stomach, the heart, the lungs, the large and small intestine, bones, the brain, the liver, the reproductive organs, and blood vessels."

Isabel: "Which system was the easiest to draw?"

Mary: "The digestive system."

Isabel: "Why was the digestive the easiest?"

Mary: "It's [gastrointestinal system] the easiest. You know like everyone has one. You see it on TV all the time and everyone eats and $%*@*%. Crap! I don't think I can say that. Sorry, I mean poops. You know what I'm saying like everyone knows about it. It's easy to draw because I remember talking about it in school and you see it on TV and a lot of people have problems."

This dialog occurred during a classmate interview between two pre-service science teachers talking about the internal anatomy of humans and pigs. Isabel was interviewing Mary about her drawing of the human body to determine which system she drew first and why. Mary clearly knew about the gastrointestinal system [digestive] and many of its organs. She identified the gastrointestinal system as the easiest to draw and identify because she thought "everyone knows about it". By allowing pre-service teachers to interview each other, they might be prompted to discuss the prior social contexts in which they learned about the systems. This chapter will discuss a study completed with pre-service middle level (ages 10–13) and secondary (ages 14–18) science teachers, in which they drew the internal anatomy of the human and the pig. The conclusions and discussion will relate this study to practical use in the classroom.

Drawing is the act or process of representing an object or outlining an idea by the means of placing lines on paper and producing a visual representation of one's thoughts (see www.merriam-webster.com, www.dictionary.com). In relation to students and their knowledge, drawing is a basic process that requires few materials and provides every student with an opportunity to share their knowledge and participate in the learning process. Moreover, drawings provide an opportunity to visualize concepts and feelings. For educators, drawings can be a window into student understanding, knowledge, and social representations and provide affective links to the topic. Drawings have been used as a method of representing information because they motivate participants to learn more than conventional teaching (Hackling & Prain, 2005), contribute to the formulation of thinking and meaning (Brooks, 2005; Brooks, 2009), and provide an individualized look at learner knowledge (concepts and misconceptions). Interest in the use of drawings in science learning has expanded because drawings reflect "new understandings of science as a multimodal discursive practice" (Ainsworth, Prain, & Tytler, 2011, p. 1097) and there has been "mounting evidence for its value in supporting quality learning" (p. 1097).

Even though drawings may be utilized to define student knowledge and learning, drawings may also be used to identifying the understandings in-service and pre-service educators have about the science topics they teach (i.e. Arslan, Cigdemoglu, & Moseley, 2012; Dikmenli, 2010; Dikmenli, Cardak, & Kiray, 2011; Kolomuç & Tekin, 2011; Patrick, 2014; Tatar, 2011; Yates & Marek, 2013; Yip, 1998). In order to add to the literature concerning pre-service teachers' concepts of the biological sciences, this chapter describes a study which visualized the way in which pre-service middle level and secondary science teachers think about the internal anatomy of the human and pig. The pig was chosen, because according to Tim Atkinson, Operations Manager of Anatomical Studies at Carolina Biological Supply Company (number one supplier of dissection specimens), still born pigs are the most dissected mammal in middle level and secondary classrooms. Mr. Atkinson affirmed that the reason still born pigs are chosen most often by teachers is because the still born pig is most closely related to humans both anatomically and physiologically (T. Atkinson, personal communication, September 15, 2014).

Even though studies have not asked participants to draw the internal anatomy of the pig, many studies exist in which participants have drawn the internal anatomy of the human body. The relevant research will be discussed in the literature review. Previous studies of the

P. Katz (Ed.), Drawing for Science Education, 41–54.
© *2017 Sense Publishers. All rights reserved.*

drawings of human internal anatomy indicate that participants concentrate on drawing the gastrointestinal and cardiovascular systems. However, these studies do not ask the participants why they drew these systems most often or where they learned about the systems. This lack of information indicates that further research is needed to better understand the context in which learning occurs, because drawings alone do not provide a context for where the pre-service science teachers believe they learned about the internal anatomy. Therefore, drawings accompanied by interviews afforded a deeper look at the knowledge of the participants and the social interactions that shaped their knowledge. The drawings and interviews were analyzed to answer the following questions: (1) Which organs and systems do pre-service science teachers draw most often in the human and pig? (2)Which system do pre-service science teachers name and describe most often in the human and pig? (3) Where do pre-service science teachers believe they learned about the systems? Do the pre-service science teachers describe social contexts?

THEORETICAL FRAMEWORK

Social Representations Theory

Teachers often subscribe to the same misconceptions as their students (Bahar, 2003; Wandersee, Mintzes, & Novak, 1994), which is of great concern considering classroom teachers are the most important factor in determining student achievement (National Research Council, 1999). The misconceptions shared by classroom teachers and students may be due to a shared cultural understanding of internal anatomy. In investigating the understandings pre-service teachers have of mammalian internal anatomy, the researcher deemed it important to frame the investigation in social representations theory. The theory of social representations (Moscovici, 1963, 2001) provides a lens through which to analyze the participants' socially constructed concept of internal anatomy. Social representations are lay theories about socially relevant objects that are collectively constructed and shared (Lorenzi-Cioldi & Cle´mence, 2004). A social representation is a mental construct shared by a social group and allows the group to communicate about a social object (see Wagner, 2012 for an example). Social objects may be a physical, figurative, or abstract entity "to which people attribute certain characteristics and therefore are able to talk about" (Hovardas & Korfiatis, 2006, pp. 417–418). Social representation theory allows the researcher to avoid unique individual instances that would be problematic to define, but at the same time offers "the theoretical justification for considering conceptual changes at the level of a learners group's collective representation(s)" (p. 418). Recently, researchers used social representations theory as a way to represent the understandings people have of environmental concepts such as biodiversity (Mouro & Castro, 2010), energy use and climate change (Fischer et al., 2012), nature (Buijs et al., 2012), and non-native species (Selge & Fischer, 2011), but to date no studies have investigated the shared social representations pre-service teachers have of human and pig internal anatomy.

Social Constructivist Perspective

When regarding the importance of understanding internal anatomy and how the body works through the lens of socially constructed representations, this study took into account how the participants were informed by the social constructivist theory. The rationale for using the social constructivist theory came from the notion that science learning occurs through socially mediated experiences such as observations, conversations, and personal experiences that transpire throughout life (Bruner, 1990; Vosniadou, 2003; Vygotsky, 1978; Wood, Bruner, & Ross, 1976). Social experiences provide people with an opportunity to access prior knowledge about a subject and build on that knowledge to construct a new understanding (Bruning, Schraw, & Norby, 2011). Idea-based social constructivism posits that certain big ideas are important foundations for learners to expand their understanding of a socially constructed concept (Gredler, 1997). In regard to this chapter, the big idea I seek to understand is how or from what sources students construct their knowledge of internal anatomy.

The cognitive tools perspective of the social constructivist theory is one way in which a researcher may attain an understanding of a participant's prior knowledge. A cognitive tool allows participants to create a product, a drawing in this study, and impose meaning on the product based on prior knowledge (Gredler, 1997). Therefore, the pre-service science teachers' knowledge of the body systems and the social sources of development that shaped their knowledge may be assessed through drawings and interviews. The interview was important to this study because the language used in the interview was assessed to reveal any knowledge the pre-service science teachers did not provide in the drawings (Gee, 2007; Lave & Wenger, 1991) and to define if there were social interactions that the pre-service teachers identified as sources of knowledge (Rogoff, 1990). Revealing the shared social representation pre-service science teachers have of the internal anatomy of the human and pig is important, because pre-service science teachers, whose inaccuracies may not be addressed, will eventually become in-service science teachers.

LITERATURE REVIEW

In relation to knowledge of the human body, drawings have been used since the mid-1900s to reveal what individuals know about internal anatomy. In 1955, Tait and Ascher designed the Inside-of-the-Body Test to determine if psychiatric patients, medical patients, and sixth graders (ages 11–12) had similar notions about the internal anatomy of the human body. Results of the Inside-of-the-Body Test revealed the heart was drawn more often than other organs and the cardiovascular and gastrointestinal systems were illustrated most often. Subsequently, the Inside-of-the-Body Test manifested as a way in which drawings may be used to determine participants' concepts of human internal anatomy.

A comprehensive literature review revealed that since Tait and Ascher's Inside-of-the-Body test 20 studies have asked participants to draw what they thought was inside of the human body, but no studies were found to ask about the internal anatomy of the pig. The information provided in Table 1 (available online at https://www.researchgate.net/publication/276206345_Table_1.Studies_in_which_ participants_were asked_to_draw_human_internal_anatomy_including_information_about_participants_methodology_and_organs_ and_systems_drawn_least_and most_successfully_%28Adapted_from_Patrick_2014%29) identifies the 22 studies and the participants, methodologies, organs drawn least and most often, and systems drawn least and most successfully in studies in which participants were asked to draw human internal anatomy. The methodologies and results were examined and used to (1) provide a historical perspective of the use of drawings in defining knowledge of internal human anatomy, (2) determine if the organs and systems drawn were similar across studies, and (3) investigate the methodology to conclude if classmate interviews were previously used as data collection tools. Studies asking participants to draw human internal anatomy have been completed in 22 countries with participants ranging in age from 4 to 76 years. The studies span six decades and represent various ages and countries and signify that the findings from Tait and Ascher's 1955 study are still valid. No matter the age or country of the drawer, the overall findings of drawing tests are similar. Nine of the studies identified the gastrointestinal system as one of the most accurately drawn systems or reported that organs from the gastrointestinal system were correctly drawn most often. In addition to the gastrointestinal system, the respiratory was reported as one of the most successfully drawn systems in six of the articles, respectively. Even though the heart was one of the most drawn organs in every study that reported data about the most drawn organ, the cardiovascular system was drawn successfully in only three studies. Ten studies reported the brain as one of the most drawn organs, while six studies identified bones as draw often. Even though the brain and some bones were reported as being successfully drawn, four studies indicated the skeletal system and one study named the nervous system as the most drawn systems. The endocrine and reproductive systems and their organs were drawn the least often.

Eleven of the studies asked participants to draw the internal anatomy, but did not include supplementary data gathering tools. Studies that included additional data gathering tools asked participants to (1) write about their drawings, (2) complete a Peabody Picture Vocabulary (Dunn, 1959, as cited in Offord & Aponte, 1967) and sentence completion, (3) participate in an interview, (4) name organs on a picture, (5) circle where organs were located on a line drawing, (6) take an open-ended questionnaire, and (7) write about the functions of the body systems. Even though studies utilized interviews, no studies were completed that asked participants to conduct classmate interviews about their drawings of the internal anatomy of the human body and describe where the participants believed they learned about the systems. The benefit of employing interviews in conjunction with drawings was of interest for this study, because the literature review suggested that when multiple data gathering tools were utilized a richer understanding of participant knowledge was established (Mathai & Ramadas, 2009; Rowlands, 2004; Texeira, 2000). On average, the information articulated during the interviews better expressed the structure and function concepts of the organs and systems than did the drawings alone.

While the 22 studies demonstrated that participants' knowledge may be obtained through drawings, questionnaires, circling the location of organs, and interviews; research is needed to further explore the intricate web of knowledge of the systems in the human body and how that knowledge may be shaped by cultural experiences. Based on the social constructivist theory the role of the researcher is to establish the source of the information in order to better appreciate the knowledge of the participant. Therefore, in addition to being asked to draw the internal anatomy of the human body, pre-service science teachers were asked to explain to a classmate which system they thought was the easiest and hardest to draw, why they thought the system was easy or difficult to draw, and where they believed they learned about internal anatomy.

METHODOLOGY

This study utilized a qualitative methodology and a social constructivist approach in order to investigate the knowledge pre-service middle level and secondary teachers have of the internal anatomy of the human and pig. In order to determine how personal experiences have impacted their knowledge, and consequently what they will teach their students, the teachers were asked to draw internal anatomy and describe their drawings.

PARTICIPANTS

This study took place during six science methods courses from fall 2007 to spring 2011 at two small suburban universities located in the southeastern United States of America. The science methods classes were made up of 148 pre-service science teachers who would be teaching middle level (students ages 11–14) and secondary science (students ages 14–18). The pre-service science teachers (ages 20–28) were in their fourth year of college and their second year in the undergraduate teacher education program and had completed an introductory biology course. The science methods course met for a three hour block once a week during the fall or spring semester. A total of 148 pre-service science teachers participated, but three drawings and interviews were removed from the study due to incomplete drawings or interviews, which left 145 pre-service science teacher participants. Due to concerns about asking participants to identify their gender and race, participants were told they could provide this data but it was not necessary. Sixty-nine percent of the participants chose not to identify their gender or race; therefore, gender and race are not reported.

DATA COLLECTION

Drawings

During each of the science methods courses, two weeks were spent discussing and practicing various types of formative assessment. Drawings and classmate interviews were discussed as an assessment technique during the second formative assessment class. In order to provide the pre-service science teachers with an opportunity to practice using drawings and classmate interviews in the classroom, participants were asked to draw what they thought was inside the human body. The pre-service teachers were given an 8.5" × 11" sheet of white paper and asked to "Draw the internal anatomy of a human." When the pre-service science teachers were finished drawing the internal human anatomy, they completed an interview with a classmate. After the interview, pre-service science teachers were given another sheet of white paper and asked to "Draw the internal anatomy of the pig." The pre-service science teachers were given as much time as they desired to draw the systems; however, the pre-service science teachers were finished with each drawing after 15 minutes. When they finished the internal anatomy of the human body drawings, they were asked to make a list of all the systems in the human body.

Interviews

After the preservice science teachers completed a drawing, they were randomly assigned a classmate, who interviewed them about the drawing. Classmate interviews were chosen because (1) interviews could be completed immediately after the drawing, (2) describing a drawing to a classmate might not be as intimidating as a teacher (King, 1989), (3) drawings allowed the candidates to practice questioning skills (King, 1994), and (4) the candidates modeled participant/participant interactions that could be used in the classroom (Webb, Nemer, & Ing, 2006).

Prior to the classmate interviews a protocol was established to ensure that the classmate partners were asking the same questions. The Internal Anatomy Interview Protocol was straightforward and contained the following directions and questions. (After each question allow your partner time to think and respond. Do not interrupt them as they speak.) (1) Tell me about your drawing. (2) Which system did you find to be the easiest to draw? Tell me why you thought that system was the easiest. (3) Which system did you find to be the most difficult to draw? Tell me why you thought it was the most difficult. (4) Where did you learn about the internal anatomy? (5) Is there anything else you would like to tell me about your drawing?

Procedure

The pre-service science teachers were given an 8.5" × 11" piece of paper and asked to draw the internal anatomy of the human and make a list of the systems. When they finished with the drawings, the pre-service science teachers were assigned a classmate partner and told that one person would be an interviewer and the other person would be the interviewee and asked about their drawing. The first interviewer was given the Internal Anatomy Interview Protocol and told to use the protocol to question the interviewee about the drawing. The classmate partners completed one interview about the human internal anatomy drawing. Because the second interview would be influenced by the first interview, one person in the group was not interviewed. After the interview was completed, the interviewee was asked to return to their seat and the same process was employed for the drawings and interviews about the internal anatomy of the pig. However, the interviewer from the human drawing interview became the interviewee in the pig drawing interview. For example, Bob and Janet were interview partners. Bob interviewed Janet about her human drawing, in turn, Janet interviewed Bob about his pig drawing. By asking Bob to interview Janet about the human and not being interviewed himself about his human drawing, the interviewee data was not influenced. The interviews were digitally recorded and lasted from 6 minutes to 17 minutes with a Mean of 10 minutes. The interviews were transcribed by the author into a Microsoft Word document and stored for data analysis. The resulting data were 145 drawings each of the internal anatomy of the human and pig with 72 human body interviews and 73 pig interviews.

Drawing named organs

After the drawings were completed, the participants were given an outline drawing of the pig and human. Participants were asked to draw the following organs in the correct locations and label them (Eiser & Patterson, 1983; Eiser, Patterson, & Tripp, 1984; Gellert, 1962): femur, gallbladder, heart, humerus, intestine, kidney, liver, ovaries, thyroid, trachea, and urinary bladder. These organs were chosen based on a study completed by Gellert (1962) and the literature review which indicated these organs were some of the most and least drawn.

DATA ANALYSIS

Drawings

First, the drawings were analyzed to determine the organs that were drawn and the systems that were listed. Second, a five point scoring system, shown in Table 2, developed from Prokop, Fancovicová, and Tunnicliffe's (2009) work was used to analyze the level at which participants drew each system. For the purpose of this study, eight systems were identified and named as Cardiovascular, Endocrine, Gastrointestinal, Muscular, Nervous, Respiratory, Skeletal, and Urogenital. To illustrate the analysis, Figure 1 presents an example of a participant's human internal anatomy drawing. The following scores were recorded for the systems in the drawing: Cardiovascular Level 4 (two organs correct position), Endocrine Level 1 (no organs), Gastrointestinal Level 5 (more than three organs correct position), Muscular Level 1 (no organs), Nervous Level 4 (two organs correct position), Respiratory Level 3 (one organ correct position), Skeletal Level 5 (more than three bones correct position), and Urogenital Level 4 (two organs correct position). The author and a science education graduate student, who had a Master's of Science in Biology, independently analyzed the drawings using the five point scale found in Table 2. They agreed on 91% of the drawings. For the drawings in which the Levels were in disagreement, the Levels were compared and finalized through discussions.

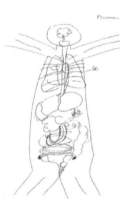

Figure 1. Example of human anatomy drawing

Table 2. Five point scale for scoring the systems. The five point scale is based on Prokop et al. (2009)

Level	Description
Level 1	No representation of organs (bones)
Level 2	One or more organs (bones) placed at random
Level 3	One organ (bone) in appropriate position
Level 4	Two organs (bones) in appropriate position
Level 5	Three organs (bones) or more in appropriate positions

The systems that the pre-service teachers listed were recorded against the eight systems that were identified for this study. For example, if the urinary system and/or reproductive system were named the system was recorded as Urogenital, the digestive system was recorded as Gastrointestinal, and circulatory was recorded as Cardiovascular. The data was placed in an Excel file as "0" not named and "1" named to determine which systems were drawn most often.

Interviews

The interviews were transcribed and the pre-service science teachers' answers were analyzed to determine which systems they found the easiest and most difficult to draw. A process of 'open coding' (Charmaz, 2006) was utilized to establish where pre-service teachers believed they learned about the internal anatomy. This resulted in the development of a list of 12 codes generated from the data along with examples of student quotations included under each code. The established codes were grouped into three major themes, including:

(1) role of school in exposing pre-service teachers to internal anatomy, (2) influence of media/technology, and (3) health experiences. Nvivo 8 software was used during the coding process to track the number of participants referring to each theme, resulting in the data that are presented in Tables 3–5 for select themes along with sample quotations for each code.

Drawing Named Organs

Figure 2 is a line drawing of the pig on which a pre-service teacher drew organs as they were named. The pre-service teacher in this drawing successfully illustrated the correct location of the heart, liver, stomach, kidney, urinary bladder, and intestine. The organs that were successfully drawn in the correct locations were recorded in an Excel file.

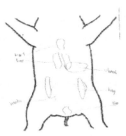

Figure 2. Pre-service teacher's drawing of pig anatomy

RESULTS

Drawings

Table 3 displays the Levels at which the pre-service teachers drew each of the systems in the human and pig. The scores offered a closer look at the organs and systems the pre-service teachers drew correctly most often and indicated that the results of the human and pig drawings were similar. The Gastrointestinal system was drawn most often in both organisms. Even though the Cardiovascular system was not one of the most correctly drawn systems, the drawings consistently represented one organ, which was the heart in all cases. Much like the Cardiovascular system, the Nervous and Respiratory systems were not the most correctly drawn systems, but the brain and lungs were among the most drawn organs. The pre-service teachers were not as successful at drawing the Endocrine, Muscular, and Skeletal systems. In fact, the Endocrine system was represented the least often.

Table 4 presents the organs that were illustrated in the drawings. The results of the drawings were similar in that the most successfully drawn organs in the human and pig were the lungs, heart, intestine, stomach, and brain. Of the organs that the pre-service teachers illustrated, the muscles, pancreas, thyroid, and appendix were the least successfully drawn organs.

Table 3. The percentage of pre-service science teachers who scored at each Level on the drawings of the internal anatomy of the human and pig. The systems are listed from most drawn to least. N=145

System	Level 1		Level 2		Level 3		Level 4		Level 5	
	Human	Pig	Human	Pig	Human	Pig	Human	Pig	Human	Pig
Gastrointestinal	4%	9%	0%	0%	18%	12%	23%	4%	58%	76%
Respiratory	4%	12%	3%	0%	61%	52%	12%	22%	19%	13%
Cardiovascular	15%	17%	0%	0%	66%	63%	16%	8%	3%	12%
Urogenital	32%	38%	0%	0%	37%	26%	19%	16%	12%	17%
Nervous	53%	49%	0%	0%	49%	49%	0%	3%	0%	0%
Skeletal	54%	52%	3%	0%	39%	41%	0%	4%	4%	1%
Muscular	95%	98%	0%	0%	3%	0	0%	4%	2%	0%
Endocrine	97%	98%	0%	0%	34%	2%	0%	0%	0%	0%

After students completed the human body drawing, they were asked to make a list of the systems in the human body. The results indicated that 92% of the pre-service teachers named the Gastrointestinal system and 90% (120) of those pre-service teachers named the Gastrointestinal system first in the list. The Cardiovascular, Respiratory, and Nervous systems were named by 92%, 90%, and 83% of the pre-service teachers, respectively and the Cardiovascular system was listed second in the list most often. These systems were

*Table 4. The percentage of pre-service science teachers who drew
each organ in the pig and pig. N=145*

Organ	# of human drawings	Organ	# of pig drawings
Lungs	92%	Lungs	88%
Heart	85%	Heart	83%
Intestine	82%	Intestine	76%
Stomach	61%	Stomach	66%
Brain	49%	Brain	52%
Kidney	27%	Liver	29%
Gall bladder	26%	Kidney	28%
Trachea	24%	Esophagus	26%
Esophagus	23%	Leg bones	26%
Liver	21%	Arm bones	23%
Ribs	21%	Ovaries	19%
Arm bones	17%	Vagina	19%
Leg bones	17%	Trachea	19%
Ovaries	17%	Urinary bladder	18%
Vagina	17%	Gall bladder	15%
Urinary Bladder	14%	Ribs	14%
Testicles	12%	Testicles	8%
Penis	12%	Penis	6%
Pancreas	6%	Muscles	4%
Muscles	4%	Pancreas	3%
Thyroid	3%	Thyroid	2%
Appendix	1%	Appendix	0%

followed by the Muscular (20%), Skeletal (15%), and Urogenital systems (14%). The endocrine system was not included by any of the pre-service teachers in the systems listing exercise.

Drawing Named Organs

When the pre-service teachers were asked to draw the location of organs that the author named, they were more likely to draw the organ in the correct place than when they were asked to "Draw the internal anatomy of…" Drawings in Figure 2 (pig) and Figure 3 (human) revealed that when pre-service teachers were asked to use outlines of the organism and illustrate specific organs in the human and pig the pre-service teachers had similar successes and failures. In the human and the pig every pre-service teacher (N=145) was able to draw the correct location of the heart, intestine, kidneys, and urinary bladder. The ovaries were drawn successfully in 84% of the human outlines and 81% of the pig outlines. The liver was depicted in 31% of the human outlines and 27% of the pig outlines, whilst the gallbladder was drawn in 27% of the human outlines and 17% of the pig outlines. Interestingly, no pre-service teachers represented the thyroid without the trachea. Even though 52% of pre-service teachers illustrated the trachea in the human and 43% in the pig when prompted, the thyroid was portrayed in 31% of the human drawings and 23% of the pig drawings, which is an increase from drawings in which students were told to "Draw the internal anatomy of…" The femur was drawn correctly in 63% of the human drawings and 45% of the pig drawings; conversely, the humerus was drawn successfully in 13% of the human illustrations and 8% of the pig illustrations.

Interviews

The three major themes that emerged from the data analysis and the results from the codes are shared below. While data were collected during interviews about the human and pig, the percentage of participants discussing each code was remarkably similar (<12% points differential for each code). Due to the similarity in the percentages, the data have been aggregated and are presented as such.

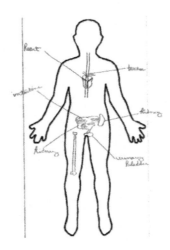

Figure 3. Pre-service teacher's drawing of human anatomy

Even though Tim's drawing of the pig in Figure 4 is not representative of the other participants, his drawing and interview do provide a different perspective of pig internal anatomy.

> When she said 'Draw what is inside the pig.' all I thought about was food. I didn't think about drawing the organs and stuff like you did. All I could think about when she asked was the stuff you can eat. I drew bacon and sausage and ham and eggs and a ham. I didn't even think about drawing anything else. I'm not sure why I drew that. That's just what I thought of when she asked. I just thought about the parts of the pig you could eat. I really like pig…bacon and ham and sausage.

As is demonstrated by the interview, when Tim was prompted to draw the internal anatomy of the pig he connected that request with the various parts of the pig that he liked to eat. Based on the rubric developed for the study, Tim scored a Level 1 (no organs represented) on every system. The drawing completed by Tim represents his view of pig internal anatomy, but may not be all the information he knew about the internal anatomy, which provides justification for utilizing additional data gathering tools when defining knowledge.

Figure 4. Tim's drawing of edible pig anatomy

Theme 1: Role of school.   The percentage of total participants who discussed each of the codes in Theme 1, role of school, is presented in Table 5. The data demonstrate that 95% of the 145 participants sampled wrote about the role of school in exposing them to internal anatomy. The highest percentage described their teacher as a source of knowledge, while a bit smaller percentage, talked about dissecting as an experience they had at school. Another significant finding was that the pre-service teachers described experiences in which teachers had taken them on a field trip to an informal science institution.

Lillian, who completed the human drawing found in Figure 5, expressed that she learned about internal anatomy from her college biology teacher and field trip experiences she had during her college biology class, as follows:

> During my college biology class, the professor taught us this song about the circulatory system. I think it was something like this… Arteries carry the blood away. Veins come back to the heart all day. Sixty thousand miles it goes. Around and through the heart it flows. I think that was it. I can't remember the rest of it, but that really helped me during the test. She also took us to the see the body exhibit. I think it was called body works or body world. Yeah it was Body World. Wow that was amazing. Have you seen it? It's like when we dissected stuff in class, but way cooler.

Table 5. Role of school in exposing pre-service teachers to internal anatomy

Theme or Code	Total/Percentage (N=145)	Example student quotes
Theme 1: Role of school in exposing pre-service teachers to internal anatomy	95%	
Code 1: Teacher	77%	I think my teacher is where I learned about it because she told stories about the systems
Code 2: Dissection	69%	In my high school biology class, we did dissections and activities about the systems
Code 3: Biology/Science book	45%	I remember the pictures in my biology book when I was in school
Code 4: Field trip	24%	When I was in the fourth grade, my teacher took us to a museum that had a program about the body

Lillian's quote is representative of a large number of participants who wrote about experiences they had at school, often with teachers. Even though a smaller number of students wrote about their experiences during field trips, the descriptions were much like the vivid memories Lillian described in her depiction of a visit to the Body World exhibit. Moreover, Lillian mentioned dissection, which was mentioned often by pre-service teachers.

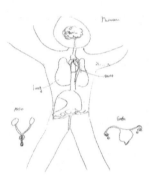

Figure 5. Lillian's drawing of internal human anatomy

A small number of pre-service teachers wrote about the information they gleaned from their biology or science textbooks as Mike, who completed the human drawing in Figure 6, demonstrates: "I remember the pictures in my science books at school. They had pictures of the inside of the body. The pictures were a human body with the organs inside."

The quotes illustrate the connections between the pre-service teachers and the social encounters they had at school or during a school sponsored event. These types of school related experiences are important to student learning.

Figure 6. Mike's anatomy drawing referencing school science books

Theme 2: Influence of media/technology. The percentages of total participants who discussed the codes in Theme 2, the influence of media/technology, are presented in Table 6. The pre-service teachers believed they learned about the internal anatomy from various forms of media/technology, including the internet, medical programming, commercials, television programs, and books other than text books. For example, in the following quote Betsy describes how she found out more about Parkinson's disease:

> My Dad found out he's got Parkinson's last year. I think. Maybe it was two years ago. Anyway, when I found out I tried to find out everything I could about Parkinson's. I knew…it makes you shake, but I really didn't know much about it so I looked it up on the internet…When I found out I had cysts on my ovaries, I looked that up too. When I want to know something I go to WebMD or the Mayo clinic website.

Even though Betsy was not asked about how she would approach teaching her students about internal anatomy, she went on to say "I think I'd use the internet and websites to teach my students about anatomy. There're a lot of good websites about diseases and there're websites that show the inside of the body virtually."

Surprisingly, many participants described medical programming and commercials as a source of knowledge about internal anatomy. In the following description, Betty (Figure 7 pig drawing) provides details about a medical program and a commercial:

I watch Dr. OZ all the time…I learn so much about stuff I can do to keep healthy…Sometimes he does funny stuff to show you how things work. Like one time he had these stuffed viruses and he put them in a box to show you how viruses reproduced. Oh yeah…and I sometimes…you see those commercials where you see the digestive system. There's also this commercial that shows how pain killers go to the brain. It's like a dotted line that goes up to the brain.

Table 6. Influence of media/technology.

Theme or Code	Total/Percentage (N=145)	Example student quotes
Theme: Influence of media/technology	79%	
Code 1: Commercials	75%	I see commercials on TV all the time with pictures of the internal anatomy
Code 2: Internet	45%	We just found out my husband has polycystic kidney disease so we looked it up online
Code 3: Medical programming	39%	I watch Dr. Oz all the time.
Code 4: Television programs	29%	I watched Nip Tuck and they showed stuff that looked real, like nose reconstruction
Code 5: Books other than text books	12%	When I was growing up my parents bought me a set of Encyclopedias and they had pictures of the human body in them

Betty followed her description of watching medical programming with her memories of commercials in which she remembered learning about the gastrointestinal and nervous systems.

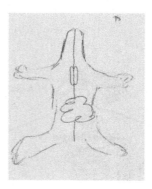

Figure 7. Betty's anatomy drawing referencing TV commercials

Theme 3: Health experiences. The percentage of total participants who discussed each of the codes in Theme 3, health experiences, is presented in Table 7. Participants commented on the influence of health related experiences on their knowledge of the human body. In discussing the influence of health related experiences upon their knowledge of internal anatomy, pre-service teachers specifically described personal health experiences as influencing their knowledge of internal anatomy and described the health experiences of family and friends as influential.

Table 7. Health experiences

Theme or code	Total/Percentage (N=145)	Example student quotes
Theme 4: Health experiences	66%	
Code 1: Personal health experiences	33%	I know where my pancreas is because I am diabetic
Code 2: Family/Friend health experiences	27%	I go to the doctor with my Dad…he has colon cancer
Code 3: Doctor	14%	Going to the doctor is another way I learn about the body, because they show you models to tell you about what is happening

When pre-service teachers explained the impact of their health experiences on their knowledge, they discussed medical issues from the past or illnesses they were currently undergoing. Moreover, some participants described interactions they had with medical doctors, as in the following quote by Tammy, who drew the pig in Figure 8:

I broke my ribs last week and it really hurt. The doctor sent me to get a chest x-ray and told me to ask for a CD of the pictures. I took the CD home and put it up on my TV. I could see my ribs, my heart, my lungs, and [a] bunch of other stuff. I know where my ninth and tenth ribs are now, because my doctor showed me on a skeleton.

Figure 8. Tammy's anatomy drawing referencing her own medical experience

Some pre-service teachers discussed medical experiences they had with a family member or friend, as Mack does here with regard to his father. The important role that family and friends play in exposing participants to internal anatomy is an important theme which deserves further exploration.

Well…hmmmm…not really sure how I know about the body. I think I just kinda know. Like I just know. You know stuff happens and then you learn about that part of the body. Like when my aunt went to the hospital they said she needed her gallbladder out. So then you know where that's at, but she also had something wrong with her pancreas…So I learned about where the pancreas is. You know it's over here on this side. I think it's near the stomach somewhere right here. One time my Dad broke his clavicle and we found out that that's the most broken bone. The clavicle's right here.

Mack's quote is representative of a number of participants who wrote about medical issues, often with family. Participants described the illnesses or diseases of family and friends and often with some detail.

CONCLUSIONS AND DISCUSSION

An analysis of the collected data provided answers to the research questions and allowed for the following conclusions. The pre-service science teachers: (1) drew the gastrointestinal, respiratory, and cardiovascular systems and their organs most often, (2) drew the muscular and endocrine system and their organs the least often, (3) had knowledge of organs that may not be represented in their drawings of human internal anatomy, and (4) described social, personal, and familial interactions as a source of knowledge.

Since the 1950's, there has been considerable interest in the knowledge held by the public of the internal anatomy of the human body; however, the studies have not attempted to define a shared social representation of human internal anatomy. The social constructivist theory posits a relationship between knowledge, personal experiences and social interactions. This study centered on discerning the knowledge that pre-service science teachers have of human internal anatomy, but was designed to engage the pre-service teachers in conversations to define the places and social experiences that pre-service science teachers deemed as important to their knowledge of the systems. Defining the shared social representation people have of internal anatomy is an important factor in supporting meaningful learning for the students and the public. Social representations of the human body are what the public develops as their shared understanding of the internal anatomy and may not be well developed. Therefore, based on the study reported here and previous studies (Patrick, 2014; Dempster & Stears, 2014), a shared social representation of the public's ideas about human anatomy is revealed. When asked to draw the internal anatomy, the drawings indicated that participants were most aware of the gastrointestinal and cardiovascular systems and the heart and lungs. Additionally, the endocrine system was not included as part of the social representation of the internal anatomy. However, when participants were asked to draw specific organs in the correct location and interviewed about their drawings, the findings were more fascinating. When asked to draw the internal anatomy participants did not draw organs representing all the systems; however, when prompted to draw specific organs participants were able to illustrate additional organs. This finding indicates that participants may have more knowledge of the internal anatomy than revealed by the drawings alone, but may not have a clear understanding of how the organs interact within a system.

Even though the participants' internal anatomy drawings and prompted organ drawings reflected some knowledge of internal anatomy, the interviews exposed additional understandings. The participants' interviews are filled with rich descriptions of 'social interactions' associated with teachers, family members, and friends and field trip and dissection experiences. Drawings are an integral part of understanding science and can deepen students' conceptual development (Ainsworth, Prain, & Tytler, 2011), but encouraging discourse may foster the recognition of inaccuracies and misconceptions and increase knowledge.

The data from this study demonstrate that a large majority of the pre-service teachers recognize the social interactions that occur in their everyday lives as a source of information. In relation to Rogoff's (1990) theory of guided participation, in which involvement of people in communication through culturally valued activities, face-to-face communication, and observation of cultural routines, it follows that the social representations of the human body held by the public are formed and reformed by their personal experiences and interactions. Taken as a group, the results suggest that participants knew more about the organs and systems that are discussed or seen in public or have been affected by illness. In Tait and Ascher's (1955) original Inside-of-the-Body Test, they discovered similar results in which medical patients drew most often their afflicted organs. Moreover, as suggested in the social constructivist theory, when interviewed the participants shared instances in which they learned during social interactions.

The findings of this study support the findings of Dempster and Stears (2014), who stated that children in Grade 1 may know more about the skeletal, gastrointestinal, and gaseous (respiratory) systems because "adults who interact with children usually have some knowledge of these systems and stories often refer to food and eating" (p. 77). Moreover, the children's awareness of their internal anatomy appears to arise more from direct experience and interaction with parents or caregivers. Similarly, Patrick (2104) found that when pre-service teachers were asked to discuss their source of knowledge about the gastrointestinal and endocrine system, they described interactions with family and friends. Based on the findings from Dempster and Stears (2014), Patrick (2014), and the current study, discourse that occurs with family members, friends and teachers, as children and adults, is an important aspect of the social interactions that construct the representations that people hold of human internal anatomy. According to Merriam (1998) knowledge is created by individuals interacting with the social world and experiences are 'lived' and 'felt' through contextual and concrete experiences. The results of this study support the supposition of Merriam (1998) that, "reality is constructed by individuals interacting with their social worlds" (p. 25). The social interactions that the pre-service science teachers describe are based on widespread cultural and societal interactions. This implies that knowledge of the two systems is explored in unique social communities (Yore, Hand, & Florence, 2004).

The pre-service teachers in this study identified the social interactions that took place at school and with teachers as one source of knowledge about internal anatomy. These findings are of concern because if the social representation pre-service teachers have of human internal anatomy does not include a well-developed understanding of the organs and their relationships within a system, then as teachers they will perpetuate these socially held concepts to their students. The role of science teachers is to prepare students to understand the natural world, biological concepts, and personal health issues; therefore, science teachers must also understand the individual roles of organs and the interdependence of organs within a system. Above all providing students with correct knowledge of internal anatomy may afford students the ability to make informed decisions about their health care.

IMPLICATIONS

An implication of this research is that the interactions and experiences students have in and out of school are important in their development of knowledge about the human body systems. The types of interactions and experiences that influence students' knowledge are different for each system; therefore, a plethora of methods will aid children [to] interpret environmental stimuli, allowing them to match their learning to their perceptual strengths. Such is the case with information about the internal body. By providing a variety of sensory experiences along with the didactic information, there is a greater likelihood that children will process such information for later recall. (Vessey, 1988, p. 265)

The findings have implications for teachers, school systems, curriculum developers and teacher preparation programs. Each group should be aware of their impact in promoting students' knowledge of the systems and, based on the data from this study, should consider ways of teaching that promote social exchanges.

I postulate that a framework of social interactions that includes a broad context (media, friends, everyday acquaintances, school, etc.) and familial relationships should be considered in the classroom. A social constructivist framework for teaching about the human body will contribute to the construction of knowledge of the systems. Students need to connect socially with each other to stimulate their thoughts about previous social situations which may lead to cognitive stimulation. Along with drawings, teachers should create social exchanges by providing first-hand experiences through authentic and computer simulated dissections and encouraging students to interact through discussion or debates related to health issues. Pre-dissection lessons should include asking students to draw what they believe is inside the body. During-dissection activities should ask students to define their ideas concerning the relationships between the organs and the organ system. Post-dissection activities should combine both drawings and reflections and encourage discourse about how the organs function within the systems.

The importance of defining students' social representation of a science concept through drawings is of great concern, because the social representations reveal their knowledge and misconceptions about a concept. Hopefully, teachers will recognize the significance of drawings and will utilize them as a supplemental evaluation of knowledge. By combining drawings with additional evaluation techniques, teachers can connect students' prior knowledge with new concepts resulting in the establishment of new social representations. These types of activities are becoming more important as teachers are faced with an increasing demand for formative assessment. Teachers need to promote thinking through drawing and social interactions, which are a crucial aspect of acquiring and discovering knowledge.

REFERENCES

Ainsworth, S., Prain, V., & Tytler, R. (2011). Drawing to learn science. *Science, 333*(6046), 1096–1097.

Arslan, H. O., Cigdemoglu, C., & Moseley, C. (2012). A three-tier diagnostic test to assess pre-service teachers' misconceptions about global warming, greenhouse effect, ozone layer depletion, and acid rain. *International Journal of Science Education, 34*(11), 1667–1686.

Bahar, M. (2003). Misconceptions in biology education and conceptual change strategies. *Educational Sciences: Theory & Practice, 3*(1), 27–64.

Berger, J. (1982). *Another way of telling.* New York, NY: Pantheon Books.

Brooks, M. (2005). Drawing as a unique mental development tool for young children: Interpersonal and intrapersonal dialogues. *Contemporary Issues in Early Childhood, 6*(1), 80–91.

Brooks, M. (2009). What Vygotsky can teach us about young children drawing. *International Art in Early Childhood Research Journal, 1*(1).

Bruner, J. (1990). Culture and human development: A new look. *Human Development, 33*(6), 344–355.

Bruning, R. H., Schraw, G. J., & Norby, M. M. (2011). *Cognitive psychology and instruction* (5th ed.). Upper Saddle River, NJ: Pearson.

Buijs, A. E., Hovardas, T., Figari, H., Castro, P., Devine-Wright, P. Fischer, A., Mouro, C., & Selge, S. (2012). Understanding people's ideas on natural resource management: Research on social representations of nature. *Society & Natural Resources: An International Journal, 25*(11), 1167–1181.

Charmaz, K. (2006). *Constructing grounded theory: A practical guide through qualitative analysis.* London, UK: Sage.

Dempster, E., & Stears, M. (2014). An analysis of children's drawings of what they think is inside their bodies: A South African regional study. *Journal of Biological Education, 48*(2), 71–79.

Dikmenli, M. (2010). Misconceptions of cell division held by student teachers in biology: A drawing analysis. *Scientific Research and Essay, 5*(2), 235–247.

Dikmenli, M., Cardak, O., & Kiray, S. A. (2011). Science student teachers' ideas about the 'gene' concept. *Procedia – Social and Behavioral Sciences, 15*, 2609–2613.

Dunn, L. M. (1959). *Peabody picture vocabulary test.* Washington, DC: American Guidance Service Inc.

Eiser, C., & Patterson, D. (1983). Slugs and snails and puppy-dog tails': Children's ideas about the inside of their bodies. *Child: Care, Health and Development, 9*, 233–240.

Eiser, C., Patterson, D., & Tripp, J. H. (1984). Diabetes and developing knowledge of the body. *Archives of Disease in Childhood, 59*(2), 167–169.

Fischer, A., Peters, V., Neebe, M., Vavra, J., Kriel, A., Lapka, M., & Megyesi, B. (2012). Climate change? No wise recourse use is the issue: Social representations of energy, climate change, and the future. *Environmental Policy and Governance, 22*(3), 161–176.

Gee, J. P. (2007). *Social linguistics and literacies: Ideology in discourses* (3rd ed.). London, UK: Taylor & Francis.

Gellert, E. (1962). Children's conceptions of the content and functions of the human body. *Genetic Psychology Monographs, 65*, 293–405.

Gredler, M. E. (1997). *Learning and instruction: Theory into practice* (3rd ed.). Upper Saddle River, NJ: Prentice-Hall.

Hackling, M., & Prain, V. (2005). *Primary connections: Stage 2 trial.* Canberra: Australian Academy of Science.

Hovardas, T., & Korfiatis, K. (2006). Word associations as a tool for assessing conceptual change in science education. *Learning and Instruction, 16*, 416–432.

King, A. (1989). Effects of self-questioning training on college participants' comprehension of lectures. *Contemporary Educational Psychology, 14*(4), 366–381.

King, A. (1994). Guiding knowledge construction in the classroom: Effects of teaching children how to question and how to explain. *American Educational Research Journal, 31*(2), 338–368.

Kolomuç, A., & Tekin, S. (2011). Chemistry teachers' misconceptions concerning concept of chemical reaction rate. *Eurasian Journal of Physics and Chemistry Education, 3*(2), 84–101.

Kukla, A. (2000). *Social constructivism and the philosophy of science.* New York, NY: Psychology Press.

Lave, J., & Wenger, E. (1991). *Situated learning: Legitimate peripheral participation.* New York, NY: Cambridge University Press.

Lorenzi-Cioldi, F., & Cle´mence, A. (2004). Group process and the construction of social representations. In M. B. Brewer & M. Hewstone (Eds.), *Social cognition* (pp. 298–320). Oxford, UK: Blackwell.

Mathai, S., & Ramadas, J. (2009). Visuals and visualisation of human body systems. *International Journal of Science Education, 31*(3), 439–458.

Merriam, S. (1998). *Qualitative research and case study applications in education.* San Francisco, CA: Jossey-Bass Publishers.

Moscovici, S. (1963). Attitudes and opinions. *Annual Review of Psychology, 14*, 231–260.

Moscovici, S. (2001). Why a theory of social representations? In K. Deaux & G. Philoge´ne (Eds.), *Representations of the social* (pp. 8–36). Oxford, UK: Blackwell.

Mouro, C., & Castro, P. (2010). Local communities responding to ecological challenges: A psycho-social approach to the Natura 2000 network. *Journal of Community & Applied Social Psychology, 20*, 139–155.

Mosely, C., Desjean-Perrotta, B., & Utley, J. (2010). The draw-an-environment test rubric (DAET-R) exploring pre-service teacher's mental models of the environment. *Environmental Education Research, 16*(2), 189–208.

National Research Council. (1999). *Foundations: Inquiry thoughts, views, and strategies for the K-5 classroom.* Washington, DC: National Academy Press.

Offord, D. R., & Aponte, J. F. (1967). A comparison of drawings and sentence completion responses of congenital heart children with normal children. *Journal of Projective Techniques & Personality Assessment, 31*(2), 57–62.

Patrick, P. (2014). Social interactions and familial relationships preservice science teachers describe during interviews about their drawings of the endocrine and gastrointestinal systems. *International Journal of Environmental & Science Education, 9*, 159–175.

Prokop, P., Fancovicová, J., & Tunnicliffe, S. D. (2009). The effect of type of instruction on expression of children's knowledge: How do children see the endocrine and urinary system? *International Journal of Environmental and Science Education, 4*(1), 75–93.

Prokop, P., Prokop, M., & Tunnicliffe, S. D. (2008). Effects of keeping animals as pets on children's concepts of vertebrates and invertebrates. *International Journal of Science Education, 30*(4), 431–449.

Reiss, M. J., & Tunnicliffe, S. D. (2001). Students' understandings of human organs and organ systems. *Research in Science Education, 31*, 383–399.

Rogoff, B. (1990). *Apprenticeship in thinking: Cognitive development in social context.* New York, NY: Oxford University Press.

Rogoff, B. (1995). Observing sociocultural activity on three planes: Participatory appropriation, guided participation, and apprenticeship. In J. V. Wertsch, P. del Rio, & A. Alvarez (Eds.), *Sociocultural studies of mind* (pp. 139–164). Cambridge, UK: Cambridge University Press.

Rowlands, M. (2004). What do children think happens to the food they eat? *Journal of Biological Education, 38*(4), 167–171.

Selge, S., & Fischer, A., (2011). How people familiarize themselves with complex ecological concepts—anchoring of social representations of invasive non-native species. *Journal of Community and Applied Social Psychology, 21*(4), 297–311.

Tait, C., & Ascher, R. (1955). Inside-of-the-body test. *Psychosomatic Medicine, 17*(2), 139–148.

Tatar, E. (2011). Prospective primary school teachers' misconceptions about states of matter. *Educational Research and Reviews, 6*(2), 197–200.

Teixeira, F. M. (2000). What happens to the food we eat? Children's conceptions of the structure and function of the gastrointestinal system. *International Journal of Science Education, 22*(5), 507–520.

Vessey, J. (1988). Comparison of two teaching methods on children's knowledge of their internal bodies. *Nursing Research, 37*(5), 262–267.

Vosniadou, S. (2003). Exploring the relationships between conceptual change and intentional learning. In G. M. Sinatra & P. R. Pintrich (Eds.), *Intentional conceptual change* (pp. 377–406). Mahwah, NJ: Lawrence Erlbaum Associates, Inc.

Vygotsky, L. S. (1978). *Mind in society.* Cambridge, MA: Harvard University Press.

Wagner, W. (2012). Social representation theory. In D. J. Christie (Ed.), *Encyclopedia of peace psychology.* Malden, MA: Wiley-Blackwell.

Wandersee, J. H. Mintzes, J. J., & Novak, J. D. (1994). Research on alternative conceptions in science. In D. Gabel (Ed.), *Handbook of research on science teaching and learning: A project of the national science teachers association* (pp. 177–210). New York, NY: Macmillan.

Webb, N. M., Nemer, K. M., & Ing, M. (2006). Small-group reflections: Parallels between teacher discourse and participant behavior in peer-directed groups. *The Journal of the Learning Sciences, 15*(1), 63–119.

Wood, D., Bruner, J. S., & Ross, G. (1976). The role of tutoring in problem solving. *Journal of Child Psychology and Psychiatry, 17*(2), 89–100.

Yates, T. B., & Marek, E. A. (2013). Is Oklahoma really OK? A regional study of the prevalence of biological evolution-related misconceptions held by introductory biology teachers. *Evolution: Education and Outreach, 6*, 1–20.

Yip, D. Y. (1998). Teachers' misconceptions of the circulatory system. *Journal of Biological Education, 32*(3), 207–215.

Yore, L. D., Hand, B. M., & Florence, M. K. (2004). Scientists' views of science, models of writing, and science writing practices. *Journal of Research in Science Teaching, 41*(4), 338–369.

Patricia Patrick
Texas Tech University, USA

5. DEVELOPMENT OF BIOLOGICAL LITERACY THROUGH DRAWING ORGANISMS

INTRODUCTION

This chapter is about how children's drawings convey their level of conceptual understanding of organisms. Drawings are a useful pedagogical tool as a window to investigate children's conceptual knowledge and the meanings they give to this form of expression. We analyzed the drawings collected from pupils living in rural areas, towns, and suburban areas in Brazil. Louv (2008) has written that young children may be out of touch with wildlife in developed countries. However, in every culture children can be seen as interested in living things, identifying, classifying, and seeking patterns, especially about animals (Tomkins & Tunnicliffe, 2007). Young children aged 4 to 15 years in every culture notice and find out about living things around them (Patrick et al., 2013). When children encounter living organisms it provides countless opportunities for understanding the natural world, contributing to their science learning (Zoldosova & Prokop, 2006). These young children are interested in a wide variety of living organisms such as plants and the animals that they encounter: insects, birds, dogs and cats. They identify, classify and notice the patterns used in grouping them (Bartoszeck et al., 2011; Patrick & Tunnnicliffe, 2011; Rybska et al., 2014). Attitudes differ. Primary and secondary school students in some countries show positive atitudes towards animals such as spiders and toads while others regard them with disgust (Prokop et al., 2010; Tomazic, 2011).

Children see live animals at home, in their backyards, in their gardens, around the local area or visits to zoos. They see plants (trees, shrubs, small flowering plants, ferns and mosses for example) at home or around where they live, or when going on trips to places such as botanical gardens (Sanders, 2007; Bartoszeck et al., 2014). They are able to identify striking features of the structures and sometimes behavior of these organisms. In this way children come to recognize the environment as a part of the natural world (Patrick & Tunnicliffe, 2011). The concept of animal and plant are fundamental ontological categories that allow children in every culture to organize the perception of the world in which they live (Angus, 1981; Wee, 2012).

Even children entering preschool around age 3 already have an early understanding of biology acquired from observing what happens in the world around them (Legare et al., 2013). It is mostly at the preschool level that children begin to develop concepts that help them give meaning to the natural world around them. As they grow we see that they are able to draw a basic representation from memory of outer features of snails, flowering plants, trees, insects, and birds (Vieira et al., 1968; Bartoszeck & Tunnicliffe, 2013; Rybska et al., 2014a, 2014b; Tunnicliffe, 2012). Research is continuing to explore what young learners are thinking about the insides of organisms (e.g. Reiss & Tunnicliffe, 1999; Bartoszeck et al., 2011a).

Children's drawings as they grow older have proven to be significant tools that may be used to evaluate their knowledge and concepts of the ecosystem and diversity of flora and fauna, as for example in the Atlantic rain forest (Schwartz et al., 2007). Childrens' drawings from memory are less accurate in detail because they are drawn from associations gathered in memory or in action in the working memory, their mental models. According to Rapp (2007) "mental models" are representations of information and experiences from the outside world. However, such drawings are often able to depict the many aspects of an object for other people to recognize (Potter, 1976; Hitch & Halliday, 1988; Morse, 1999; Pike et al., 2012; Dunning et al., 2013). A child's drawing is a way that the child may represent their mind's images (Van Driel, 1999: Lourenção van Kolck, 1981; Schnotz, 2002). Moreover, drawings (the expressed model) channel graphic information and communicate children's ideas or development of concepts (Hopperstad, 2008). The basic hypothesis of Luquet (1927/1979) is that the aim of drawings is a translation of visual properties of objects into graphics. Thus, when a child is drawing symbols she is expressing a model from the point of view of her psychologic or cognitive development (Jung, 1962; Johson-Laird, 1988; Plotkin, 1997).

Biological drawings made by pupils allow them to create their own visual representations providing evidence of their conceptual understanding of the subject that they are illustrating (Ballew, 1930; Chang, 2012). In addition to any evidence of their current thinking, drawings can be a proactive method for pupils to aid in remembering details of what they have observed. This was the case in research based on activities dissecting earthworms or grasshoppers under the extereo-microscope and identifying the parts which form the rudimentary nervous systems of these invertebrates (Freeman & Bracegirdle, 1976; Righi, 1966).

EXPLORING THE DEVELOPMENT OF CHILDREN'S DRAWINGS AS A TOOL FOR LEARNING

Children's drawings vary according to their development and what experiences they bring to school from their socio-cultural backgrounds. These are manifested in the shape of symbolic representations (Kendrick & Mckay, 2002). Drawings produced by children evolve as the child's cognitive and motor skills expand. As a starting point, scribbles are the first purposeful marks left by children when they are about 2 to 3 years of age (Figure 1). They reveal the child's capacity to form an intention and put it on paper. Later, these scribbles

P. Katz (Ed.), Drawing for Science Education, 55–65.
© *2017 Sense Publishers. All rights reserved.*

change from uncontrolled pencillings to a purposive activity where the child may assign a name to the drawing object as in Figure 2 (Burt, 1922). This begins at about 3 years of age, but varies widely. As children have increasing control and co-ordination of movements (fine and gross motor skills) and can manage the pencil in a better way, they start making their first shapes (Eliot, 1999). The child seeks to produce circles, crosses and next rectangles and triangles (Yang & Noel, 2006). Between 4 to 5 years of age children develop progressive visual control. The human figure often becomes the favourite subject, but plants and animals also appear (Figures 3 and 4).

   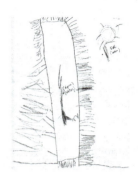

Figure 1. Drawing by 3 year old boy representing an insect *Figure 2. Drawing by a 4 year old boy of a human with the characteristics of a "tadpole man"* *Figure 3. Drawing of a bird by a 5 year old boy* *Figure 4. Drawing of a plant by 4 year old boy*

By 5 to 6 years of age children reach the "early pictorial stage." Flowers, leaves and fruit may be added when representing trees and shrubs and other seed bearing plants. By 7 years, children create a more elaborate scene, a narrative, and begin to reveal how they perceive and attach meaning to the world around them, a kind of descriptive symbolism (Bourassa, 1997; Hopperstad, 2010). However, although drawing activity is common during elementary science lessons, there is a scarcity of studies concerning the natural world (Symington et al., 1981).

Hayes & Symington (1988) proposed three stages, based on previous studies: (1) "symbolism" where the human figure depicted is reproduced with certain accuracy; (2) "intellectual realism" where children jot down what they think they know instead of what they see and try to communicate a lot of detail from memory; (3) "visual realism" where children begin drawing what they perceive from nature (Hayes & Symington, 1984; Hayes et al., 1994).

THEORY: THE NEED TO DRAW

Some researchers claim that there are similarities between the first drawings of a child and those produced by our prehistoric ancestors or by more recent preliterate oral societies, referencing Haeckel's law (that is known most commonly as "ontogeny recapitulates phylogeny") in cognitive development (Diamond, 1992; Manqueriapa & Darinquebe, 2009). There is evidence that activities such as drawing, painting and sculpting are part of human nature. We see enough samples of such work, leading us to believe that human beings have wished to communicate their experiences, dreams and thoughts to other people for thousands of years. There are prehistoric drawings dated to between 30,000 and 11,000 years ago illustrating animals such as horses, stags, and oxen. These were found painted on the walls of Lascaux and Altamira caves in Southern France and Spain, where they are well documented, but these kinds of images are found in other sites worldwide (Chauvet et al., 1996; Spivey, 2005; Kleiner, 2011). The meanings of these paintings has been interpreted as preparation for spiritual ceremonies, for successful hunting, or perhaps humankind's urge to express its imagination, reflections or dreamings creatively (Boas, 1955; Day, 1970; Leakey, 1981; Lewis-Williams, 2002).

In Brazil, prehistoric rock art featuring animal paintings (jaguar, deer, vultures) and geometric traces have been found on the walls of caves close to the towns of Piraí do Sul, Tibagi, Sengés and Jaguariaíva, Paraná State (Southern Brazil). Such paintings are presumed to have been done by hunter-gatherer Indian tribes between 12,000 and 5,000 years ago. These have been interpreted as representations depicting spiritual ceremonies, images derived from everyday activities, and/or reflections or imaginings from these populations (Cardoso & Westphalen, 1986; Parellada, 2009; Oliveira, 2014, Parellada et al., 2014). Hans Staden first reported seeing early Brazilian Indian tribal drawings of animals and plants around 1576 (Staden, 2008).

The theorists cited above consider that this ancient art, created by our ancestors, reappears as mental models in contemporary children's minds and is manifested as drawings (expressed models) which begin with the scribbling of the shape of animals (Luquet, 1923, 1927/1979; Cox, 2005). It seems that children tend to spontaneously draw people and animals because they are active and make sounds. They show less interest for plants at first (Dempsey & Betz, 2001; Villarroel & Infante, 2014; Anderson et al., 2014; Ballas & Momsen, 2014).

When children are asked to draw plants, young children frequently draw a tree or a flower, as an image of a composite flower and of a "lollipop" tree (Figures 5 and 6). Older children and adolescents notice more differences that characterize organisms, as in the example of the coconut tree below right, which is clearly a specific tree (Figure 7) or the young girl's drawing that puts an apple tree in a setting. (Figure 8).

Figure 5. Drawing by a 5 year old girl depicting her idea of a tree (Camoriu town, urban area, Brazeil).

Figure 6. Drawing by a 4 year old boy depicting an herbaceous plant (Piraquara Town, rural area, Brazil).

Figure 7. Drawing by an 8 year old boy depicting a coconut tree (Dorizon town, rural area, Brazil).

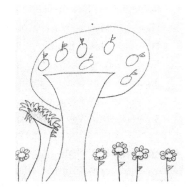

Figure 8. Drawing by a six year old girl, depciting an apple tree with other environmental elements. (Piraquara town, rural area, Brazil.

Children (ages 5–13) prefer to draw certain organisms if given free choice. An outline of animals is more frequently drawn by the youngest children (Waehner, 1946). When pupils were asked to draw what they thought was inside creatures when they were alive, they represent their idea of organs and organ systems. However, some children say that they do not have an ability to draw. Researchers also included interviews as a way for children explain their drawings and the intent, with or without their confidence in drawing skill.

Probing pupils' thinking by means of drawings is a starting point for more effective teaching in the classroom. Science teachers, even those working in preschool years, can use drawings to elicit current biological knowledge held by their pupils, gleaned from visits to science museums, zoos, botanical gardens or from "around," in addition to classroom lessons (Tunnicliffe & Reiss, 2000). Children in different cultures, whether developing countries, such as Zimbabwe and Brazil, or developed ones such as England, already had some concepts about a few internal organs when asked to draw what was inside their bodies. They knew roughly where some most commonly known organs and organ systems were located in the specimens of a bird, a fish and a small mammal, (Tunnicliffe & Reiss, 1999a, 1999b; Manokore & Reiss, 2003; Bartoszeck et al., 2008).

OUR STUDIES USING DRAWINGS

We present four different studies using drawings constructed by early learners about the external features and internal anatomy of different organisms to explore trends. In the first study we sought children's understandings of the external features of an insect, so often reprinted in early years' education as a being with a small head with antenna and a long body to which are attached two wings each with two segments, which is biologically inaccurate. In the second study we investigated what children observed about bird morphology in their local environments. In the third study we sought to gain insights into the children's understanding about the internal anatomy of specimens of vertebrate classes: a fish, a bird, and a rat. The fourth study describes what children conceptualized about the anatomy of a tree. We did the last study to include both external and internal anatomy because drawings collected previously in several studies by the authors indicated a semantics issue with the word 'inside' when associated with trees.

Insects

The samples of drawings of insects were collected in schools located in urban, suburban and rural areas to sample the social and cultural strata of the population in southern (Curitiba town, Paraná) and northern (Rio Branco town, Acre) Brazil (Bartoszeck et al., 2012; Bartoszeck & Tunnicliffe, 2011). These studies were conducted to investigate the mental models children may have held by examining their drawing. We adapted a rubric developed in previous research by one of the authors (Table 1). This rubric was developed by Bartoszeck et al., 2012 after Tunnicliffe and Reiss 1999. We scored children's levels of detail expression within that rubric of levels (Andrade, 2000; Moskal, 2000; Malini, 2007). The same type of rubric with distinct levels defined before the study by the researchers using their biological knowledge has been used for subsequent analysis of the internal complexity and biological accuracy of other organisms such as earthworms (Tunnicliffe, 2015).

Table 1. The scale used to allocating a grade to the concept of insect drawings

Level	Insect characteristics
0	Nothing recognizable
1	Scribble I
2	Scribble II with resemblance to body and appendages.
3	Has resemblance to an organism with legs and or antennae.
4	Has resemblance to a caterpillar (head/body/appendages).
5	Single body, wings representations, often as a single structure with 2 lobes and/or antennae.
6	3 parts of body and/or antennae or wings.
7	6 legs and wings or antennae.
8	3 parts body, 6 legs on thorax, 1 or 2 pairs of wings, antennae.

Children notice insects in their lives to differing extents, which may reflect the cultures in which they are immersed. See Figures 9 and 10 as examples. Drawings together with other educational tools (for instance interviews) are useful strategies to elicit children's mental models of insects and to evaluate their understanding of the natural world manifested by pictorial representations (Cinici, 2013).

 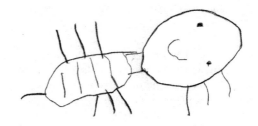

Figure 9. A drawing by a five year old girl depicting what she thinks is an insect which scored as level 5 according to the scale in Table 1.

Figure 10. A drawing by a 5 year old girl depicting what she thinks is an insect. This scored a level 3 according to the scale in Table 1.

The results for the insect drawings of external morphology are shown in Table 2, below.
Reading the results shows what was intuitively anticipated, that the children increase their understanding and more accurate knowledge of external insect morphology as they mature. However, for example, 89.0% of the drawings by 4-year-olds were not recognizable.

Birds

Bird observation only recently has been adopted in preschool and elementary school in Brazil as a strategy to improve environmental and preservation education, as it stimulates pupils' observations of organisms in the natural world and develops respect for environments

Table 2. Summary of drawings of insects by age showing different levels of understanding (%)

Age	Level	Percentage	N
4 year old	1	11%	53
5 year old	2	32%	133
6 year old	3	35%	29
Total			215

they live in. We asked children to identify morphological features related to feeding habits (e. g. beak shape) as well as their more general concept of birds in a drawing task (Bartoszeck & Tunnicliffe, 2011; Bartoszeck et al., 2011b). Analysis of the drawings collected was intended to elicit pupils' mental models of birds, similar to Luquet's (1927/1979) work considering drawing as an expressed model. After examining the birds drawn by the pupils, the authors created a simple rubric for scoring the morphological attibutes, as shown in Table 3, below (Bartoszeck et al., 2011b, 2011c.). Below the table are two examples of the scoring (Figures 11 and 12).

Table 3. Bird rubric scheme used to allocating a grade to drawings

Level	Bird characteristics
0	Nothing recognizable
1	Scribble (resemblance of a bird).
2	3 parts body, legs, wings, beak.
3	3 parts body, 2 legs on thorax, feathers, wings, tail, beak (e. g. insect catcher).
4	3 parts body, 2 legs on thorax, feathers wings, tail, beak (e.g. seed breaker).
5	3 parts body, 2 legs on thorax, feathers, wings, tail, beak long (like humming birds).

Figure 11. A nine year old girl's bird, scored at level 2

Figure 12. A bird drawn by an 11 year old girl, scoring at level 2

Table 4, summarizes the results of external morphological features of the drawings by childrens' ages. It shows the levels of understanding, by the percentages (%) of students who were scored on increasing levels for their concepts of birds.

Table 4. The scoring of bird drawings by age

Age	Level	Percentage	N
4 to 5 year old	1	75%	154
6 to 7 year old	2	17%	57
8 to 10 year old	3	6.8%	44
Total			255

Learning about birds endemic to the culture children live in is part of their learning about science in the everyday world. Birds are very much a part of this world and play important roles in ecological balance. These data show that the observations of children of such everyday organsisms increased with age. Hence, they did acquire more detailed information through formal school teaching and educational materials in venues of out of school learning where children can make firsthand observations. Teachers should take such knowledge into consideration when preparing interactive exhibits and materials for use with children so that they can construct further understanding from their baseline.

Skeletal Anatomy

In this Brazilian study of familiarity with skeletal anatomy, the pupils were shown a single preserved specimen of a laboratory (Wistar) rat (*Rattus norvegicus*), a taxidermically prepared woodpecker (*Chrysoptilus melanochlorus*), and a salt water fish corbina (*Sciaena aquila*) fresh. The Brazilian school year is organized by pupils' performance, age groups and corresponding grades. Thus, for this study we collected a total of 420 drawings from year 0 (age 4 or 5 year old, grades K-II, K-III, N = 242); year 1 (age 6 or 7, grades 1st, 2nd, N = 80); year 2 (age 8 or 9, grades 3rd, 4th, N = 98). On each occasion, the pupils were asked to draw what they thought was inside these creatures when they were alive, as presented on the set-up we brought (Bartoszeck et al., 2008). Again adapting the rubric from earlier work, we prepared Table 5, below (Tunnicliffe & Reiss, 1999). Many pupils labelled the internal structures in their drawings, and the teachers wrote labels for children who where not able to write properly (Figures 13 and 14).

Table 5. Skeleton composition ranking protocol

Level	Criteria
1	No bones
2	Bones indicated by simple lines or circles.
3	Bones indicated by "dog bone" shape and at random or throughout body.
4	One type of bone in its appropriate position.
5	At least two types of bones (e. g. backbone and ribs) indicated in their appropriate position.
6	Definite vertebrate organisation- i. e. backbone, skull and limbs and/or ribs.
7	Comprehensive skeleton- i. e. connections between backbone, skull, limbs and ribs.

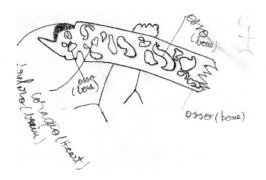
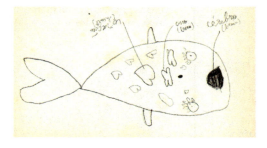

Figure 13. Drawing by four-year- old boy representing what he thinks is inside a bird. Scored level 1 for bones and level 2 for organs and organ systems (Curitiba town, urban area)

Figure 14. Drawing by a four-year-old girl representing what she thinks are the internal structures of a fish. Scored level 2 for bones and level 4 for organs and systems (Curitiba town, urban area)

In Table 6, we have summarized the mean levels from the different age groups for what their drawings indicate about their understanding of the skeletons of the vertebrates presented.

Table 6. Scores for skeletal drawings by age

Year/age	Rat	Bird	Fish	N
0 (4 or 5year old)	1.71	1.65	1.76	242
1 (6 or 7 year old)	1.64	1.62	2.16	80
2 (8 or 9 year old)	1.41	1.35	1.91	98
Total				420

Interestingly there is variation amongst the children and ages in their undertsanding of the internal anatomy of these animals and such variance could be a result of lack of exposure to the animals and lack of knowledge about their own human internal anatomy and experience. It is typical in other studies from young children and the observations of educators working with such learners that the youngest children draw the dog bone shapes particularly around the inside of the drawn outline of the animals.

When drawings are considered for other internal organs a similar pattern was identified, using the scale below (Table 7) also adapted from Reiss and Tunnicliffe, (1999b).

Table 7. Organ and organ system scoring scale

Level 1	No representation of internal structure.
Level 2	One or more internal organs (e. g. bones and blood) placed at random.
Level 3	One internal organ (e.g. brain or heart) in appropriate position.
Level 4	Two or more internal organs (stomach and bone "unit" such as ribs) in appropriate positions but no extensive relationships indicated between them.
Level 5	One organ system indicated (e. g. connecting mouth to anus).
Level 6	Two or three major organ systems indicated out of skeletal, gaseous exchange, nervous, digestive, endocrine, urogenital, muscular and circulatory.
Level 7	Comprehensive representation with four or more organ systems indicated out of skeletal, gaseous exchange, nervous, digestive, endocrine urogenital, muscular and circulatory.

We again present the summary of the mean levels by age for the scores of the children's drawings where organ and organ systems were illustrated (Table 8).

Table 8. Summary of grade mean levels (%) achieved by children defined by the scoring scale for organs and organs system

Year/age	Rat/level	%	Bird/level	%	Fish/level	%	N
0 (4 or 5 year old).	1	1.5	1	1.0	2	15.0	86
1 (6 or 7 year old).	2	8.0	2	12.0	3	12.0	32
2 (8 or 9 year old).	3	3.0	3	3.0	4	55.0	34
Total							152

These hundreds of drawings and their analysis confirm studies in other countries, particularly England by Tunnicliffe and Reiss (1999b). Children gradually become aware that there are internal organs and are able to identity the main ones. They acquire this knowledge from the activities and discussion with their families, from books and, as they get older, from electronic media as well as in schools. At first, when they are aware of internal anatomy, they do not know where the organs are located but position them randomly, gradually becoming aware of a general region where such organs are located. In our experience the brain is often the first organ to be placed appropriately, followed by the heart, which is generally represented as an iconic 'love heart' in the cultures we have studied.

Plants

Research with young children about plants as well as their understanding of the concept of plant and trees is limited (Tunnicliffe & Reiss, 2000; Bianchi, 2000; Patrick & Tunnicliffe, 2011). Children from the earliest years notice plants in their everyday lives and gradually build a memory bank of knowlwdge about adaptation to habitats as depicted in Figure 15.

Figure 15. Drawing by a five-year- old girl depicting a tree outside, scored as a level 4

It is well established by previous studies that children have a developed theory about the natural world before they experience any formal teaching in pre-school. Out of school experiences, in particular informal education, are important sources of science literacy for all gender and age groups (Knight, 2009). When children are asked to draw what they think is inside a tree they are familiar with either at the school grounds or park or home orchard, they seem to transfer the knowledge of bones, which are peculiar to vertebrates, to trees, using themselves as their templates (Carey, 1995; Tunnicliffe, 1999; Bartoszeck & Tunnicliffe, 2013). Therefore, in this research, which was conducted in the towns of Mallet, Rio Claro, Dorizon (rural area) and Curitiba (urban and suburban areas) in Brazil, we wanted to evaluate what children knew about the internal organization of trees, ecological views, and habitats associated with trees using drawings (Haene & Aparicio, 2007; Lorenzi & Souza, 2011). Children appear to have some difficulty knowing what "inside a tree" means. The term 'inside' is interpreted by many as being in between the leaves on the branches and not within the external surface of the tree (personal observations). Hence in this study an awareness of the outside features of the tree was also scored to capture what the children drew about trees, both internal and exterior. The scoring rubric is in Table 9, below.

Table 9. Scoring rubric for children's drawings of trees

Level	Source of knowledge
0	Scribble (nothing recognizable).
1	First hand observation remembered (resemblance of a tree).
2	Internal parts of a tree (water tubes, veins, heart, lungs).
3	External parts of a tree (roots, branches, leaves, fruit, bark).
4	Ecological & habitats views associated with trees (birds, ants, butterflies, nest, grass, sun, clouds).

Figure 16 is an example of a drawing depicting what a child thought was inside a tree. Sometimes, "inside" means within the branches or foliage of trees. A rubric of levels was prepared based on researchers' previous experiences in other biological fields. The scoring for the drawing is included in Figure 16.

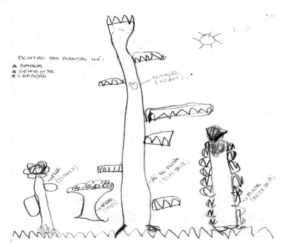

Figure 16. Drawing by a six-year-old boy, depicting what he thinks is inside a plant, scored as level 3

We again present a summary of the scored mean levels of tree drawings by age in table 10, below.

Some children were chosen randomly to be interviewed. They were prompted to explain what they thought was inside a tree depicted in their drawing. For example, during the interview a four-year-old girl, after performing her drawing, said that inside the trunk there was timber, that roots made the tree grow, and that leaves were outside the plant on the branches. A five-year-old boy said that the roots held the tree on the ground preventing it from falling, that the trunk was inside the plant, and that the apple is an inner part of the plant. A three-year-old boy from a Mallet nursery school represented the tree with structural elements and the pine fruit (pinhão in Portuguese) inside a hole in the trunk revealing his precocious natural world observation.

DISCUSSION

The work presented in this chapter indicates how much knowledge about the natural world children may learn in their lives everyday. The authors are aware and recognize that collecting drawings plus holding an interview with pupils would certainly clarify, as for

Table 10. Scored levels by age of children's illustrations of tree anatomy

Age	Level	%	N
4 year old	1	44	47
	3	19	
	4	17	
5 year old	1	41	68
	3	29	
	4	19	
6 year old	1	29	51
	3	27	
	4	12	
Total			166

example, to what inner animals' structures they are referring to or to the main features of birds, insects and the internal structures of trees. The conception of what is internal to trees is more difficult since children use themselves as a template (Carey, 1985). Observing the external qualities of plants and of all kingdoms is crucial for identification and taxonomy. Both skills are vital in conservation biology and sustainability (Pooley et al., 2013).

Although the botanical information supplied by pupils in the range of four to six years old, from this study, was not accurate, they do provide their conceptions of the environs and trees from their own observations. Additionally they need to understand the basic external anatomical features of trees and that trees may be a shelter for invertebrates and reptiles. They see that water is needed for trees to survive and produce edible fruit and timber (Anderson et al., 2014). It is evidenct that as children grew older they rearranged the representations of trees and environs, showing a progressive complexity reflecting a better grasp of internal and external parts of trees. Younger children seem to interpret "inside" as within the branches whereas older children interpret inside as actually internal to the outside to the tree, inside the trunk and branches, confirming Symington's observations that drawings progressed from scribbling to realism (Symington et al., 1981).

Interviews would be an opportunity to lessen ambiguities in the interpretation of drawings. However, interviews to be fully valuable in eliciting the understanding of the interviewee should have to be carried out soon after the pupil handed in their drawing as s/he would still have it fresh in their mind what s/he intended to depict on the sheet. We want to suggest that capturing the expressed models, i.e. representations of phenomena illustrated in drawings, should be a collaborative goal in itself and expand through other educational settings. We think that a collaborative endeavor of cross cultural investigations worldwide would be useful. Still, we do not know from where most of the subjects in this study learnt this information on organisms. School does not seem to make a difference, as usually science activities do not emphasize internal anatomy of organisms. Probing pupils' thinking in biological issues through drawings is the starting point for more effective teaching in the classroom. We would recommend that science teaching, starting in pre-school, would benefit from having the children draw. Thus, educators working with young children, eliciting their representations of the natural world, could assist pupils in constructing further understanding of living organisms. Therefore, more emphasis on the use of drawing should be added in pre-service and in-service teacher training to explore readily observable organisms such as snails, earthworms, insects, birds, common local plants and trees, particularly in developing observational skills in science learning.

REFERENCES

Anderson, J. L., Ellis, J. P., & Jones, A. M. (2014). Understanding early elementary children's conceptual knowledge structure and function through drawings. *CBE-Life Sciences Education, 13*, 375–386.

Andrade, H. G. (2000). Using rubrics to promote thinking and learning. *Educational Leadership, 57*(5), 13–18.

Angus, J. W. (1981). Children's conceptions of the living world. *Australian Science Teachers Journal, 27*(3), 65–68.

Ballas, B., & Monsen, J. L. (2014). Attention "blinks" differently for plants and animals. *CBE-Life Sciences Education, 13*, 437–443.

Ballew, A. M. (1930). An analysis of biological drawings. *School Science and Mathematics, 30*(5), 490–497.

Bartoszeck, A. B., & Tunnicliffe, S. D. (2011). Using drawings to investigate the concept of birds in the early years children in Southern Brazil. *Emergent Science Newsletter, 4*, 4.

Bartoszeck, A. B., & Tunnicliffe, S. D. (2012, Septmeber 17–21). *Visualization of insects in the early years.* European Research in Didactics in Biology 9th Conference, Berlin.(interactive poster).

Bartoszeck, A. B., & Tunnicliffe, S. D. (2013). What do early children think is inside a tree (extended abstract). *Journal of Emergent Science, 5*, 21–25.

Bartoszeck, A. B., Bartoszeck, A. C. de P. S., & Tunnicliffe, S. D. (2008). Science literacy: The development of the concept of skeletons in Brazilian students. *Educere-Revista da Educação, 8*(1), 41–65.

Bartoszeck, A. B., Kruszielski, L., & Bartoszeck, F. K. (2011a). Science literacy: The point of view of student into understanding the internal anatomy of selected vertebrates. *Educere-Revista da Educação, 11*(1), 19–49.

Bartoszeck, A. B., Silva da, I. G. M., & Tunnicliffe, S. D. (2011b, September 5–9). *Brazilian children's concept of bird: An exploratory study*. European Science Education Research Association 9th Conference, Lyon, France. (interactive poster)

Bartoszeck, A. B., Silva, B. R. da, Tunnicliffe, S. D. (2012). Children's concept of insects by means of drawings in Brazil. *Journal of Emergent Science*, (2), 17–24.

Bartoszeck, A. B., Cosmo, C. R., Silva, B. R. da., & Tunnicliffe, S. D. (2014). Concepts of plants held by young Brazilian children: An exploratory study. *European Journal of Educational Research, 4*(3), 105–117.

Bianchi, L. (2000). So what do you think a plant is? *Primary Science Review, 61*, 15–17.

Boas, F. (1955). *Primitive art*. New York, NY: Dover.

Bourassa, M. (1997). Le dessin, mieux comprendre pour mieux intervenir. *Canadian Psychology/Psychologie Canadienne, 38*(2), 111–121.

Buchholz, D. (2000). *Understanding the biological concept "bird": A kindergarten case study* (Doctor of Philosophy dissertation). Louisiana State University, Baton Rouge, LA.

Burt, C. (1922). *Mental and scholastic tests* (pp. 317–327). London: P.S. King and Son.

Carey, S. (1985). *Conceptual change in childhood*. Cambridge: MIT Press.

Chang, N. (2012). The role of drawing in children's construction of science concepts. *Early Childhood Education Journal, 40*, 187–193.

Chauvet, J.-M., Deschamps, E. B., & Hillaire, C. (Eds.). (1996). *Dawn of art: The Chauvet Cave*. New York, NY: Harry N. Abrams.

Cinici, A. (2013). From caterpillar to butterfly: A window for looking into students' ideas about life cycle and life forms of insects. *Journal of Biological Education, 47*(2), 84–95.

Cardoso, J. A., & Westphalen, C. M. (1986). *Atlas histórico do Paraná*. Curitiba: Livraria do Chain Editora (Historical atlas of Paraná State).

Cox, M. (2005). *The pictorial world of a child* (pp. 154–166). Cambridge: Cambridge University Press.

Day, M. H. (1970). *The fossil man*. New York, NY: Bantan Books.

Dempsey, B. C., & Betz, B. J. (2001). Biological drawing: A scientific tool for learning. *The American Biology Teacher, 63*(1), 271–279.

Diamond, J. (1992). *The third chimpanzee: The evolution and future of the human animal* (pp. 168–179). New York, NY: HarperCollins Publishers.

Dunning, D. L., Holmes, J., & Gathercole, S. E. (2013). Does working memory training lead to generalized improvementsin children with low working memory? A randomized controlled trial. *Developmental Science, 16*(6), 915–925.

Eliot, L. (1999). *What's going in in there? How the brain and mind develop in the first five years of life* (pp. 260–289). New York, NY: Bantam Books.

Freeman, W. H., & Bracegirdle, B. (1976). *An atlas of invertebrate structure*. London: Heinemann Educational Books.

Haene, E., & Aparicio, G. (2007). *100 trees of Argentina*. Buenos Aires: Editorial Albatros.

Hayes, D., & Symington, D. (1984). The satisfaction of young children with their representational drawings of natural phenomena. *Research in Science Education, 14*, 39–46.

Hayes, D., & Symington, D. (1988). Purpose achieved by drawing during science activities. *Research in Science Education, 18*, 104–111.

Hayes, D., Symington, D., & Martin, M. (1994). Drawing during science activity in the primary school. *International Journal of Science Education, 16*(3), 265–277.

Hitch, G. J., & Halliday, S. (1988). Visual working memory in young children. *Memory & Cognition, 16*(2), 120–132.

Hopperstad, M. H. (2008). When children make meaning through drawing and play. *Visual Communication, 7*(1), 77–96.

Hopperstad, M. H. (2010). Studying meaning in children's drawings. *Journal of Early Childhood Literacy, 10*(4), 430–452.

Johnson-Laird, P. N. (1988). How is meaning mentally represented. *International Social Science Journal, 115*, 45–61.

Jung, C. G. (1962). *Símbolos de transformación*. Buenos Aires: Editora Paidós.

Jung, C. G. (1988). *Essai d'exploration de inconsciente* (p. 181). Paris: Edition Denoel.

Kendric, M., & McKay, R. (2002). Uncovering literacy narratives through children's drawings. *Canadian Journal of Education, 27*(1), 45–60.

Kleiner, F. S. (2011). *Gardner's art through the ages* (pp. 15–23). Boston, MA: Wadsworth.

Knight, S. (2009). *Forest schools and outdoor learning in the early years*. London: Sage Publications.

Langevin, B. (2014). *Comprender los dibujos de mi hijo*. Barcelona: Ediciones Obelisco.

Leakey, R. E. (1981). *The making of mankind*. London: Sphere Books.

Legare, C. H., Zhu, L., & Wellman, H. M. (2013). Examining biological explanations in Chinese preschool children: A cross-cultural comparison. *Journal of Cognition and Culture, 13*(1–2):67–93.

Lewis-Williams, D. (2002). *The mind in the cave*. London: Thames & Hudson.

Lorenzi, H. (2011). *Árvores brasileiras: manual de identificação e cultivo de plantas arbóreas nativas do Brasil*. Nova Odessa: Instituto Plantarum (Trees from Brazil, identification guide).

Lourenção van Kolck, O. (1981). *Interpretação psicológica de desenhos* (pp. 115–119). São Paulo: Editora Pioneira (*Psychological evaluation of drawings*).

Louv , R. (2008). *Last child in the woods: Saving our children from Nature-Deficit Disorder*. Chaptel Hill, NC: Algonquin Books.

Luquet, G.-H. (1923). Le réalisme dans l'art paléolitique. *L'Antropologie, 33*, 17–48.

Luquet, G.-H. (1927/1979). *Le dessin enfantin*. Neuchâtel-Paris: Éditions Delachaux & Niestle`.

Malini, R. (2007). Effect of rubrics on enhancement of student learning. *Educational Journal, 7*(1), 3–17.

Manokore, V., & Reiss, M. J. (2003). Pupil's drawings of what is inside themselves: A case stududy in Zimbabwe. *Zimbabwe Journal of Educational Research, 15*(1), 28–43.

Manqueriapa, A., & Dariquebe, W. Q. (2009). *Wanamey: Relato de la primeira generación Wachiperi*. Cuzco: Centro de Estudios Regionales Andinos Bartolomé de Las Casas.

Morse, R. C. (1999). *The involvement of working memory in children's drawing development*. Lancaster: Lancaster University.

Moskal, B. M. (2000). Scoring rubrics: What, when and how? *Practical Assessment, Research & Evaluation, 7*(3), 1–8.

Oliveira, F. C. P. (2014). *Abrigos com pinturas rupestres em Pirai da Serra, Paraná: uma abordagem geoarqueológica* (pp. 107–296, Msc. Thesis). University of Paraná. (*Rock art in Paraná: a geoarqueological approach*).

Parellada, C. I. (2009). Arte rupestre of Paraná. *Revista Científica da Faculdade de Arte do Paraná, 4*(1), 1–25. (Prehistorical rock art of Paraná)

Parellada,, C. I., Oliveira, F. C. P., Sclvilzki, E. S. (2014). As pinturas rupestres do abrigo São José da Lagoa 2, X International Symposium on Rockart, Teresina, Piauí, Brasil, July, abstract, 1p. (Rock art in São Jose da Lagoa, Pirai do Sul, Brazil).

Patrick, P., & Tunnicliffe, S. D. (2011). What plants and animals do early childhood and primary students' name? Where do they see them? *Journal of Science and Educational Technology, 20*(5), 630–642.

Patrick, P., Byrne, J., Tunnicliffe, S. D., Asunta, T., Carvalhgo, G., Havu-Nuutinen, S., & Tracan, R. (2013). Students (ages 6, 10, and 15 years) in six countries knowledge of animals. *NorDina, 9*(1), 18–32.

Pike, A. W., Hoffmann, D. L., Garcia-Diez, M., Pettitt, P. B., Alcolea, J., De Balbín, R., González-Sainz, C., de las Heras, C., Lasheras, J. A., Montes, R., & Zilhão, J. (2012). U-series dating of Paleolithic art in 11 caves in Spain. *Science, 336*, 1409–1413.

Plotkin, H. (1997). *Darwin machines and the nature of knowledge* (pp. 179–227). Cambridge: Harvard University Press.

Pooley, S. P., Mendelsohn, J. A., & Milner-Gulland, E. J. (2013). Hunting down the chimera of multiple disciplinary in conservation science. *Conservation Biology, 28*(1), 22–32.

Potter, M. C. (1976). Short-term conceptual memory for pictures. *Journal of Experimental Psychology and Human Learning, 2,* 509–522.

Prokop, P., Talarovicova, A., Camerik, A., & Peterkova, V. (2010). High school students' atitude towards spiders: A cross-cultural comparison. *International Journal of Science Education, 32*(12), 1665–1688.

Rapp, D. N. (2007). Mental models: Theoretical issues for visualization in science education. In J. K. Gilbert (Ed.), *Visualization in science education* (pp. 43–60). Dordrecht: Springer.

Reiss, M. J., & Tunnicliffe, S. D. (1999). Conceptual development. *Journal of Biological Education, 34,* 13–16.

Righi, G. (1966). *Invertebrados: A minhoca.* São Paulo: IBECC. (Invertebrates: the earthworm).

Rioux, G. (1951). *Dessin et structure mentale.* Paris: Presses Universitaire.

Rybska, E., Tunnicliffe, S. D., & Sajkowska, Z. A. (2014a). What's inside a tree? The ideas of five year-old children. *Journal of Emergent Science, 8,* 7–15.

Rybska, E., Tunnicliffe, S. D., & Sajkowska, Z. A. (2014b). Young children's ideas about snail internal anatomy. *Journal of Baltic Science Education, 13*(6), 828–838.

Sanders, D. (2007). Making public the private life of plants: The contribution of informal learning environments. *International Journal of Science Education, 29,* 1209–1228.

Schnotz, W. (2002). Towards an integrated view of learning from text and visual displays. *Educational Psychology, 14*(1), 101–120.

Schwartz, M. L., Savegnani, L., & André, P. (2007). Representações da mata atlântica e da sua biodiversidade por meio de desenhos infantis. *Ciência & Educação, 13*(3), 369–388. (Representations of the Atlantic rainforest and its biodiversity through children's drawings).

Spivey, N. (2005). *How art made the world.* London: BBC Books.

Staden, H. (2008). *Duas viagens ao Brasil: primeiros registros sobre o Brasil* (pp. 171–178). Porto Alegre: L & PM Editores (Two trips to Brazil).

Symington, D., Boundy, K., Radford, T., & Walton, J. (1981). Children's drawing of natural phenomena. *Research in Science Education, 11,* 44–51.

Tomazic, I. (2011). Reported experiences enhance favourable atitudes toward toads. *Eurasia Journal of Mathematics, Science & Techology Education, 7*(4), 253–262.

Tomkins, S., & Tunnicliffe, S. D. (2007). Nature tables: Stimulating children's interested in natural objects. *Journal of Biological Education, 4*(94), 150–155.

Tunnicliffe, S. D. (1999). What's inside a tree. *Primary Science & Technology Today, 11,* 3–5.

Tunnicliffe, S. D. (2012). Visualisation of animals by children: how do they see birds. *C. E. P. S. Journal, 1*(4), 63–79.

Tunnicliffe, S. D. (2015). What's inside an earthworm? The views of a class of English 7 year-old children. *Journal of Emergent Science,* (9), 44–48.

Tunnicliffe, S. D., & Reiss, M. J. (1999a). Student's understandings about animal skeletons. *International Journal of Science Education, 21,* 1197–1200.

Tunnicliffe, S. D., & Reiss, M. J. (1999b). Learning about skeletons and other organ systems of vertebrate animals. *Science Education International, 10*(1), 29–33.

Tunnicliffe, S. D., & Reiss, M. J. (2000). Building a model of the environment: How do children see plants. *Journal of Biological Education, 34*(4), 172–177.

Van Driel, J. H. (1999). Teachers' knowledge of models and modelling in science. *International Journal of Science Education, 21*(11), 1141–1153.

Vieira, C. O. F., Vieira, N. B. P., & Silva, W. M. V. (1968). *Iniciação à Ciência-1.* Rio de Janeiro: FENAME (Begginer's science).

Villarroel, J. D., & Infante, G. (2014). Early understanding of the concept of living things: An examination of young children's drawings of plant life. *Journal of Biological Education, 48*(3), 119–126.

Waehner, T. S. (1946). Interpretation of spontaneous drawings and paintings. *General Psychological Monographs, 33,* 3–70.

Wee, B. (2012). A cross-cultural exploration of children's everyday ideas: Implications for science teaching and learning. *International Journal of Science Education, 34,* 609–627.

Yang, H.-C., & Noel, A. M. (2006). The development characteristics of four- and five-year-old pre-schoolers drawing: An analysis of scribbles, placement paterns, emergent writing, and name writing in archived spontaneous drawing samples. *Journal of Early Childhood Literacy, 6*(2), 145–162. doi:10.1177/1468798406066442

Zoldosova, K., & Prokop, P. (2006). Education in the field influences children's ideas and interest toward science. *Journal of Science Education and Technology, 15,* 304–313.

Amauri Betini Bartoszeck
University of Paraná (Federal) Curitiba, PR Brazil

Sue Dale Tunnicliffe
Institute of Education
University College, UK

GARY WIND

6. ANATOMIC DRAWING FOR MEDICAL EDUCATION[1]

Leonardo da Vinci said "when describing anatomy, don't trouble yourself with words unless you are talking to blind men". In communicating structural detail, a picture is indeed worth a thousand words. Humans have a long history of depicting anatomic ideas in graphic form. Rudimentary examples exist in prehistoric cave paintings. From the beginning of recorded history classical centers of civilization in Egypt, Greece, Rome, India and China recorded their concepts of anatomy on media such as stone, silk and papyrus. During the long night of the dark ages barber surgeons of Europe left scattered primitive examples of illustrations, limited by the constraints on learning imposed by the Christian church and Islam. The Renaissance brought a flourishing of intellectual curiosity characterized by direct observation and authoritative artistic depiction. The renewed blossoming of art added beauty to science. Collaboration between artist and anatomist resulted in the exquisite production of the first comprehensive, accurate anatomic opus of Andreas Vesalius which set a standard for the golden age of Italian and later German anatomy. Advances in print media made this new graphic information widely available for the first time. Modern visual representation of anatomy has advanced orders of magnitude beyond simple line drawing with the advent of photography, video and digital imaging, but drawing can still be a valuable adjunct in the learning armamentarium of the individual student as he or she internalized anatomic concepts and later communicates concepts to patients.

ANCIENT ANATOMIC DEPICTION

Early man left graphic images of the world around him from prehistoric times. Cave paintings from Lascaux France depict a bull with eviscerated intestines and one in Spain depicts a fetus in a mother's womb. Ancient Egypt in the millennia before the common era developed the process of mummification which included removing the internal organs. This knowledge of anatomy surely informed their practice of medicine as recorded in artifacts like the Smith and Ebers papyri, but they left no illustrations with these records. Egyptian tomb paintings (Figure 1) show a circumcision, but no other anatomic detail.

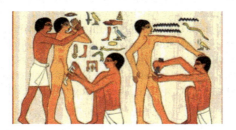

Figure 1. Egyptian tomb painting

During this early historical period, records kept in centers of civilization in India, Babylon, China and Greece documented on stone, bamboo, silk, papyrus and metal the knowledge of the time, but few graphic representations survive. The concept of the importance of illustration, however was recognized by Confucius to whom the quote "A picture is worth a thousand words" is attributed.

In Greece in the centuries before the Common Era, careful observation of surface anatomy was obvious in the superme realism of classic Greek sculpture. There is no record of the great sculptors, Praxitiles, Myron, Scopas, studying human dissections, but Aristotle is reputed to have used graphic illustrations of anatomy in his teachings. We know that human dissection on executed criminals was done in Hellenic Alexandria. Herophilus (350BCE) wrote a dissection-based text, but no illustrations survive if they existed.

Galen, a Greek physician who studied in Asia Minor and Alexandria, treated the injuries of gladiators in Rome, but because human dissection was prohibited by the Romans, his anatomic treatises were based on animal dissections, and many of his misconceptions about human anatomy held sway for subsequent centuries.

THE MIDDLE AGES

Little can be said about scientific advancement and the illustration of scientific concepts in the several hundred years of the middle ages. Surgical interventions were relegated to barber surgeons who were limited by lack of anesthesia in how deeply they could invade the body, and thus had little need for detailed anatomic knowledge. The earliest resurgence of scientific inquiry during this period arose in the 12th to 14th centuries. In these works, such as the De Arte Physicale et de Cirugia of the English surgeon John Argerne, the illustrations were primitive and non-realistic (Figure 2). Prohibitions on dissection by the Catholic church and Islam continued to obstruct scientific progress.

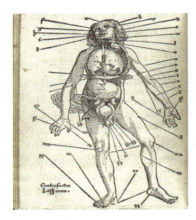

Figure 2. From the De Arte Physicale et de Cirugia by John Argerne

THE RENAISSANCE

The advent of the renaissance in the 15th century brought the confluence of several key elements of scientific progress and dissemination of information. The flourishing of the graphic and plastic arts brought a renewed interest in the form of the human body. The northern Italian artist Leon Battista Alberti wrote in Della Pittura "in painting the nude, we place first his bones and muscles, which we then cover with flesh...to understand where each muscle is beneath". Albrecht Durer (1471–1528) in Germany stressed the need for accuracy in anatomic illustration. Artistic media became more varied with woodcuts allowing for multiple copies to be made and disseminated.

By the early 16th century, church suppression of dissection began to ease, but artists of the time like Leonardo daVinci, Michelangelo and Rapheal had to keep their dissections concealed. While Michelangelo and Raphael studied anatomy primarily for artistic purposes, Leonardo delved deeply into scientific anatomic inquiry as he did in multiple other areas, and recorded his findings on structure and function extensively and beautifully in hundreds of annotated drawings (Figure 3). Leonardo devised the exploded view, cross-sectional illustration and views from four angles. This work, like many of Leonardo's endeavors, was never finished to his satisfaction and never published until rediscovered in the Royal Library of Windor castle by an English nobleman in 1636. During the renaissance, Berengario da Capri (1460–1530) produced the first illustrated text with figures alongside text. The years 1543 to 1627 were the golden age of Italian anatomy.

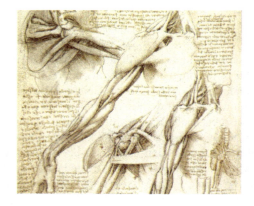

Figure 3. Sample of Michelangelo's anatomy drawings

The watershed work of this period that set the standard for anatomic study and representation was produced by Andreas Vesalius, a Belgian by birth, who dissected executed criminals, demonstrated and lectured in Padua Italy. He was a true anatomist, surgeon and was an artist himself, illustrating his early work the Tabula Sex. His breakthrough accomplishment, however, was enlisting artists from Titian's school in Venice to illustrate his great work, *De Humani Corporis Fabrica: Librum Septum* (*Seven Books on the Structure of the Human Body*) printed as giant folios in 1543 (Figure 4). Prominent among the artists who created more than 200 woodblock engravings under Vesalius' direction, was Jan Stephan von Calcar. This work dominated the study of human anatomy for the next 250 years and is still admired today.

Figure 4. From DeCorporis Fabrica Librum Septum by Vesalius

POST RENAISSANCE

In the period between the Renaissance and the European enlightenment at the end of the 18th century, many new anatomic works were illustrated and published, having the benefit of newer media like engraving and lithography, and advances in printing. Works such as William Harvey's De Motu Cordis benefited from illustration which conveyed the concept of the circulation of the blood Figure 5). Bernard Siegfried Albinus, the greatest anatomist of the early 18th century, followed Vesalius' example and employed an expert artist, Jan Vandelar to produce exquisite illustrations of his work (Figure 6). The enlightenment promulgated the philosophy that the world could be understood through rational investigation, and the quality and accuracy of anatomy depictions blossomed in turn.

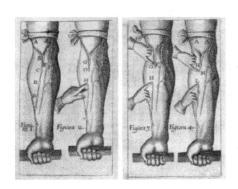 

Figure 5. From De Motu Cordis by William Harvey   *Figure 6. Jan Vandelar's illustrations for Albinus*

THE 19TH CENTURY

In the 19th century advances in printing and illustration led to an explosion of visual information for wide dissemination of information. Photoengraving (1868), halftone screen (1880) and 4 color printing (1893) allowed the mass production of illustrated books. The classic anatomic standard was produced by Henry Gray and was illustrated with 522 woodcuts by Henry Vandyke Carter, Professor of Anatomy and Physiology, in 1859. The first American edition appeared in 1878, and new editions continue to be produced.

THE 20TH CENTURY

Early in the 20th century, an illustrator named Max Brodel who trained in Liepzig Germany, was recruited to Johns Hopkins, where he observed and illustrated thousands of surgical procedures and autopsies. His lively line drawings and half-tone carbon dust on scratch-board illustrations illuminated the classic texts of the era (Figure 7). He founded the first school of medical illustration in America at Johns Hopkins in 1911. The AMI (Association of Medical Illustrators) was established in 1945, and there are now 5 accredited programs of medical illustration in the United States (Hopkins, Georgia, Michigan, Illinois, Texas) and one in Toronto.

Figure 7. An example of Max Brodel's anatomic illustration

In the early to mid 20th century, beautiful color atlases of anatomy such as Pernkopf and Sobotta were produced. An American physician named Frank Netter, who had some prior illustrating experience, finished his internship and found great demand for his medical illustration, which he then pursued full time. With the sponsorship of the Ciba pharmaceutical company, he produced monographs and collections of illustrated works in collaboration with top clinicians. These works greatly enhanced the education of recent generations of medical students. Medical photography never had the ability to clarify and convey anatomic information that illustration does, and the analytic ability of illustration was nowhere better evidenced in recent times than in Netter's work (Figure 8).

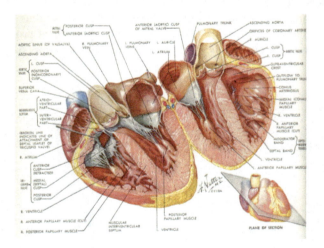

Figure 8. An example of Netter's illustration

THE PRESENT AND THE FUTURE

Digital media and delivery platforms have provided powerful new tools with which to depict anatomy, and modern imaging allows dynamic two- and three- dimensional depiction of anatomy. The use of drawing by students of anatomy can still be a vital means of internalizing structural information and concepts, especially for visual learners (Figure 9). It may even lead some to combine illustration with surgical practice (Figure 10).

As far back as I can remember I drew. In grade school I was drawing cartoons like Mickey Mouse. When I was 7 or 8 my grandfather, who had been an artist in Russia, gave me his inlaid box of artists tools including fine sable brushes, gold leaf and beautiful drawing exercise books from Vienna. My parents bought me my first oil paint set and my first effort was a credible painting of a bulldog, followed by multiple figure paintings, mainly based on National Geographic pictures. In grade school I made a bas relief of the lungs and digestive system in hardening clay and an illustration of the endocrine system which found a place on my science teacher's wall. In the same time period I experimented with papier-mâché, creating a tiger, and started carving balsa which produced an African head, an

 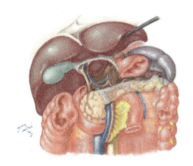

Figure 9. Drawing to learn medicine in contemporary studies   *Figure 10. Example of Wind's contemporary illustration*

antelope and my first carving knife wound in my thigh. The second target was my left hand. My attempt at hemostasis in the absence of my parents was to put my hand in the freezer, which not surprisingly did not work. Two stitches did the trick.

A major epiphany happened early in high school when, studying in the school library, in a frequent moment of my ADD distraction, I looked up on the cubicle shelf and saw Vesalius in large letters on the spine of a large format book. It blew me away. I subsequently made ink line drawing copies of many of the magnificent woodcuts, and if I wasn't totally hooked on anatomy before, there was no turning back thereafter. I always knew I wanted to be a surgeon and avidly dissected frogs, fetal pigs and whatever I could get my hands on, including road kill, at every opportunity. I imbibed and vividly remember every medical Life magazine spread which included a cover story on Michael DeBakey's pioneering vascular work, a premonition of my popular book *Anatomic Exposures in Vascular Surgery* and my endeavors as a microvascular course director.

In college my favorite courses were comparative anatomy and mammalian anatomy. During the latter, I enjoyed the luxury of being the sole dissector of the latex-injected cat specimen since my lab partner had a tremor due to a football neck injury. I made multiple drawings of the revealed anatomy as my study guide for the practicums. My art progressed during my college years to large format acrylic paintings, mainly figurative.

Medical school was where my drawing skills were invaluable. Anatomy was taught in the first half of the first year, and I filled a three-ring notebook with extensive illustrations drawn from all the classic anatomy atlases and particularly from Frank Netter's clinical symposia and Ciba Collections of his illustrations. I submitted watercolor Netter-like educational illustrations to local competitions and earned much needed cash by doing lettering for a major Philadelphia medical publishing house.

My illustrations greatly impressed my interviewers for internship, and a major vascular surgeon who interviewed me asked (or told) me on the spot if I would illustrate a technique book he had in mind. During my residency I did line-drawing illustrations for multiple papers which I co-authored and for others.

My postgraduate evolution progressed through line-drawing to acrylic to computer graphic illustration for my own books and for others. Now in the electronic era, I illustrate digitally with all the computing power to do layering, transparency and three dimensional graphics. The output is web-based and portable to multiple electronic platforms. A long journey from Mickey Mouse.

NOTE

[1] This chapter was written in Dr. Wind's private capacity and does not represent the views of the Uniformed Services University or the Department of Defense.

REFERENCES

Ackland Robert, D. (2010). *Ackland's video atlas of human anatomy*. Philadelphia, PA: Wolters Kluwer/Lippincott Williams & Wilkins. Retrieved from http://www.aclandanatomy.com/?adid=20110825_v001
Crosby, R. W. (2012). *Max Brodel: The man who put art into medicine*. New York, NY: Springer Verlag.
Hale, R. B., & Coyle, T. (2003). *Albinus on anatomy*. New York, NY: Dover.
Loechel, W. (1960). The history of medical illustrtion. *Bulletin of the Medical Library Association, 48*(2), 168–171. Retrieved from http://www.ncbi.nlm.nih.gov/pmc/articles/PMC200463/
Netter, F. (2014). *Atlas of human anatomy*. Amsterdam, The Netherlands: Elsevier Science Health.
Norman, J. (1986). *The anatomical plates of Pietro da Cortona*. New York, NY: Dover.
O'Malley, C. (2007). *Andreas Vesalius of Brussels*. New York, NY: Dover.
Pernkopf, E. (1979). *Atlas of topographical and applied human anatomy, Vol.2: Thorax, abdomen and extremities*. Vienna: Urban & Schwarzenberg.
Standring, S. (2008). Gray's Anatomy the anatomical basis of clinical practice (150 Anniversary Ed.). Amsterdam, The Netherlands: Elsevier Science Health.
Tsafrir, J., & Ohry, A. (2001). *Medical illustration: From caves to cyberspace*. Retrieved from http://onlinelibrary.wiley.com/doi/10.1046/j.1471-1842.2001.d01-16.x/full

Gary Wind
Walter Reed National Military Medical Center, USA

AMY DAI

7. LEARNING FROM CHILDREN'S DRAWINGS OF NATURE

INTRODUCTION

This study investigated children's ideas about "nature" as they drew them around the time they entered formal school education. It suggests how school education can scaffold learning from those ideas. Some studies suggest that children's understanding of nature is not necessarily age-related (Shepardson et al., 2007; Littledyke, 2004; Loughland et al., 2002) and that even young children may have expansive conceptions of the environment (Cohen & Horm-Wingerg, 1993; Phenice & Griffore, 2003).

Studies show that most children think of nature as a place where animals and plants live (Phenice & Griffore, 2003; Bonnett & Williams, 1998; Littledyke, 2004; Shepardson et al., 2007). Children also hold different feelings toward nature – some relate it to a place to relax or quiet down, but some relate it to danger or fear. Anthropocentric or biocentric are other lenses that are often used to examine children's views of nature (Bonnett & Williams, 1998; Hyun, 2005; Kahn & Lourenço, 2002). Children may value nature from the perspective that nature provides entertainment, learning, physical and emotional experiences, and resources for them or other organisms.

A preponderance of research suggests that children learn about the environment and nature from direct experience such as sensory or first-hand interaction (Hyun, 2005; Kellert, 2002; Kalvaitis, 2007; Sebba, 1991). However, in our modern lives, children may learn more about nature from the media, adults, and their peers than from direct experience (White, 2006; Louv, 2005; Littledyke, 2004; Walker & Loughla nd, 2003; Kellert, 2002; Rickinson, 2001; Bonnett & Williams, 1998; Payne, 1998; Cohen & Horm-Wingerg, 1993). What they learn from the media can sometimes be contradictory to their own daily life experiences and understanding of nature (Payne, 1998).

After starting school, children also learn more about nature and the environment from the school curriculum, projects, and other activities such as recycling (Bonnett & Williams, 1998; Littledyke, 2004). They start to shape their learning into cognitive models rather than perceptions. Those cognitive models assist them in developing scientific understanding of the natural world beyond first-hand sensory and interactive experiences (Hyun, 2005; Wilson, 2006). However, because environmental education is often not mandatory in school curricula, children's varied degrees of understanding nature mainly depend on their different life experiences (Littledyke, 2004). Cobern and his colleagues (1999) found that ninth graders in the United Stated still did not talk much about their ideas of nature learned from school after nine years of schooling. Rather, they linked nature with personal life experiences that were not related to school science knowledge.

We can argue that children's conceptions that are learned from either direct or indirect experience *are* their understanding of what is nature. It would also be hard to tease out different sources from firsthand exposure to nature or secondhand information from the media. Thus, following the question of how children define nature, I proposed to ask the question, "What are children's *relationships* with nature?" This approach might show a sense of what nature personally means to children in this study's particular urban context and reflect their interpretations of nature closer to daily life. Otherwise, the definition given by children could come from a textbook rather than from their experience.

This study was done in Taiwan, an island located in East Asia, which has a rich biodiversity due to its unique landscape. The plains have, however, been heavily exploited. As a result, most children, especially those in the cities, do not have much access to nature. There have been no previous studies about how Taiwanese children perceived nature in this context (Chou, 2003).

On the other hand, credentialism is deeply embedded in Taiwanese society. In the very competitive Taipei City, many children live under the pressure of getting good grades in order to finally earn a diploma from universities that seem to promise better career choices and higher socioeconomic status. This social belief has been criticized for a long time for distorting the purpose of education and destroying young people's lives in many aspects. Preparing young people as future citizens with a more realistic and comprehensive education has become a strong voice in the society. The ongoing educational reform in Taiwan began in the mid-1990s. Following the Environmental Education Curriculum Guidelines, environmental education is now required in school curricula. By knowing what children think and what concepts they bring with them to school, educators can use that information as the foundation of biology education or environmental education. Therefore, in this study I explored Taiwanese children's ideas and definitions of nature. Children's ideas can include knowledge, understanding, feeling, or anything that makes children think of the word *nature*.

LITERATURE REVIEW

While children's conceptions about nature touch on an array of ideas, animals and plants are often the main characteristic in children's mind about nature. Secondly, sometimes older children describe nature using its interrelations. Thirdly, children show different positive or negative affection toward nature. Finally, how children define and view nature may vary depending on their perspectives.

P. Katz (Ed.), Drawing for Science Education, 73–86.
© *2017 Sense Publishers. All rights reserved.*

Animals and Plants

Children have diverse ideas about what nature is. One salient theme that emerged from these ideas is that many children thought nature was the place where animals and plants lived (Phenice & Griffore, 2003; Bonnett & Williams, 1998; Littledyke, 2004; Shepardson et al., 2007). In a study by Phenice and Griffore (2003), more than one hundred 32- to 72-month-old children were interviewed about their perception of and their relationship to nature. In this study, 76% of the children answered "Yes" to the question "Are trees part of nature?" while 74% said "Yes" to the question "Are animals part of nature?" Also, 70% and 66%, respectively, said "Yes" to the questions "Are plants part of nature?" and "Are humans part of nature?" From the discussions of a series of photographs with fifth- and sixth- graders, Bonnett and Williams (1998) observed that some children thought nature was only plants, but many thought animals were inseparable from nature. They had different views about whether human beings belong to nature. Some children thought of both animals and human beings as parts of nature, because human beings and animals have similar needs. Shepardson et al. (2007) found four different mental models emerging from children's drawings and writings of what constitutes the environment and from their justifications for whether a series of photographs depicted the environment. More than half of the students conceptualized the environment as a place where animals and plants live without human beings. Many fewer children thought of the environment as a place modified by humans, or as a place where humans, animals, and plants lived.

Littledyke (2004) interviewed first to sixth graders with the question, "When people talk about the environment, what do they mean?" and found that children had all sorts of answers across ages. During the interview, children spent a lot of time defining the environment as the world around, animals and plants, and environmental problems. Loughland et al. (2002) interviewed more than 2,000 students from both elementary and secondary schools in Australia with the question of what they thought the word "environment" meant. They concluded that six conceptions were present in the students' responses, divided into two major groups. One was "object focus," including conceptions that the environment is "a place," "a place that contains living things," and "a place that contains living things and people." The second group of conceptions in this study was "relational focus."

Interrelations

Loughland et al. (2002) included in "relational focus" the ideas that "the environment does something for people," "people are part of the environment and are responsible for it," and "people and the environment are in a mutually sustaining relationship." The authors stressed that even young children could see the environment as an interactive and holistic model from its attribute of interrelationship.

Bonnett and Williams (1998) reported that children thought nature was important for many reasons. They thought trees were important because they provide food, shelter, and oxygen for animals. Animals need plants as food or places to live and humans, likewise, need plants. Yet according to the authors, some children might not have seen the overarching idea of the interrelations in nature, because what they learned from schools and the media is not well connected or applicable to their daily life. It could also be that they have not experienced enough to see the underlying relations in nature.

In Shepardson's (2007) study of children's mental models of the environment, 20% of the children had the concept that the environment supported the resources necessary for life. These children saw both abiotic and biotic factors in nature and included human beings in the environment. Only about 3% of the students in the study knew the cycle of matter or energy in the environment: the sun provides energy to plants, plants provide energy for animals.

Having the ideas of interrelations, some children were aware that they could take action to make changes regarding some environmental issues. Littledyke (2004) concluded that some older students articulated attitudes of sharing and responsibility for protecting the environment. Most children had an opinion on their environment and were willing to take action to make changes (Kwan and Miles, 1998; Littledyke, 2004).

Affections

Children reported their emotions when they talked about nature. One student in the Shepardson et al. (2007) study drew three people with one of them flying a kite and labeled them as a "happy family." In the interview of Bonnett and Williams' (1998) study, some children valued nature as a quiet and relaxing place for leisure activities. A boy said that nature was sometimes where "You get away from your troubles."

Children also frequently connected nature with their play. The researchers suggested that children talk about different environments by thinking about what they can do there. Wals (1994) studied middle school students' perceptions and experiences of nature in the city of Detroit, United States. These urban adolescents thought many activities were more enjoyable in nature, but not required to be in nature. On the other hand, some children suggested that nature (woodland and meadow) would be so boring that they would not like to stay very long. Some children associated nature with the danger of being mugged or with anxiety about being alone.

Perspectives

Bonnett and Williams (1998) found that children thought of themselves in some sense as part of a natural process and interdependent with it. They knew that humans need nature for life. On the other hand, children also thought that nature was sometimes a sanctuary for getting away. It is separate from their everyday life.

Payne (1998) found most children in his Australian sixth grade believed that nature was the same as the environment, and that nature did not include human-made objects. He also had children draw a picture of their local environment as seen from the schoolyard. Then, he asked them to list things that they left out of the drawings. Payne sought to discover whether children's conceptions of nature and the environment remained the same when the context was narrowed to their local environment from the general idea of "the environment." About half the children began listing some human-made objects but left out others, sometimes without supporting reasons. The rest of the children continued to exclude humans and human-made objects in their drawings. The study concluded that sixth-grade children's views on nature were not fully developed or consistent across different contexts. However, other studies also show that adults may have different views about how many human-made things could be included in their definition of nature (Ma, 2009; Liu & Lederman, 2007).

METHODS USED TO INVESTIGATE YOUNG CHILDREN'S IDEAS OF NATURE

Naturalistic Observation

Payne (1998), as both a teacher and researcher, unobtrusively collected data from his students' conversations about nature, writing, and drawings. Hyun (2005) analyzed her field-based vignettes to reflect how 3- to 5-year-old children's thinking process about nature is different from adults' thinking in their daily lives. The observed occasions happened in natural settings such as the playground, home, or parks. As an acquaintance of the children, the observer's presence was unobtrusive and the dialogue between children and adults was collected over a span of 8 years. The author argued that adults might easily impose their own frame of understanding on children and ignore the children's competence or epistemology.

Content Analysis—Drawing

Many researchers used drawing as a way for children to communicate and demonstrate their understanding of nature (Bonnett & Williams, 1998; Kalvaitis, 2007; Payne, 1998; Sebba, 1991; Shepardson, 2002, 2005; Shepardson et al., 2007). Drawing was believed to be a child-friendly means that could be used particularly for young children with limited language skills to demonstrate their mental model (Shepardson, 2007). Bonnett and Williams (1998) used the drawing data collection method as a way to warm up at the beginning of interviews. Children were first asked to draw their favorite place (which was not limited to natural places) because the researchers intended to see if nature appeared in children's minds without prompting. Drawing can serve as a buffer that allows children to get settled and familiar with the interview situation and later have something about which to talk. Since some ideas are hard to express in a drawing, providing children the opportunity to write or talk about their drawing could potentially allow them to reveal more of their ideas to others.

Content Analysis—Writing

Written pieces were also for children to clarify their concepts in drawings and validate the meaning for the researchers (Payne, 1998; Shepardson, 2007). Besides drawing, Kalvaitis (2007) asked children to write about their drawings and their relationship with nature. The materials were later used in the interviews. Bonnett and Williams (1998) asked fifth- and sixth-graders to write down things in general that worried them and what they would like to see changed or stopped and also the things that they thought were important and would be upset about if they changed or stopped. Children from upper elementary schools to high school in Kwan and Miles's (1998) study listed three things that they treasure very much, they would like to change, they think is important, annoy them most, and finally, that worry them a lot beyond their local areas. Students were encouraged to provide reasons for each item.

Interview

All the studies that interviewed children used group interviews rather than one-on-one style interviews. Littledyke (2004) argued that group interviews can stimulate ideas and extend the discussion among peers. Many strategies were used to foster children's expressions of their ideas such as providing a trustful and secure atmosphere. Children were grouped with others they knew and sat in a circle, with no obvious authority. The interview time was limited in terms of children's attention spans. Age-appropriate language was used to communicate with children.

Cohen and Horm-Wingerg (1993) also used a series of illustrations for their interviews. They found that 3-year-olds were not quite able to articulate needed information in their study. Four- and 5-year-olds, however, were capable of responding to interview questions.

This study had been designed to use both individual and group interviews. However, I decided to drop the latter after conducting three group interviews. First of all, the children surprisingly repeated the exact same answers in the group interviews as in the individual interviews. The group conversation did not provide any richer data than did the individual interviews. Second, the opportunity to have fun with classmates and be away from the authority of the teachers caused the children to act very differently in group interviews than they had in individual interviews. This could be a cultural phenomenon. In Taiwan children are not well skilled in the practice of group discussion and are more used to following instruction from one authority.

Photographs/Illustrations

Like children's drawings, photographs and illustrations were also used frequently in communicating with children. Cohen and Horm-Wingerg (1993) used a series of photographs in their research on 3- to 5-year-old children's ecological awareness. First, in "picture discrimination," they asked children to look at six pairs of pictures and choose which is "nicer" from each pair. The researchers designed the paired illustrations with the nicer ones being those that are not polluted. Second, in the "picture comprehension" tasks, children were asked "What's wrong here?" while looking at pictures of human actions--for instance, a person throwing trash out of a car. Their tests met the reliability criteria and were age-appropriate tasks for revealing children's rich resources for ecological thoughts.

Bonnett and Williams (1998) used photographs throughout their interviews as a talking point to initiate conversation among fifth- and sixth-graders. They wanted children to use their own words to express their understanding and concerns for the environment, rather than having adults' words imposed on them (Kwan & Miles, 1998).

To study children's mental models of the environment, Shepardson (2007) presented to fourth- to twelfth-graders photographs of "natural and human-managed environments: desert plants in the desert, rows of urban houses, bears in a stream, a woodland stream, cornfields with farmstead, an industrial plant with trees in the background, and a deciduous forest." Students needed to tell the researchers if each photo represented the environment and to provide their justifications.

CONTEXT AND METHODOLOGY

Schools in This Study

Kindergartens in Taiwan usually take students from age 3 to 5. Attendance is not compulsory, but the enrollment rate for 5-year-olds in the school year 2009 to 2010 was 92.12 % (Ministry of Education, 2010). There is no national curriculum standard to follow before elementary school. In Taipei City, both kindergarten and elementary school outdoor spaces are fairly small in size. Children usually play or do homework indoors after school and have limited access to outdoor spaces.

In this study, efforts were made to select four schools with varied characteristics in order to include a wide range of children's ideas about nature (Rickinson, 2001). Two independent and two public schools in different districts of the city were chosen to include different families and their chosen school education systems. Gu-Shin is an independent elementary school; Ge-Chen is a public kindergarten; Lu-Dye is a public elementary school; and Pu-Lin is an independent kindergarten.

Participant Selection

This study targeted twelve children from their last year in kindergarten or their first year in elementary school (N=12) as participants for this study. Data from four more participants than the targeted number was collected in case any of the original participants withdrew from the study. Thus, my flexibility to select cases that would provide the richest information was increased.

Before I went to Taiwan for data collection, teachers were told to select children according to criteria that would provide rich information. First, the children had to be able to express themselves in front of strangers. Second, they should select some children with special interests in nature and some without. Third, two girls and two boys would be needed from each class (school). Fourth, teachers should try to select children from families of different socioeconomic status or with different beliefs about nature education—such as families that often participate in nature-oriented activities.

Data Collection

I decided to use a variety of means to understand children's views and to allow children to express themselves. Various means also helped me to triangulate children's understanding of the phenomena from different layers of constructions.

I asked for drawings with the assumption that children have an inner representation, a mental model, as their understanding of a phenomenon (Moseley et al., 2010; Greca & Moreira, 2000; Shepardson et al., 2007; McClary & Talanquer, 2011). This model is constructed from one's conceptions and experiences and may change over time with new experience and knowledge. We can learn the children's conception of nature from what they include in the drawings and can understand their relationship with nature from how they situate themselves in the picture. Although verbal communication served as a means to express ideas, share information, and mediate through the socialization process, what children expressed in the interview was what they were able to express at that particular moment or in that sociocultural context. There might be ideas that they were not able to fully express by spoken language or intellectual resources that they were not able to retrieve and assemble as efficiently as adults (Shepardson, 2002; 2007). I had to be aware that those cultural representations—languages and illustrations—are in some ways limited for measuring children's intellectual resources. However, Shepardson (2002) suggested that some time spent probing can cue children's additional thoughts or help interviewers confirm what they hear and want to know about more.

In this study, each child participated in the tasks of drawing, being interviewed, and interpreting photographs during January of 2010. They were taken to a quiet room, such as the library, activity room, or conference room, during the school day. Crayons were supplied for them to do the drawings. A drawing prompt was used in this research: "Please draw a picture of yourself with your family" followed by "Please draw a picture of yourself in nature." The purpose of drawing families was to warm up the conversation. Most children understood the prompts well and started their drawings immediately.

The drawings served as a talking point for the semi-structured interview that began upon completion of the drawing. Sample questions included: "Tell me about your drawing," "What are you doing there?," "What is nature?," "How do you feel in nature?," "Do you like it?" The interview questions were designed to reflect different aspects of the Contextual Model of Learning (Falk & Dierking, 2000) which structured the entire larger project. I believed children's daily lives and thoughts can be learned from natural conversations guided by semi-structured interviews. I also tried to ask more questions when a child brought up some experiences related to nature to see if that could elicit more details.

To prevent a situation in which the children have no clue about what nature is and to continue the study, eleven photographs were prepared to provide scaffolds for children without defining nature for them. Examples of photographs were prairies, cities, deserts, ocean, an elementary school campus, a living room, and natural trails as shown in Figure 1. The decision making in selecting the particular photographs was to show a wide range of scenes that included different landscapes and varied degree of human-made and natural elements. From the first interview, I decided to ask all the children to interpret these photographs to enrich the data. Children were asked, "Is this nature?" and "Why?"

After the interviews, I gave the children little gifts to thank them for their participation and cooperation. I used a digital recorder and also took notes during the interviews. The drawing and interview took about 30 to 45 minutes.

Figure 1. Examples of photograph used in the interview

Data Analysis

All drawings were coded, and all the codes were counted. The photograph interpretations were coded by children's responses to the Yes or No question, "Is this nature?", and their explanations to support their response were counted. Both drawings and photograph interpretations were also quantified into numerical items based on a scoring rubric. The higher the score, the more complex and consistent were the child's understandings of nature. Using the rubric, the drawing and photograph interpretation methods were also compared side by side to reveal if either method can better retrieve children's intellectual resources. The scores were then compared according to different school systems, genders, and ages, so that I could examine whether there was any trend.

The children's interviews were coded, and the codes were modified and re-grouped several times every time I re-read the transcripts. The themes from the interviews are reported only when they are closely related to the results from children's drawings and responses to the research question.

RESULTS

Definition of Nature

Five themes emerged from the children's conceptions of nature: (1) Children use different elements to define nature. (2) Plants create the space called nature. (3) Nature sometimes contains different degrees of natural and artificial elements. (4) Nature grows and moves. (5) Human beings are not nature. Finally, the complexity and consistency of how a child held his or her definition of nature were

A. DAI

Table 1. Drawing coding sheet

1 Tone	1.1 Positive: Smiling figures		
	1.2 Unclear		
	1.3 No facial expression		
2 People	2.1 Self		
	2.2 Family	2.2.1 Dad	2.2.3 Sister
		2.2.2 Mom	2.2.4 Brother
	2.3 Friends		
	2.4 Farmers		
3 Natural elements	3.1 Plants	3.1.1 Trees	
		3.1.2 Grass	
		3.1.3 Flowers	
		3.1.4 Falling leaf	
	3.2 Animals	3.2.1 Bees	3.2.5 Ladybug
		3.2.2 Butterfly	3.2.6 Snake
		3.2.3 Beetles	3.2.7 Fish
		3.2.4 Ant	3.2.8 Squirrel
	3.3 Abiotic elements	3.3.1 Sun	
		3.3.2 Clouds	
		3.3.3 Wind	
		3.3.4 Sky	
		3.3.5 Water	
4 Human-made elements	4.1 Buildings	4.1.1 Home	
		4.1.2 Other buildings	
	4.2 Planter		
	4.3 Airplane		
	4.4 For activities	4.4.1 Bike	
		4.4.2 Frisbee	
		4.4.3 Chess	
5 Activity	5.1 Physical	5.1.1 Biking	
		5.1.2 Playing Frisbee	
	5.2 Interaction with and observation of living things	5.2.1 Observing animals	
		5.2.2 Looking at trees	
		5.2.3 Looking at flowers	
		5.2.4 Looking at grass	
	5.3 Leisure	5.3.1 Looking at nature	
		5.3.2 Sun bathing	
		5.3.3 Watching sky	
		5.3.4 Posing for a photo	
		5.3.5 Resting	
		5.3.6 Spacing out	
	5.4 Intellectual	5.4.1 Playing chess	

compared over the different school systems, gender, and age. In terms of children's feeling toward nature, most children expressed positive feelings about nature. They enjoyed nature because of its aesthetic and social value as well as the chance to interact with living things.

Different elements of nature. Drawing was used as a starting point for the interview. Ten of the twelve children started the drawings immediately after the prompt. Exceptions to this reaction included Chi-Z and Jin-Ruei. Chi-Z said that he only knew how to draw planes. I let him draw a plane. In later conversation, he provided me with a verbal answer of his definition of nature. The other child, Jin-Ruei, responded that she did not know enough about nature to draw the picture. I showed her the eleven photographs before beginning the drawing. She got the idea from the photographs without my further explanation of nature and continued her drawing and interview.

Children's drawings were analyzed using a coding system modified from Kalvaitis' (2007, p. 207). Many items identified in Kalvaitis' study were also identified in mine. In addition, his way of categorizing the codes was very similar to the way I wanted to group the items shown in my children's drawings. Elements in all drawings were categorized and are listed in Table 1. Each drawing was coded. Examples of the coding of An-Jhen's and Ning-Chen's drawings are shown later in Table 3. Next, all the element codes were counted, as summarized in Table 2. People were counted only when someone other than the child was included, since the prompt clearly asked the children to draw themselves in the pictures. Three children included someone else in their drawings of nature. Fifty-two counts of natural elements and eight counts of human-made elements showed in children's drawings in this study. Among the natural elements of plants, animals, and abiotic elements, plants were the most common element with a count of 26 in children's drawing of nature.

Table 2. Summary of elements included in children's drawing of nature

Coding category	Counts
2 People (other than self)	3
3 Natural elements	52
3.1 Plants	(26)
3.2 Animals	(10)
3.3 Abiotic natural elements	(16)
4 Human-made elements	8

Nature is the space plants create. In the photograph interpretation, I counted children's reasons for judging the photographs as nature or not. Trees (51 counts), flowers (29 counts), and grasses (27 counts) were the elements most often used to explain why they thought the photograph represented nature. This result that plants were essential in defining nature matches the results from the drawings where I counted 26 plants (as shown in Table 2). Eleven of the twelve children included trees, grasses, or flowers in their drawings. The one who did not include any plants was the one who drew only a plane.

Plants created the space in which children can play, do things with families, or observe living things. Plants do not just *live* in nature (Littledyke, 2004; Shepardson et al., 2007), but they themselves *are* nature. When I asked if there were any nature close to home, Suan-Hui said "Hmm… yes. Like the sidewalk in Yu-Chen Park near our home--there are rows after rows of big trees." De-Lu described the nature close to her home as "the big area of grass." Si-Chen, pointing to the world map on the wall of the library, said, "That prairie is nature. Yeah, prairie is nature. You see Africa with its prairies? That's nature. Mountains are nature, too, because there are many trees in the mountains. There are fewer trees in the high mountains. But it is nature too." They all expressed the ideas that plants themselves are nature.

While many children thought of plants as nature, some seemed to have a sense of difference in the amount of naturalness. They said that there has to be lots of grass (De-Lu, Chen-Yu, Jin-Ruei), lots of trees (Chi-Z, Ge-Jin, Chen-Yu, Jin-Ruei), and lots of flowers (Jin-Ruei) to be nature. Si-Chen told me that it has to have a lot of building to not be nature.

Different Degrees of Nature. It seemed to the children in my study that as long as plants were the main elements in a space, it could be called nature. In children's minds, nature can include things that are not natural and it is just a matter of proportion of the vegetation.

When he talked about the photograph of the beach, Si-Chen said, "This! This! This is nature! You see, there are no houses at all. There is nothing. Nature is what has been there for a long time. Cities are built later. Nature is the entire area with no houses. Sometimes there are some houses, but not many houses. Like the ones full of houses—it's a city. Like Taipei City is a city."

I found that when the children were asked where they saw nature, parks were often mentioned. Yet, it seems as if parks in the city are not 100% nature, so that a child could sound conflicted. When I tried to affirm Yen-Pin's ideas, she sounded unsure.

Amy: So there is not much nature around your home?
Yen-Pin: Um. Only in our community [the park].
Amy: What's in your community?
Yen-Pin: There are swing seats.
Amy: Are swing seats nature?
Yen-Pin: (Shakes head)
Amy: So what's nature in your community?
Yen-Pin: Places to rest.

Nature moves and grows. Nature apparently links to living things. "This is [nature]. Trees…and trees and…the leaves on the trees *move* when the wind blows." Ning-Chen thought things that grew and moved are nature. Electricity poles are not nature because "they aren't plants and they don't move." As the conversation went on, Ning-Chen stated "Human beings move. They're half [nature]…. Because human beings are not plants…also they are not the things that grow things."

Suan-Hui also mentioned that trees and flowers are nature because they grow from the soil. It is informative that the children who talked about nature as it moves and grows are all from the same kindergarten, Ge-Chen. The explanation could be that they believe nature is somehow living or, rather, they mix up the definition of living things with nature. To these kindergarteners, nature is associated with living things. Another example that children link nature to living things is Huan-Mong's statement that "the entire earth is nature, because there are many living things in it."

There is a cultural bias here. In Chinese the character for animals is 動物. The first Chinese character means "move," and the second character means "things." Literally, animals are the "things that move." In this study, seven out of twelve children included animals in their drawings, but interestingly two out of the seven said animals are not nature when interpreting the photographs.

Humans are not nature and not related to nature. Only four children thought human beings were nature. Yu-Ting said that human beings are nature because human beings are animals. Others either did not know or thought human beings were not nature. Conversely to Yu-Ting's explanation, some children said human beings are animals, but not nature. (These children also did not think animals were nature).

A few children included other people in their drawings. However, in the interviews, they clearly told me they do not think human beings are nature. Instead, the humans in the drawings represented to them social interaction in nature. Several explained that humans were not nature because they do not grow grass or they have no flowers (Ning-Chen, De-Lu, and Chen-Yu). Chen-Yu used a unique way to describe how animals are nature, but human beings are not. He said "deer…should be [nature]… Yeah, it doesn't grow grass. But it is nature because it walks in forests… Human beings want to take… [When] human beings want to take a walk, they take a walk. So they are not [nature]." As the interview went on, he evolved his definition of nature from things that grow grass to include the animals that *live* in forests. The "plant is nature" theme was clear to children. However, although they believed human beings are animals and animals seem to be nature, they got confused as to whether human beings are nature.

Amy (Interviewer): So living things are nature, right?
Huan-Mong: Animals are [nature] too.
Amy (Interviewer): But you just said human beings are not nature. Is a human being an animal?
Huan-Mong: Yes.
Amy (Interviewer): So human beings are not nature but other animals are?
Huan-Mong: Some [animals] are and some are not….

Children hesitated to claim human beings are nature and they in general have not grasped the relationship between humans and nature. Only a very few children thought humans were related to nature when I brought up this topic. When I asked Si-Chen if he thought he was related to nature, he responded that "Yes. We all need nature so we can walk for pleasure. Like there is lots of exhaust gas on the streets. Who can stand that? In nature, then you can chat, chat with others. And it can…produce carbon dioxide. And the trees keep absorbing it and emit good air."

Comparing Children's Definition of Nature with Other Factors

To see how children's definition of nature is affected by other factors, I quantified their definitions into numerical items so that it would be easier to examine any trends (Moseley at al., 2010). Their drawings and the photograph task were then scored based on the rubric I created, as follows:

5: Consistently includes animals (A), plants (P), abiotic elements (B), and excludes human-made material (M), with a consistent and correct overarching way to define nature (C)

4: Consistently includes animals, plants, and abiotic elements and excludes human-made material

3: Any three of the A, P, B, M, or C

2: Any two of the A, P, B, M, or C
1: Any one of the A, P, B, M, or C
0: Only human-made things

Table 3 shows examples of how each coding in a drawing was rated as a numeric score.

Table 3. Children's drawings code and rated score examples

Children's name and drawing	Coding of drawing	Items included	Score
Ning-Chen	3.1.2 Grass 3.1.3 Flowers 3.2.4 Ant 3.3.1 Sun 4.2 Planter	APB	3
De-Lu	3.1.1 Trees 3.1.2 Grass 3.1.3 Flowers 3.2.2 Butterfly 3.2.6 Snake 3.3.1 Sun 3.3.2 Clouds	APBM	4

The coding for A (animals) is entirely based on animals (coding category 3.2) not people (coding category 2). The children who have drawn families and friends were representing the social function of nature as shown in Figure 2. Both children told me that human beings are not nature.

Figure 2. Children's drawings with other people. Left: Si-chen's drawing (me, mother); right: Jin-ruci's drawing (farmer, me friend)

In addition, all responses from the photographs were coded and listed in a table to see if a child's definition of nature was consistent over the eleven photographs. Item C exclusively applied to the photographs because there was no consistency issue for a drawing. Offering a consistent idea about nature showed that that child had developed a more mature overarching understanding of nature than those who just looked at separate elements in the photographs and changed their ideas from photograph to photograph. Of the twelve children, three got a C and scored 5. Si-Chen defined nature as "that has been there for a long time." Chi-Z thought, "It is not nature if it is human–manipulated." Yu-Ting claimed that anything *made* is not nature and used that concept throughout the interview.

As listed in the first three columns in Table 4, each child received three scores: one for the drawings, another for the photographs, and the last to combine the two. That is, the combined score tried to include the child's definition from both methods, since the different methods were designed to understand children's ideas of nature from different perspectives. The difference between the drawings and

A. DAI

photographs is listed in the last column in Table 4 to show if some ideas about nature are easier to discover in drawings or through photographs. The results show that excluding human-made things (M) is the one definition most often used either only in drawings or only for photographs. Children more often did not include human-made things (in the drawings) when I did not prompt the question. However, in the photographs, whether or not to include human-made things became confusing for children in defining nature. Children started to sense the different degrees of naturalness in photographs and sometimes got confused as to whether human-made things were or were not nature.

Table 4. Children's scores for definitions from drawings and photographs

Children	Drawings	Photographs	Combined	Difference between photographs and drawings
An-Jhen	3APM	4APBM	4	B
Yen-Pin	2PB	3APB	3	A
Si-Chen	1P	5APBMC	5	ABMC
Huan-Mong	4APBM	2AP	4	BM
Ning-Chen	3APB	3APB	3	
Suan-Hui	3PBM	3APB	4	AM
De-Lu	4APBM	1P	4	ABM
Chi-Z	0	5APBMC	5	APBMC
Yu-Ting	4APBM	4APBC	5	MC
Ge-Jin	3PBM	3APB	4	AM
Chen-Yu	3APM	3APM	3	
Jin-Ruei	3APB	3PBM	4	AM

In this sample, the children from public schools received a higher average score (4.59) than the ones in independent schools (3.88). Girls got a higher average score (3.59) than boys (3.00). First graders got a higher score (4.59) than kindergarten children did (3.59). Moreover, different methods (drawings or using photographs) did not change these results. This is, children in public school had a higher average score than those in independent schools for both drawings (4.33: 2.5) and photographs (4.44:3.50).

Since the study sample size is so small, the trend cannot lead to a conclusion or be generalized to other populations. But because the data collection process endeavored to balance the children's schools, gender, and grades, it is worth noting that these factors could affect children's understanding of nature and be used as variables in a future study.

Children's Feelings about Nature

Children were asked to draw two pictures at the beginning of the interview. One was of themselves with the family and the other was of them in nature. All children who actually drew the family pictures showed a smiling face. Comparing each child's two drawings, only those of An-Jhen and Chen-Yu did not show a smiling face in the drawing of nature as they did in the drawing of their families (Figure 3). But neither was their facial expression negative (Figure 3). And in the interviews when asked about what their mood was or how they felt in the drawings, both An-Jhen and Chen-Yu responded that they were very happy, as did most other children.

It is apparent that children easily connect nature with a delightful mood. The reasons varied. Three thought that nature was beautiful, three felt happy because of observing or interacting with living things, and one said that there were friends (in her drawing) that she can play with. Explaining the good mood in nature, Yu-Ting said: "Because you can see many beautiful things. Flowers are beautiful. Grass is beautiful. Big trees are beautiful." Suan-Hui likes nature "'cause you can do some wonderful things--like...you can play with the ducky in the pond." Ge-Jin often used "good weather" to define nature. Later in the interview, he explained that good weather makes people feel good. In the interviews, only one child (Huan-Mong) used "It's okay" to describe how he was feeling in his drawing of nature. He also said "[I do not like being in nature] when there is nothing to see."

Yu-Ting seemed to have a unique bond with trees at school and at home. She seemed to have an intimate connection with trees. The starting point was a school lesson that introduced her to the idea of hugging trees. More than just observing or interacting with living things, this relationship showed a deeper emotional bond with plants.

I found that some negative feelings were also expressed in the conversations. One type of negative feeling was mainly directed toward ants, bees, mosquitoes, or caterpillars-- insects that are typically viewed by Taiwanese as pests. Another was a kind of more general fear and wish to avoid danger and even dirtiness in nature. Ning-Chen said that there were trees at grandma's place, but she

Figure 3. Examples of children's drawings of themselves with families and in nature

could not climb them because they're dirty and it's dangerous. Yen-Pin explained desert is not nature "because there is no water. And it's strange, unless you bring your own water."

DISCUSSION

An Already Developed Understanding of Nature

Children at the year before and after entering elementary school showed that they already have a basic conception of what nature is as well as an understanding of the word itself. In Littledyke's study, only five out of 46 children were able to provide an answer to the question, "What do people mean when they talk about the environment?" Louv (2005) also discussed the nature-deficit disorder phenomenon of children in the United States, where children in modern society are severely lacking in outdoor free-play time. Another concern is that five- and six-year old children might not be familiar with the Chinese term nature 大自然 and not be able to express their conceptions regarding nature. However, while some ideas might not have been developed enough to provide an overarching definition of nature, none of the children were so far afield that they could not respond to all of the questions on the topic.

In addition, children's overall scores of drawings and photographs showed that children at this age had a varied complexity of understanding nature. My intention was not to judge if the child had correct *science-based knowledge* (Hart, 2007, p. 700) or how knowledgeable he or she was. Rather, I tried to use the rating to determine the complexity of the children's ideas of nature and how solid their belief was in their definition.

Daily Life Reflected in Conception of Nature

None of the children in this study drew wild animals (e.g., tigers) or landscapes (e.g., rainforests) that are not often seen in their own living environments. Littledyke (2004) argues that including animals is influenced by children's frequent contact with pets and anthropomorphic representations of animals in children's books and television programs. Rickinson (2001) and Walker and Loughland (2003) also found evidence of the vital impact of the media on children's ideas of nature. Yet all the children in this study drew small animals that are often encountered in the city.

Their daily lives and immediate environment also reflect on the coding system which was developed based on children's drawings in the United States. I removed elements such as evergreen plants, cactus, pets, snow, sports, and work (academic and chores). Lack of evergreen plants, cactus, and snow reflects the climate of Taipei City. Things that are often connected with nature in the United States, such as a tree house or backyards, did not appear in these children's drawings.

What children are doing in the drawings of nature is also very similar to what they told me they did in nature in the interviews. In their drawings, they were biking with mom, posing for pictures, watching the sky, playing Frisbee with friends, watching flowers and observing ants, resting, and spacing out. In the interviews, they also mentioned doing physical activities, enjoying the beauty of nature, observing living things, and interacting with other people in nature.

Interrelation of Humans and Nature

The literature indicated that children were able to see the interrelation of humans and nature (Shepardson et al., 2007; Loughland et al., 2002; Bonnett & Williams, 1998). Loughland et al. (2002) found that primary school children in the United Kingdom more often used objects than relationships to define the environment than secondary school children did. Littledyke (2004) also concluded that children learn from their local environment first and gradually move to an understating of the complex relationships in the environment. In this study, the drawings and interview did not show how humans are related to nature or how living and abiotic things are interdependent. In the drawings, it is also hard to observe the relationships between themselves and nature, especially when most children did not draw themselves moving or add much description to their drawings. Conferring with the teacher in Lu-Dye elementary school, I learned that most children at this age draw human figures standing upright without much action drawn or description written (Shepardson et al., 2007).

Beginning to understand human–nature interrelation is important for children at this age in order to be competent in environmental literacy as it is designed in the curriculum guidelines. Pozarnik (1995) also argued that the human-nature relationship is the basis for children's future development of environmental ethics. My study aimed to investigate children's understanding of nature as it is the fundamental basis for environmental education. I argue that children's sense of the different degrees of nature found in this study can be a discussion point to start the conversation about the human role in the environment. First, many children do not think humans are part of nature or are related to nature. Second, children seemed unsure if nature should include human-made things even though they have a sense of the different degrees of naturalness. School teachers and curriculum developers need to emphasize human beings' possible roles in the environment.

Comparing Curriculum Guidelines with Students Existing Ideas

I compared the current environmental education curriculum standard in Taiwan with the results from this study to see if the curriculum standard design is based on and expanded from children's existing concepts. Competence indicators for environmental education are listed under five categories of learning goals: Be perceptive and sensitive to the environment, environmental concepts and knowledge, environmental value and attitudes, environmental action skills, and environmental action experience. Examples of competence indicators are as follows: To use the five senses to experience and explore things in the environment (1a); To know the surrounding natural and human-made environment around animals, plants, and microorganisms, and their interrelations (2a); To understand what role human beings play in the ecosystem and the relationship between the natural environment and human beings (3b); and To participate in community environment protection activities with families or teachers (4a).

This study suggests that children's existing ideas may easily transit into the school environmental education. Children in this study already showed some degree of understanding of their competence. They used their senses to explore nature. They were understanding nature from their surrounding environments. They had curiosity about living things. They can use language and drawings to express their ideas. It appears that there could be greater achievement for first and second graders as they begin their nine years of compulsory education. None in this study mentioned ideas about microorganisms. The interdependency of nature and the roles of human beings still need to be learned.

Implications

Based on the results from this study, I suggest that urban designers add more easily accessed green space in the city. Many of the children thought green areas were essential in nature, that plants created the space called nature. In fact, connected green spaces in a city attract more animals and allow them to move from habitat to habitat. This way, the natural interrelations among living things and nonliving things can grow from these green spaces and provide chances for children to learn about nature.

Schools could develop a school-based and community-based curriculum that included learning about children's immediate environment. In this study, children's understandings of nature were mostly from their direct contact with nature, so it is important to maximize the use of children's surrounding environment for learning about nature. The national curriculum guidelines also expect children of about this age to learn about the organisms around them.

White (2008) also argued that environmental education programs that are beyond children's cognitive ability and understanding, such as teaching rainforest destruction in the classroom, are not appropriate for young children. Rather, learning about the local natural environment that is part of their regular experience is more likely to produce environmental protection in the future (Chawla, 2006). Lindemann-Matthies' (2005) investigation of children's perception of biodiversity also found that children can be interested in creatures other than pets or exotic species as long as they get to learn something about those local species.

Both pre- and in-service teachers need to learn about local environments to engage students in learning about nature around them. Community professionals and informal science and environmental education institutes such as parks or environmental centers can provide classes for family outings and teacher development. Home is also one of the most important places for children at this age. It would be even better if the school curriculum would include family practice for sustainability

Future investigators may be aware that both drawing and the use of photographs were shown to be appropriate for learning ideas from children at this age. Most children in my study started their drawings right away without much shyness or hesitation. Since most children at this age have not learned to write many Chinese characters, adding labels to the drawings were seen less. However, when we try to understand how children define nature by its interrelations, we need to keep in mind that interrelation might be more difficult to show via drawings. In addition, the underlying interrelations may not be the first thing that comes to students' minds when they are asked about what the environment is. Different children's ideas can be elicited through different methods, thus helping to triangulate and clarify children's thoughts. Comparing results from the same child enables researchers not to miss intellectual resources embedded in the various methods. If we interpreted results only from one method, we would probably miss much of the children's interpretation of nature.

These different methods may also help children evolve their definition of nature within the interview process. Yu-Ting at the beginning explained her ideas of nature "[This is nature] because it is city. Many houses. But there are trees here." For another photograph, she determined, "This is nature too. But the leaves have all fallen. Falling leaves is also a natural…phenomenon!" To the photograph of the living room, she started to use the word *made*. She said, "This is not. Because chairs and sofa were *made*. And houses were built. So they are not nature. Only those flowers behind are." She was still inconsistent about whether houses are nature or not, but she started to say "desert is [nature], because sands are not made." I asked her again if cars and houses are nature. She asserted they are not because they were *made*. I was inspired by this evolution that a child can immediately grasp new ideas and reconstruct meanings in the interview process, and hope that what she took away was an overarching concept about how to make a definition rather than detailed facts about what is made and what is not.

MY CHANGING DEFINITION OF NATURE

Even though this study was planned to understand children's ideas, I thought about my own definition of nature before the data collection process began. I thought that nature is everything except human-made things and the unity that these things together create. After this study, I have somewhat changed my own thinking about nature. The idea of nature in my mind probably does sometimes include human-made things. Does a human-made trail or a gazebo in the mountains make the environment not nature? But how do we determine the limits for human-made things and still deem an area nature? Are the parks in urban areas nature? I now believe they should not be excluded from children's nature and environmental learning. Teachers and parents should use these places more often. In addition, the government should consider opening more green places like these to provide children with a place to play and to learn.

REFERENCES

Bonnett, M., & Williams, J. (1998). Environmental education and primary children's attitudes towards nature and the environment. *Cambridge Journal of Education, 28*(2), 159–174.

Chawla, L. (2006). Learning to love the natural world enough to protect it. *Barn, 2*, 57–78.

Chou, S. (2003). *Young children's conceptions and thinking of natural science* (in Chinese). Taipei, R.O.C.: Psychological Publishing.

Cobern, W. W., Gibson, A. T., & Underwood, S. A. (1999). Conceptualizations of nature: An interpretive study of 16 ninth graders' everyday thinking. *Journal of Research in Science Teaching, 36*(5), 541–564.

Cohen, S., & Horm-Wingerg, D. (1993). Children and the environment: Ecological awareness among preschool children. *Environment and Behavior, 25*(1), 103–120.

Directorate-General of Budget, Accounting and Statistics, Executive Yuan, R.O.C. (2009). *Average family income & expenditure per household by districts in Taiwan—Year 2009 report.* Retrieved November, 23, 2014, from http://win.dgbas.gov.tw/fies/214.asp

Falk, J. H., & Dierking, L. D. (2000). *Learning from museums visitor experiences and the making of meaning.* Walnut Creek, CA: AltaMira Press.

Greca, I. M., & Moreira, M. A. (2000). Mental models, conceptual models, and modelling. *International Journal of Science Education, 22*(1), 1–11.

Hart, P. (2007). Environmental education. In S. Abell & N. Lederman (Eds.), *Handbook of research on science education.* Mahwah, NJ: Erlbaum.

Hyun, E. (2005). How is young children's intellectual culture of perceiving nature different from adults'? *Environmental Education Research, 11*(2), 199–214.

Kahn, P. H., & Lourenço, O. (2002). Water, air, fire, and earth: A developmental study in Portugal of environmental moral reasoning. *Environment and Behavior, 34*, 405–430.

Kalvaitis, D. (2007). *Children's relationship with nature: An exploration through the drawings and voices of young children* (Unpublished doctoral dissertation). Utah State University, Logan, UT.

Kellert, S. R. (2002). Experiencing nature: Affective, cognitive, and evaluative development in Children. In P. H. Kahn & S. R. Kellert (Eds.), *The human relationship with nature: Development and culture.* Cambridge, MA: The MIT Press.

Kwan, T., & Miles, J. (1998). In the words of children and young people: The opinions and concerns about their environments of some Brisbane school students. *Australian Journal of Environmental Education, 14*, 11–18.

Lindemann-Matthies, P. (2005). 'Loveable' mammals and 'lifeless' plants: How children's interest in common local organisms can be enhanced through observation of nature. *International Journal of Science Education, 27*(6), 655–677.

Littledyke, M. (2004). Primary children's views on science and environmental issues: Examples of environmental cognitive and moral development. *Environmental Education Research, 10*(2), 217–35.

Liu, S. Y., & Lederman, N. (2007). Exploring prospective teachers' worldviews and conceptions of nature of science. *International Journal of Science Education, 29*(10), 1281–1307.

Loughland, T., Reid, A., & Petoc, P. (2002). Young people's conceptions of environment: a phenomenographic analysis. *Environmental Education Research, 8*(2), 187–197.

Louv, R. (2005). *Last child in the woods: Saving our children from nature-deficit disorder.* Chapel Hill, NC: Algonquin Press.

Ma, H. (2009). Chinese secondary school science teachers' understanding of the Nature of Science—emerging from their views of nature. *Research in Science Education, 39*, 701–724.

McClary, L., & Talanquer, V. (2011). College chemistry students' mental models of acids and acid strength. *Journal of Research in Science Teaching, 48*(4), 396–413.

Minister of Education. (2010). *2010/2011 Education in Taiwan*. Taiwan: Ministry of Education. Retrieved November, 16, 2014, from http://english.moe.gov.tw/public/Attachment/012131727571.pdf

Moseley, C., Desjean-Perrotta, B., & Crim, C. (2010). Exploring preservice teachers' mental models of the environment. In A. M. Bodzin, B. S. Klein, & S. Weaver (Eds.), *The inclusion of environmental education in science teacher education*. New York, NY:Springer.

Payne, P. (1998). Children's conceptions of nature. *Australian Journal of Environmental Education, 14*, 19–26.

Phenice, L., & Griffore, R. (2003). Young children and the natural world. *Contemporary Issues in Early Childhood, 4*(2), 167–178.

Pozarnik, B. M. (1995). Probing into pupils' moral judgment in environmental dilemmas: a basis for "teaching values". *Environmental Education Research, 1*(1), 47–57.

Rickinson, M. (2001). Learners and learning in environmental education: a critical review of the evidence. *Environmental Education Research, 7*(3), 207–320.

Sebba, R. (1991). The landscapes of childhood: The reflection of childhood's environment in adult memories and in children's attitudes. *Environment and Behavior, 23*(4), 395–422.

Shepardson, D. P. (2002). Bugs, butterflies, and spiders: Children's understandings about insects. *International Journal of Science Education, 24*(6), 627–643.

Shepardson, D. P. (2005). Student ideas: What is an environment? *Journal of Environmental Education, 36*(4), 49–58.

Shepardson, D. P., Wee, B., Priddy, M., & Harbor, J. (2007). Students' mental models of the environment. *Journal of Research in Science Teaching, 44*(2), 327–348.

Wals, A. E. J. (1994). Nobody planted It, It just Grew! Young adolescents' perceptions and experiences of nature in the context of urban environmental education. *Children's Environments, 11*(3), 177–193.

Walker, K., & Loughland, T. (2003). The socio-cultural influences on environmental understandings of Australian school students: A response to Rickinson. *Environmental Education Research, 9*(2), 227–239.

White, R. (2006). Young children's relationship with nature: It's importance to children's development & the earth's future. *Taproot, 16*(2).

White, R. (2008). Nurturing children's biophilia: Developmentally appropriate environmental education for young children. *Collage Magazine*. Retrieved from http://www.communityplaythings.com/resources/articles/environmentaleducation/Biophilia.html

Wilson, R. A. (2006). The wonders of nature: Honoring children's ways of knowing. *Early Childhood News, 18*(1), 14–19.

Amy Dai
Science Education Researcher
Taipei, Taiwan

8. THE UNDERSTANDING OF HUMAN ANATOMY ELICITED FROM DRAWINGS OF SOME BANGLADESHI VILLAGE WOMEN AND CHILDREN

INTRODUCTION

There are a number of methods to obtain information about a person's understanding of science (White & Gunston, 1992; Tunnicliffe & Reiss, 1999a). Drawings are considered one useful tool (Haney et al., 2004). Most techniques require respondents to talk or write their answers to questions. Osborne and Gilbert, 1980 used oral questions whilst written responses have been analysed, for example by Lewis, Leach and Wood-Robinson, 2000. Tunnicliffe and Reiss (1999b) elicited children's spontaneous conversations about learners' interpretations of brine shrimps. An increasingly popular technique in eliciting learners' understanding of ideas is the concept map introduced by Novak (1990). This technique is much used and modified as mind maps and is focused not on words but on a visual representation, which is a universal transcending language. Reiss and Tunnicliffe have postulated that different aspects of the understanding of an individual of a particular phenomenon are revealed through using different methodologies. In this study we recognise that the drawings indicate only one aspect of the understanding of the participants of the internal anatomy of the human body. Using drawings has advantages over written responses because drawing is without the need for language, although interviews can enhance the level of participants understanding despite language limitations. There are, of course, always the provisos about the subject's technical and manipulative skills of drawing. Hence we chose an outline of the organism being considered and refer to this as a "supported" drawing. We see that a drawing framework (not unlike a table or other organizer to assist learners) helps focus the drawer on the concepts about which you are seeking their understanding.

The mental models drawn by the child in a drawing are representations of an object or an event. The image that the drawer is seeking to produce is formed by the process of mental modeling. Duit and Glynn (1996) state that the process of forming and constructing models is a mental activity of an individual or group. The models are personal and unique, their own knowledge of the phenomenon, animals, plant, human, or habitat seen, formed in these everyday environments, museums, nature parks, zoos or representations in books and in the electronic media observed. Their constructed models are in contrast to the conceptual knowledge learnt through formal education. Rapp (2007) refers to mental models as "memory structures that can be used to extrapolate beyond a surface understanding of presented information, to build deeper comprehension of a conceptual domain" (p. 43). However, there is a relationship between the mental model, habitats, organisms or human, looked at (the trigger or real object) and what the child comments upon (the expressed model – in words, models, or drawing). Brooks (2009) suggests that through visualization and expression through representation of ideas the essence that has been understood is early focused in consciousness. She suggests that a drawing is an externalization of a concept or idea. Thus drawings are products of the drawer's imagination and memory as expressed models (Reiss, Boulter, & Tunnicliffe, 2007; Gilbert & Boulter, 2000). As Brooks (2009) points out, drawings and visualisations can also help young children to shift from everyday or spontaneous concepts to more scientific concepts whilst their construction also enables children to come to terms with spatial visualisations, interpretations, orientations, and relations. She claims that when children are able to create visual representations of their ideas they are more able to work at a met cognitive level.

When subjects are asked about their understandings of anything, they respond by presenting "representations" of various genres, verbal, three-dimensional, described by gestures, symbols, or by drawings, depending on the topic, the interviewees, and the objectives of the interviewers. We must acknowledge the limitations that adults and children can achieve in the technical and manipulative skills of drawing as well as their personal subject knowledge. Whatever form they take, these representations can be considered as expressed models generated from the mental model, the personal cognitive representations held by individual subjects.

USING DRAWINGS ABOUT ORGANISMS TO IDENTIFY UNDERSTANDING

Research using the drawings of children to access their ideas have became more frequent. Children's drawings provide a 'window' into their thoughts and feelings, mainly because they reflect an image of his/her mind (Pridmore & Bendelow, 1995). However, using someone's drawing to elicit the person's understanding of a given phenomenon or process depends on how the researchers interpret the end product and the skill of the person making the drawing. It can be a more difficult task for a younger or inexperienced adult drawer because of their lack of experience in using drawing tools and lack of this type of representation in their society.

Some children find it easy to draw their ideas; others do not. While many children dislike answering questions, drawings can be completed quickly, easily and in an enjoyable way. However, Strommen (1995) found that children's drawings of forests yielded less information than interviews. Combining drawings with subsequent interviews (Tunnicliffe & Reiss, 2014) can yield richer information.

P. Katz (Ed.), Drawing for Science Education, 87–93.
© 2017 Sense Publishers. All rights reserved.

Symington et al. (1981) proposed three stages in the development of the ability of children to draw, starting with the youngest with "scribbling", the result being unintelligible to adults. Secondly a child enters a stage in which drawings shows very little resemblance to the object and the picture is used more as a visual representation of the child's ideas, a symbol. An older child shows "visual realism", where the object and the drawings are identifiable, bearing a closer resemblance. Earlier than the age of 6, children know there are some different organs. Hatano and Inagaki (1993, 1994) working with young Japanese children, suggest at this age the learners form biology as an autonomous domain but until about that age children talk about the organs as independent creatures that have needs and initiative. Through their observations and hearing comments by their community, children become aware of the existence of organs in their bodies (Cuthbert, 2000) and this they apply to other organisms. Tunnicliffe and Reiss (1999a) found that English children in their first week of school (5 yrs) already knew there were a few internal organs. Brain, bones, stomach, and heart were drawn from information gleaned in their everyday lives from family, friends and media.

Children see objects and organisms from their earliest years and can begin making representations, which become more recognizable as they acquire manipulative skills so they can represent them. Krampen (1991) suggests that one way of looking at and drawing conclusions about the drawings of children is to focus on one figure, such as the human. He reports that it was soon discovered that such drawings change from the tadpole man to a realistic presentation. The ability of young children to draw a human as a "Tadpole man" is a definite stage in achieving a realistic representation that can be recognised and identified by others (Figure 1).

Figure 1. "Me" drawn by Luc, age 4, a Welsh boy

However, the question to subjects of what is inside organisms is a relatively new area of study amongst biologists. Several researchers have recently studied children's understanding of the anatomy organs of invertebrates. Bartozeck et al. (2011) used drawings to elicit children's understanding of the external anatomy of insects. Rybsyka et al. (2014) used drawings and interviews to elicit the understanding held by 5, 7 and 10-year-old Polish children of the internal anatomy of snails. The most often drawn organ was a heart although all the children drew organs in the foot of the mollusk and not within the shell.

The understanding of internal organs of vertebrates, beginning with bones, was elicited by Tunnicliffe and Reiss (1999) who then studied understanding of organs in some vertebrate specimens from fish to humans (Reiss & Tunnicliffe, 2001a). These researchers showed real specimens of a fish (fresh, a herring), a bird, and preserved specimens, before they asked the children of ages 5, 8, 14, and undergraduates about internal organs of these vertebrates. Subsequently Reiss and Tunnicliffe et al. (2002) conducted an international comparison of the understanding using analysis of drawings of 15-year-olds from a variety of countries, some Western and some from Asia.

A South Africa regional study by Dempster and Stears (2014) found, as did other researchers, that children were able to identify and draw familiar organs but not relationships between them as a system and that such information was acquired out of school. Their results showed that most of the children draw bones as lines throughout the body. The ribs are the first bones they know apart from bones in legs and hands. The heart and the brain are the first organs they illustrate, and they know that we need to eat healthy food to become big and strong. Occasionally, Reiss and Tunnicliffe (2001), Reiss, Tunnicliffe, et al. (2002) found that children drew separate organs and labeled them as in a key it a map. On interview, these children, when shown an outline of a body, could indicate the appropriate location of the organs that they had drawn within the outline.

Some studies have looked at one particular organ or systems. Bahar et al. (2008), for example, looked at student teachers' understanding of the heart. Teixeira (2000) looked at Brazilian children's understanding of the digestive system. Tunnicliffe (2004) looked at pre-secondary children's understanding of the urinary system and its connection with the digestive system and found a greater understanding of the digestive system than of the excretory one. Ozsevgec (2007) asked different aged Turkish pupils to make two drawings each, one of the bones and one of the organs in humans. The children were interviewed about the function of the bones and organs. The children were also given a cracker and a glass of water and asked to describe the way the food goes from the mouth and onwards. A good summary of studies where drawings have been used to gather human body concepts is found in Patrick (2013).

There are a few studies we have found of the understanding of human anatomy that have been conducted other than in the USA and UK. Ozsevgec (2007) carried out work in the Black Sea region of Turkey from twelve- and fourteen-year-old pupils who drew and then wrote about the content of their drawing. Prokop et al. (2007) studied the understanding of Slovakian children aged 6–16 years of internal anatomy, finding that the size of the animal affected the understanding of skeletons but not organs systems. Reiss, Tunnicliffe et al. (2002) considered drawings of seven-year-olds and fifteen-year-olds from 11 different countries, namely, England, Denmark, Northern Ireland, Portugal, Iceland, Taiwan, Russia, Australia, Zimbabwe, Uganda and Ghana. Although the samples were small, the data show that although the fifteen-year-olds had more knowledge of organs, they had little understanding of the organs as part of a system. Furthermore, Óskarsdóttir (2013) explored what kind of ideas a class of Icelandic four-year-old children have about the location, structure and function of bones and certain organs. Manokore and Reiss (2003) compared the understanding as shown through the analysis of the content of drawings of both genders of seven-year-olds and fifteen- year-olds in Zimbabwe. Dempster and Stears (2014) study elicited the understanding of Zulu children in South Africa.

THE RESEARCH STUDY

The study we present was conducted at Sreepur village in Bangladesh. Sreepur is a purpose built village off the Mymensingh Road, north of Dhaka, in the Gazipur District. It aims to house destitute women and their children while the women learn a trade. They can then return with their children to their communities and earn a living. The women, and their children, were all volunteers and the study was conducted in their free time. Hence it is a self-selected sample. Thus it is an exploratory study.

In this study we collected two expressed models:

a. Drawings from mothers from rural villages in Bangladesh who had not received formal education and some of the children of the mothers who are receiving local state education.

b. The words the participants used to describe and explain their drawings. They were interviewed in their first language of Bangla. The interviewer then translated the responses into English and annotated their drawing as the participants indicated.

The majority of the women have received no schooling. A few of the mothers at the village have experienced limited years of primary education and occasionally some secondary education, but they did not volunteer (Tunnicliffe, 2013). The children attend a state primary school in the village whilst older children attend the local secondary schools. Extension education activities are provided and the "Talking Science" project is one such. It is a voluntary activity. The facilitator, one of the authors, a recent graduate in agricultural science from a Bangladesh university, delivers the project with frequent discussion with the other author who is not local. He has other duties in the village, such as teaching the participants how to grow simple crops so that they can grow vegetables when they return to their communities.

We were interested to find out the human biology understanding of these women and decided that using drawings would be the most appropriate way of doing this. We wanted to obtain drawings from school-aged children living in the village so we could compare the understandings. A total of 17 women volunteered to participate in this project. Five of the woman also had their sons with them and agreed that they too could share their knowledge of human anatomy through this drawing technique. Twenty-five children in all participated. Forty-two drawings were constructed and analysed.

Drawing was not a technique with which the participants were familiar. The participants were provided with an A4 sheet of paper with the outline of the human body in lateral views (Figure 2, a supported drawing). They were asked to fill in by drawing on the given sheet what they knew of the internal anatomy of a human body. One of the authors then interviewed each mother to clarify what organ or system they had indicated. As they named the organs, that was written by the interviewer in English. The children of some of the women who lived at the village were also asked if they would complete the task. Only five mothers and their own children participated.

S. D. TUNNICLIFFE & A. SARKER

An individual interview was conducted with each participant after they had finished inserting organs on their outline drawing (Figures 2–5). During this time the facilitator wrote the name of the organs on the paper in English. Each participant was asked, in Bangla, some questions when they had identified the parts. Five questions were asked. The first question asked was, "How did you know inside parts of human body?" All but one of the women drawers replied that they knew from hearing others talk. L. Begum said that she compared herself with what she knew about the inside of other animals, such as hen and duck. None of the mothers learnt about inside the parts of human body from any schooling. The interview answers were collated and summarized. Below is a photograph of the women working on their anatomy illustrations (Figure 6).

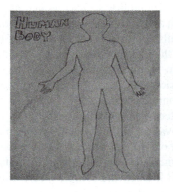
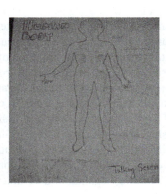

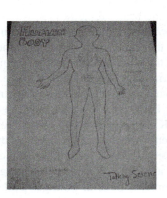

Figure 2. Outline of body   *Figure 3. Drawing by R. Soran, 25*   *Figure 4. Drawing by N. Begun, 37*   *Figure 5. Drawing by L. Begum, 19*

Figure 6. Photograph of Mother's drawing

ANALYSIS

There are a variety of methods of analysing the internal organs shown though drawings The most often used is that introduced by Reiss and Tunnicliffe (2001), (Tables 1 and 2). In this analysis technique letters stand for organs with a system as defined by Reiss and Tunnicliffe (2001). An organ that is a component of a system is indicated by a lower case letter, e.g., n = nervous system, s = skeletal system, r = respiratory system, u = urogenital system, d = digestive system. A capital letter indicates the presence of a complete system. Accordingly, if the skeletal system as a whole were indicated, it would be denoted by a capital S. The system and organ rubrics are defined in Table 1 (Reiss & Tunnicliffe, 2001). No complete organ systems were recorded here, hence only lower case letters are used and shown in the results tables.

In this work we identified the organs and counted them.. We then work out the percentage of occurrence in the drawings, although since the numbers are small, we show both numbers and percentages. We also identified the system to which the organ belonged. Furthermore, we identified the number of organs within a system that these participants identified

Table 1. Definition of systems (Reiss & Tunnicliffe, 2001)

Skeletal system (s)	Skull, spine, ribs and limbs
Respiratory system (r)	Two lungs, two bronchi, windpipe which joins to mouth and/or nose
Nervous system (n)	Brain, spinal cord, some peripheral nerve (e.g., optic nerve)
Digestive system (d)	Through tube from mouth to anus and indication of convolutions and/or compartmentalisation
Endocrine system (e)	Two endocrine organs (e.g., thyroid, adrenals, pituitary) other than pancreas (scored within digestive system) or gonads (scored within urinogenital system)
Urinogenital system (u)	Two kidneys, two ureters, bladder and urethra or two ovaries, two fallopian tubes and uterus or two testes, two epididymis and penis
Muscular system (m)	Two muscle groups (e.g., lower arm and thigh) with attached points of origin
Circulatory system (c)	Heart, arteries and veins into and/or leaving heart and, at least to some extent, all around the body

Table 2. Definition of level (Reiss & Tunnicliffe, 2001)

Level 1	No representation of internal structure
Level 2	One or more internal organs (e.g., bones and blood) placed at random
Level 3	One internal organ (e.g., brain or heart) in appropriate position
Level 4	Two or more internal organs (e.g., stomach and a bone unit such as the ribs) in appropriate positions but no extensive relationships indicated between them
Level 5	One organ system indicated (e.g., gut connecting head to anus)
Level 6	Two or three major organ systems indicated out of skeletal, respiratory, nervous, digestive, endocrine, urinogenital, muscular and circulatory
Level 7	Comprehensive representation with four or more organ systems indicated out of skeletal, respiratory, nervous digestive, endocrine, urinogenital, muscular and circulatory

RESULTS

Both authors analyzed the drawings separately by inspection for indication of organs and systems, using the rubric above. The number of organs indicated and their position on the drawing indicate the Level of knowledge (Table 3). However, the organs of the digestive system that were mentioned were stomach, liver, and occasionally esophagus and bowel. Bones shown were rib but no sternum or limb bones. Some drawings indicated the navel but as a surface feature, so we did not included this. Note that only six of the eight systems had representatives in this study. No representative of the muscular or endocrine system was drawn.

Table 3. Data from all mothers and all children. All at Level 4

Drawer	Average age	n	s	r	u	c	d
Mothers N = 17	28.8	17 (100%)	17 (100%)	3 (18 %)	6 (35%)	0	9 (53%)
All children n = 25	10	25 (100%)	25 (100%)	5 (20%)	13 (52%)	2 (8%)	15 (60%)
TOTAL 42		42 (100%)	42 (100%)	8 (19%)	19 (45%)	2 (5%)	24 (57%)

Of the organs of the digestive system, indicated as "d" in the table, which does not indicate the number of organs cited, bowels and intestines were most often mentioned. Women indicated a liver also in the correct position. Of the bones mentioned, they were drawn in units, such as arm bones, leg bones (upper limb, lower limb with one bone each), similar hand or feet bones. Chest bones, indicating sets of ribs but no sternum, all floating and as 2 sets, one on each side of the chest, with the correct number of ribs indicated. Of the nervous system it is the brain in the correct position. It is interesting that in all other data collected elsewhere the kidneys are drawn. Two mothers indicated them in the correct position but no ureters and bladder were shown. According to the Reiss and Tunnicliffe analysis two or more component organs of the digestive system (d) shown at the approximate correct position would be at level 4 and the other systems, nervous, urogenital, would be level 4 with only one organ belonging to that system indicated in the appropriate position.

Table 4 Summary of data of five mothers and their sons compared (numbers of occurrence not of organs in the system)

Drawer	Average age	n	s	r	u	c	d
Mothers N = 5	32.4 yrs	5	5	0	0	0	5
Their sons N =5	10 yrs	5	5	4	0	1	5

The sons had received some primary education where they apparently learnt about the lungs and one drew a heart. Inspection of the drawings showed that the digestive system had the most organs known. But although the esophagus, stomach, intestines and bowel were mentioned by many participants, a complete system (according to the Reiss and Tunnicliffe definition) was not indicated. Likewise no bone systems (skeleton) was drawn, but 3 bone sets, each counted as an organ, were mentioned. However, these were drawn in isolation in the appropriate location within the body. These "bone sets" were, chest bones, leg bones, and arm bones.

The participants, not the mothers with their sons, but the other twelve women, were asked 5 questions:

1. Do you know about the inside parts of the human body?
2. How did you draw the inside parts of the human body?
3. Did you look at a picture of the inside parts of the human body before?
4. Do you know how the inside parts of the body work?
5. Do you want to learn internal anatomy?

The facilitator wrote down their responses in English. The answers presented are those of twelve mothers who participated voluntarily but without their children. They all answered "No" to the first question. However, in response to the second question, ten mothers said that they just assumed the information but two said they had known it before. Every mother replied negatively to the third question whilst the responses to question 4 about their understanding of the workings of the body varied. Two of them replied that they worked it out by what they thought human internal anatomy would be by extrapolating from that of animals that they knew, presumably from cooking and looking after goats. Four mothers had heard from others of their family and six responded that they did not know All the mothers replied positively to the last question, which asked if they wanted to learn more about the human body. The children were not asked these questions.

The knowledge, accurate or otherwise, in a community is the most frequent source of information mentioned. However, two residents said they had worked out the anatomy by applying their practical knowledge learnt from cooking animals. Women who had come from one region in Northern Bangladesh, which people visit to purchase kidneys, had knowledge of kidneys. This fact had not been noticed in the literature of other countries

DISCUSSION

Examination of these data show sons knew more than their mothers. The sons had all attended school. These children had more knowledge of the inside of the human body than did their mothers. All children knew more than the women. The women did not learn about the inside parts of the human body from any school, but from their communities and their own observations. Indeed, it was noticed whilst they were filling in their body outline drawing that they felt bones in their own bodies to find out where bones are before they inserted representation on their drawings.

All of the mothers knew the same organs, bones, brain and bowels (organ of digestive system). Several mothers knew about kidneys and the correct location. The age of the mother is not a factor in the level of knowledge about the inside parts of the human body. Four out of five of the sons knew that we have lungs, and two out of five sons knew that we have kidneys. One out of five sons knew that we have a heart. The age of sons appears to be a factor about knowing about the inside of the human body, but these children have attended schools while their mothers had not.

The evidence from the data from the drawings reinforces the observations of Hipkins et al. (2000) that context is important when teaching systems and reinforces the suggestion, first voiced by Tunnicliffe and Reiss and reiterated by Manokore and Reiss (2002), that teaching organs of the human body should begin, as learners do spontaneously, with learning the organs and assembling them into a system, rather than by breaking up systems into component organs.

The work reported in this chapter indicates how much human anatomy is learnt in the everyday. Children of the same women who were receiving education knew a few more organs than their mothers but again no systems. The knowledge of kidneys amongst

THE UNDERSTANDING OF HUMAN ANATOMY ELICITED FROM DRAWINGS

a group of women hailing from the same northern rural area of the country is explained anecdotally through two different personal communications from local people that villagers in these areas are encouraged to sell a kidney; hence the kidney's location and name are known in the community. The study indicates the knowledge of human anatomy that is acquired from public understanding and own observations amongst members of communities where participants have received no formal education. But it highlights the increased understanding held by children of these participants who have received formal schooling. These data have implications for the various health programmes, which are developed in countries for people with little schooling. Information needs to consider the everyday understanding, and, when related to internal anatomy and physiology, start with what the participants have found out already.

REFERENCES

Bartoszeck, A., & Tunnicliffe, S. D. (2013). What do early years children think is inside a tree. *Journal of Emergent Science*, 21–25.

Bartoszeck, A. B., Rocha da Silva, B., & Tunnicliffe, S. D. (2011). Children's concept of insect by means of drawings in Brazil. *Journal of Emergent Science*, (2), 17–24.

Brooks. M. (2009). Drawing, visualization and young children's explorations of big idea. *International Journal of Science Education, 31*(3), 319–343.

Buckley, B., Boulter, C., & Gilbert, J. (1997). Towards a typology of models for science education. In J. Gilbert (Ed.), *Exploring models and modeling in science and technology education* (pp. 90–105). Reading: University of Reading New Bulmershe Papers.

Carey, S. (1985). *Conceptual change in childhood.* Cambridge, MA: MIT Press/Bradford.

Carivita, S., & Falchetti, E. (2005). Are bones alive? *Journal of Biological Education, 39*(4), 163–170.

Cuthbert, J. (2000). Do children have a holistic view of their internal body maps? *School Science Review, 82*(299), 25–32.

Duit, R., & Glynn, S. (1996). Mental modelling. In G. Welford, J Osbourne, & P Scott (Eds.), *Research in science education in Europe. Current issues and themes.* London: Routledge Falmer.

Dempster, E., & Stears, M. (2014). An analysis of children's drawings of what they think is inside their bodies: A South African regional study. *Journal of Biological Education, 48*(2), 71–79.

Gilbert, J. K., & Boulter, C. (2000). *Developing models in science education.* Dordrecht: Kluwer.

Guichard, J. (1995). Designing tools to develop the conception of learners. *International Journal of Science Education, 17*, 243–253.

Haney, W., Russel, M., & Babell, D. (2004). Drawing on education: Using drawings to document schooling and support change. *Harvard Educational Review, 74*(3), 241–271.

Hatano, G., & Inagaki, K. (1994). Young children's naive theory of biology. *Cognition, 50*, 171–188.

Hipkins, R., Bull, A., & Joyce, C. (2008). The intrepaly of contex and concepts in primary chidlren's systems thinking. *Journal of Biological Education, 42*(2), 73–77.

Inagaki, K., & Hatano, G. (1993). Young children's understanding of the mind-body distinction. *Child Development, 64*, 1534–1549.

Krampen, M. (1991). *Children's drawings: Iconic coding of the environment.* New York, NY: Plenum Press.

Lewis, J., Leach, J., & Wood-Robinson, C. (2000). All in the genes? Young people's understanding of the nature of genes. *Journal of Biological Education, 34*(2), 74–79. doi:10.1080/00219266.2000.9655689

Luquet, G.-H. (2001[1927]). *Children's drawings (Le Dessin Enfantin)* (A. Costall, Trans.). London: Free Association Books.

Manookere, V., & Reiss, M. J. (2003). Pupil's drawings of what is inside themselves: A case study in Zimbabwe. *Zimbabwe Journal of Educational Research, 915*(2), 29–43.

Mintzes, J. J. (1984). Naïve theories in biology: Children's concepts of the human body. *School Science and Mathematics, 84*(7), 548–555.

Novak, J. (1990). Concept mapping: A useful tool for science education. *Journal of Research in Science Teaching, 27*(10), 937–949. doi:10.1002/tea.3660271003

Osborne, J., Wadsworth, P. O., & Black, P. (1992). *Processes of life: Primary space project research report.* Liverpool: Liverpool University Press.

Óskarsdóttir, G. (2013). "The brain is so we can listen and see the colour of the dress". The ideas four year old children have about the inside of their bodies. *BARN – Forskning om barn og barndom i Norden,* (2).

Patrick, P. (2013). Social interactions and familial relationships preservice science teachers describe during interviews about their drawings of the Endocrine and Gastrointestinal systems. *International Journal of Environmental & Science Education* (2014), *9*, 159–175.

Pridmore, P., & Bendelow, G. (1995). Images of health: Exploring beliefs of children using the `draw-and-write' technique. *Health Education Journal, 54*, 473–488.

Prokop, P., Prokop, M., Tunnicliffe, S. D., & Diran, C. (2007). Children's ideas of animals' internal structures. *Journal of Biological Education, 41*(2), 62–67. ISSN: 0021-9266.

Rapp, D. N. (2007). Mental models: Theoretical issues for visualization in science education. In J. K. Gilbert (Ed.), *Visualization in science education* (pp. 43–60). Dordrecht: Springer.

Reiss, M. J., & Tunnicliffe, S. D. (2001). Students' understandings of human organs and organ systems. *Research in Science Education, 31*, 383–399.

Rybyska, E., Tunnicliffe, S. D., & Sajkowska, Z. A. (2014). What's inside a tree? The ideas of five year-old children. *Journal of Emergent Science, 8*, 7–15.

Rybyska, E., Tunnicliffe, S. D., & Sajkowska, Z. A. (2014). Young children's ideas about snail internal anatomy. *Journal of Baltic Science Education, 13*(6), 832–838.

Symington, D., Boundy, K., Radford, T., & Walton, J. (1981).'Childrens' drawings of natural phenomena. *Research in Science Education,* (11), 44–51.

Tunnicliffe, S. D. (1999). What's inside a tree. *Primary Science and Technology Today 11*, 3–5.

Tunnicliffe, S. D. (2004). Where does the drink go? *Primary Science Review*, 8–10.

Tunnicliffe, S. D. (2013). *Talking and doing science in the early years.* Abingdon, NY: Routledge.

Tunnicliffe, S. D. (2013, September). *Talking science- a project in rural Bangladesh to increase self esteem of women though heightening their awareness of their knowledge of science and technology from their everyday lives and talking to their children.* Talk give at ICASE world conference Kuching, Malaysia. (Book of Abstracts.)

Tunnicliffe, S. D., & Reiss, M. J. (1999). Learning about skeletons and other organ systems of vertebrate animals. *Science Education International, 10*(1), 29–33.

Tunnicliffe, S. D., & Reiss, M. J. (1999a). Students' understandings about animal skeletons. *International Journal of Science Education, 21*, 1187–1200.

Usak, M. (2008). Science student teachers' ideas of the heart. *Journal of Baltic Science Education, 7*(2).

Sue Dale Tunnicliffe
Institute of Education
University of London, UK

Angshuman Sarker
Teacher at Shishu Polli Plus School, (Sreepur Village)
Tengra, Gazipur, Bangladesh

SECTION TWO

DRAWINGS IN A SERIES TO EXAMINE CHANGE

9. DRAWING EXPERIENCES IN MARINE CONSERVATION

The UK National Marine Aquarium in Plymouth has the usual large display tanks of animals but also has an education programme that explores the local and tropical marine environment and conservation issues through creative art and drawing. The National Marine Aquarium also offers a Conservation through Tourism Award. Assessing the learning that has occurred in an informal science environment, such as an aquarium or a hotel, can be difficult without resorting to complex and intrusive questioning. By asking children and adults to illustrate their knowledge of the marine environment before and after a guided visit to the aquarium or before and after training, and by developing a robust assessment strategy, for paired before and after drawings, it was possible to begin to assess the degree of learning that had occurred as result of the education programmes provided by the aquarium.

INTRODUCTION

The National Marine Aquarium (aquarium), Plymouth, UK, opened in 1998 and remains Britain's largest aquarium. It has the charitable aims of: Education, conservation and research (National Marine Aquarium [NMA], 2011). The aquarium mission statement of "Driving marine conservation through engagement" (NMA, 2011) is achieved through education to engage visitors with marine conservation. The aquarium is an organisation committed to conserving the marine environment and encouraging others to do the same by promoting a sympathetic understanding of the sea, both nationally and internationally. The overall goal is to foster a connection with the marine environment that results in pro-conservation behaviour changes, on any scale. The aquarium strives to use the exhibits on display to promote a more sympathetic and in-depth understanding of the sea. Additionally a comprehensive schools programme is designed to complement the UK National Curriculum. In order to determine the effectiveness of the schools programme, an assessment of the children's visit was undertaken using pre- and post-visit drawings (Cainey et al., 2012).

Since 2012, the aquarium has developed a Conservation through Tourism Award. This award scheme encompasses education and conservation elements that encourage organisational transformation in the hotel industry while supporting tourism activities on Mauritius, an island in the Indian Ocean. The island is part of the Mascarene Islands (Mauritius, Reunion and Rodrigues) and surrounded by fringing coral reefs, making it a popular tourist destination. The Conservation through Tourism Award is achieved through a three part programme: a bronze training programme for hotel staff, including guidance on engaging visitors in marine conservation, a silver training programme with actions for targeting impacts for the long term economic sustainability of the hotel, and a gold level to engage the local community and businesses. The bronze training programme for hotel staff was assessed using the pre- and post-training drawings (Jensen, 2012).

The global marine environment is critically threatened by pollution, over-fishing, tourism and climate change (Boyle, Bolze, & Koontz, 1995; Wetzel & O'Brien, 1995; Graham et al., 2007; Hoegh-Guldberg & Bruno, 2010; Cinner et al., 2012), all of which can be directly or indirectly attributed to man's impact on the marine environment.

Pollution, such as run-off containing high levels of nutrients (fertilizers), encouraging blooms of marcoalgae and change the chemistry of the affected area (Halpern et al., 2008). Over-fishing dominates in regions of the ocean neighbouring high populations (e.g. UK, Halpern et al., 2008) and tourism impacts especially on coral reefs with an increase in boat traffic and the presence of divers, who may directly damage the reef (Halpern et al., 2008).

Climate change caused by increasing levels of anthropogenically derived gases, such as carbon dioxide and methane, places stress on oceans and in particular sensitive ecosystems such as coral reefs (Hoegh-Guldberg & Bruno, 2010). The stresses arise from three sources: increased levels of dissolved carbon dioxide in the ocean results in acidification, which hampers the ability of marine organisms to assemble calcium carbonate skeletons and shells (Doney et al., 2009); increases in sea surface temperatures drive conditions away from the optimum for biological processes and result in coral bleaching; and increased sea levels, which changes the exposure to storms and light levels (Hoegh-Guldberg & Bruno, 2010).

Additionally marine biota such as micro- and macro-algae have a role in regulating climate through the production of gases that result in cloud condensation nuclei for clouds and damage to the marine ecosystem may limit this natural regulation process (Cainey, 2007).

DEVELOPING AN ASSESSMENT PROGRAMME FOR INFORMAL LEARNING AT THE AQUARIUM

In 2009, the aquarium developed a programme to assess the learning during school visits based on pre- and post-visit drawings (Cainey et al., 2012). The aquarium has a systematic evaluation process for all guided school visits, which includes the opportunity for children to draw or write about their experiences post-visit. Prior to Cainey et al. (2012) the role of drawings in assessment at the aquarium was based on research by Bowker (2007) that demonstrated drawings were a useful tool for assessing learning experiences in informal education environments. However, the aquarium had only collected drawings post-visit and therefore had not been able to quantitatively assess the degree of learning resulting from children visiting on a guided tour.

The aquarium hosts visits from over 30,000 children a year and it is not possible to assess the experiences of all children who participate in a school visit, but by using drawings as part of all visits, combined with questionnaires, and paired pre- and post-visit drawings for a selection of school visits, it is possible to make assessments about the learning resulting from the aquarium's education programme.

The aquarium, through its schools programme, uses the exhibits to demonstrate marine environments and put marine issues in context of the species and environments they affect. The programme ultimately aims to use the enjoyment and inspiration of the setting to deliver key information that may lead to a change in attitudes and values towards the marine environment and consequently a change in behaviour. Key to achieving these aims is improving the initial knowledge and understanding of the marine environment, developing skills in communication and observation and engaging audiences to promote enjoyment and foster learning about the local and wider marine environment (Ballantyne & Packer, 2005; Ballantyne, Packer, Hughes, & Dierking, 2007; NMA, 2011).

Aquaria have very specific learning outcomes for visitors that need to be achieved, as does the NMA, defined in their Global Learning Outcomes (GLOs):

1. Knowledge and understanding;
2. Skills;
3. Attitudes and values;
4. Enjoyment, inspiration and creativity;
5. Activity, behaviour and progression.

These GLOs overlap with the aquarium mission statement of "Driving marine conservation through engagement" (NMA, 2011). The aquarium strives to use the exhibits on display to promote a more sympathetic and in depth understanding of the sea through the charitable aims.

The challenge is to ensure that these outcomes are achieved through a delivery approach that must accommodate the widest range of learning styles (Hein, 1999). The aquarium also facilitates the ability of children to freely discuss their experiences with their peers, which results in co-construction of learning centred around the environment in which that learning occurs (Anderson, Lucas, & Ginns, 2003; Driver, Asoko, Leach, Mortimer, & Scott, 1994; Falk & Dierking, 2000; Kola-Olusanya, 2005; Rojas-Drummond, Mazon, Fernandez, & Wegerif, 2006, Papandreou, 2014).

The assessment programme using pre and post-visit drawings developed by Cainey et al. (2012) sought only to address the degree of learning that resulted from guided educational visits of the aquarium and so focused on GLOs 1, 2 and 4, which were selected on the basis that they could be monitored using drawings.

DRAWINGS AS AN ASSESSMENT TOOL

One of the barriers to utilisation of learning science outside the classroom is the difficulty of assessing the degree of learning that occurs in the informal or non-formal environment (Rennie & McClaffery, 1995). Assessment of learning is a significant facet of education. Informal learning, with its child-led unstructured approach, does not lend itself to assessment without disrupting the perceived benefits that arise from such learning (Dowling & Brown, 2000; Wellington, 1990). Formal tests and questions do not necessarily reveal the learning that occurs in an informal setting (Birney, 1995), since what was learnt from a visit is highly personal and to accurately assess this learning has been described as being tantamount to getting inside a learner's head (Rennie, Feher, Dierking, & Falk, 2003). Various strategies have been developed and continue to be developed (Bowker, 2007; Brody, 2005; Falk & Adelman, 2003; Rennie et al., 2003, Haring & Reesa, 2014) to allow learning in informal environments to be gauged.

The use of children's drawings to assess the psychological state of a child is well studied (Thomas & Jolley, 1998) and drawings have been used to assess children's perceptions of teachers and scientists (e.g. Newton & Newton, 1992; Kesicioglu & Deniz, 2014), however the use of children's drawings to assess learning is less well studied.

Drawings were selected as the tool to assess learning at the aquarium as they allow children the freedom to express their knowledge without limitations of language (Alerby, 2000) and without the imposition of question-defined boundaries.

Children recognise the ability of drawings to represent their thoughts and feelings and can be in control of the drawing process and its outcomes (Cox, 2005). Children's drawings allow them to actively define reality rather than reproducing a given reality (Brooks, 2009; Cox, 2005). Butler, Gross and Hayne (1995) found that, in children over the age of 4, drawing enhanced the verbal recall of an event, both immediately after the event and one month later. Drawing not only allows a child to record their thoughts, but also enhances the memory and learning process (Anning & Ring, 2004; Brooks, 2009; Butler et al., 1995). Piaget and Inhelder (1971) suggest that images allow a child to gain knowledge by conceptualising an object or information and Brooks (2009) suggests that drawings offer a link between a child's thoughts and speech to build meaning. Haring and Reesa (2014) found that assessing children's drawings in three broad categories (content, interpretation and development) provided great insights in the learning and development of children.

Therefore drawings are a particularly useful tool to assess learning, as shown by Bowker (2007) when drawings were used to assess the degree of learning following a visit to the Humid Tropic Biome at The Eden Project, Cornwall. Further examples include Rennie and Jarvis (2006) who studied primary-aged (7–11 years old) children's use of drawings to assess understanding of technology and Alerby (2000) who used drawings to assess children's views about the environment. Tranter and Malone (2004) compared children's drawings of the existing playground to drawings of an improved playground to assess their responses to their immediate school environment. Reiss and Tunnicliffe (2001) used students (4 years to undergraduate age) drawings to assess the degree of knowledge students had about the human body. The content of the drawings was scored based on defined levels and defined descriptors of the organs and systems.

This approach has been used to assess other biological phenomena (Prokop & Fancovicova, 2006; Reiss & Tunnicliffe, 1999). Prokop and Fancovicova (2006) suggest that some children may have difficulties expressing their knowledge through drawings or be limited by their drawing skills. This expresses the distinction proposed by Luquet (2001) between visual realism and intellectual realism. In many of these studies the drawing obtained is believed to represent knowledge. Ehrlen (2009) used drawings and interviews to assess knowledge of children (aged 6–9), suggesting that this combined method of assessment gave a better indication of a child's concept of the Earth, however during the interviews, many children modified their drawings in response to the questions asked (Ehrlen, 2009). To minimise the complications of assessing knowledge from a drawing that may have been produced using different conceptual frameworks (Ehrlen, 2009; Luquet, 2001), this study assessed and compared the pre-visit drawing with the post-visit drawing from the same child and assuming that the conceptual framework and level of skill of the drawer remained unchanged between the two drawings, then the changes in the content of the drawings relate to the learning that had occurred between the pre-visit drawing and the post-visit drawing, as a result of the visit to the aquarium. O'Byrne (2009) used pre- and post-teaching drawings to assess children's (aged 6–8) learning about wolves and these paired drawings gave an insight into children's thinking, with the post-teaching drawings showing a significant refinement in concept.

Assessment of Drawings – Aquarium

During the week 16–20 March 2009, primary school groups between the ages of 4–11 that had booked a guided session with the aquarium were asked if they would allow each child to create drawings on two subjects, prior to the visit to the aquarium:

- The underwater life off the Devon coast (approximating the Atlantic Reef tank) and;
- The underwater life on a Coral Reef (approximating the Coral Reef tank).

Children were given 15–20 minutes for each drawing and were encouraged to use colour. These pre-visit drawings were created at school and there was to be no input from teachers on the content of the drawings (e.g. indications of what kind of things to include in drawing) to allow an independent assessment of each child's prior learning. However, children were asked to "Draw a picture of what you would expect to find in the sea off the Devon coast and "Draw a picture of what you would expect to find in a coral reef". In all cases, the children were asked to draw the local (Atlantic Reef) scene first. After the visit to the aquarium, the same process was repeated with children again providing two unassisted drawings (Atlantic Reef and Coral Reef), with 15–20 minutes for each drawing. Children were asked to name their drawings so that the pre- and post-visit drawings could be paired for assessment.

Two of the school groups (Schools 1 and 3) were local to the aquarium and 85–90 % of the children had previously visited out of school time. School 4 was local to Devon (55 miles from the aquarium) and 70% of the children had previously visited the aquarium independently. All of the schools had predominately white British populations. At school 1 the number of children receiving free school meals was higher than average, while at School 4 this figure was below average. All of the schools had been assessed as good or outstanding by the national inspectorate (Ofsted).

Table 1. Drawings collected as part of assessment

School	Age – years old	Atlantic reef		Coral reef		Focus	Previous visit to aquarium
		Pre-visit	Post-visit	Pre-visit	Post-visit		
School 1	5–6	33	30	29	30	General	90%
School 3	4–5	29	28	29	29	General	85%
School 4	9–10	30	32	31	32	Pollution	70%

In addition, the school groups were observed during their visit to the aquarium to determine their levels of engagement and also to record the information provided to the children by the aquarium team member. School 1 (5–6 years) were observed while they completed their post-visit drawings and the only discussion between children and adults was to identify isolated features in the drawings and to determine prior knowledge (see Figures 1a and 1b showing adult annotations).

Drawings

Cainey et al. (2012) collected over 360 drawings from the three school groups, with the ages of the participating children ranging from 4–11 years old. The pre-visit drawing from a given child was paired with the post-visit drawing from the same child. Only 276 drawings could be paired, due to the non-return of some of the drawings. This allowed a direct assessment of informal learning as a result of the visit to the aquarium, using 138 pairs of before and after drawings: 72 pairs for the Atlantic Reef and 66 pairs for the Coral Reef tank. These drawings were further split into Key Stage 1 (KS1, including Foundation Stage) encompassing ages 4–6 and Key Stage 2 (KS2) encompassing ages 7–11, with a total of 94 paired drawings from KS1 and 44 paired drawings from KS2. The post-visit drawings of Schools 1 and 4 were completed at the aquarium immediately following the guided visit. School 3 completed their post-visit drawings a few days after the visit and this had no impact on recall (Haney et al., 2004; Cainey et al., 2012).

Analysis

The aquarium had previously incorporated drawings into its post-visit assessment programme prompted by the work of Bowker (2007) and extended through implementation of the Inspiring Learning for All Framework (ILfA). The assessments of drawings contribute to the IlfA framework for the development of exhibits and learning programmes that better engage all visitors (Taylor, 2009). For consistency with this existing assessment, the analysis of the current drawings was also based on the same method detailed in Bowker (2007). Each of the drawings were scored for three categories: breadth, extent and detail (analogous to "depth" in Bowker (2007). The sum of the scores in each of the categories gave the mastery for each drawing. Bowker (2007) expressly avoided reducing the complexity of children's drawings to a single number. However, the NMA wanted a quantitative technique to assess their schools programme and so the overall mastery score was used to give a quantitative assessment of learning. The mastery score for the pre-visit drawing was subtracted from the mastery score for the post-visit drawing to give a quantitative assessment of the change in mastery, representing the degree of learning resulting from the visit to the aquarium.

a. Breadth was defined as the number of themes included in a drawing and in this research the five themes assessed under "breadth" were:
   Fish (excluding Rainbow Fish)
   Non-fish marine animals
   Involvement of man (excluding mermaids)
   Habitat
   Relationship to surrounding environments (air, land etc.)
   The incorporation of each of the features above scored 1 mark out of a possible total of 5.
b. Extent was defined as the number of different marine animals represented in each drawing, to a maximum score of 5. Where an animal was drawn
   more than once, it was counted only once. On the few occasions that animals were shown in the incorrect environment (e.g. Clown Fish on the
   Atlantic Reef), this was given a negative score.
c. Detail was defined as the level of accuracy of the drawing and used a scale of 1 to 5. The description of the scale is shown below (Table 2) after the drawing samples.
   Specific aspects looked for in the drawings included:
   Appropriate use of colour
   Sharks with 5 gill slits
   Octopuses with 8 tentacles
   Starfish with 5 or more obvious arms
   Crabs with pincers
   Fish shown with distinct fins/tails
   Use of specific features (e.g. teeth on sharks, textures, patterns)
   Turtle shell detailing scutes

Examples of Children's Drawings

The Atlantic Reef drawings of child HC13 (KS1, aged 5–6 years old) showed significant changes between the pre- and post-visit (Figures 1a and 1b):
   The pre-visit drawing is cartoon-like in nature and vibrantly colourful (pinks and yellow). In keeping with many children from this school, a mermaid was shown, while there was a complete absence of fish. The inclusion of an imaginary marine creature in the pre-visit drawing is similar to the representation of wolves in pre-teaching drawings and indicates the sources of prior learning (O'Byrne, 2009).

 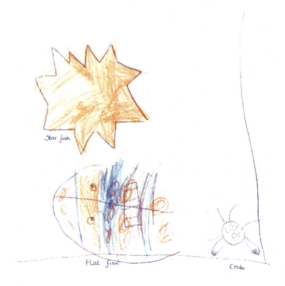

Figure 1a. Pre-visit drawing (HC13)   *Figure 1b. Post-visit drawing (HC13)*

In the post-visit drawing, the mermaid was absent and the palette used was more appropriate to the local marine environment (brown/beige). The level of detail shown in the drawing of the flatfish and the crab indicated significant recall of observations. Both the starfish and the flatfish were targeted in the tour, with children being asked to (a) count the number of arms a starfish has and (b) describe what a flatfish looks like in respect to colour and pattern.

In the post visit drawing the crab has pincers and the starfish has 10 obvious arms, close to the number of arms (12) that could be observed on the Sun Star in the rockpool area. The flatfish is shown in the correct "pancake" shape, with the speckled camouflage pattern also detailed. There are possibly gill slits shown, which are not appropriate for a flatfish, but for a ray. It would be hard for a young child to distinguish between the underside of a ray and a flatfish (both fish did move through the tank, allowing viewing of their undersides). However the drawing of gill slits, even if associated with the incorrect animal, indicates a high level of observation while viewing the Atlantic Reef tank.

The pre-visit drawing had a mastery score of 0, while the post-visit drawing had a mastery score of 10 resulting in a change between pre- and post-visit mastery scores of 10 and this was the most significant change in all assessed paired drawings.

Occasionally the presentation of the animals and their tank engages children more than the contents of the tank itself. The Atlantic Reef drawing of a 5–6 year old (HC-15) shows the exact detail of the rocks and vegetation in the Atlantic Reef tank (Figures 2a and 2b):

The pre-visit drawing shows fish with heads and bodies and they are coloured bright orange (perhaps related to "Nemo"). A seahorse is shown out of context, however after the visit the fish are drawn more accurately and the palate used is more appropriate. The creatures are shown in less detail when compared to the detail of the individual rocks of the tank habitat, still the pre-visit drawing had a score of 5, while the post-visit drawing had a score of 11 demonstrating an improvement following the visit to the aquarium.

The pre-visit drawing of the Atlantic Reef from child F-17 (9–10 years old) shows the transition between the atmospheric and marine environment (Figures 3a and 3b). The presence of rubbish is not unsurprising since this group of children were studying the impact of pollution on the marine environment. Only a single fish and a crab is shown, but man (an anchor) and ducks are also incorporated, suggesting a good understanding of the links between the non-marine and marine world.

The post-visit drawing incorporated much more detail, with rays, a variety of fish (unidentified), a crab, now with eight legs, a shrimp, a starfish and an octopus (with eight tentacles) are shown. Nets and human legs are included keeping the drawing on theme with the work the group were doing, but rubbish is now absent. The comparison between the two drawings shows an increase in mastery score of 8, with detail and extent showing the greatest improvements.

This child used little colour in both drawings, apart from the rubbish. Lack of colour may indicate reticence in drawing or it may just indicate a lack of time, with the child unable to add colour within the timescale set for the drawing task.

The following child, F-1 (aged 9–10) provided a pre-visit drawing of a Coral Reef that was nearly devoid of colour, but the post-visit drawing is saturated with colour (Figures 4a and 4b.

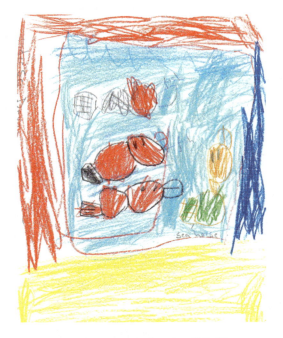

Figure 2a. Pre-visit drawing (HC-15)

Figure 2b. Post-visit drawing (HC-15)

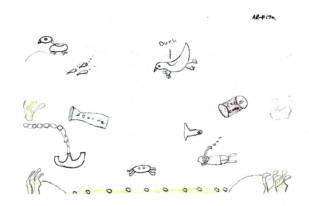

Figure 3a. Pre-visit drawing (F-17)

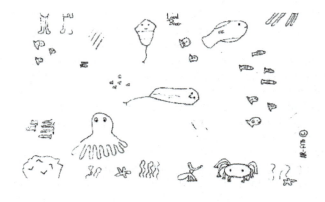

Figure 3b. Post-visit drawing (F-17)

Figure 4a. Pre-visit drawing (F-1)

Figure 4b. Post-visit drawing (F-1)

In addition to the post-visit drawing being more colourful, there is greater detail shown in the animals drawn: The sharks are drawn with black tips to their fins and tail (black tip reef shark) and the turtle shows scutes on its shell. The detail of the sharks is interesting since this group of children also spent time visiting a tank of larger sharks (Sand tigers), which are uniformly grey. While the pre-visit drawing shows either vegetation or coral, the post-visit drawing clearly shows both vegetation (green) and coral, with some attempt to show the detail of the coral structure. Many more creatures are shown, including angel fish (drawn with a more correct shape that the "Nemo" type fish of the pre-visit drawing) and crabs (with 8 limbs, including pincers). The post-visit drawing showed a mastery of 12, an increase of 5, resulting from improvements in detail and extent.

DISCUSSION

Cainey et al. (2012) performed statistical assessment on the scores and observed nearly a doubling in mastery scores when comparing pre-visit to post-visit drawings, regardless of the age of the children. Older children demonstrated increased prior knowledge, but still achieved significant mastery scores following a trip to the aquarium. The "detail" aspect should the greatest improvement, 4 times better, between pre- and post-visit drawings suggesting learning through observation, reinforced by children seeking further information by questioning the aquarium team. The increased extent score indicates an increased understanding of the variety of marine life. Both detail and extent are targeted by the "challenges" children are set during their visit, such as to find out how many arms a starfish has or describe what a flatfish looks like.

It is also critical to understand sources of prior knowledge as this influences the content of drawings (Braund & Reiss, 2006, Cainey et al., 2012). The pre-visit drawings, particularly of School 1, demonstrated the influence of three sources of prior knowledge. Even though the majority of children from both Schools 1 and 3, 5–6 and 4–5 years old respectively, had visited the aquarium outside of school, their drawings showed the influence of two films, "Finding Nemo" and "The Little Mermaid". "The Little Mermaid" was re-released in December 2008 and many of the children had recently seen this film. While Nemo was not specifically drawn, there were many drawings that showed orange fish and the tanks containing Clown Fish excited the children. Many rainbow fish also appeared in the pre-visit drawings and this was related to the picture storybook "The Rainbow Fish", which had been recently read to the children.

Older children (9–10 years old) showed over double the prior knowledge (Mastery score of per-visit drawing) than younger children (4–6 years old) and Cainey et al. (2012) attributed this to age related drawing skills (Alerby 2000; Barraza, 1999; Kola-Olusanya, 2005). It is therefore important to know the age of the artist when assessing drawings. The KS1 category comprised of a class of Year 1 children (5–6 years old) and a class of EYFS children (4–6 years). The Mastery scores for the EYFS children were lower than the Mastery scores for the Year 1 children. This might be expected as a result of both the lower expected drawing skills and prior knowledge of the younger children (Barraza, 1999; Prokop & Fancovicova, 2006). Additionally the Year 1 children showed a greater improvement in Breadth for the Coral Reef drawing than was demonstrated by the EYFS children. The greater increase in Detail may be attributed to the difference in drawing skills between the two ages of children (Barraza, 1999; Prokop & Fancovicova, 2006), while the increased Breadth shown by the older children may be related to the higher level of prior knowledge of a marine environments.

Additionally Cainey et al. (2012) assessed the robustness of the scoring system for the assessment of the drawings using the post-visit drawings for the Atlantic Reef of School 4. Using the criteria detailed above, the drawings were assessed independently by two different pairs of people. There were no significant differences in scoring (P>0.05) for breadth, extent, detail and mastery suggesting that the system is robust and independent of the assessor.

By assessing pre- and post-visit drawings it was possible to understand the impact that the visit to the aquarium had had on children. A key learning outcome (GLO 1) for the aquarium is the broadening the knowledge of the marine environment and associated species (Taylor, 2009) and the increased extent score clearly demonstrates that children are increasing their knowledge of species of marine animals. The increased breadth score demonstrates a greater understanding of the marine environment, although few children showed an awareness of their relationship to the marine environment since their post-visit drawings did not show people or land.

The aquarium hopes to target awareness and behaviour (conservation) through GLOs 3 and 4. School 4 was undertaking a specific visit programme on pollution and many of the pre-visit drawings showed rubbish and nets, however the post-visit drawings did not, accurately representing what the children saw during their visit. However the visit did not allow an opportunity to observe the relationship between man and the marine environment and while the relationship and conservation issues are discussed during the visit it is clear the aquarium will need to do further work to better address GLOs 3 and 4.

Table 2. Changes in mastery score resulting from informal learning at the aquarium

School	*Atlantic reef mastery scores*			*Coral reef mastery scores*		
	Pre-visit	*Post-visit*	*Average change*	*Pre-visit*	*Post-visit*	*Average change*
School 1 (HC) KS1	3.2	7.0	+3.8	2.2	5.9	+3.7
School 3 (KB) KS1	3.4	6.5	+3.1	4.5	7.4	+2.9
School 4 (F) KS2	6.1	10.2	+4.1	7.1	10.9	+3.8

Another key learning outcome desired by the aquarium is to develop skills (GLO 2) such as observation and communication (Taylor, 2009) and it is clear from the enhancement in detail scores that the educational visits are achieving this outcome well.

Additionally the comparison and assessment of pre- and post-visit drawings allowed an insight into the learning process that occurred as a result of the visit and the improvement in the representation of the marine environment, in particular the animals in that environment, suggest that the learning was a step-wise process, which was proximal to the prior knowledge held by students (O'Byrne, 2009) and enhanced by the informal nature of the setting which promoted shared talk to allow co-constructed knowledge (O'Byrne, 2009; Papandreou, 2014).

It was not possible to assess changes in attitude (GLO 3) to the marine environment with regards to marine conservation from the drawings, but this learning outcome is targeted in the aquarium post-visit evaluation form.

THE REEFS IN MAURITIUS

The original approach of paired pre- and post-visit drawings detailed in Cainey et al. (2012) has been extended to other informal education contexts, such as a longleaf pine centre (Dentzau & Gallard Martínez, 2014) and summer camps in Greece (Flowers et al., 2014). Additionally the approach of using pre- and post-learning drawings (Cainey et al., 2012) has been extended to the formal education environment and is used in classrooms in Singapore (Ow & Bielaczyc, 2013). The aquarium has also used this assessment method as part of a training programme for tourism providers on Mauritius.

Mauritius is an island in the Indian Ocean, forming part of the Mascarene Islands (Mauritius, Reunion and Rodrigues). It is almost completely encircled by fringing coral reefs, making it rich in marine life. As a result of its natural beauty, this tropical destination attracts thousands of tourists each year.

However, the local coral reefs are subject to some domestic and agricultural pollution, with sediments and fertilizers causing eutrophication (Ahamada et al., 2002). The local population lives by subsistence fishing, which has depleted fish stocks, although the fisheries are now managed to minimise impact (Ahamada et al., 2002). The fishery environment contributes significantly to the success of tourism in Mauritius and therefore biodiversity conservation must be undertaken (Sobhee, 2006).

The reefs of Mauritius escaped the coral bleaching, which occurred in the Indian Ocean in 1998 (Ahamada et al., 2002), as it is located further south, however the widespread publicity of the event resulted in a reduction in tourism income of US$3.0 M (<1%, Westmacott et al., 2000). While in some areas the coral and biodiversity remain largely unaffected by tourism activities (Graham et al., 2007), there is strong evidence that some practices, such as removing seagrass bed (for a more pleasant swimming experience) and the development of a water skiing lane have major impacts on the environment in specific localised areas (Daby, 2003; Sobhee, 2006; Graham et al., 2007).

Approximately 28% of the Mauritian national economy is based on travel and tourism, with just under 1 million visitors in 2013 (Statistics Mauritius, 2013a), with a growth of 3% over the preceding year, with the reefs a specific attraction, with 45% of visitors being divers. With a resident population of 1.26 million (Statistics Mauritius, 2013b), tourism represents a significant proportion of the economy, with the greatest increases in the southern hemisphere summer (December), with tourists representing 9% of the population at this peak time (Westmacott et al., 2000; Statistics Mauritius, 2013a).

The health of the coral reefs around Mauritius has a significant impact on the local economy, with tourism representing close to US$350 M (7% of GDP, Statistics Mauritius, 2013b) and additionally 94% of hotels on the island are located in beachside locations, indicating that the sea and coastal views are highly valued by holidaymakers coming to the island (Prayag et al., 2010). The strong link between economic and conservation needs motivated the development of the conservation engagement programme: the National Marine Aquarium's (NMA) Conservation through Tourism Award.

This is a new business conservation project developed by the aquarium. This initiative encourages businesses and hotels to recognise coral reefs as assets that should be protected for a more productive commercial future, with the added bonus of conserving reefs for their aesthetic appeal and ecosystem services (NMA, 2012). This educational and pragmatic programme is made up of three levels of achievement – Bronze, Silver and Gold. Each level is designed to engage participating hotels, their staff, holiday makers and the local community in a progressing process of education, conservation and restoration:

> Education (level 1 – Bronze)
> Conservation (level 2 – Silver)
> Restoration (level 3 – Gold)

The bronze level has its foundation solely in education of managers, front of house personnel and boat house operators. The purpose is to provide an understanding of corals, the coral community and the importance and value of this community to the tourist sector, thereby facilitating engagement with the community and protecting the economic benefits of this asset. The recruitment and education of enthusiastic people who can drive the momentum forward and bring about real change is an essential component in making this level a success.

The silver level takes the knowledge and understanding gained to assess and actively reduce the impact of the hotel on the ecosystem. Additionally, the hotel uses this new knowledge to promote the importance of the coral reef to the wider community. This includes not only visitors to resorts but other businesses, other hotels, schools and community groups so that those living nearest to the reef become involved in caring for the reef as well. Any steps taken by the hotel to become more sustainable will be met with praise by visitors and also lead guests to feel that they are in some way a part of that process. This can only be a benefit in an age where the general public are becoming much more environmentally aware, indicated by the range of "green schemes" globally (travellife.org).

At the centre of this process, the hotel becomes the hub that brings these groups together. Other hotels that are introduced to the scheme may then choose to undertake the bronze training for themselves, further contributing to protecting the economic potential that a reef system provides. This level can only be achieved by completing the bronze training.

The highest level of achievement, the gold award, is centred on restoration of the reef system. The hotel is introduced to possible avenues of restoration, one of which may be to team up with Corals for Conservation and their Coral Gardener programme. Active restoration should involve the designation of marine parks, and employment of coral gardeners to manage the recovery of reef systems and become further involved in engaging the local community. There are also avenues whereby guests of a hotel may be able to participate in activities like coral gardening, extending the reach of the programme and raising awareness.

This level is dependent on completion of bronze and silver levels, governmental support and the willingness of the hotel to provide employment for required people.

This programme has already been accredited by the Mauritian government and it has also been robustly evaluated at the bronze level by Jensen (2012).

The first participant in the Conservation through Tourism Award programme was a hotel on Mauritius (Shandrani Resort & Spa). Shandrani Resort shares the coastline with Blue Bay Marine Park, one of only two government protected marine parks on the island. This marine park attracts tourists to the region and consequently the hotel. The manager of the hotel was concerned to see that the marine park (and its associated coral reef species) was under threat from increasing boat use, and what they perceived to be ineffective government management and lack of enforcement of the regulations in place to preserve the area (Ahamada et al., 2002). He was also concerned about his hotel's impacts on the local marine environment and a lack of marine knowledge amongst hotel staff taking guests into the park. The hotel was apprehensive that an overall decline of the Marine Park posed a risk to the hotel's long-term business interests, namely its ability to attract holidaymakers. To address the hotel's interests, the following needs were identified:

A training programme for hotel staff
Guidance on engaging visitors in marine conservation
Targeting impacts for the long term economic sustainability of the hotel.

The aquarium's interests are, of course, distinct from those of a hotel chain. However the needs of the hotel business and the aquarium intersect with the global issue of coral reef conservation. Coral reefs worldwide are under threat. Scientists estimate as much as 10 % of coral reefs have already been irreversibly damaged with little hope of recovery, 30 % are in critical condition and may die within 10 to 20 years. If current pressures are allowed to continue unabated, 60 % of global coral reefs may die completely by 2050 (CRTF, 2000). These unique habitats must be preserved for their contribution to global marine biodiversity and the wealth of ecosystem services they provide, including those underpinning the tourism industry and hotels such as Shandrani Resort & Spa (Prayag et al., 2010).

The training programme commenced in the off-season of October/November 2012 and lasted 6 days. Hotel staff were drawn from a broad range of departments within the hotel to ensure the broadest impact on hotel operations and staff were encouraged to volunteer for the programme or were offered the training as a reward for good service. This resulted in 14 highly motivated and enthusiastic participants in the programme, ranging in age from 25 to 52 years old (average 38 years old), who, following the programme, were designated as "Shandrani Rangers".

The staff at the hotel are predominately drawn from the local population. Many of the staff had low levels of formal education, with some participants in the training having only completed primary education, while some had degrees. The average time spent in education by the participants was 13 years (up to the age of 16). Therefore, the training needed to take varying starting levels and learning requirements into consideration and a combination of formal teaching elements with more hands-on activities outside of a classroom setting was developed, with the more formal sessions occurring in the morning and informal mentoring time spent on boat excursions to the reef with guests to practice enacting the knowledge gained each day. This helped to put the content of the course into a familiar context, helping them to link what participants were seeing in their local environment to what had been talked about that morning. The practical afternoon session also gave participants the opportunity to practice incorporating their new knowledge into their normal daily work activities, thereby starting them on the path towards long-term adoption of this new approach to engaging guests with marine conservation.

Additionally the first languages for hotel staff were either French or Creole and while some of the participants had a working knowledge of English, communication was sometimes problematic. To help overcome this potential language barrier to effectively communicate scientific concepts relating to conservation, the course was delivered in English but by a provider who had a good working knowledge of French. For individuals who could not understand English or French or had limited reading and writing skills, other hotel staff members were able to provide additional assistance.

Communication was a critical issue since, following training, the participants would need to be able to convey conservation ideas, correct behaviour, and impart knowledge to hotel guests. To ensure that Bronze level training outcomes were met, the programme was assessed by Jensen (2012) using two techniques:

J. CAINEY ET AL.

Each participant filled a questionnaire (available in French or English) before and after training, which was assessed qualitatively using "thought-listing", with the results displayed as pre- and post-training word clouds (Jensen & Holliman, 2009).

Each participant prepared pre- and post-training annotated drawings, which were also assessed qualitatively. Participants had access to coloured crayons and pencils, but they all chose not to use colour, unlike the aquarium drawings by children that are often rich in colour (see Figure 4(b)). This difference in the use of colour between adults and children may relate to adults (And older children) being "reluctant" artists (Anning & Ring, 2004).

The Bronze level training had specific learning goals (Jensen, 2012) covering biodiversity on a coral reef (types of corals, fish and invertebrates) and conservation (threats and protection activities). Analysis of the pre- and post-training questionnaires showed increased elaboration of the role coral reefs play in providing habitat for marine creatures and the need to protect the environment that humans depend upon (income via tourism and physical protection of land). Participants showed a greater focus and degree of understanding of the need for the conservation of coral environments (Jensen, 2012).

The pre- and post-training drawings of coral demonstrated a significant modification in the participants thinking about coral, indicating gains in the different types of coral and the separate drawings related to fish showed increased awareness of the number of different types of fish and their particular features. While invertebrates were also covered in a separate series of pre- and post-training drawings, only limited changes could be evidenced from the drawings, with plankton receiving the most positive increase in awareness (Jensen, 2012).

In the pre-training assessment, Anne has drawn quite a comprehensive coral scene showing that her starting knowledge was quite extensive to begin with, perhaps from her own observations. The detail that this drawing lacks is in the specifics of the corals. In her post drawing, there is still quite a broad range of detail but there is a substantial improvement in identification of corals e.g. branching, table, foliose etc. Additionally, there is evidence of more scientific terminology such as "school of fish", plankton and identification of specific anatomical features (gender of octopus) (Figures 5a and 5b).

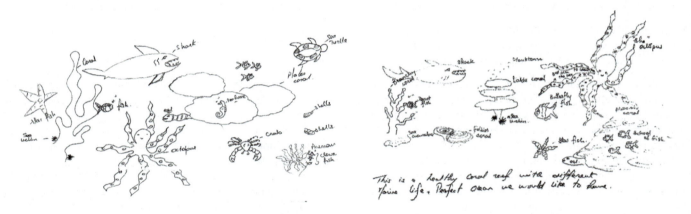

Figure 5a. Anne's pre-training diagram *Figure 5b. Anne's post-training drawing*

Alain drew a scene with representative of coral and fish in his pre-training drawing (without annotations) but the post-training drawing has considerable improvements. There is evidence of invertebrates where they were absent before (starfish, sea urchins, shells, octopus), names of some fish (banner fish) and specific mention of types of coral (table, branching) (Figures 6a and 6b).

 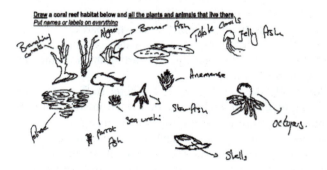

Figure 6a. Alain's pre-training drawing *Figure 6b. Alain's post-training drawing*

106

Georges drew a single starfish in his pre-training drawing. His post-training drawing is very much focused on the corals themselves (branching, flower, table, massive), the structure (barrier reef) with only two other marine species present. This indicates an increase in knowledge pertaining to corals but there is still a fundamental lack in understanding of how these intersect to create a habitat for other marine species (Figures 7a and 7b).

Figure 7a. Georges' pre-training drawing *Figure 7b. Georges' post-training drawing*

Catherine was able to draw a very basic coral habitat pre-training (sand, seaweed, massive coral) as well as some marine organisms within the habitat. Post-training, there is evidence of increased knowledge of coral types (foliose, tabular), some invertebrates (sea cucumber, octopus), some fish (butterflyfish and parrot fish) and while these are not detailed images, they do indicate an expansion of knowledge. She also uses scientific terminology e.g. biodiversity, in her description of the drawing and notes zooplankton and phytoplankton (Figures 8a and 8b).

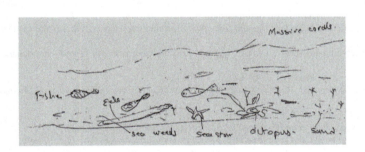
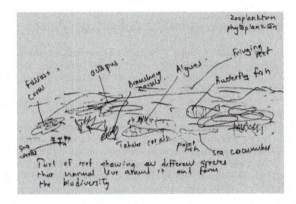

Figure 8a. Catherine's pre-training drawing *Figure 4b. Catherine's post-training drawing*

The participants understanding of conservation was also explored using pre- and post-training drawings, but the results were ambiguous. Only one of the participants (Bruno) showed four clearly identified threats to coral in his pre-training drawing, but nothing in his post-training drawing, preferring to focus on marine biodiversity in his post-training drawing. This is likely to be the result of representing conservation measures in a drawing, without significant annotation, which is difficult in language-limited situations. The drawings were particularly good at demonstrating substantial improvements in scientific and species knowledge relating to coral reefs (Jensen, 2012). The training course included glass-bottom boats trip and snorkelling, which allowed the participants to experience the coral reef directly. This activity may also have reinforced the "scientific" learning from the more formal parts of the course, while facilitating discussions on the appropriate behaviours related to coral reefs. Indeed, the participants reported in their post-training questionnaires that the "doing" aspects of the training were most rewarding (Jensen, 2012). However, it is difficult to draw "behaviours" and much easier to draw "things". This is an important aspect to consider, when using drawings to assess learning and understanding.

The hotel undertook Silver level training in 2013, but needed further support to achieve success and the hotel was recently reassessed by the aquarium (2014) and was successful in achieving the Silver Award (Beachnews, 2014). The hotel participants not only educate tourists, but also communicate their knowledge of the local coral reef to the wider community, including local schools, resulting in more sustainable behaviour (Evasion, 2014).

CONCLUSIONS

Drawings are a versatile tool that can be used as part of the assessment process for education and training programmes, for both children and adults. Drawings allow for an assessment of learning that can be independent of language and initial educational skills and is an assessment process without the rigours of a test or questionnaire. By pairing pre- and post-learning drawings, the skill of each artist is accommodated.

The aquarium has a well-developed series of programmes for both schools and the tourism industry that have specific learning outcomes focused on broadening knowledge of the marine environment and associated species, developing observation and communication skills and enhanced empathy and respect for the marine environment. The assessment of drawings clearly demonstrates that a visit to the aquarium promotes children's understanding of the marine environment and schools can be confident that not only is a visit to the aquarium enjoyable and exciting, but also results in significant learning.

Additionally, the use of drawings in an adult training programme, where participants had English as a second or third language and where formal education rates were low, demonstrated, along with verbal surveys, that the aquarium's Conservation through Tourism Award programme also met the key learning outcomes, particularly those related to increasing knowledge and understanding of marine habitat and creatures, which is a learning outcome (GLO 1) shared with the school education programme.

It was difficult to use drawings to assess conservation attitudes (GLO 3). In the school programme this aspect was explicitly not assessed with drawings, but the training programme at the Hotel did attempt to use drawing to assess changes in conservation approaches and this produced ambiguous results. Verbal and written questionnaires were much more successful at gauging the changes in conservation approaches as a result of the Conservation through Tourism Award training.

Drawings are a good tool to assess the increased scientific knowledge gained as a result of education or training programmes. Using drawings creates an inclusive and accessible assessment process, accommodating a broad range of ages (4–52 years old) and education level (1–19 years), which can be further enhanced by annotation or qualitative questioning.

REFERENCES

Ahamada, S., Bigot, L., Bijoux, J., Maharavo, J., Meunier, S., Moyne-Picard, M., & Paupiah, N. (2002). Status of coral reefs in the south west Indian Ocean island node: Comoros, Madagascar, Mauritius, Reunion and Seychelles. In C. R. Wilkinson (Ed.), *Status of the coral reefs of the world* (pp. 79–100). Townsville: Australian Institute of Marine Science.

Alerby, E. (2000). A way of visualising children's and young people's thoughts about the environment: A study of drawings. *Environmental Education Research, 6*, 205–222.

Anderson, D., Lucas, K. B., & Ginns, I. S. (2003). Theoretical perspectives on learning in an informal setting. *Journal of Research in Science Teaching, 40*, 177–199.

Anning, A., & Ring, K. (2004). *Making sense of children's drawings*. Maidenhaed, UK: McGraw-Hill International.

Ballantyne, R., & Packer, J. (2005). Promoting environmentally sustainable attitudes and behaviour through free-choice learning experiences: What is the state of the game? *Environmental Education Research, 11*, 281–295.

Ballantyne, R., Packer, J., Hughes, K., & Dierking, L. (2007). Conservation learning in wildlife tourism settings: Lessons from research in zoos and aquariums. *Environmental Education Research, 13*, 367–383.

Barraza, L. (1999). Children's drawings about the environment. *Environmental Education Research, 5*, 49–66.

Beachnews. (2014). *Shandrani rangers – Conservation through tourism award programme*. Retrieved from https://www.facebook.com/notes/beachnews/shandrani-rangers-conservation-through-tourism-award-programme/857546274277033

Birney, B. (1995). Children, animals and leisure settings. *Society and Animals, 3*, 171–187.

Bowker, R. (2002). Evaluating teaching and learning strategies at the Eden project. *Evaluation and Research in Education, 16*, 123–135.

Bowker, R. (2007). Children's perceptions and learning about tropical rainforests: An analysis of their drawings. *Environmental Education Research, 13*, 75–96.

Boyle, P., Bolze, D., & Koontz, F. (1995). COWRI: Critical Ocean Wildlife Recovery Initiative. *International Zoo Yearbook, 34*, 25–30.

Braund, M., & Reiss, M. (2006). Towards a more authentic science curriculum: The contribution of out-of-school learning. *International Journal of Science Education, 28*, 1373–1388.

Brody, M. (2005). Learning in nature. *Environmental Education Research, 11*, 603–621.

Brooks, M. (2009). Drawing, visualisation and young children's exploration of "Big Ideas". *International Journal of Science Education, 31*, 319–341.

Butler, S., Gross, J., & Hayne, H. (1995). The effect of drawing on memory performance in young children. *Developmental Psychology, 31*, 597–608.

Cainey, J. (2007). Understanding the origin of clouds. *Environmental Chemistry, 4*, 141–142.

Cainey, J., Bowker, R., Humphrey, L., & Murray, N. (2012). Assessing informal learning in an aquarium using pre-and post-visit drawings. *Educational Research and Evaluation, 18*(3), 265–281.

Cinner, J. E., McClanahan, T. R., Graham, N. A. J., Daw, T. M., Maina, J., Stead, S. M., Wamukota, A., Brown, K., & Bodin, Ö. (2012). Vulnerability of coastal communities to key impacts of climate change on coral reef fisheries. *Global Environmental Change, 22*(1), 12–20.

Coral Reef Task Force (CRTF). (2000). *The national action plan to conserve coral reefs*. Washington, DC: CRTF.

Cox, S. (2005). Intention and meaning in young children's drawings. *International Journal of Art and Design Education, 24*, 115–125.

Daby, D. (2003). Effects of seagrass bed removal for tourism purposes in a Mauritian bay. *Environmental Pollution, 125*(3), 313–324.

Dentzau, M. W., & Gallard Martínez, A. J. (2014). The development and validation of an alternative assessment to measure changes in understanding of the longleaf pine ecosystem. *Environmental Education Research*, (ahead of print) 1–24.

Doney, S. C., Fabry, V. J., Feely, R. A., & Kleypas, J. A. (2009). Ocean acidification: The other CO2 problem. *Annual Review Of Marine Science, 1*, 169–192.

Dowling, P., & Brown, A. (2000). A grand day out: Towards and interrogation of non-school pedagogic sites. *The Curriculum Journal, 11*, 247–271.

Driver, R., Asoko, H., Leach, J., Mortimer, E., & Scott, P. (1994). Constructing scientific knowledge in the classroom. *Educational Researcher, 23*, 5–12.

Ehrlén, K. (2009). Drawings as representations of children's conceptions. *International Journal of Science Education, 31*(1), 41–57.

Evasion. (2014). *Beachcomer Hotel Magazine, 38* (April), 6–11.

Falk, J. H., & Dierking, L. D. (2000). *Learning from museums*. Walnut Creek, CA: AltaMire Press.

Falk, J. H., & Adelman, L. M. (2003). Investigating the impact of prior knowledge and interest on aquarium visitor learning. *Journal of Research in Science Education, 40*, 163–176.

Flowers, A. A., Carroll, J. P., Green, G. T., & Larson, L. R. (2014). Using art to assess environmental education outcomes. *Environmental Education Research*, (ahead-of-print), 1–19.

Graham, N. A., McClanahan, T. R., Letourneur, Y., & Galzin, R. (2007). Anthropogenic stressors, inter-specific competition and ENSO effects on a Mauritian coral reef. *Environmental Biology of Fishes, 78*(1), 57–69.

Haney, W., Russell, M., & Bebell, D. (2004). Drawing on education: Using drawings to document schooling and support change. *Harvard Educational Review, 74*(3), 241–272.

Haring, U., & Reesa, S. (2014). The CID lens: Looking at children's drawings using content, interpretive, and developmental methods. *International Journal of Arts Education, 8*(3), 15–29.

Hein, G. (1999). The constructivist museum. In E. Hooper-Greenhill (Ed.), *The educational role of the museum* (pp. 73–79). London: Routledge.

Hoegh-Guldberg, O., & Bruno, J. F. (2010). The impact of climate change on the world's marine ecosystems. *Science, 328*(5985), 1523–1528.

Jensen, E. (2012). *External evaluation report: Conservation through tourism award.* Coventry: National Marine Aquarium and University of Warwick.

Jensen, E., & Holliman, R. (2009). Investigating science communication to inform science outreach and public engagement. In R. Holliman, E. Whitelegg, E. Scanlon, S. Smid, & J. Thomas (Eds.), *Investigating science communication in the information age: Implications for public engagement and popular media* (pp. 55–71). Oxford; Milton Keynes: Oxford University Press; Open University.

Kesicioglu, O. S., & Deniz, U. (2014). Investigation of pre-school children's perception of teacher in their drawings. *Creative Education, 5*, 606–613.

Kola-Olusanya, A. (2005). Free-choice environmental education: Understanding where children learn outside of school. *Environmental Education Research, 11*, 297–307.

Luquet, G. H. (2001). Children's drawings [Le dessin enfantin] (A. Costall, Trans., introduction and notes). London: Free Association Books. (Original work published 1927)

National Marine Aquarium. (2011). *About the national marine aquarium.* Retrieved from http://www.national-aquarium.co.uk/what-you-can-see/marine-conservation

National Marine Aquarium. (2012). *Conservation through tourism award.* Retrieved from http://www.national-aquarium.co.uk/research/conservationtta

Newton, D. P., & Newton, L. D. (1992). Young children's perceptions of science and the scientist. *International Journal of Science Education, 14*(3), 331–348.

O'Byrne, B. (2009). Knowing more than words can say: Using multimodal assessment tools to excavate and construct knowledge about wolves. *International Journal of Science Education, 31*(4), 523–539.

Ow, J., & Bielaczyc, K. (2013, August 6–9). *"Drawing out" students' voices: Students' perceptions about learning science through ideas first, a knowledge building approach.* Presented at Crossing the Educational Chasm: From Basics to Creative Work with Ideas, Puebla, Mexico.

Papandreou, M. (2014). Communicating and thinking through drawing activity in early childhood. *Journal of Research in Childhood Education, 28*(1), 85–100.

Piaget, J., & Inhelder, B. (1971). *Mental imagery in the child.* New York, NY: Meridian Books-World Publishing Company.

Prayag, G., Dookhony-Ramphul, K., & Maryeven, M. (2010). Hotel development and tourism impacts in Mauritius: Hoteliers' perspectives on sustainable tourism. *Development Southern Africa, 27*(5), 697–712.

Prokop, P., & Fancovicova J. (2006). Students' ideas about the human body: Do they really draw what they know? *Journal of Baltic Science Education, 2*, 86–95.

Reiss, M. J., & Tunnicliffe, S. D. (1999). Learning about skeletons and other organ systems of vertebrate animals. *Science Education International, 10*, 29–33.

Reiss, M. J., & Tunnicliffe, S. D. (2001). Students' understandings of human organs and organ systems. *Research in Science Education, 31*, 383–399.

Rennie, L., & Jarvis, T. (2006). Children's choice of drawings to communicate their ideas about technology. *Research in Science Education, 25*, 239–252.

Rennie, L., & McClafferty, T. (1995). Using visits to interactive science and technology centers, museums, aquaria and zoos to promote learning in science. *Journal of Science Teacher Education, 6*, 175–185.

Rennie, L., Feher, E., Dierking, L., & Falk, J. (2003). Toward an agenda for advancing research on science learning in out-of-school settings. *Journal of Research in Science Teaching, 40*, 112–120.

Rojas-Drummond, S., Mazon, N., Fernandez, M., & Wegerif, R. (2006). Explicit reasoning, creativity and co-construction in primary school children's collaborative activities. *Thinking Skills and Creativity, 1*, 84–94.

Sobhee, S. K. (2006). Fisheries biodiversity conservation and sustainable tourism in Mauritius. *Ocean & Coastal Management, 49*(7), 413–420.

Statistics Mauritius. (2013a). *Monthly tourist arrival.* Ministry of Finance & Economic Development, Mauritius. Retrieved from http://statsmauritius.gov.mu/English/Publications/Pages/Monthly-Tourist-Arrival.aspx

Statistics Mauritius. (2013b). *Republic of Mauritius – Mauritius in figures.* Ministry of Finance & Economic Development, Mauritius. Retrieved from http://statsmauritius.gov.mu/English/Publications/Documents/MIF/MIF2013.pdf

Taylor, L. (2009). *National marine aquarium generic learning outcomes* (Unpublished manuscript). Schools Programme, National Marine Aquarium, Plymouth, UK.

Thomas, G., & Jolley, R. (1998). Drawing conclusions: A reexamination of empirical and conceptual bases for psychological evaluation of children from their drawings. *British Journal of Psychology, 37*, 127–139.

Tranter, P., & Malone, K. (2004). Geographies of environmental learning: An exploration of children's use of school grounds. *Children's Geographies, 2*, 131–155.

Wellington, J. (1990). Formal and informal learning in science: The role of the interactive science centers. *Physics Education, 25*, 247–252

Westmacott, S., Cesar, H. S., Pet-Soede, L., & Lindén, O. (2000). Coral bleaching in the Indian Ocean: Socio-economic assessment of effects. In H. S. J. Cesar (Eds.), *Essays on the economics of coral reefs* (pp. 94–106).

Wetzel, J. A., & O'Brien, M. (1995). Aquariums: A look to the future. *International Zoo Yearbook, 34*, 1–6.

Jill Cainey
CSIRO Marine and Atmospheric Research
Aspendale, Australia

Lauren Humphrey
Conservation through Tourism Award, National Marine Aquarium
Plymouth, UK

Rob Bowker
Graduate School of Education, University of Exeter
Exeter, UK

10. DISCOVERING CHILDREN'S SCIENCE ASSOCIATIONS UTILIZING DRAWINGS

THE ROLE OF STUDENTS' CONCEPTIONS IN PHYSICS EDUCATION

Some concepts in science and especially physics, in particular, seem to be hard to fully comprehend. A lot of research has been done to find out effective ways to support students when they are being confronted with certain subject matters. A major impact factor that influences how difficult (or easy) a specific concept appears to students is how well the students' own conceptions match the scientific ideas. In a lot of cases, the students' ideas are far-removed from the scientific concepts that the teachers want to impart. In this case, we often call these ideas *misconceptions* in order to stress this wide divergence between the students' ideas and the scientific concepts. Table 1 gives you some examples of typical misconceptions from various fields of science that pose a challenge when teaching these specific topics. More examples of students' conceptions can be found in research literature. For a detailed introduction we recommend Rosalind Driver's book (Driver, 1985) that is not only geared towards researchers but practitioners as well.

Table 1. List of typical students' conceptions compared to the scientific ideas

	Typical students' idea	Scientific idea
Electricity	In an electric circuit, the electrons flow from the power source to the bulb and are then used up (Shipstone et al., 1988).	In an electric circuit, the current (=number of electrons per second) before and after the bulb stays the same.
Optics	In a totally dark room, you will eventually see the surrounding objects if you just give your eyes enough time to adapt (Guesne, 1985).	In order to see an object, light must be reflected (or emitted) by it. If there is no light entering the room, it is impossible to see any objects (that are not light sources themselves), no matter how long you wait.
Astronomy	It is summer when the Earth is closer to the Sun, due to the Earth's elliptical orbit (Baxter, 1989).	The reason for the seasons is not the distance between the Earth and Sun but the tilt of the Earth's axis. The Earth's orbit is almost perfectly circular.
Mechanics	An object will only stay in motion if you apply a constant force on it (Gunstone & Watts, 1985).	An object will stay in constant motion if there are no external forces acting on it.
Thermodynamics	A scarf keeps you warm. This is why an ice cube melts very fast when you wrap it in a scarf (Lewis & Linn, 1994).	A scarf consists of air pockets that act as bad thermal conductors. This is why the scarf slows down thermal heat exchange and melting will occur very slowly. This is also why you don't lose as much body heat if you wear a scarf.

For a teacher who wants to teach these scientific concepts to her students, it is of the upmost importance to not only be aware of the most widespread misconceptions, but also to be mindful about methods to support her students in overcoming them. Although science education research has been very busy in this field of study, in a lot of cases the teacher is unable to draw upon research results since typical misconceptions have not been scrutinized in all scientific fields (and even less so in the humanities). This is why teachers who are aware of this challenge will find it useful to explore methods that they can use themselves to find out about their students' ideas.

The most important advice for teachers who are interested in learning more about their students' misconceptions is to use methods in their teaching that will give the students a lot of opportunities to be active and express themselves. Just by listening to answers that might sound incorrect and carefully analyzing what kind of misconceptions could be behind them, teachers can already discover a large number of students' ideas. Teachers who are interested in a more systematic approach and are willing to spend some time on scrutinizing what conceptions their students have (e.g. before introducing a topic or after having discussed it) will probably use established research methods. Teachers usually do not have the time to perform in-depth interviews with all of their students as is the case in most science education research projects. A repertoire of quick, yet efficient, methods suitable for this purpose can be found in the available literature (e.g. White & Gunstone, 1992).

Why Students' aAssociations Matter

One of the methods that White and Gunstone recommend in their book is the method of using children's drawings. As is already laid out in several other chapters of this book, children's drawings can be an interesting way of assessing students' understanding of scientific concepts. But drawings can also help us in the very beginning by finding out what students associate with different terms before we start discussing these topics in science lessons. A number of misconceptions can be traced back to the fact that a word we use in science is also regularly used in everyday-life but albeit with a (slightly) different meaning. Here are some examples:

- The word *radiation* refers to several different types of energy transfer. Whereas to a scientist it is clear that light is a type of radiation, the majority of laypeople would not agree. To them, radiation only designates something that is not visible to the human eye (such as X-rays or gamma radiation).
- The word *chemical* is a rather neutral term for a scientist. Every form of matter that surrounds us consists of distinct chemicals: Water, for instance, is a typical example of a chemical. To a non-scientist, the term has an extremely negative connotation – most people associate the word chemical with substances that can be harmful to the human body, such as chlorine, bleach, or hydrochloric acid.
- The word *force* has a distinct meaning in physics: it is used to describe an interaction between two objects. In everyday language, the word has a slightly different connotation: People usually think of force as something that one can possess. A body-builder, for instance, might be said to have a lot of force stored in his muscles.

In order to combat potential misconceptions, finding out about students' associations with a certain term appears to be crucial before teachers introduce a new topic.

How to Find out about Students' Associations

Several methods seem to be suitable to discover what children associate with a particular term (White & Gunstone, 1992, pp. 142–157): The teacher can, for instance, moderate a brainstorming session, during which the students can prepare a list of words, or the class can be divided up into groups to find as many words as possible that have to do with this term. Discussing the results (e.g. by clustering the associations and categorizing them) helps the students reflect on their ideas later on.

The previously mentioned ideas, however, also have their limits; in some cases, it might be better to implement a different method entirely: letting the students draw. First, hand them a blank sheet of paper and invite them to draw whatever comes to their minds when confronted with a certain scientific term. Writing this word on the board might be useful for your students. Then, after 10–15 minutes, collect the drawings (putting their names on the drawings is not required) and use them in the next lesson to start a discussion about this specific term based on the students' associations. The discussion can, for instance, focus on:

- What was the most common motif found in the children's drawings?
- What was the reason for the students to include motif XY?
- Do the objects drawn by the students show any emotional reaction to this term?
- Are there any prevailing colors that students chose? Why did students choose those?
- Are the motifs that students drew similar to the images found in their science textbooks?
- Were there any objects that the students had on their minds but were unable to draw (e.g. because drawing these objects would have been too difficult)?

Benefits of Using Drawings in Educational Research and Implementation at School

There are several good reasons to implement drawings when attempting to find out about preconceptions. The most apparent advantage is that drawing provides a more playful and creative alternative, especially when compared to methods in which students have to answer either written or oral questions. Students in science courses are used to writing texts, filling out worksheets and writing lab reports. When they are told that the next activity will require them to draw something, the reactions are generally quite positive. The drawing method can simply help to diversify science lessons. This also holds true if you implement drawings in your research: Students who are asked to contribute to educational research usually have to fill out questionnaires or give interviews. The fact that they can participate in a scientific study just by drawing will probably be something new to them.

Another benefit of using drawings becomes apparent when you teach or do research on younger children: At a certain age, drawing is simply easier than writing. Children don't have to worry about spelling or about technical terms they don't know yet – they can just jot down whatever comes to mind. In our research study, we encountered this fact several times when we let 10-year old children explain their drawings. Some of them were not able to find the correct technical terms (e.g. power plant, remote control, etc.) but their drawings were surprisingly accurate and easy to decipher.

We also came across another positive aspect: Apparently, children who are usually more reluctant to participate in the lesson showed great willingness to contribute drawings. This seems to be essential for teachers whose goal it is to actively include all students in their lessons. Some students just prefer methods that do not require verbal engagement. In this context, the students might also benefit from the additional time this method gives them to come up with ideas. While the usual time for devising word lists amounts to 5–10 minutes, the drawing method necessitates more time and therefore fosters children who prefer to have more time.

There was an additional advantage of using drawings that we discovered after taking a closer look and interviewing the students regarding their drawings. In some of them, deeper concepts of understanding were revealed and provided us with the chance to discuss them with the students. In one drawing of an electric circuit, for instance, the student not only drew a battery, a light bulb and wires but he also depicted what he thought was going on inside the cables. Little particles were not only moving from the plus pole of the battery to the light bulb but also from the minus pole until they met in the light bulb. He then explained to us, during our interview with him, his idea that the glowing of the light bulb's filament happened because these particles crashed together. Also, one student depicted how she envisaged the propagation of light: She drew little balls and a wave that was curving around the balls. The interview with her revealed that, in her science textbook, she once saw light depicted as a wave but evidently did not know the reason for this representation. In her opinion, light always travels in a straight line but as soon as it encounters other particles (she described the little balls in the drawing as oxygen particles in the air), light bends around them like a wave.

What to Look out for When Using Drawings to Find out about Students' Associations

Just as with any other method, there are some pitfalls to be mindful of. First of all, make sure that the students' age is suitable for the use of drawings. As we said before, the younger the students are, the more eager they are to use their colored pencils. We observed that between the ages of 12–13, the students' enthusiasm for drawing significantly plummeted. It might still be possible to find some students within this age group who love drawing but the majority will not feel comfortable about their individual talent any more. In this case, you might want to consider implementing a different method for discovering students' associations such as word lists or concept maps.

One of the drawbacks of utilizing drawings, however, is the fact that some students might choose to draw objects that are easy to depict, rather than their immediate associations. When confronted with the word *physics*, they might think of Albert Einstein first, but then decide not to draw him because sketching things like magnets or lab equipment is easier or more fun than drawing a person. You can try to circumvent this problem by allowing the students to also use words in their drawings or by inviting them to label their motifs. This issue can also be addressed if you take the time to discuss the results of the students' drawings with the class. This can be a welcome opportunity for them to add other associations that they did not find easy enough to draw. Of course, this step requires the students to openly engage in class discussions.

Another important piece of recommendation, especially when using the drawings for research purposes, is to find a way of verifying your interpretations. Sometimes it might be hard to decipher the motifs in a child's drawing, while in other cases you cannot be sure if your interpretation matches the intention of the student. If possible, getting justification and further explanation live from the illustrator is the safest option. Usually, short interviews are a suitable method for the classroom as well as in a research project. In our study, for example, the problems we faced due to misinterpretation were surprisingly rare. In an overwhelming number of cases, the drawings were easy to interpret (for counter-examples, see fig. 1 and fig. 2) and the children agreed with our interpretations during the subsequent interviews. In some cases, however, we had to slightly alter our inferences: Some children who drew mobile phones and surrounded them with curved lines, for instance (see fig. 3), wanted to signify the vibration that takes places while the phone is ringing. Other children, however, drew similar lines to show the radiation emitted by the phones.

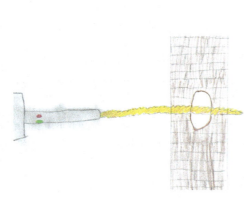
Figure 1. Drawings can be difficult to interpret: A laser beam penetrating a wall

Figure 2. Are the spirals meant to be water vapor or radiation?

Figure 3. Do the curved lines signify radiation or the vibrations of the phone?

We would like to use the rest of this chapter to give some concrete examples of how drawings were used to find out about students' associations. We will start with two practical examples from school and present an overview of our research study that also used drawings in the last section.

Practical Application 1: ENERGY

Our first example of teachers implementing drawings in their science lessons took place in a 6th grade classroom with 11–12 year old students. In this specific case, the drawings were used not to elicit the students' immediate associations but to find out what the students' associations were after a short input phase. The input phase, however, did not include concrete examples because the teacher wanted to see what the students would come up with on their own afterwards.

The two participating classes were physics introductory courses in their first month of lessons following the summer holiday. After one lesson of discussing organizational details and one lesson of talking about characteristics of physics compared to other natural sciences, the teacher[1] gave the classes a short general introduction about energy. For this, she used a science website (http://www.kids.esdb.bg/) as the main resource for her input. The key ideas the teacher delivered in this input phase were the following:

- Energy is the main driving force in our universe. It is what makes all the different processes in our universe possible.
- Energy can come in a lot of different forms that can be transferred between each other.
- The total amount of energy in our universe remains constant.

After this input, during which the teacher avoided giving any specific examples of energy types or sources, the teacher handed out blank sheets of paper and wrote the word "energy" on the board. She asked the students to draw whatever comes to mind and allotted them ten minutes before she collected the drawings. All students had given their permission to use the drawings for research purposes and also to potentially publish some of the drawings in this book.

We were able to categorize the 43 drawings we received into eight main categories: electric wires showing the transport of electrical energy, wind turbines, light bulbs or other forms of lamps, bodies of water such as rivers or waterfalls, solar cells, lightning bolts, means of transportation (such as cars, planes or trains), and motifs related to nuclear energy.

Other motifs that only occurred in singular drawings (e.g. a magnet, a Newton's cradle, a hamster in a wheel) or motifs that did not show a direct connection to the topic but were rather drawn as part of the environment (such as clouds, houses or green meadows) were not taken into account.

Fig. 4 gives an overview of the typical objects that students drew, each representing one of the eight different categories.

Figure 4. Categories of depicted objects that students associated with "energy"

The analysis of the drawings revealed that the pictures showed a variety of different objects but overall, the production, transport and use of electricity was a recurring theme (also see Figure 5). In 44% of the drawings, devices used to transport electricity (wires, cables, power lines) were shown. Power plants were also a reoccurring theme in many children's drawings. Wind power plants appeared in 35% of the drawings, hydro-electric power plants and streaming rivers in 26%, and solar cells in 23%. Motifs denoting nuclear power, however, only showed up in 12% of the drawings. Objects that could be interpreted as devices that "use" energy, such as light bulbs and means of transportation, were represented in 30% and 12% of the drawings, respectively. Bolts of lightning also made an appearance, showing up in one fifth of the drawings. While they mostly originated in clouds, these lightning bolts were utilized several times to demonstrate the power of magnets or electricity.

What is most striking from the results is the fact that students' associations with energy were largely dominated by the field of electricity. Fossil fuels, the main source of energy on the global (as well as the national) scale were not explicitly found in any of the drawings at all. Our individual source of energy, food, also failed to appear. These results provided an interesting starting point for the teacher-initiated discussion in the next lesson. As it turns out, not only had the students not included food or fossil fuels in their drawings, but most of them were absolutely unaware of the fact that food, for instance, is an important source of energy.

A second remarkable aspect that the teacher, as well as the research team, came across in the drawings was that, in spite of the fact that wind and solar power plants make up only a very small percentage of Austria's electricity production sector,[2] students tended to depict these kinds of power plants much more often than others (fossil-fueled power stations, for instance). This might stem from the

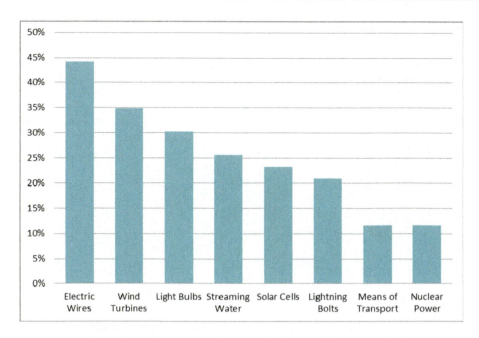

Figure 5. Motifs students included in their drawings about energy

fact that the discussion of sustainable energy resources makes up a large share of the Austrian teaching curriculum regarding energy. Another possible explanation could be that students tend to draw objects that they frequently see in their everyday lives. Although wind power plants and solar cells do not contribute greatly to Austria's electricity production, they can be seen quite often in the students' surroundings. Solar cells are mounted on public buildings and private houses and wind turbines are eye-catching buildings in the country side. Thermal power plants, however, are harder to locate.

Practical Application 2: CHEMISTRY

The other example that we would like to present in this chapter stems from an introductory chemistry course.[3] Since chemistry is not introduced before 8th grade in the Austrian school system, the students were 13–14 years old. As mentioned above, students at this age might already be a bit more hesitant to draw. In the three classes that took part in this case study, however, this was not the case and the students welcomed the drawing task as a pleasant change in their daily school routine.

The teacher of this chemistry class used the drawing method to find out what her students associated with the word *chemistry* in general. For this purpose, she asked her students in the very first chemistry lesson to fill the blank sheets of paper she provided with whatever comes to mind when they hear the word *chemistry*. The teacher announced that she would allocate the students ten minutes time for this task and would then collect the drawings. She also mentioned that she would like to scan in the drawings for research purposes in order to coincide with the research ethos. She also underscored that the drawings would be used as a springboard for discussions in the next lesson and that they would not be used to assess the students in any way.

All in all, the teacher received drawings from 77 students and met with the research team afterward in order to analyze them together. We reached a consensus on the following categories into which we could classify the majority of the motifs drawn by the students:

- Lab equipment (such as test tubes, flasks, forceps, …)
- Explosions (or a fire, e.g. as a result of mixing two substances together)
- Chemical formulas or symbols (e.g. specific elements, reactions)
- Radioactivity (usually in the form of the hazard symbol for ionizing radiation)
- People engaged in lab work (e.g. the chemistry teacher, students or a "stereotypical" scientist)

Figure 6 shows representative examples of motifs classified into these categories

A frequency analysis of the motifs showed the following results (see also Figure 7): In all of the 77 drawings that we received, students included lab equipment: mostly test tubes and flasks. There was literally not a single drawing we received that did not have any lab equipment in it. The second most popular motif (chosen by 71.4% of the students) was an explosion or a fire which was usually drawn as a result of a chemical experiment. Some students even drew a whole comic strip portraying the events during a chemical reaction (e.g. mixing two liquids together in a test tube which leads to an explosion). Nearly a third of the students (32.5%) included some kind of chemical formulas in their drawings (either compounds or elements), closely followed by motifs related to radioactivity

Figure 6. What students associate with "chemistry" – 5 main categories

(28.6%). Drawings depicting people occurred in only one fifth of the sample (data) set and they were mostly depicted as stereotypical chemists in white lab coats.

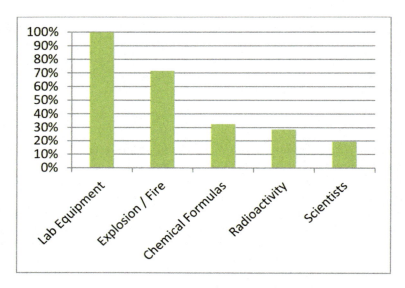

Figure 7. Frequency analysis of the motifs students chose

Some details about the drawings that do not show up in the frequency analysis above but gave us some interesting insights in the study also include the following:

Three students drew the element symbols "Br" and "Ba" and aligned them in the shape of the logo of the TV series *Breaking Bad*[4] (see Figure 8). One more student included little crystals in her drawings that she labelled as "drugs". In the discussion that took place during the next chemistry lesson, several other of the students affirmed that their associations also stemmed from the TV series *Breaking Bad*, which lead to a conversation about the role of chemistry in the series.

It was especially interesting to us, as well as to the teacher, to see what the motifs of the fifth category ("people related to chemistry") looked like. In most cases, the drawings exhibited male characters dressed in lab coats performing chemistry experiments (sometimes equipped with safety goggles). Some of these representations could definitely be described as the stereotype of a nerdy scientist with glasses and disheveled hair. This result is very familiar to science education researchers as it has been found in extensive studies examining the image that comes to mind when students are asked to consider a "typical scientist" (Chambers, 1983; Finson, 2002). Also, only three of the depicted people involved in chemistry work were found to be female (one involved a female student and two showed the female chemistry teacher of the class).

Figure 8. One example of the impact of media on students associations

Associations with the word chemistry, however, can also go into a totally different direction, as shown in Figure 9. One student not only drew lab equipment and the periodic table of elements but also portrayed two people with hearts between them – apparently, the chemistry is right between the two of them.

Figure 9. The chemistry seems to be right

DRAWINGS IN SCIENCE EDUCATION RESEARCH

Example: RADIATION

Knowing about students' associations helps teachers create suitable learning environments. As we shall see in the next section, discovering associations can also help science education to learn more about students' misconceptions. Drawings can be used as a tool to find these associations and provide researchers with a well-supported and substantiated database. In this section, we will present an overview of our research concerning associations and misconceptions about *radiation*. For a more detailed presentation of our research, we would like to draw the reader's attention to our publication (Neumann & Hopf, 2013).

Our motivation to do research in the field of students' conceptions about radiation was our observation that many media reports, as well as typical students' comments, did not align with the scientific definitions. Not only did we find a lot of newspaper articles that used the word *radiation* interchangeably with *radiating particles* but we also came across the fact that, very often, journalists do not differentiate between different types of radiation. Since most of the articles discussing the effects of radiation in newspapers and magazines deal with ionizing radiation (and definitely not with visible radiation or infrared radiation), it comes as no surprise that a common misconception about radiation is the alleged fact that radiation is always harmful. Also, the fact that the media seems to deal much more frequently with the risks of different types of radiation, rather than their benefits, supports this conception.

Following these initial impressions that supplemented previous research results (Acar Sesen & Ince, 2010; Lijnse, Eijkelhof, Klaassen, & Scholte, 1990; Rego & Peralta, 2006), we became curious to see what findings the analysis of children's drawings could provide in this context. Our main hypothesis was that the drawings would also demonstrate that the word "radiation" was strongly connected to something harmful, rather than something beneficial to mankind. We formulated our research questions as follows:

- What do younger students (between 9–12 years old[5]) associate with the term "radiation" before having learned about it in the science classroom?
- Do these associations vary according to age?
- Do boys and girls associate different things with the term "radiation"?

As our first data collection took place in December 2009 and data evaluation and presentation proceeded parallel to the incident at the Fukushima nuclear power plant (March, 2011), we decided to include a fourth research question that related to the possible changes of associations before and after Fukushima.

- Did the students' associations change as a result of to the Fukushima disaster?

Our Arguments for Using Drawings as Our Preferred Research Method

Although the implementation of word lists to find out about children's associations was also very tempting, we decided to use drawings in our study. The main reason for this decision was the fact that we wanted to focus on younger children (between 9–12 years old) who we expected would eagerly embrace drawing rather than writing a text. Also, this method helped our research to be a little bit disconnected from traditional methods in school, with the hope that the children would not necessarily relate their ideas exclusively to school but felt free to also include non-school experiences. For us as researchers, the main benefit of the drawings was that we could not only use them to count how often the children drew certain motifs, but we could also discover more hidden concepts in the drawings – things that words would not have been able to reveal as easily.

The Set-Up of Our Study

To find answers to our research questions, we asked teachers from different types of schools in an urban area of our country to perform the following procedure: The teachers should distribute blank sheets of paper and write the word *Strahlung* (= radiation[6]) on the board. Then they should ask the children to draw whatever comes to mind. After 10–15 minutes, the children should be told to write their names and class on the back (in order to facilitate interviews in case clarifying questions proved necessary) and the sheets of paper should be collected. The teachers were asked not to answer any subject-related questions and also to avoid any scientific input whatsoever (this was achieved, for instance, by not having the drawing sessions take place during science lessons or not having them moderated by science teachers).

The collection of drawings was supported by short, follow-up interviews with a sub-set of the students. These interviews served a variety of purposes: They made it possible to compare our interpretations of the drawings to the children's true intentions (as it turns out, we only misinterpreted the children's drawings in 2 out of 103 cases); it provided us the opportunity to ask the children to go into more detail about their ideas and perceptions; and we were able to inquire about their sources of information.

Evaluation of the Drawings

All in all, we received n = 509 drawings in the first round (15 months before the Fukushima accident) and n = 516 drawings 2 years later in the second round (9 months after the Fukushima disaster). The distribution of these drawings among the different age groups as well as the ratio of girls vs. boys was more or less statistically even.

In order to analyze the more than 1000 drawings we received, we focused on the motifs that the children had drawn. Our research team, supported by additional independent advisors (one psychologist and one teacher), categorized the motifs into the following five main categories:

- The Sun
- Artificial light sources
- Motifs related to radioactivity
- Mobile phones
- PC screens and TV monitors

Figure 10 gives you an impression of what typical examples of these five main categories looked like:

Figure 10. Typical examples from our five main categories: the Sun, artificial light sources, radioactivity, mobile phones, TV/computer screen

Analysis of the First Study – What Students Drew as Associations with the Term "Strahlung" (=Radiation)

When we analyzed the drawings from the first study, we found that nearly 70% of the children chose the Sun as one of their motifs (see also Figure 11). For international readers, this might be very surprising, but can be easily explained by the linguistic background that the study was performed in: The German word "Strahlung" (= radiation) that was used as the basis for this study is used both as a technical term for invisible types of radiation as well as an everyday word in terms like "Sonnenstrahlung" (= sunshine). Only about a quarter of the students chose artificial light sources such as lamps, flashlights, or mobile phones. Drawings related to radioactivity only amounted to 18%. Upon closer analysis of the data, it became clear that the associations drawn by the students were largely influenced by their age. As Figure 12 shows, younger children nearly exclusively included the Sun in their drawings whereas older students had more diversified associations with the term "radiation".

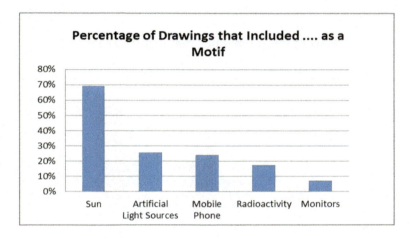

Figure 11. Frequency analysis of the children's drawing (from the study conducted in 2009)

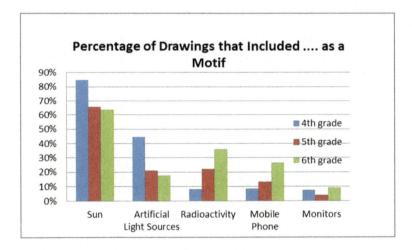

Figure 12. Associations with the term "radiation", analyzed by age

Apparently, as students get older, they are more likely to associate radiation with invisible sources such as radioactivity and/or mobile phones. Younger children, however, tend to associate radiation with visible sources such as lamps or the Sun. These results were also supported by the short interviews: The older and more educated the students were, the more they were aware of the existence of harmful, invisible forms of radiation--sometimes focusing solely on these associations and neglecting the association to visible light. The outcomes of this study were also reinforced by a different research study we performed: an extended interview study with 15 year old students (Neumann & Hopf, 2012). Using interviews, we were also able to show that feelings about the term "radiation" tended to be limited to the association that radiation is always something invisible, man-made, and harmful to the human body. Hardly any of the 15 year old students still associated radiation ("Strahlung") with something warm and pleasant like the Sun.

After analyzing the frequency of the objects drawn according to the third research question that dealt with gender differences, we did not find many discrepancies between the choices of the boys and those of the girls. The only motifs that boys drew much more frequently were objects related to radioactivity, but all of the other categories showed no highly significant differences between the two sexes.

Change in Associations: Before and After Fukushima

The specific time frame of our study made it possible for us to scrutinize the influence of an exterior event, the tragic events in Fukushima, Japan, in March 2011 on children's associations with the term "radiation". Nine months after the accident that led to worldwide intensive media coverage about potential hazards of nuclear power plants and ionizing radiation, we decided to replicate the study and compare the results. For this purpose, we asked children from the same grades and the same schools as in the previous study in 2009. The set-up, as well as the evaluation of the drawings were identical to the first part of the study.

The results showed that the percentage of drawings that were categorized as "motifs related to radioactivity" almost doubled (see Figure 13). This was the case among all three grades and for both sexes. Also, the short follow-up interviews that we performed with a sub-set of the children showed that their associations between radiation and nuclear power plants (or radioactivity) had become much more prominent.

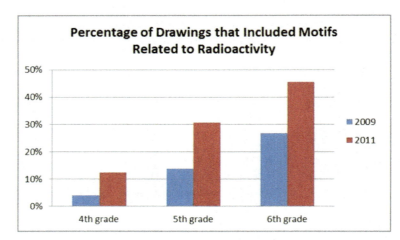

Figure 13. In 2011, many more students drew objects related to nuclear power plants and radioactivity

Some examples of typical drawings related to radioactivity that we received in the second part of our study (after Fukushima) can be seen in Figure 14. Most of them showed how menacing the term "radiation" was perceived by the students. This negative impression that we got from the drawings was reinforced during the short interviews.

Figure 14. Some typical drawings related to radioactiviy (after the events at Fukishima)

We would like to encourage the reader to experiment with the method of using drawings for research or teaching purposes. Although we were aware of certain drawbacks regarding our decision to use drawings as our primary research method, we were, generally, positively surprised by the benefits of utilizing this approach. Apart from the fact that the drawings revealed a number of, what might otherwise have been, hidden thoughts and concepts, we really appreciated the ease with which the teachers – and especially the children – could contribute to scientific research while enjoying themselves at the same time.

As demonstrated time and again throughout the existing literature, as well as in our own studies described above: discovering students' associations is essential for effective teaching. The reactions of the teachers in our case studies, as well as our research results described in part three of this chapter, both show that drawings can offer a viable, effective, and easy method of identifying students' ideas and associations. This provides a solid foundation for planning suitable lesson concepts that will be beneficial to all students.

NOTES

[1] Special thanks to Waltraud Leger-Felber, the physics teacher who organized and carried out the "energy case study".

[2] Electricity production in Austria currently focuses on hydro-electric power plants (62%) and thermal power plants (36%), whereas wind and solar power plants together only amount to 3% of the total electricity production. Austria does not produce any electricity from nuclear power

[3] We would also like to express our gratitude to Claudia Aumann, the chemistry teacher who conducted this case study.

[4] The TV series Breaking Bad deals with a chemistry teacher who uses his subject knowledge to produce crystal meth in order to earn money for his cancer treatment.

[5] In the Austrian school system this is the equivalent of grades 4–6. The Austrian science curriculum introduces the concept of radiation in grade-7 (thermal radiation) and in grade-8 (nuclear radiation).

[6] As the research took place in Austria, where German is spoken, the actual word written on the board was *"Strahlung"*, which corresponds to the English word "radiation" as in *elektromagnetische Strahlung = electromagnetic radiation*.

REFERENCES

Acar Sesen, B., & Ince, E. (2010). Internet as a source of misconception: "Radiation and Radioactivity". *Turkish Online Journal of Educational Technology – TOJET, 9*(4), 94–100.

Baxter, J. (1989). Children's understanding of familiar astronomical events. *International Journal of Science Education, 11*, 502–513.

Chambers, D. W. (1983). Stereotypic images of the scientist: The draw-a-scientist test. *Science Education, 67*(2), 255–265.

Driver, R., Guesne, E., & Tiberghien, A. (Eds.). (1985). *Children's ideas in science*. Milton Keyes: Open University Press.

Finson, K. D. (2002). Drawing a scientist: What we do and do not know after fifty years of drawings. *School Science and Mathematics, 102*(7), 335–345. doi:10.1111/j.1949-8594.2002.tb18217.x

Guesne, E. (1985). Light. In R. Driver (Ed.), *Children's ideas in science* (pp. 10–32). Milton Keyes: Open University Press.

Gunstone, R., & Watts, M. (1985). Force and motion. In R. Driver (Ed.), *Children's ideas in science* (pp. 85–104). Milton Keyes: Open University Press.

Lewis, E. L., & Linn, M. C. (1994). Heat energy and temperature concepts of adolescents, adults, and experts: Implications for curricular improvements. *Journal of Research in Science Teaching, 31*, 657–677.

Lijnse, P. L., Eijkelhof, H. M. C., Klaassen, C. W. J. M., & Scholte, R. L. J. (1990). Pupils' and mass-media ideas about radioactivity. *International Journal of Science Education, 12*(1), 67–78.

Neumann, S., & Hopf, M. (2012). Students' conceptions about 'Radiation': Results from an explorative interview study of 9th grade students. *Journal of Science Education and Technology, 21*(6), 826–834. doi:10.1007/s10956-012-9369-9

Neumann, S., & Hopf, M. (2013). Children's drawings about "Radiation"—Before and after Fukushima. *Research in Science Education, 43*(4), 15. doi:10.1007/s11165-012-9320-3

Rego, F., & Peralta, L. (2006). Portuguese students' knowledge of radiation physics. *Physics Education, 41*(3), 259–262.

Shipstone, D. M., Rhoeneck, C., Jung, W., Karrqvist, C., Dupin, J. S., Joshua, S., & Licht, P. (1988). A study of students' understanding of electricity in five European countries. *International Journal of Science Education, 10*, 303–316.

White, R. T., & Gunstone, R. F. (1992). *Probing understanding*. London & New York, NY: Falmer.

Susanne Neumann
University of Vienna, Austria

Martin Hopf
University of Vienna, Austria

KATRINA ROSELER AND MICHAEL DENTZAU

11. USING DRAWINGS TO DEMONSTRATE INFORMAL SCIENCE LEARNING EXPERIENCES THROUGH THE CONTEXTUAL MODEL OF LEARNING

INTRODUCTION

Everyday activities engage learners in scientific practices in multiple contexts over time through various experiences. These everyday activities provide opportunities to engage in scientific practices in relaxed but informative environments. In these environments, individuals can develop knowledge and skills over time, spanning a multitude of topics and in varied contexts. Commonly, out-of-school learning experiences are described as informal learning. When you consider that less than 8% of the life of an average 18 year-old student is spent in formal classroom settings, and only a fraction of that time devoted to science (Ellenbogen & Stevens, 2005), the contributions of informal settings to science experiences and ultimately learning are clear.

Informal learning is often characterized as being voluntary, open ended, and removed from curriculum and standards of the traditional school environment, including high stakes accountability measures (Dierking, Falk, Rennie, Anderson, & Ellenbogen, 2003; Ellenbogen & Stevens, 2005; Foutz & Stein, 2009; Rennie, 2007). For the purposes of this chapter, informal learning is more broadly defined as any learning that occurs outside of a traditional, formal, school environment. While this may take place in structured settings such as museums, it also includes unstructured environs, recreation and "play". The term 'museum' is used to describe informal science institutions including but not limited to: museums, science centers, aquaria, zoos, environmental centers, botanical gardens, and national parks. There is a body of research devoted to learning in museums and given that learning spans multiple formal and informal contexts over a lifetime, a theoretical framework that pays attention to these varied contexts is helpful for understanding the learning contributions from these multiple settings.

CONTEXTUAL MODEL OF LEARNING

Research on informal learning, given its variety of forms, intensities and durations, is often framed by the Contextual Model of Learning (e.g. Phipps, 2010). The Contextual Model of Learning ("Contextual Model") was developed by John Falk and Lynn Dierking (2000) and describes learning as a process that results from "complex phenomenon situated within a series of contexts" and rises from "interactions between an individual's personal, sociocultural and physical contexts over time" (Falk & Storksdieck, 2005, p. 745). In the Contextual Model, the personal context draws from a constructivist learning perspective which considers prior knowledge and experience as factors that influence individual interpretation and learning and how these variables are integrated in informal settings. Through a sociocultural context, learning is influenced by social interactions; not only upon our prior and cultural and social underpinnings, but also based on the interaction that occurs during learning between learners. The physical context acknowledges that learning occurs in a physical environment, and that setting affects what is learned and why it is learned. Finally, all of these contexts are at play over time, essentially throughout the life of the learner. Through the frame of the Contextual Model, learning occurs in overlapping contexts (see Figure 1) suggesting that learning research needs to address these contexts which occur in various settings, including informal environments.

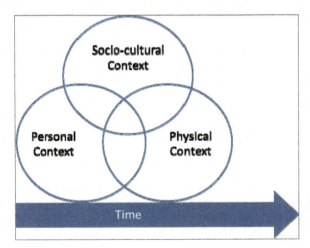

Figure 1. Contextual model of learning as proposed by Falk & Dierking (2000)

DRAWINGS: A TOOL TO DEMONSTRATE LEARNING IN VARIOUS CONTEXTS

Researchers have used various means to capture information regarding the impacts of informal science experiences, including surveys, interviews, video/audio recordings and drawings. Drawings, as a data collection tool, have been used "to record what [students] had done or what they [had] discovered during science activities" (Symington & Hayes, 1991, p. 39). Drawings have also been found to be "an efficient and effective [data collection] method: efficient in that they contain much information … and effective, in that they are easily assimilated by the person looking at them" (Bowker, 2007, p. 105). In addition, drawings are open-ended, with fewer restrictions than other forms of data collection and may provide insights not available by other means (White & Gunstone, 1992). Research using drawings has been used to demonstrate shifts in understanding in pre/post situations (Bowker, 2007; Dentzau & Gallard, 2014; Trundle, Atwood, & Christopher, 2006). In addition, drawings have also been used to demonstrate science conceptions at a specific point in time (Alerby, 2000; Chang, 2012; Dove, Everett, & Preece, 1999; Ehrlen, 2009). In certain situations, the usefulness of drawings has been enhanced when participants have the opportunity to further explain the thinking that supports the images (Copeland & Agosto, 2012; Rennie & Jarvis, 1995).

METHODS

In this chapter we discuss the way that drawings have been used in two research contexts in an effort to understand informal science experiences within vastly different settings. The first research context calls upon a sample of undergraduate students to reflect upon a time that they remember engaging in science outside of school and to depict an experience through drawing. The second research context looks at the impacts of an environmental education experience on the developing understanding of a local ecosystem. This second research context involves a sample of 4th Grade students (approximately 10 years old) who were asked to draw an image of a longleaf pine ecosystem both before and after participation in series of guided environmental education experiences Although the driving questions for each study were vastly different, we have chosen to analyze the data through the lens of the Contextual Model, namely the physical setting of learning, personal contributions to learning, the socio-cultural interactions of learners, and the influence of time on the learning experience. The methodology behind each setting and study are presented individually. In contrast, the results will incorporate evidence from both studies to demonstrate the multiple learning contexts described in the Contextual Model and how drawings are able to communicate learning from within these overlapping contexts.

UNDERGRADUATES DOING SCIENCE OUT-OF-SCHOOL

A total of 184 drawings from a mix of undergraduate science and non-science majors from a large southeastern university representing themselves engaged in science outside of school were collected and analyzed. Each participant completed the 'Draw Yourself Doing Science' instrument, (developed for this research), which prompted participants to "Draw a picture (or write) of a time when you thought you were participating in science or doing something scientific outside of school". No restrictions were placed upon the content of the drawings, and all participants were asked to label features of their drawings and provide a short narrative explaining their drawings. This draw-and-write technique was aimed at encouraging participants to explain the thinking embedded within the drawings created.

Similar to others that have used drawings in research (see Alerby, 2000; Dove, Everett, & Preece, 1999; Ehrlen, 2009; Symington, et al., 1981; Hayes & Symington, 1984), participants in this research were asked to make one drawing. In order to ensure instructions were clearly interpreted by the participants, the phrase "out-of-school" was used in place of "informal" learning experience. By requesting participants to draw themselves doing science, the researcher sought to capture perceptions of what participants understood science to be and how they identified themselves with science.

Qualitative analysis procedures were used to analyze the drawings; facilitated through the use of QSR NVivo 10 data analysis software. Structured coding, guided by the Contextual Model, was completed on each drawing (i.e., physical context, personal context sociocultural context, and time). Each drawing was analyzed for each of the contexts of the Contextual Model and parameters for these codes were provided by Falk and Dierking (2000) as part of their description of the model.

4TH GRADE STUDENT ENVIRONMENTAL EDUCATION EXPERIENCE

The data for this study included 293 students approximately 10 years of age over 2 distinct years that attended an out-of-school environmental education program at the E.O. Wilson Biophilia Center ("Center") that focused on learning about the longleaf pine ecosystem. This ecosystem which once covered vast areas of the southeastern United States is now present in only 3% of its historic range in disjunctive populations (Frost, 1995). The Center's environmental education program was provided to students from local school districts, but it was not a mainstream curriculum used by the schools, and was based on the goal of the Center to educate about and connect with the local ecosystems and biodiversity (E. O. Wilson Biophilia Center at Nokuse Plantation, n.d.). Students attended the Center on 4 days, generally spread out over the duration of a month or longer.

The Draw a Longleaf Pine Forest Ecosystem (D-LLPFE) tool was designed as a pre and post measure to evaluate the impact of the experience on ecologically important criteria of the longleaf ecosystem (Dentzau & Gallard, 2014). Prior to attending the Center, students were asked to produce a drawing that represented their impression or understanding of a longleaf pine ecosystem that is typical of north Florida. The specific prompt was as follows:

On the back of this page please draw what you understand the longleaf pine forest (ecosystem) to look like in northern Florida. Please include the plants, animals and processes that you feel are part of this natural community. Please feel free to label any part of your drawing or to add comments to make your drawing clearer.

Each student was provided with a standardized drawing sheet containing the above instructions and places for a name and date. This tool and prompt were administered by the students' individual teacher prior to attending the first day of the Center activities. After the last day at the Center, the students were again given the prompt and asked to repeat the exercise. All drawings were completed at the students' individual schools and the researcher was not present during the in school activities to verify the fidelity of teacher implementation.

Each drawing was analyzed using a validated and reliable rubric (Dentzau & Martinez, 2014), focusing on key identifying characteristics of the longleaf pine ecosystem including flora, fauna, distinct life stages, adaptive features, community diversity and ecosystem function. The intent behind the use of the drawings was to highlight changes in student understanding of the longleaf pine ecosystem and from these shifts determine the impact of the experience on the students. In addition, the drawings were also reviewed to detect emerging themes not fully captured by the rubric. These themes emerged and became stable through a constant comparative coding methodology (Lincoln & Guba, 1985).

Analysis/Results

In order to demonstrate the flexibility of drawings to provide evidence of the impact of informal science learning experiences through the lens of the Contextual Model we present the analysis and results of the two studies simultaneously.

Personal Context. The personal context, in addition to considering prior knowledge and experience also addresses personal interest and therefore motivation, which are interwoven in the context of informal learning (Falk & Dierking, 2000). When considering the undergraduate study it can be assumed that all drawings reflected the personal context because the prompt specifically asked to remember a time out of school that "you" thought you were doing something scientific. More specifically, however, drawings coded "personal context" can further reflect the participant engaged in an informal science experience independent of others (i.e., the participant engaged in the experience alone). Seventy-one drawings indicated informal science experiences where the participant engaged in learning alone. Figure 2 provides an example where the participant represents herself independent of others engaging in the act of cooking.

Figure 2. Drawing data coded "personal context" represented here as the participant engaging in the activity of cooking alone

Other than cooking, examples of the personal context were exemplified in drawings where participants described connecting ideas together (i.e., thinking), media consumption (reading, watching TV), making observations of phenomenon, sports activities (i.e., fishing, SCUBA diving, dancing) and testing ideas through experimentation. Given the prompt provided to students, reflections of individuals engaging in in these free-choice activities demonstrates the interest and motivation components of the personal context dimension of the model.

The drawings of the 4th Grade students highlighted the personal context in a slightly different way. From the drawings that preceded the environmental instruction, one was able to get a glimpse into prior knowledge, most importantly student alternative conceptions. For example, in the pre-drawings there were 41 distinct representations of animals inappropriate for a longleaf pine forest ecosystem in northern Florida, including monkey, koala, moose, sloth, boa constrictor, shark, dolphin, ape, jaguar, flying marsupial, lion, tiger, cheetah, gorilla, and leopard.

Alternative conceptions of the ecosystem were also common representations by students in the pre-drawings. These were characterized by the absence of animals in the drawing (an ecosystem consists of flora, fauna and abiotic constituents), the inclusion of atypical physical elements (e.g. snow-capped mountains that are not found in a state with the highest elevation of 345 feet above mean sea level (USGS, n.d.)), as well as plants and animals that are generic representations and could be generally found in most North American ecosystems. Figure 3 provides such an example that was common, showing what was characterized by the researcher as "lollipop" trees. Compare that to the same students post-drawing (see Figure 4) that depicts specificity through inclusion of identifying characteristics of the longleaf pine (e.g. needles extending from the terminus of the branches) and iconic species (e.g. – harvester ants represented by the mound and tracks along the left center of the drawing).

Figure 3. Pre-drawing highlighting alternative conceptions of the longleaf pine ecosystem

Figure 4. Post-drawing from the same student as depicted in Fig. 3 showing a more sully developed representation of the community

Sociocultural Context. The sociocultural context suggests that learning is a function of an individual's cultural and social lenses, and/or the interactions that occur with others during the experience (Falk & Dierking, 2000). Undergraduate drawings coded as "sociocultural context" most commonly represent multiple individuals engaging in the informal science experience along with the participant. Commonly, the other individuals who are identified in the drawings are friends and/or family. Ninety-nine drawings demonstrate informal science experiences incorporating individuals besides the participant. Figure 5 is an example of an undergraduate drawing that was coded "socio-cultural context". In this drawing the participant indicates that the informal experience (i.e., making ice cream), is a social activity occurring with his/her mother and brother. Other examples of activities depicted in drawings that were coded sociocultural context include camping, hiking/nature walks, testing ideas (experimenting) and/or building.

The relevance of the socio-cultural context, however, is also represented through more subtle, often implied, examples that stem from the individuals cultural assets. In this manner a community influences individual thinking in a particular context. Figure 6 is an additional example from the undergraduate research study that demonstrates such a sociocultural experience. In this drawing, the participant describes a family practice or culture of working on a cooperative farm. The participant indicates that working on the farm was expected and because of the experience, he learned about the science associated with farming.

In the 4th grade student drawings evidence of the sociocultural context of the learning was not particularly prevalent, though some examples showing their classmates engaged in activities or references to the informal educators at the Center are present. In Figure 7 the student's drawing depicts one of the educators at the Center known to all the children as "Turtle Bob". Turtle Bob introduced the students to different kinds of native reptiles with live exhibits and the opportunity to interact with these animals on a limited basis. The most curious aspect of this drawing, however, is that it represented a pre-drawing before the student actually had the opportunity to

USING DRAWINGS TO DEMONSTRATE INFORMAL SCIENCE LEARNING EXPERIENCES THROUGH THE CONTEXTUAL MODEL OF LEARNING

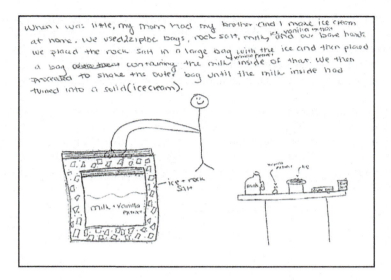

Figure 5. Drawing data coded as sociocultural context, represented here by references to "mom" and "brother"

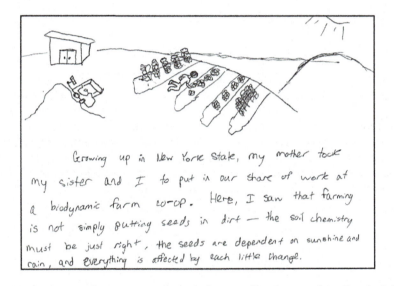

Figure 6. Second undergraduate drawing demonstrating the code "socio-cultural context" implies the influence of family culture

Figure 7. Pre-drawing referencing an instructor the student was informed would be present during her/his visits to the center

meet Turtle Bob. This suggests another dimension of the sociocultural context wherein students' expectations of their upcoming visits were influenced by older students that had experienced the Center in the one or two years prior. At the time of this study, these students represented the third cohort of 4th Grade students visiting the Center, which at that time was open to the public only for these coordinated trips. Also of note is the reference to a dog, which is not a typical resident of the longleaf pine forest. It is likely that this dog was meant to represent "Roscoe" a stray dog that found its way to the Center and has become a lovable fixture that accompanies students on field hikes.

Physical Context. The physical context is the place or the surroundings in which learning is situated (Falk & Dierking, 2000). The undergraduate participant drawings represent the physical context as various locations including museums, indoor spaces (i.e, home, dance studio), outdoor spaces, summer camps, and work/volunteer experiences. Nearly all of the drawings were coded as occurring in a particular physical context. Drawings that could not be coded for physical context demonstrated no indication of the location of the activity, merely the activity itself, void of any physical context. Figure 8 is an example of a drawing that was coded for its physical context. In this drawing the participant draws herself engaging in an informal science experience in an outdoor location, specifically at the ocean.

Figure 8. Drawing data demonstrating the code "physical context", represented here as an outdoor location (i.e., the ocean)

The importance of the physical context is also illustrated in the 4th Grade student drawings. Remembering that students were prompted to draw their understanding of the longleaf pine forest again after their last visit to the Center, the inclusion of specific activities, people (e.g. Figure 7), and structures emphasize the sometimes overriding importance of the setting for the learning. Figure 9 is one student's post-drawing focused entirely on the Exhibit Hall filled with animal exhibits, interactive displays and dioramas. Included are the snapping turtle enclosure, photosynthesis exhibit, observation bee hive, and oversized models of a gopher tortoise and harvester ant.

Figure 9. Student's post-response to the prompt to draw his/her understanding of the longleaf pine forest

Time. Time is another factor that impacts learning in informal settings, and the two research examples provide different perspectives of the role of this dimension. The undergraduate participant drawings represent time in multiple ways through the specific activities, and this element was largely an inferred component. For example, it was assumed that cooking occurred in a short period (i.e. less than one day), while growing plants occurred over an extended time period. Thirty drawings indicated multiple independent informal experiences occurring at various times, while 35 drawings indicated that the participant engaged in similar or the same experience on multiple occasions. While all of the activities depicted in the drawings required time in order to occur, only those that represented multiple experiences or multiple repetitions were coded for time. Figure 10 is a drawing coded for its representation of time; over both multiple experiences and multiple repetitions. In this drawing, the participant indicates two different informal science experiences as well as suggests that these experiences occurred frequently.

Figure 10. Drawing demonstrating the code "time", represented through multiple representations and multiple repetitions

More significantly, however, is that all of the undergraduate students in the drawings, and the text that accompanied them, were reflecting on a prior time of engaging in science that was meaningful to them in one way or another. Perhaps it was the activity, the personal involvement, the social interaction or the physical context that were memorable; but in all cases the experience occurred in the past, sometimes long in the past. The act of recalling an experience from the past reinforces the power of the dimension of time in these informal science experiences. Figure 11 is an example of such an activity. In this drawing, the participant represents herself as a child viewing what is inferred to be a composite representation of the multiple visits she had to particular museum throughout her childhood.

Figure 11. Drawing demonstrating the impact of time on an informal learning experience

The time factor was once again reflected slightly differently in the 4th Grade student participants. Instead of providing insight over a period of years, as with many of the undergraduate students, the 4th grade participants provided a pre-post instruction view that spanned a median time between drawings of 42 days.

Using the rubric, the researcher was able to demonstrate evidence of increasing understanding of the essential ecological characteristics of the longleaf pine ecosystem by the students ($t = -15.03$, $p < 0.001$); a statistical difference supported by a large effect size (Cohen's $d = 1.095$). Figures 12 and 13 are pre and post-drawings from a single student that embody this shift. The pre-drawing contained minimal representation of animals and no important processes associated with the ecosystem. The post-drawing (Figure 13) referenced enhanced biodiversity, iconic species including the gopher tortoise and the harvester ant (as indicated by the two burrow systems), and an acknowledgement of the importance of fire in the perpetuation of the ecosystem. In addition to the validated rubric for the drawing assessment (Dentzau & Gallard, 2014) the qualitative analysis of the drawings identified emerging themes including increasing biodiversity, species specificity (e.g. red cockaded woodpecker replaced unidentified bird); and decreasing representation of alternative conceptions/misconceptions.

The 4th grade drawings demonstrate the impact of time demonstrated as learning about the longleaf pine ecosystem. Given the growth and complexity of understanding that are demonstrated in the pre and post drawings, and the scarcity of such content in the formal educational setting, the time that the students spent at the Center, engaged in activities, impacted their understanding of the ecosystem.

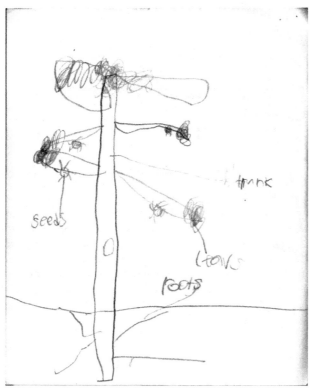

Figure 12. Pre-drawing that received a score of 5 out of 18 based on the rubric

Figure 13. Post-drawing from same student that was scored a 15

Discussion

The results from these studies, from vastly different settings indicate some of the benefits of using drawings to inform understanding about learning in informal contexts. Drawings are an excellent means to capture evidence of learning through the multiple lenses of the Contextual model. Also, drawings provide a means to capture details about an informal science experience that might be missed if collected through other means.

Drawings capture details that other metrics may not. We believe that drawings are able to capture nuanced information about the learning experienced by the participants that may be missing in other types of inquiries. For example, had the 4th grade students been asked to describe the longleaf pine ecosystem, either verbally or in writing, we question whether the subtleties of prior knowledge and alternative conceptions would have been evident. Both drawings represented in Figure 14 are representations of a forest with large pine trees; yet it is clear that in the drawing on the left the student was heavily influenced by prior knowledge which is best classified as a representation of a cartoon pine forest or trees more typical of northern latitudes, while the student on the right represents characteristics unique to the longleaf pine.

Figure 14. The image of the forest on the left contains animals and pine tree, but clearly the pines are alternative conceptions based upon prior knowledge that is not consistent with the characteristics of a natural longleaf pine forest. The image on the right reflects a model of the forest more consistent with ecologists

Similarly, the undergraduates' draw-and-write data provided detailed accounts of experiences that might otherwise be lost if asked to complete only a written or oral account of their informal experience. Figure 15 demonstrates how the draw-and-write technique was used by one participant to demonstrate a personal understanding of the connection between composting and gardening. In this drawing the participant shows how she uses specific types of household garbage ("i.e., biodegradable waste) to produce soil that is then used to grow herbs (i.e., basil and cilantro).

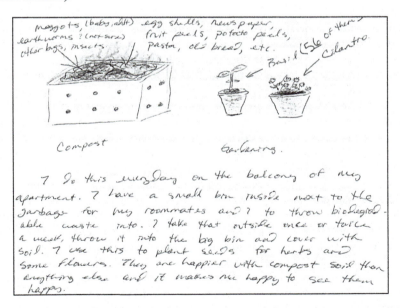

Figure 15. Drawing demonstrating the connection between composting and gardening as practiced by one undergraduate participant

Drawings capture learning as framed by the Contextual Model. Drawings are also excellent vectors for demonstrating the impacts of informal science experiences through the lens of the Contextual Model; specifically the three learning contexts (i.e., personal, socio-cultural, physical) and time. Both samples (i.e., undergraduate drawings and 4th grade drawings) demonstrate evidence of the

131

differing importance of these contexts to the individual learner. In addition, that these contexts were represented differently in the two studies only enhances the value and adaptability of drawings in assessing knowledge and impact of informal science experience.

Personal context. The role of the personal context in informal science learning was demonstrated in drawings by knowledge gains between the pre/post drawings (4th Grade), the eliciting of alternatsive science conceptions (4th Grade), connecting prior knowledge (undergraduate and 4th Grade), and representations of engaging in the practices of science individually (undergraduate). Consider also, how drawings are able, largely from a personal context perspective, to show how learners in informal environments make meaning from the connection of ideas. For the 4th Grade students, the conversion of alternative conceptions to those more closely aligned with accepted scientific doctrine are prime examples. Using a pre and post drawing format automatically captured the impacts of learning over a period of time as demonstrated by the 4th grade data sample. The time-lapse between the two drawings suggest that the intervention at the Center provided participants with an opportunity to expand their understanding of the longleaf pine ecosystem therefore impacting the personal context (i.e, learning). In addition, we find that the relative scarcity of an overt personal content in the drawings on the longleaf ecosystem to also be informative. Does the virtual absence of personal representation within the longleaf pine ecosystem suggests that participants view themselves as separate from the environment, as has been suggested by other researchers (e.g. Shepardson, Wee, Priddy, & Harbor, 2007). The consequences of such a position may indicate that Center may wish to stress the connection between the environment and our role within the environment and as stewards of the same.

Undergraduate drawings demonstrated the personal context of learning in a different manner. Many drawings represented the participant engaging in an informal experience alone, which the researcher coded as "personal context". This surface level analysis does little to illuminate the impact of these experiences on personal learning. However, further consideration of the data coded "personal context" revealed a subset of the drawings that indicate some level of meaning making (i.e., thinking) being done by the learner. In this subset of drawings, the undergraduates generally describe connecting one learning experience with another (e.g., applying what was learned in school to what is observed in nature). So, although not explicitly captured in a pre/post fashion, one-time drawings can demonstrate personal meaning making as described by the Contextual Model.

Time. While the undergraduate participants were instructed to represent only a point in time, many chose to represent multiple experiences or similar repetitive experiences. Those that represented multiple experiences provide evidence of the impact of informal experiences over time; these informal science experiences are memorable and, for the purposes this particular research context, demonstrate some level of personal connection to science understanding. Even without a pre/post format, drawings can demonstrate the impact of time on learning.

The 4th grade data demonstrated the impact of time on learning through the data collection method. By choosing to collect pre and post data from the participants around their participation at the Center, the research was designed to capture the impact of the experience as it unfolded over time.

Sociocultural context. From a sociocultural perspective, most support for this framework was offered by the undergraduate student drawings which often described their informal science learning experiences as occurring within a group or resulting from an assumed cultural lens. The relative absence of this in the 4th Grade drawings may have resulted from the framing of the prompt. The open-ended drawing prompt provided to the undergraduates provided opportunities to demonstrate interactions between personal and sociocultural contexts for learning. In some undergraduate cases, the sociocultural dimension of the informal experience supported individual learning (i.e., personal context). An example of this is the use of personal observations to connect to scientific ideas in a social setting. When in the presence of others, one person independently observes the world around them (i.e., you can only see, hear, smell and taste with your own senses). Even when you are surrounded by others, your experience is individualized and subject to prior knowledge and experience. Similarly, when engaging in activities with others you connect ideas in a different manner than others who are engaging in the same experience.

Analysis of the undergraduate drawings also demonstrated the cultural influence of learning during informal experiences, particularly from family. The analysis of undergraduate drawings suggests that informal science experiences carried a particular level of participation or expectation with regard to the family unit. Family vacations, cooperative farming and fishing are examples of how the undergraduate participants demonstrated family influence (i.e., culture) for engagement during the experiences represented in the drawings. The cultural piece was demonstrated through an implied expectation or role that the participant assumed as represented in their drawing(s).

Physical context. Most evident of all, however, is the importance of the physical context for learning science in informal settings. The process of learning has long been connected with place or the location. Lave and Wenger (1991) advocate the theory of situated learning, in which learning occurs within a situated activity that is embedded within a particular social and physical environment. The concept of situated learning "implies that understanding and experience are in constant interaction – indeed, are mutually constitutive" (Lave & Wenger, 1991, pp. 52–53). Learning is considered to be embedded with the specific context of delivery and is effective only through active participation (Greeno, 1998).

As mentioned previously, nearly all of the undergraduate students identified themselves engaged in science in a particular physical setting. Sometimes this setting was integral, as in a specific location of a museum or a national park, and other times it was less obvious such as a reference to being indoors or in a kitchen. Clearly "doing" science and therefore learning science is inextricably tied to place. While at first glance, the importance of physical setting might appear less clear in the 4th Grade student examples, careful review of the drawings show elements of their experience in their drawings. Sometimes it is a reference to an activity completed by the students or a tree that formed the focus of a particular stop on one of the hikes. In virtually all cases, however, the images offered were strongly influenced by the experiences while at the Center. The "long" needles of the namesake pine, the mounds characteristic of the harvester ant (a focus of one of the lessons), reference to specific animals that were only observed in diorama displays, and of course the inclusion by over 30% of the students in the post drawings of either the gopher tortoise and/or its iconic burrow, are all products of the experiences that occurred in the physical setting that is the Center.

We believe we have demonstrated the value of drawings in eliciting the impact of informal science experiences. Just as these experiences are varied and cross a huge spectrum, so is the information that is contained in drawings whether dealing with adolescents or adults. Using drawings has the ability to illuminate complex and nuanced understanding of informal science learning experiences that might otherwise be hidden from an educator or researcher. We see drawings as powerful tools worthy of broader implementation.

REFERENCES

Alerby, E. (2000). A way of visualising children's and young people's thoughts about the environment: A study of drawings. *Environmental Education Research, 6*(3), 205–222.

Bowker, R. (2007). Children's perceptions and learning about tropical rainforests: An analysis of their drawings. *Environmental Education Research, 13*(1), 75–96.

Chang, N. (2012). The role of drawing in young children's construction of science concepts. *Early Childhood Education Journal, 40*(3), 187–193.

Copeland, A. J., & Agosto, D. E. (2012). Diagrams and relational maps: The use of graphic elicitation techniques with interviewing for data collection, analysis, and display. *International Journal of Qualitative Methods, 11*(5), 513–533.

Dentzau, M. W., & Martínez, A. J. G. (2014). The development and validation of an alternative assessment to measure changes in understanding of the longleaf pine ecosystem. *Environmental Education Research,* (ahead-of-print), 1–24.

Dierking, L. D., Falk, J. H., Rennie, L., Anderson, D., & Ellenbogen, K. (2003). Policy statement of the" informal science education" ad hoc committee. *Journal of Research in Science Teaching, 40*(2), 108–111.

Dove, J., Everett, L., & Preece, P. (1999). Exploring a hydrological concept through children's drawings. *International Journal of Science Education, 21*(5), 485–497.

Ehrlen, K. (2009). Drawings as representations of children's conceptions. *International Journal of Science Education, 31*(1), 41–57.

Ellenbogen, K. M., & Stevens, R. (2005). *Informal science learning environments: A review of research to inform K-8 schooling.* Washington, DC: National Research Council Board on Science Education – Science Learning K-8.

E. O. Wilson Biophilia Center at Nokuse Plantation. (n.d.). Retrieved from http://www.eowilsoncenter.org/welcome.html

Falk, J. H., & Dierking, L. D. (2000). *Learning from museums: Visitor experiences and the making of meaning.* Lanham, MD: Altamira Press.

Foutz, S., & Stein, J. (2009). Visitor studies. In M. Bates & M. Maack (Ed.), *Encyclopedia of library and information sciences* (3rd ed., pp. 5556–5563). London: Taylor & Francis.

Falk, J., & Storksdieck, M. (2005). Using the contextual model of learning to understand visitor learning from a science center exhibition. *Science Education, 89*(5), 744–778.

Frost, C. (1995). Four centuries of changing landscape patterns in the longleaf pine ecosystem. In S. I. Cerulean & R. T. Engstrom (Eds.), *Proceedings 18th Tall Timbers Fire Ecology Conference, May 30–June2, 1991* (pp. 17–43). Tallahassee, FL: Tall Timbers Research, Inc.

Greeno, J. G. (1998). The stativity of knowing, learning, and research. *American Psychologist, 53*(1), 5–26.

Hayes, D., & Symington, D. (1984). The satisfaction of young children with their representational drawings of natural phenomena. *Research in Science Education, 14*, 39–46.

Lave, J., & Wenger, E. (1991). *Situated learning: Legitimate peripheral participation.* New York, NY: Cambridge University Press.

Lincoln, Y. S., & Guba, E. G. (1985). *Naturalistic inquiry.* Newbury Park, CA: Sage.

Phipps, M. (2010). Research trends and findings from a decade (1997–2007) of research on informal science education and free-choice science learning. *Visitor Studies, 13*(1), 3–22.

Rennie, L. (2007). Learning science outside of school. In S. K. Abell & N. G. Lederman (Eds.), *Handbook of research on science education* (pp. 125–167). Mahwah, NJ: Lawrence Erlbaum.

Rennie, L. J., & Jarvis, T. (1995). Children's choice of drawings to communicate their ideas about technology. *Research in Science Education, 25*(3), 239–252.

Shepardson, D. P., Wee, B., Priddy, M., & Harbor, J. (2007). Students' mental models of the environment. *Journal of Research in Science Teaching, 44*(2), 327–348.

Symington, D., & Hayes, D. (1991). Drawing for a purpose. *Australian Journal of Early Childhood, 16*(3), 38–40.

Trundle, K. C., Atwood, R. K., & Christopher, J. E. (2006). Preservice elementary teachers' knowledge of observable moon phases and pattern of change in phases. *Journal of Science Teacher Education, 17*(2), 87–101.

USGS. (n.d.). Retrieved from http://geonames.usgs.gov/apex/f?p=gnispq:3:0::NO::P3_FID:1851954

White, R. T., & Gunstone, R. F. (1992). *Probing understanding.* London: Falmer Press.

Katrina Roseler
Chaminade University of Honolulu, USA

Michael Dentzau
Oxbow Meadows Environmental Learning Center
Columbus State University, Georgia, USA

12. APPROPRIATE INTEGRATION OF CHILDREN'S DRAWINGS IN THE ACQUISITION OF SCIENCE CONCEPTS

WHY CHOOSE TO WORK WITH DRAWINGS?

If drawings are integrated into science education, not only can they assist young children in the development of scientific literacy, but they also can benefit them for the following reasons:

- Many young children produce drawings effortlessly (Kress, 1997) and love to draw (MacKenzie, 2011). Drawing is children's play (Copple & Bredekamp, 2009), an activity that is rarely refused by young children.
- It has been commonly recognized that while drawing, young children are able to develop their fine motor skills. The act of drawing helps increase muscle strength and good eye-hand coordination, which enable young children to engage in more advanced skills later in school such as writing with a pencil (NAEYC for families, n.d.). Oken-Wright (1998) further noted that drawing is a precursor to writing.
- Copple and Bredekamp (2009), Hopperstad (2010), Kress (1997), and Kress and van Leeuwen (2006), however, held a different view; they perceived that drawings contain meanings.

I conducted a study (2011) and found that drawing could also make children's learning educational and enjoyable. The study was intended to examine pre-service teachers' perceptions of drawing included in science instruction. Seventy pre-service teachers participated in the study. They worked with 140 young children from ages 4 to 7 across four semesters (fall, 2004, to spring, 2006) from a Midwest comprehensive university. Each of the students was required to teach two young children a science concept with drawing utilized as pre- and post-assessment tools. Prior to a student interacting with a child, he or she must know in what a child was interested. Based on the child's interests, a lesson plan was developed. All the students were required to submit reports following the interactions with the young children. One of the findings is that some children did not feel that they were being tested while drawing. For instance, Josiah (J), a six-year-old boy, drew a picture of the life cycle of an apple after the instruction. After he was asked to explain the drawing, the child did not seem to believe that the lesson was over (Figures 1 & 2):

S: Can you tell me about your picture?
J: First the seed came, then the tree, then the bud, then the flower, and then the apple.
S: Beautiful. Alright, that is all for today. Thank you so much for your help.
J: Is that it? (Chang, 2011, p. 12)

Figure 1. Josiah's first drawing of the life cycle of an apple   *Figure 2. Josiah's second drawing of the life cycle of an apple*

As reported by Sabrina, Josiah enjoyed drawing pictures. Drawing could give rise to a cathartic effect, helping reduce the degree of uneasiness and nervousness of both an adult and a child in the teaching and learning of science. The involvement of drawing in science education could situate both adult and child in a low-stress learning environment (Chang, 2011).

Historically, drawing has long been the center of interest of many educators and researchers. In 1885, Cooke believed that children's drawings reflected the unique quality of their minds (in Strommen, 1988). This was supported by Piaget and Inhelder (1967), who posited that a drawing represented a child's mental image of the world, although there was a disparity between an image on paper and that held by a child in the mind (in Strommen, 1988). Racci (1887) additionally noted that what young children expressed through drawings was what they would otherwise wish to write in words (in Strommen, 1988).

APPROPRIATE INTEGRATION OF DRAWINGS INTO SCIENCE EDUCATION

If drawing is used by young children as a medium to express their inner world, such a medium can be utilized to inform teaching and to facilitate learning in various subject areas. Yet, incorporating drawing in a subject area such as science needs to be implemented appropriately for the success of children's acquisition of science concepts. Since there exist misconceptions and misunderstandings in terms of appropriate integration of drawings into science instruction, it is my view that taking a close look at the following six areas is of great necessity. The discussion of these six areas could also help advance relevant knowledge of those working with young children and stimulate a promising discussion for the best interest of young children. The six areas are (1) Stating clear objectives, (2) Having a clear conceptual learning purpose for drawing, (3) Centering on science concepts, (4) Implementing collaborative and cooperative learning through drawing, (5) Knowing spontaneous concepts through drawing, (6) Focusing on conceptual understanding.

Stating Clear Objectives

While objectives may often be determined by Common Core Standards and/or by state standards, they must be stated clearly and be measurable and achievable. Objectives could metaphorically be referred to as a light at the end of a bleakly dark tunnel, making one become motivated and energized to get out of the frightening situation. In this sense, objectives work as a guide to instruction and assessment, informing a teacher of what to teach and what to assess. Clearly stated objectives can also guide a teacher to modify and improve his or her performance.

Copple and Bredekmap (2009) wrote that young children learned things quickly, but their narrow attention could only allow them to learn or pay attention to one thing at a time. Therefore, objectives need to focus on one science concept at a time to be in line with developmentally appropriate practice.

Here is an example that may aid the reader in understanding the issue. I will first offer an objective and then elaborate it. The objective is, "The students will be able to describe, in order, five stages of the life cycle of a green frog (egg, tadpole, tadpole with front legs, tadpole with hind legs, and adult frog) by drawing and oral explanation." This objective is narrow, measurable, and achievable, although seemingly challenging. Moreover, this objective does not indicate what children will *do* but rather what they will *know*. Mentioning in this objective what children are going to do, i.e., drawing and oral explanation, serves the purposes of having children construct the science concept and of having a teacher know how much young children have learned following the instruction.

Having a Clear Conceptual Learning Purpose for Drawing

Since conceptual development is of the center of a lesson, requesting children to draw pictures should aim at children's conceptual learning that is consistent with a clearly stated objective. In other words, requesting a drawing as part of a lesson should have a conceptual learning purpose.

David's drawings (Figures 3 & 4) display how much he had known about the science concept before the instruction and how much he learned after instruction. The drawings by David demonstrate they could assess a child's conceptual learning. In addition, since drawing works as a vehicle to display a child's mental construction (Piaget & Inhelder, 1966/1971), having David draw also provided an opportunity for the child to construct the science concept. While David was drawing, the process of drawing "forced" him to review what he had learned, thus providing an avenue for David to reinforce or relearn the science concept. Therefore, having a clear conceptual learning purpose when a drawing is requested could enable the teacher to know whether or not a clearly stated objectives is met and allow a child to construct a science concept (Chang, 2007, 2011, 2012).

While having a clear conceptual learning purpose for children to draw, the clear purpose could also help focus a child's attention on learning. In other words, when a child is asked to draw a picture of a science concept and later to talk about his or her drawing prior to instruction, the child is likely to start thinking of the science concept. In this sense, the unfamiliarity with the science concept could easily place the child in a disequilibrium state, which tends to trigger his or her inner desire to learn (Charlesworth & Lind, 2013). For example, Kevin, a five-year-old child, was asked by Heather, an adult, to draw a picture of the physical characteristics of a spider before instruction. After the completion of the drawing, Kevin was asked to explain his drawing. The following is the conversation between Heather (H) and Kevin (K):

Figure 3. David's frog lifecycle before instruction

Figure 4. David's frog lifecycle after instruction

H: Please tell me about your drawing.
[Kevin looks intently at his drawing.]
K: It has eight legs, two eyes, and um…
H: What's this? [pointing to the circle]
K: It has a head.
H: What are these? [pointing to four dots]
K: Um. Noses.
H: Noses?
K: Hmm Hmm.
H: Thank you for the explanation. Now, let's read a book to find out what a spider looks like.

While Heather just started reading *The Spiders* by Monica Hughes, published by Raintree, Kevin quickly grabbed his picture.

H: What have you noticed about the spider?
K: Oh, I forgot something (while responding, Kevin added another circle immediately next to the bigger circle). (Chang, 2012, p. 188)

Apparently, the drawing made Kevin wonder about the science concept. With his eagerness to learn the science concept, Kevin's attention was consequently drawn to the book to be read by Heather. Therefore, Kevin's emotion or affect for learning was at work, which drove Kevin to amend his drawing. At this point, Keven had already understood that a spider has two body parts even before Heather started instruction. Kevin's drawing following the instruction along with his oral explanation of the drawing (Figures 5 & 6) reveals his level of understanding of the science concept.

H: Please tell me about your picture.
K: It's a spider.
K: And it's hairy.
K: It has four eyes. And it has four noses. And it has eight legs. And it has two body parts. And that's all. (Chang, 2012, p. 188)

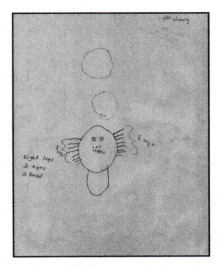 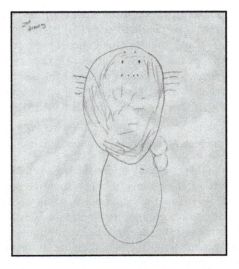

Figure 5. Kevin's spider drawing before instruction *Figure 6. Kevin's spider drawing after instruction*

137

The drawing allowed the teacher to assess how well she had taught and how well the child had learned in light of the objective. Needed adjustment to a next lesson and teaching strategies could then be made for the child's desirable learning and for his positive affect for learning.

Centering on Science Concepts

The previous section addresses the need for a clear conceptual learning purpose when a teacher requests a child to draw. This subsection takes a further look at the issue, which is vital to success of teaching and learning.

When requesting children to draw, the teacher must place the emphasis on a science concept rather than on art elements or on how to conventionally utilize art elements to correctly represent a science concept. When attention is paid to how to artistically represent a science concept while children are making drawings, it could become distracting. This practice departs from the notion by Copple and Bredekamp (2009) that children are able to learn effectively when they focus on one thing at a time. Therefore, in integrating children's drawings into science instruction, priority should be given to having children center on a science concept in drawing in order for a teacher to evaluate the status of teaching and learning.

I have so far addressed how drawing works as an assessment tool, rendering how much children know about a science concept. Yet, children are actually more capable than many adults would imagine when it comes to choosing and organizing resources, i.e., color, size, arrangement of features on paper, to represent their understandings (Kress, 1997). Here is an example. If a science concept is the lifecycle cycle of a penguin, the narrow, measurable, and achievable objective of the lesson may be "The students will be able to identify three stages of the life cycle of a penguin in order (egg, chick, adult penguin) with the use of drawing and oral explanation."

Figure 7 shows that a child had a little understanding of the concept. Why? Based on the theory of Kress (1997) and Kress and van Leeuwen (2006), the child depicted a little figure that is tucked at the very right bottom corner of the page, which could indicate the child's vague understanding of the science concept. It could also be viewed as a shot by a camera positioned at a higher-up angle to signify a sense of intimidation, the child's uncertainty about this science concept.

The child's lack of the science concept could further be assumed by a large space left empty between the sky and ground. According to Kress and van Leeuwen (2006), the empty space, a salient element, serves the purpose of capturing a viewer's attention. That is, facing the large empty white space, the viewer would then start looking for existing features in the drawing, which could well be the little figure tucked in the right bottom corner. Viewing this little figure, the viewer would seem to get a message: "I do not know the life cycle of a penguin" due to where this figure is positioned and to the size of the figure. A further look at the little figure would allow the viewer to receive another message: "Please teach me; I want to know the science concept." According to Kress and van Leeuwen (2006), the pair of eyes of the little figure appeared to directly look at the viewer, signaling the viewer that the child author is demanding something from or inviting an interaction with the viewer.

Standing in stark contrast to Figure 7, Figure 8 made by the same child following the science instruction is evidence of the child's mastery of the science concept. The drawing seems to show the child's certainty and boosted confidence. The sizes of the elements are much larger than those in Figure 7. A large figure in the center, a salient element, works as a departure point of viewing. The viewer then moves to his or her left to view the rest of the drawing, which include an egg and a smaller figure. While the egg seems disproportionate with the next figure, a chick, the viewer could sense the child's author's intended emphasis on this element, due to her pride in knowing something new. In terms of drawing elements, the child author noticeably used shapes, colors, and lines to represent her understanding of the science concept.

Figure 8 also shows the child's level of awareness of the physical characteristics of penguins, which definitely is a by-product of this particular lesson and which is not discerned at all from Figure 7. The notable addition could imply that an instructional tool, a non-fictional children's picture book, might have an impact on the child's mental schema.

In sum, this child's two distinctive, but remarkable drawings could tell us that although the child was five years of age, she was competent to use available resources to aptly and plausibly symbolize her intended meanings (Kress & van Leeuwen, 2006). Drawing is the window into a child's inner world. Centering on a science concept could yield much information needed by an adult about a child's learning level. The quality of artful representation is here not the issue.

Implementing Collaborative and Cooperative Communication through Drawing

Collaborative learning should not merely be considered as children reporting their discoveries or sharing their drawings with their peers during a whole group time, after a discovery or investigative activity involved with drawing is completed. It is inappropriate to assume that higher levels of learning would take place as a result of such group sharing. In other words, having children share each other's drawings, for example, as a whole group following an individual or small group investigation of a topic should, by no means, be the sole focus. Instead, collaborative learning needs to embrace an inextricably important element: the teacher's presence. A teacher should not detach her- or himself from the time when children are sharing their drawings or reporting their discoveries. Conversely, the presence of the teacher should see the teacher paying attention to every child's explanation of his or her drawing and then appropriately guide children's learning to either enhance the development of science concepts in light of the stated objectives or to prevent misconceptions

 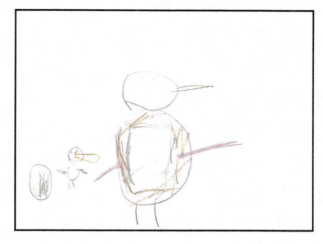

Figure 7. Penguin drawing by child prior to instruction   *Figure 8. Penguin drawing by the same child after instruction*

from taking place. Rice (2002) cautioned that once misconceptions were established, it can be very difficult to remove them from young children.

Likewise, cooperative communication should not be characterized as an interactive occasion between a teacher and a child, where a teacher would randomly ask the child a few questions about his or her drawing that have little relevance to the stated objectives. Nor should the teacher take no follow-up action on the child's answers in an effort to clarify or to facilitate the child's understanding of the science concepts according to the objectives. Cooperative communication, to all intents and purposes, should be an occasion where a teacher poses questions germane to stated objectives either to seek a child's level of understanding of science concepts prior to teaching or to grab a teachable moment to enhance the child's knowledge or to eliminate his or her misconceptions after an investigation is done. In short, questions raised to children should aid in reaching learning objectives.

For example, a group of six kindergarteners was acquiring a science concept of the life cycle of a penguin with the assistance of a teacher. Centering on the objective, prior to the instruction, the teacher asked the children to draw pictures of what they knew of the science concept. Then, organized by the teacher, the children shared their drawings with one another. While the children were sharing their drawings, the teacher asked the children individual questions to fully understand each child's drawing so as to make an informed decision as to how to adjust the prescribed lesson. After the lesson, the teacher then asked the children to show on paper what they knew about the science concept of the life cycle of a penguin to make a further decision as to how to improve the next lesson.

Through this lesson, the children did share their drawings among the group members, but the sharing was also centering on the science concept based on the objective. The sharing was focused, purposeful, and intentional with the presence of the teacher's support. While sharing was going on, the teacher also engaged the children in cooperative communication by asking each individual child questions for better instruction and learning. All in all, asking children to share drawings, without the intention of improving learning, should be avoided. Likewise, it is not useful to ask questions to a child about his drawing for the sake of asking without referencing an objective. Collaborative and cooperative communication about drawings is for the advancement of teaching and learning and for maximizing children's positive desires to learn.

Knowing Spontaneous Concepts through Drawing

Young children come to school with a variety of concepts and understandings about science, as young children are inherently curious about the world around them (NSTA, 2014). They have acquired these understandings more or less independently through their interactions with people and the environment. In view of Vygotsky's (1978) Zone of Proximal Development (ZPD), however, children need external assistance to reach their full potential (in McLeod, 2014), although they are able learn on their own to a certain extent. What children have obtained through their self-initiated explorations become their background knowledge and life experiences, which Halliday (1993) referred to as spontaneous concepts. Among these spontaneous concepts, some may continuously interest young children, which could then become bases for cultivating children's scientific concepts or higher mental functions. Drawing, as a tool to convey a child's inner world, could allow a teacher to know a spontaneous concept.

For example, Josiah's teacher developed a lesson plan on the science concept of the life cycle of an apple basing on her intimate knowledge of the child, who liked apples. With the use of a non-fiction children's picture book about the science concept, cooperative communication through the child's drawing, and a hands-on activity, Josiah reached a higher level of comprehension of the science concept (above in Figures 1 & 2).

Focusing on Conceptual Understanding

Children's drawings can express how much they know and how much they have learned about a science concept. The focus of drawing in this context should be on conceptual understanding. Observational drawings, therefore, should entirely be sidestepped. Observational drawing is a drawing made while a child author is looking at a certain object or pictorial material in an attempt to advance a child's artistic skills. The results of an observational drawing would not be helpful for a teacher to determine if a child has understood a science concept and if and how the teacher needs to adjust the next lesson, to reteach, and/or to modify teaching strategies. For that reason, a child author's conceptual understanding is a teacher's major concern; how well a child author can draw is not.

For example, Josiah did not make his drawings while looking at any concrete or pictorial objects. Instead he transformed 3-dimensional mental images relating to the life cycle of an apple onto a 2-dimensional medium, paper. The drawings reflected Josiah's conceptual understanding, the science concept of the life cycle of an apple as stated by the lesson's objective. The drawing also reflects Josiah's ability to think abstractly, his higher mental function. The teacher could thus modify her subsequent instruction according to the information obtained from the drawings, which was the concern of the teacher.

Figures 9 and 10 were produced by Gabby, a five-year-old child. These pictures both demonstrate the child's conceptions of the sequential colors of the rainbow before and after instruction. Yet, none of the pictures was made by the child being exposed to any concrete references. In other words, her drawings are not observational drawings; rather they are drawings that could inform the teacher that Gabby needed a lot of help in acquiring the science concept (see Figure 9) and that the child mastered the science concept (see Figure 10). In short, focusing on conceptual understanding rather than on artistic skills via observational drawing is what a teacher should pursue when drawing is integrated into science education.

 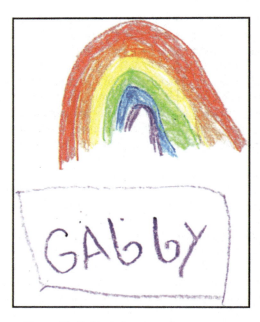

Figure 9. Gabby's drawing prior to instruction   *Figure 10. Gabby's drawing after instruction*

INSIGHTS ABOUT SCIENCE EDUCATION GAINED FROM DRAWING RESEARCH

In the following section, I would like to share with the reader the following four aspects gained from drawing research, which I believe are beneficial and essential to the appropriate integration of drawings into science education and to the success of teaching and learning: (1) How to ask for drawing, (2) How to look at or interpret drawing, (3) Roles adults play in children's science inquiry and (4) Integrated curriculum.

How to Ask for Drawing

How to ask for drawings could be fairly easy, because a teacher could simply say to her children, "Please draw a picture of … (a science concept)." However, when a request for drawing comes very abruptly, children may not be willing to cooperate. Failure to understand the purpose is likely to happen. Therefore, in asking young children to make drawings, a teacher should have a clear understanding that content learning needs to connect with children's background knowledge (Neuman, 2006; Walsh, 2003) and to be based on their interest. Built on something they know, it would be quite easy and enjoyable for children to learn something they do not know (MacKenzie, 2011). Hence, the premise is that a teacher should know children well before designing a lesson and that a teacher should have a clear focus and a clear purpose when designing a drawing activity. At the onset of implementing the lesson, a teacher should captivate young children's attention and then ease them gradually into the drawing process. To pre-assess children's knowledge of a particular science concept, a teacher then asks children to show what they know of the concept on paper. To post-assess children's learning after the lesson, a teacher could utilize a similar approach to requesting a drawing.

Here is an example to support the reader's understanding. Through the interaction with young children, a teacher gets to know that the majority of young children in her class are interested in and able to recognize green frogs. A theme of green frogs is identified. A webbing or a concept map is laid out. The teacher, based on the children's interest, decides to start the theme with a science lesson on the life cycle of a green frog. It is my view that the teacher should start the lesson with something that could potentially capture the attention of a small group of young children and then gradually ease them into the main topic of the lesson. Specifically, the teacher might start the lesson by asking, "Who can tell me what you see on the screen?" On the screen a green frog is projected. Children's responses to this question should not be unpredictable based on the teacher's knowledge of the children. But waiting time is still needed. After the responses, the teacher continues, "Who could share with me and the group where you saw a green frog?" Again, waiting time is necessary. Please note, I have found that the time spent on asking warm-up questions should neither be too short nor too long. The purpose of a warm-up time is for children to mentally get ready for the science concept. If the warm-up time is too short, children may not feel they are mentally ready for learning. Or they may feel that a drawing is requested too abruptly. If the warm-up time drags on for too long, children's attention may be distracted by questions and answers, which may also make them become weary. Hence, it is vital for a teacher to make an appropriate decision as to when drawings are requested for the purpose of pre-assessment.

In requesting a drawing, a teacher could say: "Thank you for answering my questions. Now, I would like to ask you to draw a picture of the life cycle of a green frog. That is, I would like you to tell me and your friends on paper what you think the life cycle of a green frog is." This request could serve a twofold purpose: (1) Children could be indirectly informed of what they are going to learn through this lesson and (2) Children could be placed in a disequilibrium state that is likely to increase their desire to know and to learn. In asking for drawings after instruction, the teacher could say something similar: "Now, I would like you to tell me and your friends on paper what you know of the life cycle of a green frog."

How to Look At/Interpret Drawing

To understand children's drawings, it is inappropriate for an adult to merely rely on his or her own guesses or arbitrary interpretations. Arbitrary interpretations could easily misstate children's intended meanings, if adults just construe children's drawings in light of artistic technique criteria used for measuring visual images produced by adult artists. It is equally inappropriate to judge a drawing by determining whether or not a drawing is aesthetically pleasing to human eyes and/or whether or not drawn objects or people look real. Furthermore, it should not be a teacher's central concern about whether or not children portray certain things with certain shapes, lines, and colors. Even if adults are able to 'read' children's drawings based on the grammar of visual design addressed in detail by Kress and van Leeuwen (2006), the complete meanings embedded in children's drawings still might not be laid bare. Thus, the questions now are how teachers can know the content of children's drawings and why.

Over the years, my own research (Chang, 2007, 2011, 2012, 2013) and review of a wealth of relevant literature have informed me that the desirable way to interpret children's drawings is to talk with young children about their drawings. Launching conversations with young children is of the utmost importance for the following reasons: (a) Steering away from adults' arbitrary interpretations, (b) Facilitating oral language skills, (c) Impacting children's learning, (c) Increasing visual literacy, (d) Promoting language arts, and (e) Meeting the needs of today's rapid growth of multimedia dominated world. In the passage below, I will explicate each of them:

Steering away from adults' arbitrary interpretations. Without an explanation given by a child author, what would you think Figure 11 was? This drawing was created by a four-year-old child, MyKaila, in response to an adult's request: "Show what you think [an ant] looks like?" After the drawing was done, the child explained, "This's a leg and that's a leg. Some are a little big. Looks a little bit green, yellow and that color and that color ..." (in Chang, 2011, p. 11). Following the science instruction, MyKaila produced another drawing. Here is her explanation of the drawing of the physical characteristics of an ant: "Hard body. This is the hard body. Three legs. Three on this side and three on this side ... And this is the door for them to come into their house' (see Figure 12).

If these drawings were measured based on artistic technique criteria, they were definitely not up to par. For example, the shapes and colors were all artistically off. Nonetheless, although Mykaila's drawings were not realistically recognizable, thanks to her oral explanations, Mykaila's representations revealed what she knew about the science concept before and after the instruction. Therefore, it is of essence to have a child explain his or her drawing at each completion.

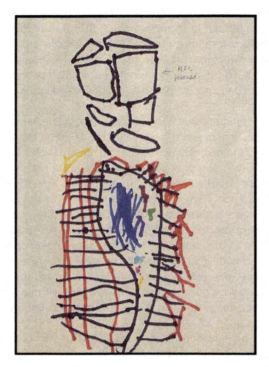 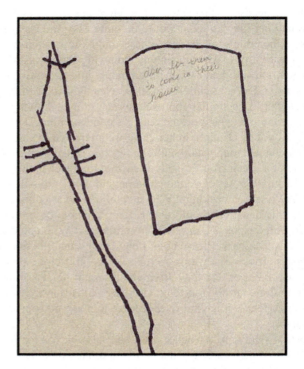

Figure 11. MyKaila's drawing of an ant prior to instruction   *Figure 12. MyKaila's drawing after instruction*

Facilitating oral language skills. Talking about drawing allows a child author to express him- or herself, which in turn helps facilitate the child's oral language skills. For example, Mykaila's explanation of or reading aloud her own products enabled her to use oral language to express herself, facilitating the child's oral language development (Chang & Cress, 2013). The four-year-old child had to think about how to make her thoughts clear to the adult, who appeared interested in her drawing. The cooperative communication between the adult and child could also provide scaffolding for the child to increase not only science knowledge but also vocabulary.

Impacting children's learning. Talking about drawing also enables an adult to obtain reliable information regarding the status of the child's learning. For example, with the visual image and her accompanying interpretation, the teacher was able to aptly adjust the instruction. For example, Mykaila's first drawing, as pre-assessment (Figure 11), informed the adult that the child did not know much about the science concept. Consequently, to effectively aid the child in learning, the teacher emphasized each of the physical characteristics of an ant when teaching: hard body, three legs on each side, and two antennas.

Mykaila's explanation of Figure 11 also enabled the teacher to know she needed to make an additional effort to help the child meet the objective. That is, in Mykaila's drawing, there seemed to be two antennas, but her oral explanations and answers to the adult's additional questions were not in tune with the drawing, indicating that the child had not yet totally comprehended the science concept.

Increasing visual literacy. Talking about drawing also helps enhance children's visual literacy skills (Chang & Cress, 2013). Visual literacy encompasses viewing and visually representing. It is characterized as one's capability to read and interpret visual images. Viewing and visually representing appear to already be part of children's life experiences (Kress, 1997). For example, although Mykaila was only four years old, she was evidently capable of visually telling the adult what she knew of the physical characteristics of an ant before and after the science instruction. With the requests made by the teacher, the child was effortlessly able to explain or read aloud her drawings. Therefore, including drawing in science instruction is likely to help promote and facilitate children's development of visual literacy.

Promoting Language Arts. Talking about drawing also allows for promoting language arts for the following reasons: Visual literacy consists of two modes of language in the language arts: viewing and visually representing. As designated by the National Council of Teachers of English (NCTE) and the International Reading Association (IRA), there are six modes of language in the language arts, including listening, speaking, reading, writing, viewing, and visually representing (National Council of Teachers of English, 2015). As has been mentioned above, for example, Mykaila along with other children, such as David, Josiah, and Gabby, already demonstrated remarkable abilities to visually represent and then view their own drawings. Before entering schools, many young children are already able to talk and listen, view and make signs. Furthermore, visual literacy is central to children's learning how to write (Mackenzie, 2011). Therefore, integrating drawing into science education could help facilitate not only scientific literacy but also language arts.

Meeting the needs of today's rapid growth of a multimedia dominated world. It is important for us to realize that in today's public communication landscape, there is no single mode of language used as an avenue of expression and communication (Kress, 1997). There are a multiplicity of modes used to disseminate information and communicate messages in everyday life. For example, it would be fairly hard to find one single textbook from preschool to 16th grade or even beyond that contains no visual images. Visual aids have been determined to be useful and helpful for learners to comprehend the content of a text. Therefore, "viewing and visually representing have become more important as means of communicating" (Roe & Ross, 2010).

Kress (1997) and Kress and van Leeuwen (2006) underscored the importance of developing the ability of both children and adults to utilize various modes other than speaking, reading, and writing to communicate and represent meanings. Therefore, integrating drawing into science instruction, such as sign making and talking about signs to learn a science concept, is apparently one way to reach children and is supportive of this grand goal.

Roles Adults Play in Children's Science Inquiry

When it comes to integrating drawing into science education, my research shows that what teachers do and how they do it matter a great deal. Therefore, I feel strongly that this issue is worth an extensive discussion.

The position statement set forth by the National Science Teachers Association NSTA (2014) stated, "an adult prepares the environment for science exploration, focuses children's observations, and provides time to talk about what was done and seen…" These roles are congruent with Piaget's (1959) theory that cognitive development largely derives from independent explorations, where children learn through self-discovery by interacting with materials in an environment arranged by teachers (McLeod, 2014). Such a way of learning has been and is still commonly deemed as child-centered or independent learning, through which young children construct knowledge on their own (in McLeod, 2014).

While these practices have their own value, I also think what is missing is appropriate guidance and instruction rendered by a teacher in the process of children's learning, which I would like to call "teachers' deep involvement" in children's learning. I would like to focus on the following two aspects to address it: (1) children's interests and (2) what they know.

Children's Interests. The NSTA (2014) called upon teachers and caregivers to "foster children's curiosity and enjoyment in exploring the world around them and lay the foundation for a progression of science learning in K–12 settings and throughout their entire lives." To this end, it is my belief that children's curiosity and enjoyment in learning are inseparable from children's emotion or affect for learning, which are inextricable from teachers' deep involvement. A teacher should develop an intimate knowledge of her children and be aware of their current knowledge. Children's drawings could be used to reach this end. Grounded on children's interests and learning levels, suitable and stimulating curriculum could thus be created, which could serve the purpose of sustaining and escalating children's enjoyment in learning, the essence of lifelong learning (NSTA, 2014).

What children know. Teachers' deep involvement is also reflected through knowing what their children know. Similar to the benefits of knowing what children are interested in, a teacher also needs to know children's prior background knowledge or life experiences. Building science lessons on what young children already know tends to increase not only their knowledge about science, but also their vocabulary and other language arts related skills (Neuman, 2006; Walsh, 2003).

Teachers' deep involvement is also reflected through knowing what children know before and after instruction. That is, with drawing used as pre-assessment and post-assessment tools to show how much children know about a science concept in light of objectives, a teacher should then utilize the obtained information to inform teaching, amending the lesson plan and teaching strategies during and after the lesson. By no means pre-fixed, this kind of teaching and learning is reciprocal and non-linear, an upward spiral, centering on the children's actual learning status.

Teachers' deep involvement in children's learning is also embodied through the reciprocal interaction with children about their drawings. Asking children questions about their drawings needs to be intentional and purposeful in light of a clearly stated objective with drawings as a common referent (Otto, 2008).

Adults play important roles in children's learning. Now only do they know children's interests and what children know, but also develop and modify lessons and teaching strategies to fit their students' learning needs and levels. All serve the purposes of fostering children's curiosity and enjoyment in exploring the world around them and in laying the foundation for a progression of science learning in K–12 settings and throughout their entire lives (NSTA, 2014).

Integrated Curriculum

Drawing incorporated into science education itself signifies integrated instruction, a combination of visual arts and science. However, an inclusion of children's trade books or non-fiction children's picture books (hereafter referred to as children's trade books or trade books) into science education would strengthen the integration more.

In terms of science education, Cox (n.d.) supported the NSTA's (2014) recommendation of placing a focus on an inquiry-based or a discovery-focused instructional approach to science. However, she also discerned that that approach was not the only recommended approach. There exist a range of materials and strategies to teach science conceptual knowledge and skills addressed in the science standards. Cox stated, "… using hands-on learning in science is not a guarantee of inquiry and discovery outcomes …" Saul and Dieckman (2005) contended that it might not be feasible for every adult to find appropriate science inquiry activities for young children to do all the time, which may partially explain why some teachers see teaching science is challenging. Therefore, the integration of trade books could have many advantages.

The inclusion could help young children clearly see that it is equally useful and important to engage in inquiry with the use of books, because in reality scientists need to be equipped with theories and knowledge before operating experiments useful for their scientific discoveries (Cox, n.d.). Since young children do not have adequate exposure to informational texts in the early grades (Duke & Block, 2012), it is beneficial to help young children acquire science concepts or develop scientific literacy through children's trade books.

Many young children grow up with children's trade books and are, therefore, familiar with them. Trade books written particularly for young children are colorful, beautifully composed, and attractively illustrated (Arizpe & Styles, 2003; Ebbers, 2002), making reading an enjoyable experience. Trade books, connecting to children's lives and prior experiences, often carry and communicate information about the natural world (Rice, 2002), a gateway to the wonder of science (Saul & Dieckman, 2005). More importantly, graphic representations in trade books can also help young children form mental images (Saul & Dieckman, 2005), can help them understand abstract and difficult science concepts (Rice, 2002), and are useful for the development of visual literacy and listening, speaking, reading, and writing. Furthermore, trade books help advance children's abilities of viewing and visually representing. All in all, integrated curriculum including children's trade books in science education coupled with children's drawings could make children's conceptual learning enjoyable and non-threatening (Chang, 2011).

CONCLUSION

To many young children drawing pictures is not at all a daunting task. Conversely, most young children are competent and experienced in representing their inner world through drawing upon entry into formal school settings (Kress, 1997). Children's natural inclination to express themselves with the use of drawings is developmentally appropriate for elementary learners of all ages (Fello, Paquette, & Jalongo, 2007). The process of drawing is able to bring about a variety of benefits: Drawing contains meanings, which unveil children's inner world and feelings. Some researchers view drawing a precursor to writing. Drawing also enables children to develop fine motor skills and make a learning environment enjoyable. That is why drawing should be included in science education.

While it makes a lot of sense to use drawings as pre- and post-assessment tools to know how much children knew prior to instruction and how much they have learned after instruction about a science concept, it is vital to integrate drawing into science education appropriately. Clearly stated objectives are central to instruction and assessment. The focus of drawing should be placed on a stated science objective rather than on arts elements or on observational drawing made in reference to an object or pictorial material.

In interpreting children's drawings, adults should avoid arbitrary interpretation based on their own criteria or on artistic standards. What is important is the invitation to a child author to explain his or her drawing.

Talking about drawing engenders many benefits: This process enables children to use oral language. Talking about drawing encourages children to think about how to explain their drawings clearly. With the interactive communication with an adult, children's oral language can be impacted and facilitated. With the accurate information from child authors' oral explanations of their drawings, a teacher is able to adjust or readjust a lesson plan and/or teaching strategies for desirable learning outcomes and to positively affect learning.

In science education, what is paramount is a teachers' deep involvement in children's science learning. With this involvement, the teacher not only can determine what to teach based on children's interest and their prior knowledge, but also can decide how to use children's drawings in science education to maximize teaching and learning.

Integrating drawing into science education results in a visual-reading integrated curriculum of two modes of expression, as does the combination of the two along with the inclusion of children's trade books. The integrated curriculum not only can help young children develop scientific literacy, but also can facilitate language arts. Both drawing and children's trade books are quite familiar to many young children, making their acquisition of science concepts easy and joyful.

Situated in the multimedia dominated world, young children need to know how to express and communicate linguistically. At the same time, expression and communication made in visual images with or without conventional texts are significant. Including drawing in science education is helpful for children not only to advance content knowledge, but also to communicate their understandings in visual images.

Therefore, it is time for teachers and teacher educators to rethink and reexamine science curriculum in order to include children's drawings in their acquisition of science concepts. However, it is imperative that the integration be implemented appropriately in order not only to promote scientific literacy, but also to cultivate children's sense of curiosity and enjoyment for learning science during pre-K to 12 and beyond in the multimedia dominated world.

REFERENCES

Arizpe, E., & Styles, M. (2003). *Children reading pictures: Interpreting visual texts.* New York, NY: RoutledgeFalmer.

Chang, N. (2007). *Embracing drawings in instruction and learning of young children on a scientific concept: A grounded theory.* Paper presented at the meeting of the American Educational Research Association, Chicago, IL.

Chang, N. (2011). What are the roles that children's drawings play in inquiry of science concepts? *Early Child Development and Care, 182*(5), 621–637. doi:10.1080/03004430.2011.569542

Chang, N. (2012). The role of drawing in young children's construction of science concepts. *Early Childhood Education Journal, 40,* 187–193. doi:10.1007/s10643-012-0511-3

Chang, N., & Cress, S. (2013). Conversations about visual arts: Facilitating oral language. *Early Childhood Education Journal, 42*(6), 415–422. doi:10.1007/s10643-013-0617-2

Charlesworth, R., & Lind, D. (2013). *Science & math for young children* (7th ed.). Albany, NY: Delmar Publishers, Inc.

Copple, C., & Bredekamp, S. (2009). *Developmentally appropriate practice in early childhood programs: Serving children from birth through age 8* (3rd ed.). Washington, DC: National Association for the Education of Young Children.

Cox, C. (n.d.). *What the research says about literature-based teaching and science.* Retrieved from Reading Rockets website: http://www.readingrockets.org/article/42288

Duke, N. K., & Block, M. K. (2012). Improving reading in the primary grades. *The Future of Children, 22*(2), 55–72.

Ebbers, M. (2002). Science text sets: Using various genres to promote literacy and inquiry. *Language Arts, 80*(1), 40–50.

Fello, S. E., Paquette, K. R., & Jalongo, R. (2007). Talking drawings: Improving intermediate students' comprehension of expository science text. *Childhood Education, 83*(2), 80–86.

Halliday, M. A. K. (1993). Towards a language-based theory of learning. *Linguistics and Education, 5,* 93–116.

Hopperstad, M. H. (2010). Studying meaning in children's drawings. *Journal of Early Childhood Literacy, 10*(4), 430–452. doi:10.1177/1468798410383251

Kress, G. R. (1997). *Before writing: Rethinking paths to literacy.* New York, NY: Routledge.

Kress, G. R., & van Leeuwen, T. (2006). *Reading images: The grammar of visual design.* New York, NY: Routledge.

MacKenzie, N. (2011). From drawing to writing: What happens when you shift teaching priorities in the first six months of school? *Australian Journal of Language and Literacy, 34*(3), 322–340.

McLeod, S. (2014). Lev Vygotsky. *Simply Psychology.* Retrieved from http://www.simplypsychology.org/vygotsky.html

NAEYC for families. (n.d.). *Helping your child build fine motor skills.* Retrieved from http://families.naeyc.org/learning-and-development/child-development/help-your-child-build-fine-motor-skills

National Council of Teachers of English. (2015). *NCTE / IRA standards for the english language arts.* Retrieved from http://www.ncte.org/standards/ncte-ira

Neuman, S. (2006). How we neglect knowledge–and why. *American Educator, 30*(1), 24–27.

NSTA. (2014). *NSTA position statement: Early childhood science education.* Retrieved from http://www.nsta.org/about/positions/earlychildhood.aspx

Oken-Wright, P. (1998). Transition to writing: Drawing as a scaffold for emergent writers. *Young Children, 53*(4), 76–81.

Otto, B. (2008). *Literacy development in early childhood: Reflective teaching for birth to age eight* (3rd ed.). Upper Saddle River, NJ: Pearson Education Inc.

Piaget, J., & Inhelder, B. (1966/1971). *Mental imagery in the child.* New York, NY: Basic Books.

Rice, D. C. (2002). Using trade books in teaching elementary science: Facts and fallacies. *The Reading Teacher, 55*(6), 552–565.

Roe, B. D., & Ross, E. P. (2010). *The language arts.* Retrieved from http://www.education.com/reference/article/language-arts/

Strommen, E. (1988). A centure of children's drawing: The evolution of theory and research concerning the drawings of children. *Visual Arts Research, 28,* 13–24.

Walsh, K. (2003). Basal readers: The lost opportunity to build the knowledge that propels comprehension. *American Educator, 27*(1), 24–27.

Ni Chang
Indiana University, South Bend, USA

MICHÈLE STEARS AND EDITH ROSLYN DEMPSTER

13. CHANGES IN CHILDREN'S KNOWLEDGE ABOUT THEIR INTERNAL ANATOMY BETWEEN FIRST AND NINTH GRADES

INTRODUCTION

Effective teaching in science requires insight into students' personal understanding of natural phenomena (Bennett, 2003). Students come to school with numerous personal experiences and beliefs as well as personal knowledge about how the world works. Such personal knowledge may be regarded as their own scientific ideas (Colburn, 2000). Children's own ideas tend to persist after formal instruction because they are based on their everyday experience of these natural phenomena. Duit and Treagust (1998) refer to such personal ideas as mental models of the world stored in students' mental systems. This notion that students actively construct knowledge based on their own experiences, has implications for schooling and has become a foundation for child-centred pedagogies. This is especially pertinent to science education where students are continually exposed to natural phenomena.

Although the construction of knowledge is personal, the way students make meaning of their 'mental models' is also influenced by social and cultural factors. Vygotsky's (1986) work is influential in this regard and is supported by Meacham (2001) who takes the view that learning does not take place in cognitive isolation, but within the context of activities and social interaction, informed by the day-to-day contingencies of culture. Vygostsky (1986) was of the view that school learning is informed by the interaction between the conceptual domains of the community and the school. While the conceptual domain developed through the community is often unstructured and the school domain is formal and structured, the two domains are connected as formal concepts are grasped through informal frameworks (Vygotsky, 1986).

McCaslin and Hickey (2001) give considerable attention to 'scaffolding' as a way of guiding conceptual change. Drawings are one way of gathering valuable information of students' informal knowledge that teachers may use in the process of scaffolding to effect conceptual change. Teaching should begin with students' personal mental models and move outwards from that point in an effort to replace students' intuitive conceptions with scientifically acceptable conceptions.

Much research in science education has been conducted in an effort to determine what students understanding of various phenomena are (Desautels & LaRochelle, 1998; Gao, 1998; Hendry & King, 1994; Gess-Newsome & Lederman, 1993). Driver, Squires, Rushworth and Wood-Robinson (1994) collated a number of research findings on children's understanding of a variety of scientific phenomena. However none of the research studies reported on by Driver et al. (1994) included students' understanding of their own body systems.

Traditionally, methods of investigating students' understanding of scientific phenomena involve written answers to diagnostic questions, interviews and concept mapping (Bennett, 2003). These approaches do not always give an accurate account of what students really understand. Language competence hinders children's ability to articulate what they know about a phenomenon. This dilemma has led to a plethora of research on alternative ways of gaining information about students' understanding (Cerrah Ozsevgeç, 2007; Clements & Barret, 1994; Fleer & Hardy, 1993; Guichard, 1995; Nakhleh, 2011; Novak & Musonda, 1991; Ören, 2011; Prokop & Fancovicová, 2006; Tunnicliffe & Reiss, 1999). Drawings as a tool to understand children's conceptions have gained much attention. Although different approaches have advantages as well as disadvantages, the use of drawings as a tool in the classroom to obtain information is very useful in contexts where students speak a language other than the language of instruction. Drawings are also a useful technique in research; for instance where the participants speak a different language to the researchers. Research by White and Gunstone (1992) has shown that drawings often reveal unsuspected understandings that are disguised in verbal responses. This finding is supported by further research by Reiss and Tunnicliffe (2001). Both these findings support the view that drawings reveal facets of understanding that may not be revealed by other methods.

Drawings as a tool to investigate students' understanding may be used in different contexts and for different purposes. By using drawings, students are asked to present their mental models as 'pictures' rather than as verbal or written explanations. In this study, as in related studies, we wanted to find out what students know about their internal organs and organ systems. The particular focus of this study was to find out about students' understanding of what is inside their bodies at two stages in their education: pre-formal instruction (first grade, age 6–8 years) and post-formal instruction (ninth grade, age 14–16 years). The intention of the study is to establish South African children's intuitive understandings of their internal anatomy, and to record how their intuitive understandings have changed after nine years of schooling. We used drawings to elicit students' understandings in an attempt to ameliorate the effect of language. While a number of research studies have investigated the use of drawings to probe students' understanding of biological phenomena (Bahar, Prokop, & Usak, 2008; Garcia-Barros, Martínez-Losada, & Garrido, 2011; Manokore & Reiss, 2003; Reiss & Tunnicliffe, 2001), the number of South African studies is limited.

P. Katz (Ed.), Drawing for Science Education, 147–154.
© 2017 Sense Publishers. All rights reserved.

Different views exist about the ways in which young children come to acquire ideas about their bodies. Teixera (2002) in his study of what happens to the food we eat, draws from the work of Carey (1985), Keil (1992), as well as Hatano and Inagaki (1997), to explain how children develop that biological knowledge. One view is that children under the age of ten have intuitive knowledge which emerges from an intuitive psychology. This view implies that children have no accurate knowledge of biology till they are formally taught it. An opposing view is that an autonomous domain of biological knowledge exists even in young children, acquired through daily experience. However, the socio-cultural context in which this learning occurs is critical in the acquisition of more advanced biological concepts at a later stage. Mintzes (1984) agrees that children acquire knowledge in their early years through personal experience or knowledge gained in a social rather than formal context. In this way children become aware of the existence of organs in their bodies (Cuthbert, 2000).

Research with regard to what students think is inside their bodies have produced different results. Enochson, Redfors, Tibell, and Dempster (2012) found that students appeared to have a better understanding of the digestive system than any other system, while research by Garcia-Barros et al. (2011) with 4–7 year-olds revealed that the children in their study had different levels of knowledge of the different systems, however as in the Enochson et al. (2012) study, all children appeared to have more knowledge of the digestive system. An interesting aspect of the Garcia-Barros et al. (2011) study was that students had poorer knowledge of the respiratory system which persisted for a number of years without improvement. Reiss and Tunnicliffe (2001) found that young chidren all have knowledge of bones and the heart and most have knowledge of a wide variety of organs, but do not understand how these organs are linked to form systems. Manokore and Reiss (2003) also found that generally Zimbabwean children have a better understanding of individual organs than organ systems.

A further aspect that needs clarification is the different levels of understanding between 7-year-olds and 15-year-olds. While it is reasonable to assume that 15-year-olds have been exposed to the structure of the human body in the formal schooling context, it is generally accepted that 7-year-olds have not. The international study by Reiss et al. (2002) used drawings to obtain information across eleven countries. A small sample of children in each country participated in the study. Students produced drawings that included organs from eight different systems in the human body. The drawings showed significant differences in how well students understood the different systems. Generally the best understood systems were the digestive system, the gaseous exchange system and the skeletal system. Very few of the drawings showed the muscular system, the endocrine system or the circulatory system. In cases where only organs, rather than organ systems were represented the heart was usually included as an organ of the circulatory system while organs of the digestive and /or skeletal system were also commonly included.

Although specific differences between countries were difficult to identify, a number of interesting aspects particular to certain countries emerged, which were linked to students experiences in their particular contexts- either during informal learning or as a result of particular pedagogies (eg teaching systems as separate entities and never presenting all systems as a functional whole). The overall results show that children in Reiss et al.'s study (even 7 year olds) have a broad knowledge of their internal structure and are aware of a number of organs. However, as in previously mentioned studies, they have a poor understanding of the relationship between organs in a system. While 15 year olds had better knowledge of the different organs, most had little understanding of organ systems.

Reiss et al. (2002) found that although most 15 year-olds obtained higher scores than 7 year-olds, this was not the case in Iceland and Taiwan. While the Iceland results were difficult to explain, Taiwanese 7 year olds were formally taught about human systems. The international study also showed that gender differences were generally insignificant although there were a few exceptions and in such exceptions males produced drawings of better biological quality than the drawings of females. For instance in Ghana, Iceland and Russia, 15 year-old males had higher scores for biological quality than girls, while in Taiwan, 7 year-old males had higher scores than 7 year old girls. The results for all countries also show that only a minority of students were able to produce drawings that could be classified as systems.

The various research studies reviewed in this introduction showed that although common trends were identified, individual differences were noted. These differences may be due to the way in which curricula of different countries conceptualise the study of the human body. For example, an international comparison of six Biology curricula for the last three to four years of schooling revealed significant differences among examining bodies (Umalusi, 2010). The curricula studied were South Africa National Curriculum Statement, Cambridge International General Certificate in Secondary Education, Cambridge Advanced Level, Namibian Senior Secondary Certificate in Education and International Baccalaureate Standard Level and Higher Level core curricula. Averaging across all six curricula, the order of depth to which each body system was studied, from greatest depth to least depth, is circulatory system and nervous system, gaseous exchange system, excretory system and reproductive system, digestive system, endocrine system, and finally musculoskeletal system. A comparison of four science curricula for roughly years four to six (South African National Senior Certificate, British Columbia, Singapore and Kenya) reveals considerable variation in the order and importance given to life processes in humans in different curricula (Umalusi, 2014). South Africa, British Columbia and Singapore introduce the musculoskeletal system in Year 4 or 5, while Kenya begins with the respiratory and digestive systems in year 5. British Columbia introduces the gaseous exchange, circulatory, digestive, excretory and nervous systems in year 5, while Singapore introduces the digestive system and gaseous exchange systems in years 3–4, adding the circulatory system and more detail of the gaseous exchange system in years 5–6. Kenya progresses to the reproductive system in year 6.

The present study hopes to elucidate the sequence in which students develop understanding of their internal anatomy by comparing first-grade and ninth-grade students' understanding of their internal anatomy. The drawing technique is highly appropriate in the South African context, with eleven official languages and English as the official medium of instruction beyond the fifth grade.

DESIGN AND METHODS

The method used in this study was adapted from that developed by Reiss and Tunnicliffe (2001) and used in the international study conducted by Reiss et al. (2002) and Manokore and Reiss (2003). Data were collected as independent research projects by senior teaching students enrolled in various teacher education qualifications at the University of KwaZulu-Natal. Each researcher collected data in the school where they normally teach, or where they conducted their teaching practice in the case of pre-service students. Convenience sampling was applied, since teachers had little choice about where it was possible to collect data.

Researchers were asked to collect data in either first grade or ninth grade. First Grade is the second year of schooling, after the reception year. However, the reception year, as a compulsory first year of schooling, has not been firmly established in South Africa, with the result that many of the grade one learners in this study never attended the reception class and were therefore in the first school year. Students are, on average, seven years of age. Grade nine is the ninth year of compulsory schooling, and usually the second year of secondary school. Students are, on average, 15 years of age. The ninth grade is the final year of compulsory schooling, and the last year in which science is a compulsory subject in the curriculum. The choice of these two age-groups for study provides a measure of the impact of life experience and formal teaching on the development of children's ideas about their internal anatomy.

Eleven researchers collected data in the ninth-grade, and eight collected data in the first grade. Schools where data was collected represented the full socioeconomic range of schools in South Africa. The researchers were instructed to give children an A3 sheet of paper, which bore two outline images of a human body, front and back view. The outline images were provided by the project coordinator. Each child was given four coloured wax crayons, and asked to draw what they think is inside their bodies. Researchers were asked to give the following instructions, adapted from Reiss et al. (2002) in whatever language was appropriate for the class:

1. *Please write your name clearly at the top of the page.*
2. *Please write how old you are in years.*
3. *Please also write whether you are a boy or a girl.*
4. *I would like each of you to do a drawing of what you think is inside yourself.*
5. *This is not a test or an examination, but please don't copy each other's work.*
6. *You can have 30 minutes.*
7. *(Ninth grade only) Please label your drawing.*

Researchers were instructed not to assist the students at all, and if asked questions to answer by saying "*It's up to you*". They were told to reassure students who were anxious about their drawing skills by telling them that we were not interested in how well they could draw, but in what they think is inside their bodies.

Instructions were translated into isiZulu and isiXhosa so that all students participating in the study received the same instructions. First-grade students were not required to label their drawings, but researchers were told to clarify with students what they had drawn, where the identity of an organ was unclear. Researchers were told to use the words "*Can you tell me what you have drawn here*". They were specifically instructed not to ask suggestive questions such as "*Is this a heart?*"

At the end of the project, all the drawings were collected, giving a total of 233 first grade drawings from eight schools, and 305 ninth grade drawings from 11 schools. Each drawing was analyzed by two expert analysts, and checked by a third analyst where the coding of the two experts differed. Table 1 describes the criteria used when coding the drawings.

Organs were identified by what the researchers or children had written on the drawings, or by location of the organ or its shape. Many students labelled their drawings in their home language. Translations were used to check that drawings were accurately interpreted by the analysts.

Each drawing was coded three times, firstly for representation of systems, and secondly for representation of organs belonging to a system. By default, if a learner drew a system, they also scored organs in that system. As the analysis progressed, it became evident that many children drew a liver, often without connection to a digestive system. A code was created to capture the number of drawings in which the liver as an individual organ was represented.

The third coding involved a level which scored the biological quality of the drawing, using the system developed by Reiss and Tunnicliffe (2001). This is reproduced in Table 2 for clarity. Illustrations of the coding of four drawings are shown in Figures 1 and 2.

Table 1. Criteria for coding organ systems (adapted from Reiss & Tunnicliffe, 2001)

System	Description
Skeletal system	Backbone, ribs and bones in both arms and legs. The skull was not required.
Digestive system	Through tube from mouth to anus, with an indication of intestines or some compartmentalization of the tube. The order mouth-oesophagus – stomach – intestines – anus did not have to be correct.
Gaseous exchange	Trachea, dividing into two bronchi connected to two lungs. Many children drew a single tube extending from the mouth and connecting to the lungs and to the stomach. It was sometimes recognizable as the trachea (bands were drawn around the tube), or it was labeled as either trachea or oesophagus. The single tube was counted as both trachea and oesophagus, since the body outline made it difficult for children to show both tubes simultaneously.
Reproductive system	Two ovaries, two fallopian tubes, uterus and vagina, OR two testes, two epididymes and penis. Where only a penis was drawn, this was scored as a reproductive organ.
Circulatory system	Heart and blood vessels that are joined to the heart and extend around the body.
Nervous system	Nervous system: Brain, spinal cord, and some peripheral nerves. The brain had to be clearly identifiable, since some children coloured in the head to represent hair.
Urinary system	Two kidneys, two ureters, bladder and urethra.
Muscular system	Muscular system: two muscle groups in different parts of the body with attached points of origin and insertion.
Endocrine system	Two endocrine organs (e.g. thyroid and pituitary) other than the pancreas or gonads.

Table 2. System used to score each biological drawing

Levels	Description
1	No representation of internal structure
2	One or more internal organs placed at random.
3	One internal organ in appropriate position in the body
4	Two or more internal organs in appropriate positions but no extensive relationships indicated between them.
5	One organ system indicated.
6	Two or three major organ systems indicated as defined in the list above.
7	Four or more organ systems drawn, as defined above.

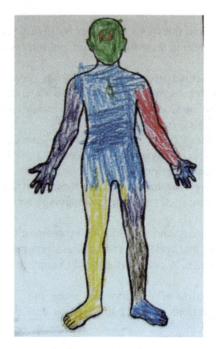 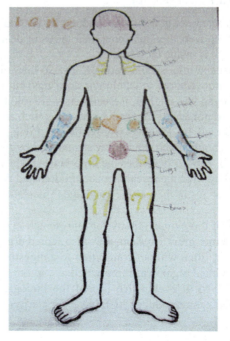

Figure 1. Drawings made by first-grade students: a) No representation of internal structure (Level 1); b) no systems, but three organs in appropriate positions: bones, kidneys and brain. Stomach, heart, and lungs incorrectly placed. Level 4 drawing

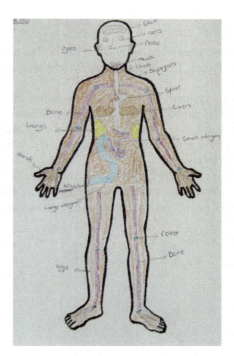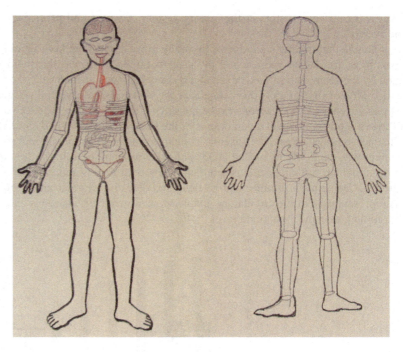

Figure 2. Drawings made by ninth-grade students a) showing digestive system, and organs of the gaseous exchange system (lungs), skeletal system (bones), liver and nervous system (brain). Level 5 drawing. b) Front and back view drawings made by a ninth-grade student, showing skeletal, digestive, gaseous exchange, urinary, and reproductive systems, as well as organs of the nervous system (brain) and circulatory system (heart). Level 7 drawing

RESULTS

The nineteen schools in which data were collected covered the full socio-economic range of South African schools, from the poorest to the most affluent. No school provided data for both first and ninth grade.

Very few first grade students drew systems, although just under 10% drew sufficient bones to qualify for the skeletal system. The drawings of ninth grade students were more detailed and showed more awareness of systems than first grade students. Figure 3 shows that the skeletal system was the most likely to be drawn in first grade and ninth grade, followed by the digestive system. Thereafter, a small number of first-graders drew the gaseous exchange system and circulatory systems. No other systems were identified in first-graders' drawings.

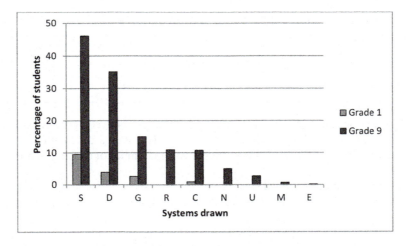

Figure 3. Percentage of students showing each system in their drawings. S = skeletal, D = digestive, G = gaseous exchange R = reproductive, C = circulatory, N = nervous, U = urinary, M = muscular, E = endocrine

The proportion of students who drew a skeletal system increased to 46% in the ninth grade, with 35% drawing the digestive system. About 15% of ninth-grade students drew the gaseous exchange system, while 11% drew circulatory and reproductive systems. Less than 5% drew the nervous system or the urinary system. A very small percentage drew the muscular system, and only one showed an endocrine system.

Figure 4 shows that organs were drawn by many more students at both Grade levels than were complete systems. The circulatory system was most frequently represented by a heart-shaped heart, as illustrated in Figure 1b). The nervous system was frequently represented by the brain, and gaseous exchange system by lungs or trachea.

More than 50% of first-graders drew organs of the skeletal, digestive and circulatory systems. Thereafter, the frequency of inclusion of organs was nervous (33%), gaseous exchange (28%), liver (21%), reproductive (13%), muscular (7%) and urinary (7%).

Over 90% of ninth-graders included organs of the skeletal, digestive and circulatory systems. Over 75% of the drawings included an organ of the nervous system and the gaseous exchange system. Urinary and reproductive organs were shown in about 50% of drawings, while the liver was explicitly identified in 33% of drawings, and muscles in 22% of drawings.

The order in which students demonstrate familiarity with organs and systems is thus similar in first-grade and ninth-grade students, with all students being most familiar with skeletal and digestive systems and organs. Thereafter, students are likely to show a heart and a brain as representative of the circulatory and nervous systems. The gaseous exchange organs and system is also relatively familiar to students at ninth grade and first grade level.

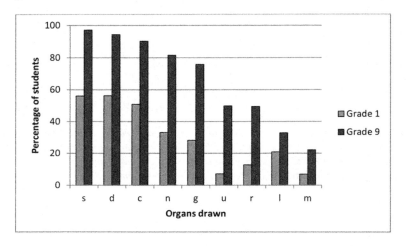

Figure 4. Percentage of students showing organs in their drawings. s = skeleton, d = digestive, c = circulatory, n = nervous, g = gaseous exchange, u = urinary, r = reproductive, l = liver, m = muscular

Ninth-grade students are more likely to draw urinary and reproductive organs and systems than first-grade students. First-graders are more likely to draw a liver than either urinary or reproductive organs, whereas the reverse is true of ninth-graders. Muscles and endocrine organs are least likely to be drawn in both grades.

Table 3. Mean levels achieved by Grade 1 and Grade 9 students

	n	Mean level	SD	Minimum	Maximum
Grade 1	233	3.6	1.0	1.0	6.0
Grade 9	310	5.1	0.8	3.0	7.0

The average level achieved by first-grade students was 3.6, corresponding to between one and two internal organs in appropriate positions in the body, but lacking extensive relationships between them. The standard deviation of 1 shows that 67% of students achieved a level between 2.6 and 4.6. Individual scores ranged from 1 to a maximum of 6. Three schools had students who produced a drawing classified as level 6.

In the ninth-grade sample, the average level achieved was 5.1, which corresponds to at least one organ system indicated. Scores for individual drawings ranged from 3 (one internal organ in an appropriate position) to 7 (four or more organ systems drawn).

DISCUSSION AND CONCLUSION

The results show significant differences between first grade and ninth grade students' presentations of what is inside their bodies. By the time students have reached ninth grade, many were able to demonstrate that they understood that their bodies contained organs, and that organs are arranged into systems. The average levels achieved by first grade children in the present study were at the upper end of the range achieved by children in other countries (Reiss et al., 2002). Ninth grade children in the present study achieved higher scores than all other countries included in Reiss et al.'s international comparison. This result is likely due to the provision of an outline of a human body in the present study, whereas Reiss and Tunnicliffe (2001) and Reiss et al. (2002) provided a sheet of blank paper. Providing a reference point activated children's ideas about their body parts, and facilitated the placement or organs in appropriate positions in the body.

Our results agree with those of other researchers, in that the systems best known to children in first grade and ninth grades are the skeletal, digestive and gaseous exchange systems. At the opposite extreme, the systems least likely to be drawn were the muscular and endocrine systems. Systems represented frequently by single organs were the circulatory system, where the heart was shown, and the nervous system, represented by the brain. All of these results are similar to the general findings in Reiss et al.'s (2002) international study, and point to a universal sequence of conceptual development about children's internal anatomy.

Awareness of the skeleton is expected because it can be felt inside the body, and the heart can be heard and felt to be beating. Movement of the ribcage during breathing also creates an intuitive awareness of lungs. The digestive system is associated with daily body functions such as eating and defaecating. Awareness of other internal organs is less intuitive, since the organs cannot be seen or felt. Growing awareness of one's internal anatomy arises from exposure to pictures in books, or television programmes, or talking about internal anatomy. Life experiences such as observing a chicken being gutted in preparation for cooking may be a source of information for rural children. This is supported by the observation that many children drew a structure in the throat which they labeled "gizzard". However, it must be assumed that students transfer knowledge of the internal anatomy of a chicken to their own anatomy.

A famous quote from the psychologist Ausubel (1968) states "… *the most important single factor influencing learning is what the learner already knows. Ascertain this and teach him accordingly*" (p.vi). The present study and others agree that children are most familiar with their skeletons and digestive organs. Science curriculum should begin the study of human systems with the skeletal system and digestive system. Thereafter, the circulatory and gaseous exchange systems should be taught. Other systems are relatively poorly understood, even at ninth grade level. The sequence in which they are taught could follow the development of understanding of individual organs, such as the brain (nervous system), urinary and reproductive systems and finally endocrine system.

The musculoskeletal system should be re-visited later in the curriculum sequence, to establish the connection between muscles and bones. The musculoskeletal system is omitted entirely in curricula for the Cambridge IGCSE and A-level (Umalusi, 2010). Enochson et al. (2012) found that students had difficulty making connections between different systems, such as the digestive system and the urinary system. Current curriculum practice is to teach each body system independently, rather than in an integrated manner. There is clearly room for improvement.

Unusual observations, not reported in other countries, were found in the South African study. The liver featured prominently in many drawings, often in isolation from the rest of the digestive system. This observation was not reported by Reiss et al. (2002). Awareness of the liver among South African students was also found in a multiple choice question from the TIMSS 2003 study, in which students were asked to identify which of five organs was not situated in the abdomen. Options given were liver, kidney, stomach, bladder and heart. Internationally, 66% of students choose the correct answer, which is heart. In South Africa, only 29% of students chose the correct answer, and 19% selected the liver, compared with 3% of students internationally. A sample of isiZulu-speaking students interviewed after answering this question said they did not know the word "abdomen" and one student did not know the word "bladder", but "kidney" sounded familiar, so she chose that answer (Dempster & Zuma, 2010). However, awareness of the liver specifically in South African students deserves further investigation.

Reiss et al. (2002) identified some unusual elements in the drawings made by children included in their international study. We also noted unusual elements in the drawings, particularly in the first grade drawings. A few children drew food inside their bodies, blood was commonly shown as dispersed throughout the body, and one 10-year-old girl drew a baby in the abdomen of her figure. Many students in first and ninth grade drew external parts of their bodies, such as buttocks, breasts, knees, ankles, elbow, hair and facial features. A few students from two different schools drew worms, snakes and snakes' eyes inside their bodies. This phenomenon merits further investigation. A common misconception among ninth grade students was that a single tube extends from the mouth to the anus, with lungs and sometimes kidneys branching off the tube. There appeared to be confusion between the liver, lungs and kidneys, and structures that were clearly one of these organs were labeled as another. This is illustrated in Figure 2a).

The most significant and pleasing finding for us was that using drawings to express their ideas of their internal anatomy removed the marked distinction between affluent and poorer schools that was obvious in text-based assessment of children's scientific knowledge (Reddy et al., 2012; Dempster & Reddy, 2007). While the drawings from the affluent schools stand out because of their accuracy and level of detail, some less affluent schools produced drawings that were scored above the level of affluent schools. It was clear, however, that the quality of ninth-grade students was affected by experience of textbook drawings or wall-charts. The absence of textbooks in South African schools is a cause for ongoing concern.

The findings of this study indicate that asking children to draw rather than to write about their internal anatomy has the potential to access the knowledge that children have, but that they cannot articulate because of the language barrier. The findings, taken in conjunction with those of other similar studies, suggest a sequence for teaching human body systems based on what children know of their bodies at two different stages in education.

ACKNOWLEDGEMENTS

This research was supported by a SIDA-NRF grant. We thank the many colleagues, students and children who participated in the study. The research was conducted under Ethical Clearance Number HSS/06321.

REFERENCES

Ausubel, D. (1968). *Educational psychology: A cognitive view*. New York, NY: Holt, Rhinehart and Winston.

Bahar, M., Ozel, M., Prokop, P., & Usak, M. (2008). Science student teachers' ideas of the heart. *Journal of Baltic Science Education, 7*(2), 78–85.

Bennett, J. (2003). *Teaching and learning science*. London: Continuum.

Cerrah Özsevgeç, L. (2007). What do Turkish students at different ages know about their internal bod parts both visually and verbally? *Journal of Turkish Science Education, 4*(2), 31–44.

Clements, W., & Barrett, M. (1994). The drawings of children and young people with Down's Syndrome: A case of delay or difference? *British Journal of Educational Psychology, 64*(3), 441–452.

Colburn, A. (2000). Constructivism: Science education's "Grand Unifying Theory". *Clearing House, 74*, 9–12.

Cuthbert, A. J. (2000). Do children have a holistic view of their internal body maps? *School Science Review, 8*, 25–32.

Dempster, E. R., & Reddy, V. (2007). Item readability and science achievement in the TIMSS 2003 study in South Africa. *Science Education, 91*, 906–925.

Dempster, E. R., & Zuma, S. C. (2010). Reasoning used by isiZulu-speaking children when answering science questions in English. *Journal of Education, 50*, 35–39.

Desautels, J., & La Rochelle, M. (1998). The epistemology of students: The "Thingified" nature of scientific knowledge. In B. Fraser & K. Tobin (Eds.), *International handbook of science education* (pp. 115–126). Great Britain: Kluwer Academic Publishers.

Driver, R., Squires, A., Rushworth, P., & Wood-Robinson, V. (Eds.). (1994). *Making sense of secondary science: Research into children's ideas*. London: Routledge.

Duit, R., & Treagust, D. (1998). Learning in science– from behaviourism towards social constructivism and beyond. In B. Fraser & K. Tobin (Eds.), *International handbook of science education* (pp. 3–25). Great Britain: Kluwer Academic Publishers

Enochson, P. G., Redfors, A., Dempster, E. R., & Tibell, L. (2012, October 29–November 3). *Ideas about the human body among secondary students in South Africa and Sweden*. Paper presented at the XVth Symposium of the International Organisation of Science and Technology Education (IOSTE), Yasmin Hammamet, Tunisia.

Fleer, M., & Hardy, T. (1993). How can we find out what 3 and 4 year olds think? New approaches to eliciting very young children's understanding in science. *Research in Science Education, 23*, 68–76.

Gao, L. (1998). Cultural context of school science teaching and learning in the peoples' republic of China. *Science Education, 82*, 3–13.

Garcia-Barros, S., Martínez-Losada, C., & Garrido, M. (2011). What do children aged four to seven know about the digestive system and the respiratory system of the human being and of other animals? *International Journal of Science Education, 33*(15), 2095–2122.

Gess-Newsome, J., & Lederman, N. G. (1993). Preservice biology teachers' knowledge structures as a function of professional teacher education: A year long assessment. *Science Teacher Education, 77*(1), 25–45.

Guichard, J. (1995). Designing tools to develop the conceptions of students. *International Journal of Science Education, 17*(2), 243–253.

Hendry, D. G., & King, R. C. (1994). On theory of learning knowledge: Educational implications of advances in neuroscience. *Science Education, 78*, 223–253.

McCaslin, M., & Hickey, D. T. (2001). Educational psychology: Social constructivism, and educational practice: A case of emergent identity. *Educational Psychologist, 36*, 133–140.

Meachum, S. J. (2001). Vygotsky and the blues: Re-reading cultural connections and conceptual development. *Theory into Practice, 40*, 190–197.

Mintzes, J. J. (1984). Naive theories in biology: Children's concepts of the human body. *School Science and Mathematics, 84*(7), 548–555.

Manokore, V., & Reiss, M. (2003). Pupils' drawings of what is inside themselves: A case study in Zimbabwe. *Zimbabwe Journal of Educational Research, 15*, 28–43.

Nakhleh, M. B. (2011). *Using external representations as a research tool*. Workshop held at the 19th conference of the Southern African Association for Research in Mathematics, Science and Technology Education (SAARMSTE), Mafikeng.

Novak, J. D., & Musonda, D. (1991). A twelve-year longitudinal study of science concept-learning. *American Education Research Journal, 8*, 117–153.

Ören, F. S. (2011). An analysis of pre-service teachers' drawings about the digestive system in terms of their gender, grade levels, and opinions about the method and subject. *International Journal of Biology Education, 1*(1), 1–22.

Prokop, P., & Fancovicová, J. (2006). Students' ideas about the human body: Do they really draw what they know? *Journal of Baltic Science Education, 2*(10), 86–95.

Reddy, V., van der Berg, S., Janse van Rensburg, D., & Taylor, S. (2012). Educational outcomes: Pathways and performance in South African high schools. *South African Journal of Science, 108*. Retrieved June 9, 2013, from http://dx.doi.org/10.4102/sajs.v108i3/4.620

Reiss, M. J., & Tunnicliffe, S. D. (2001). Students' understanding of human organs and organ systems. *Research in Science Education, 31*, 383–399.

Reiss, M. J., Tunnicliffe, S. D., Anderson, A. M., Bartoszeck, A., Carvalho, G. S., Chen, S- Y., Jarman, R., Jónsson, S., Manokore, V., Marchenko, N., Mulemwa, J., Novikova, T., Otuka, J., Teppa, S., & Rooy, W. V. (2002). An international study of young people's drawings of what is inside themselves. *Journal of Biological Education, 36*(2), 18–22.

Teixera, F. M. (1998). *What happens to the food we eat? Children's conceptions of the structure and function of the digestive system*. Proceedings of the second conference of European researchers in didaktik of Biology, University of Göteborg, Sweden.

Tunnicliffe, S. D., & Reiss, M. J. (1999). Students' understandings about animal skeletons. *International Journal of Science Education, 21*, 1187–1200.

Umalusi. (2010). *Evaluating the South African National Senior Certificate in relation to selected international qualifications: A self-referencing exercise to determine the standing of the NSC*. Pretoria: Higher Education South Africa.

Umalusi. (2014). *What's in the CAPS package? Natural sciences* (pp. 24–92). Pretoria: Umalusi Council for Quality Assurance in General and Further Education and Training.

Vygotsky, L. (1986). *Thought and language* (A. Kozulin, Ed.). Cambridge: The MIT Press.

White, R., & Gunstone, R. (1992). *Probing understanding*. London: Falmer Press.

Michèle Stears
University of KwaZulu-Natal, Pinetown and Pietermaritzburg, South Africa

Edith Roslyn Dempster
University of KwaZulu-Natal, Pinetown and Pietermaritzburg, South Africa

TERRENCE MCCLAFFERTY AND LÉONIE RENNIE

14. LEARNING PHYSICS AT SCIENCE CENTERS

Use of Visitors' Drawings to Investigate Learning at an Interactive Sound Exhibit

Science centers and museums use interactive exhibits to teach visitors about scientific concepts. Feher (1990) referred to such exhibits as "powerful learning tools", and stated that "for the user they constitute an independent, teacher-free, learning device; and for the researcher they are the means for rendering explicit user's conceptions and studying the learning process" (p. 46). It is important for the center and museum managers, and the exhibit designers, to understand the exhibit's effectiveness. They need to ask, "How are visitors using the exhibit and are they learning the exhibit's intended learning outcomes?" This chapter reports a study that used observations, interviews, drawings and visitors' annotations of them to investigate their interactions with a sound exhibit, and their understanding and learning of the scientific concepts presented. As the purpose of the study was to investigate the visitors' success with working the exhibit, empirically determine the scientific concepts visitors' associate with the exhibit and measure the visitors' learning from the exhibit, a two stage process was used. The first stage identified the concepts and skills that visitors were learning from a sound exhibit and the second stage used drawings and visitors' annotations of them to measure their learning of the scientific concepts and the skills necessary to successfully use the exhibit. Two similar exhibits, *Whispering Dishes* at Scitech, a science center in Perth, Western Australia, and *Parabolic Reflectors* at Questacon, Australia's National Science Center in Canberra, ACT were used in the study.

The exhibits' educational or behavioral learning objectives had not been described at either of the two centers, so in the first stage it was important to determine what objectives could be achieved by visitors interacting with those exhibits. Consequently, visitors were observed to determine their success using the exhibit and later interviewed to identify the scientific concepts they associated with the exhibit. This information from the first stage identified the concepts that could be learned from the exhibit and these were represented in the drawings used in the second stage to investigate visitors' understanding of sound and their use of the exhibit. The first stage was undertaken at Scitech and had three research questions that investigated:

1. What is the visitors' success with the *Whispering Dishes*?
2. How do visitors learn to use the *Whispering Dishes*? and,
3. What scientific concepts do visitors associate with the operation of the *Whispering Dishes*?

  The second stage investigated the nature of the visitors' learning in more detail using visitors annotations on drawings and was undertaken at Questacon. The research question of Stage 2 was:

4. Do visitors learn the scientific concepts and the skills to use the exhibit through their experience with the *Parabolic Reflectors*?

PROBING VISITORS' LEARNING USING DRAWINGS

White and Gunstone (1992) state that there is a "heavy reliance on words in most commonly-used tests of understanding" (p. 98) and the purpose of this chapter is to demonstrate that visitors' drawings and their annotations provide a useful and relevant way to probe the concepts understood and learned from an interactive exhibit.. Written probes can range from multiple-choice questions, which are the most limited in how responses can be made, to open-ended responses, which allow unlimited responses. Asking visitors to make drawings also provides an unlimited way for visitors to respond, however in this study it was important that the visitors' responses be limited in order to focus on the relevant concepts. It was decided to present them with a partly completed diagram and require them to annotate and add to the diagram as a way to describe their understanding of the phenomena occurring. This approach allowed the visitor to reveal their understandings about the exhibit in a more focused way than might be found using a written probe. Occasionally, the visitors' drawings and annotations can uncover unsuspected misconceptions about the concepts being investigated, and again, written responses or verbal questioning may not identify these.

DESCRIPTION OF EXHIBITS

The *Whispering Dishes* and the *Parabolic Reflectors* both consist of two fiberglass parabolic dishes of 2 m diameter mounted on platforms in Scitech, or high on a gallery wall in Questacon, and the pair of dishes are approximately 50 m apart (Figure 1). The dishes are aimed at each other and the exhibit has an implicit objective of presenting sound wave reflection and focusing so that visitors can project their voice across the room to the other dish. Each whispering dish has a circular metal frame of 10 cm diameter located at the focal point of the parabola, suspended by three metal rods radially anchored on the perimeter of the dish. At Scitech, visitors either placed their ear to listen or their mouth to speak at this circular frame, and a small step-stool allowed children to reach the frame. At

P. Katz (Ed.), Drawing for Science Education, 155–167.
© 2017 Sense Publishers. All rights reserved.

Questacon, each of the parabolic reflectors is mounted 2 m high on a gallery wall and has a 10 cm diameter flexible voice tube or snorkel at the focal point. Visitors standing below either hold the snorkel to their mouth or ear (See Figure 1). Visitors who are skilled in using either exhibit sometimes spend 2–10 minutes conversing with each other.

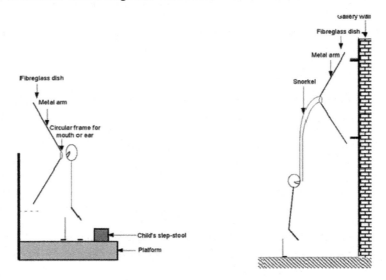

Figure 1. Exhibit forms at centers

STAGE 1 – WHISPERING DISHES: VISITORS' UNDERSTANDING OF EXHIBIT'S CONCEPTS

Visitors ($N = 280$) were observed interacting with the *Whispering Dishes* by an observer who was located unobtrusively in a nearby canteen with an unhindered view of the exhibit. Activities of visitors were recorded on a data collection form as they attempted to get the exhibit to work and an exhibit interaction was recorded as successful if the visitor was able to communicate to another at the corresponding whispering dish on the other side of the gallery. If the visitor was successful in communicating to another visitor ($n = 165$), the visitor was briefly interviewed before leaving the exhibit's platform. Children were interviewed following permission from parents or responsible accompanying adults. Successful visitors were asked four questions:

1. *How old are you?*
2. *Can you tell me how the Whispering Dishes work? How could you hear others on the other side?*

Visitors were categorised into four age cohorts of 7–10 years, 11–14 years, 15–34 years and 35 years and older (Table 1).

Table 1. Sample composition of visitors to whispering dishes

Visitors (N = 280)	7–10 yrs	11–14 yrs	15–34 yrs	35 yrs or older	n	
Male	50	30	31	49	160	58%
Female	33	21	41	25	120	42%
Visitors (n)	83	51	72	74	280	
	30%	18%	26%	26%		100%

Visitors' Understanding of the Exhibit

The final question for successful visitors was, Can you tell me how the *Whispering Dishes* work? Most visitors gave a short response and the responses were classified into six categories. Visitors' explanations displayed an understanding of either waves (10%), or waves and reflection (10%), or waves, reflection and focusing (13%) Table 2 shows the remaining visitors either offered no reason (50%), described what they did (7%) or provided a misconception (10%). Examples of the visitors' responses, grouped by their response description, are provided below.

Visitors' responses displaying knowledge of waves:

Well...it's hard to explain...the sound waves go from this dish to the other dish. (girl, 10-year-old)

Next, visitors' responses displaying knowledge of waves and reflection:

You speak into it and it bounces the sound waves over to the other side. (boy, 12-year-old)

Visitors' responses displaying knowledge of waves, reflection and focusing:

The focal point...it's the dish...it is curved so that the waves are focused into another point on the other side, and the dishes have to be the right distance

apart. They're sound waves. (female, 30-year-old)

A few visitors described how you operate the *Whispering Dishes* but failed to describe how the exhibit actually worked. An example of the visitors' responses categorised as describing what you do follows.

Well, you put your ear up to here and somebody else whispers in the other end and you can hear them. [How can you hear a whisper over a long distance?]

*...don't know. (*girl, 9-year-old)

Other visitors provided misconceptions, and described wires under the floor or hidden microphones and speakers. The final category was visitors who responded that they had no knowledge or understanding as to how the exhibit worked. Examples of these responses include:

It is impossible...I am not sure how it works...I could not believe I could hear her voice...I don't know how it works. (male, 60-year-old)

Table 2. Visitors understanding of the whispering dishes (percentage)

Visitors Understanding (N = 165)

Waves	Waves & reflection	Waves, reflection & focusing	Described activity	Misconception	Did not know
10	10	13	7	10	50

Identification of the Exhibit's Concepts

The visitors' explanations were arranged into a six level knowledge hierarchy (Perry, 1993) that began with three levels that describe no understanding of the exhibit's operation, a description of what you do to use the exhibit, and an incorrect explanation or misconception. The next three levels were the correct explanations of how the exhibit worked and were the scientific concepts the visitors associated with the exhibit. These concepts were sound waves, wave reflection and wave focusing. The knowledge hierarchy for the *Whispering Dishes* is listed on Table 3.

Table 3. Knowledge hierarchy for whispering dishes

Level	Description
0	No awareness of how the sound was being projected across the room
1	An explanation of what you had to do, but not how it operated
2	An explanation, but incorrect (misconception)
3	An understanding that sounds or sound waves travelled across the gallery
4	An understanding that sound waves were reflected by the dish
5	An understanding that sound waves were reflected and focused

The identification of the three scientific concepts in Stage 1 provided a means to investigate the visitors' learning from the exhibit. Visitors' learning can be determined by measuring the visitors' prior knowledge of the three concepts and comparing it to their knowledge after their exhibit experience. Stage 2 was undertaken to complete this task and it used a pretest and posttest, each based around diagrams, to measure visitors' knowledge before and after using the exhibit. Visitors' annotations on these diagrams were used to investigate their knowledge of these concepts.

T. MCCLAFFERTY & L. RENNIE

STAGE 2 – PARABOLIC REFLECTORS: MEASURING VISITORS' LEARNING FROM THE EXHIBIT EXPERIENCE

The second stage of the study investigated the learning of the three concepts using visitors ($N = 126$) experiencing the *Parabolic Reflectors*. Acknowledging the reactive effects of pretesting and therefore sensitising visitors to the concepts within the exhibit, the context of the pretest was earthquakes, explosions, collisions, light and the operation of a satellite television system. The pretest consisted of five questions that required the visitor to explain a diagram or write a few words or a sentence, or annotate and complete a diagram as a way to explain their understanding of the science concept or phenomena. Question 2 investigated the visitor's knowledge of waves, and had no illustration. Descriptions of the pretest questions are listed below.

Pretest

Question 1 (Earthquakes)
Earthquakes are natural phenomena, and if very large can result in substantial damage to property and the death of many people. When earthquakes occur in one region the tremors can be felt in cities far away from the center of the earthquake.

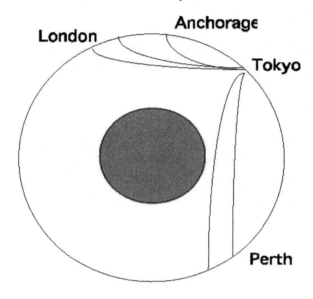

Figure 2. Section of EARTH

Special devices (seismometers) in London, Anchorage and in Perth detect that an earthquake has occurred in Tokyo. What do these devices detect
travelling through the earth?

Question 2 (Blasting)
In open cut mining and in quarries, large amounts of explosives are used to break up the rock for removal. Preparation is by drilling long holes and filling these holes with explosives. An expert wires up the explosives and blasts the rock to break up the rock. If you are in a mining area you will hear the sirens and all workers leave the mine site and move to a safe area far away from the blast. You will probably hear the blast. How are you able to hear the blast? What travels through the air which allows you to hear the blast?

Question 3 (Bouncing balls)
When you throw a ball at a wall it will bounce off and keep moving. The diagram (Figure 3) shows a soccer ball which is being kicked at a wall. Draw a line to show the direction you expect the ball to follow after hitting the wall.

Question 4 (Flashlight)
A flashlight is being shone onto a mirror in the direction of the arrow (Figure 4). Draw a line to show the direction of the beam after striking the mirror.

Question 5 (Satellite TV)
Soon, many Australian homes will have a satellite dish to receive many TV Stations from all over the world. The signals are relayed by a satellite in space to large areas of Australia. These large areas are called the satellite "footprint". Already, many towns and pastoral

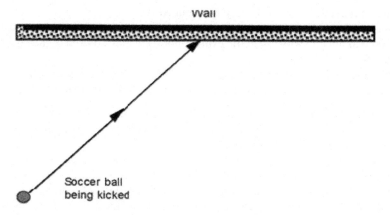

Figure 3

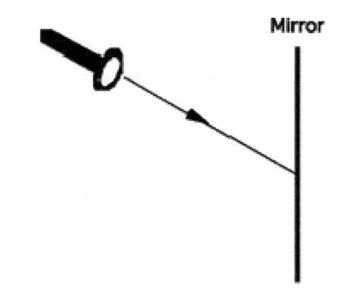

Figure 4. Flashlight shone on mirror

stations in remote Australia receive TV via satellite from AUSSAT. On the diagram below (Figure 5), draw LINES to show the signal going from the satellite to the pickup on the dish. (use arrows to show direction)

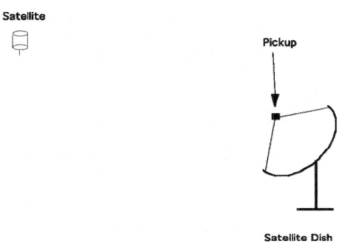

Figure 5. Side view of satellite TV transmission

Visitors completed the pretest, proceeded into the gallery and handed the pretest to the researcher who checked that the visitor had indicated their age and affixed a numbered badge to the visitor to enable the their pretest and later posttest to be linked whilst retaining anonymity. Visitors were not asked to interact with a specific exhibit, nor were they advised of the posttest, however the researcher noted the visitor's number if they used the *Parabolic Reflectors*.

After completing their visit to the gallery, visitors who used the *Parabolic Reflectors* were asked to complete a posttest designed to assess their knowledge after using the exhibit. It contained four questions and investigated the visitors' knowledge of:

1. Waves, by asking visitors how their partner's voice travelled across the gallery.
2. Wave reflection, by asking visitors how the exhibit's dish reflected their voice across the gallery. In this question, visitors were asked to draw lines on an exhibit diagram to explain the process.
3. Wave focusing, by asking visitors how their partner's voice can be heard in the snorkel tube. In this question, visitors were asked to draw lines on an exhibit diagram to explain the process.
4. Wave transmission, reflection and focusing, by asking visitors how the two reflectors operated together. In this question, visitors were asked to draw lines on a diagram that showed two persons, one listening and the other talking, on two opposing dishes.

Posttest

The posttest is provided below:

Question 1 (Communicating Across the Room)
You were able to hear your partner speaking from the other side of the room. Your partner spoke from their dish and you listened. How does their voice get to you from the other side of the room as you listen?

Question 2 (Speaking into the Dish)
For your partner to hear you, you have to put your mouth at the mouthpiece and speak into the voice tube. How does your voice get to your partner when you speak into the dish? On the diagram right (Figure 6) draw lines to show what is happening as you speak into the voice tube.

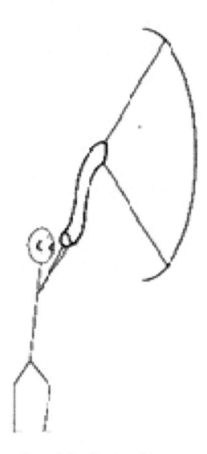

Figure 6. Speaking into dish

Question 3 (Listening from the Dish)
For you to hear your partner from across the room you placed your ear near the mouthpiece and listened (Figure 7). How does their voice get to your ear when you listen? On the diagram right (Figure 7) draw lines to show what is happening as you listen from the voice tube.

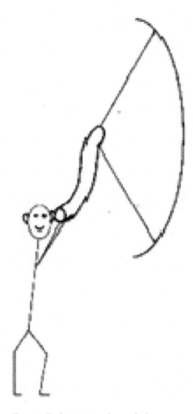

Figure 7. Listening from dish

Question 4 (Getting It to Work)
If you would like to, use the diagram below (Figure 8) to show how one person can hear the other on the *Whispering Dishes*.

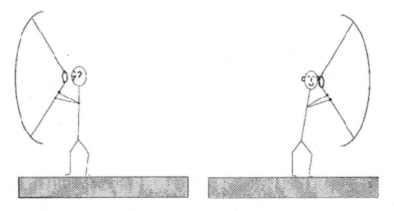

Figure 8. Getting it to work

Visitors' Responses to Pretest

The pretest's first two questions, Earthquakes and Blasting, investigated visitors' prior knowledge of the concept waves. Acceptable responses were those that implied a wave or a vibration had been transmitted through the Earth, for the former question, or air for the latter. Below are examples of visitors' responses listing acceptable and unacceptable responses.

Purpose To determine visitors' knowledge of waves or vibrations travelling through the earth.
Question: "What do these devices detect travelling through the Earth?"
  Acceptable visitors' responses to this question included:

Waves. (male, 11–14 years)
Waves created by tremors when continental plates collide or separate at stress points. (male, 15–34 years)
Shock waves. (female, 35–70 years)
Vibrations. (male, 7–10 years)
Reverberations. (male, 35–70 years)

Many visitors provided incorrect responses and some stated misconceptions. Unacceptable visitors' responses included:

Electromagnetic waves. (female, 35–70 years)
Electricity. (female, 15–34 years)
Gravity. (girl, 7–10 years)

Purpose To determine visitors' knowledge of waves or vibrations travelling through the air.
Question: "How are you able to hear the blast? What travels through the air which allows you to hear the blast?"
  Acceptable answers included:

Shock waves... Vibrations. (female, 35–70 years)
You can hear the sound because of soundwaves travelling through the air. (boy, 11–14 years)
Soundwaves expanding and contracting as they move. (female, 15–34 years)
Compression waves travelling through the air. (male, 15–34 years)

Unacceptable answers included:

Pressure. (male, 35–75 years)
With your ears. (female 15–34 years)
Noise. (male, 11–14)
Wavelengths. (male, 15–34 years)

The next two pretest questions, Bouncing balls and Flashlight, investigated visitors' prior knowledge of reflection and required visitors to complete a diagram.

Purpose To Determine Visitors' Knowledge of Wave Reflection.
Task: "Draw a line to show the direction you expect the ball to follow after hitting the wall, or the direction of the lightbeam after striking the mirror."
  Acceptable drawings were those that showed the ball's direction and the light's beam path that followed a line from the point of collision at the wall or mirror, and reflected at an angle approximating the Law of Reflection (see Figure 9 for examples).

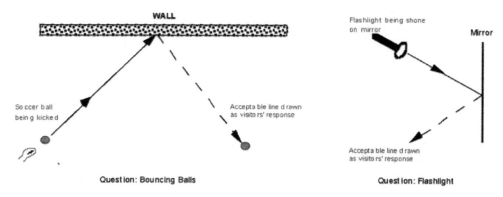

Figure 9. Acceptable responses to pretest questions for reflection

The final pretest question, Satellite TV, requested visitors to explain the operation of satellite dishes used in communication, predominantly domestic television satellite systems. Again, no written responses were requested and visitors drew lines to show the signal going from the satellite to the pickup on the dish.

Purpose To Determine Visitors' Knowledge Of Wave Focusing using a PARABOLIC DISH.
Task: "Draw lines to show the signal going from the satellite to the pickup on the dish." An acceptable drawing displayed the signal from the satellite to the dish, reflected at the dish and focused to the pickup or antenna (Figure 10).

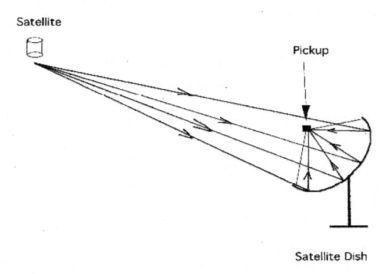

Figure 10. Acceptable response to pretest question for focusing

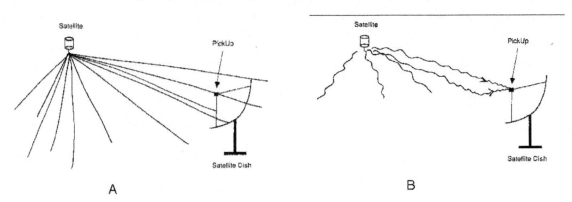

Figure 11. Unacceptable responses to pretest question for focusing

Some visitors could not explain diagrammatically the operation of satellite dishes and how waves are reflected and focused. In Figure 11 visitors failed to show that the waves are reflected by the dish to the pickup and displayed no understanding of the receiving dish's role. In item A of Figure 11 the visitor drew waves passing through dish with no reflection or focusing, and in item B, the visitor drew the waves being directly received at the pickup.

Visitors' Responses to Posttest

Visitors' learning was investigated using a posttest of four questions that assessed visitors' understanding of (1) sound waves, (2) wave reflection, (3) wave focusing and (4) wave transmission. Wave transmission was defined as the operation of dishes; here sound waves created by visitors are reflected, transmitted, reflected and focused to allow their partner to hear. The questions provided the visitors with multiple examples to display their understanding of the concepts. Question 1 required a written response, Questions 2 and 3 required a written response and annotation of a diagram (Figures 6 & 7), and Question 4 required diagram annotations (Figure 8). A visitor was recorded as understanding a concept when one acceptable response was provided. Examples of acceptable visitors' responses, both written and diagrammatic, are included below:

Purpose: To determine visitors' knowledge of waves.
Question: "How does their voice get to you from the other side of the room as you listen?"

Vibrations in the air are picked up by the dish and channelled by the tube to your ear. (boy, 11–14 years)
Bounces sound waves off one dish [and] collects on the other side. (male, 35–70 years)
The pipe carries the sound waves through to the ear. (boy, 11–14 years)
They speak into pipes and the pipe carries sound all the way through [to] the listening end. (boy, 11–14 years)
Through the tube — vibrations, sound waves carried like a telephone. (female, 15–34 years)

Purpose: To determine visitors' knowledge of waves.
Question: "How does your voice get to your partner when you speak into the dish?"

Vibrations are collected and sent via air, then collected and channelled to your ear. (boy, 11–14 years)
It travels through pipes [and] through to the other end of the pipes. (boy, 11–14 years)
My sound waves bounce out of the tube and onto the dish which spreads them out. (female, 15–34 years)

Purpose: To determine visitors' knowledge of waves and wave reflection
Question: "How does their voice get to your ear when you listen?"

The sound bounces off their dish to mine and then down the tube. (girl, 11–14 years)
The vibrations are collected and rebound to your ear. (boy, 11–14 years)
The dish reflects the waves into the tube and into the ear. (male, 15–34 years)

Purpose: To determine visitors' knowledge of wave transmission, which includes waves, wave reflection and wave focusing.
Question: "If you would like to, use the diagram below to show how one person can hear the other on the *Whispering Dishes*?"

Examples of visitors' responses acceptable for the understanding of waves, reflection, and focusing are shown on Figures 12 and 13. In Figure 12, the drawings show waves (Item A), waves and reflection (Item B) and reflection (Item C). Figure 13 shows visitors' responses to the posttest figure for wave transmittance that displayed an understanding of waves, reflection and focusing. A few visitors responded with misconceptions for the transmission of sound across the room. These visitors believed that their voice was transmitted along the steel frame that secured the snorkel tube to the focal point. They responded to the pretest question by drawing arrows (Figure 14: Item A) or waves (Figure 14: Item B) down the steel arms showing the wave direction.

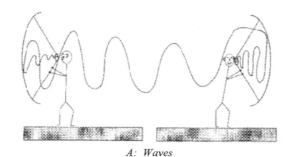

A: Waves

B: Waves and Reflection

Figure 12. Posttest responses showing correct responses for waves and wave reflection

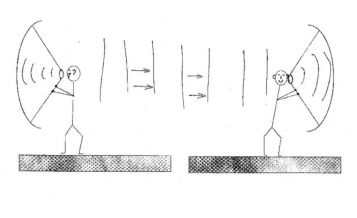

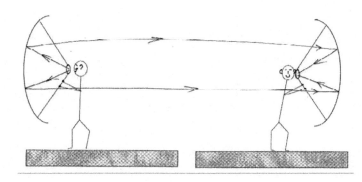

Figure 13. Posttest responses showing correct responses for waves, reflection and focusing

Figure 14. Posttest responses showing misconceptions for Parabolic Reflectors

Measuring Visitors' Understanding

The visitors' results for each of the concepts of waves, reflection and focusing for the pretest and posttest are listed on Table 4. The percentages of visitors who knew about a concept before their exhibit experience are listed on Table 4 as the "know" group for the pretest. The results of the pretest show that the concept that was most understood by all visitors was reflection and 78% of all visitors knew about it. The least understood concept was focusing and only 21% of visitors understood it. The posttest investigated the visitors' understanding of the three concepts in the context of the *Parabolic Reflectors*. The total percentages of visitors who understood a concept after using an exhibit are obtained by adding the proportions for the transfer and gain groups. The posttest's results show that the concept waves, as measured by the posttest, had the highest level for visitor understanding, as 78% of visitors understood waves after their exhibit experience. The concept focusing had the lowest level (61%) of visitors understanding focusing in the exhibit's context (Table 4).

T. MCCLAFFERTY & L. RENNIE

Visitors' Learning

The results show that some visitors are learning and this is noted by the proportion of visitors who were categorised in the "don't know" group of the pretest, and later were identified in the gain group of the posttest. It is the "don't know" group which is of interest, for this is the group who interactive science and technology centers hoped to have instructed through the exhibit experience. These visitors after using the exhibit either learn the concepts (gain) or fail to learn (no gain).

Table 4 shows that approximately half the visitors who did not initially understand a concept presented by the *Parabolic Reflectors* understood the concept after their exhibit experience. For example, 30% (n = 39) of the visitors had no understanding of the concept of waves, as measured by the pretest. After their exhibit experience, 15% (n = 20) of these visitors knew that it used sound waves for communication, that is, half of the 30% group learned about waves, and the cohort is 15% learned (gain) and 15% did not learn (no gain). Focusing was the least understood concept, with 79% of visitors (n = 103) did not understand about the focusing of waves as measured by the pretest. However, after their exhibit experience 40% (n = 53) of the don't know group understood the focusing of waves (gain) as measured by the posttest.

It was the young adult group (aged 15 - 34 years) who experienced the highest learning of the three concepts of waves, reflection and focusing. This group in the pretest had 74% persons not knowing the three concepts, however, following use of the exhibit, 52% gained, a success of 70% of the visitors (Table 4).

Table 4. Results for pretest and posttest for each concept at parabolic reflectors for visitors (percentage)

Age Cohort (years)	n	Waves						Waves and Reflection						Waves, Reflection and Focusing					
		Pretest		Posttest				Pretest		Posttest				Pretest		Posttest			
				Know		Don't Know				Know		Don't Know				Know		Don't Know	
		Know	Don't Know	Transfer	No Transf	Gain	No Gain	Know	Don't Know	Transfer	No Transf	Gain	No Gain	Know	Don't Know	Transfer	No Transf	Gain	No Gain
								Visitors											
7 – 10	14	50	50	50	0	23	27	65	35	32	33	21	14	17	83	17	0	27	56
11 – 14	30	59	41	46	13	22	19	77	23	67	10	6	17	11	89	11	0	42	47
15 – 34	40	80	20	75	5	10	10	88	12	80	8	10	2	26	74	26	0	52	22
35+	42	88	12	76	12	7	5	84	16	64	20	9	7	30	70	30	0	35	35
Total	126	70	30	63	7	15	15	78	22	63	15	10	12	21	79	21	0	40	39

STAGE 2: SUMMARY OF FINDINGS

Stage 2 assessed the effectiveness of the *Parabolic Reflectors* to teach visitors the three concepts of waves, reflection and focusing that were identified in Stage 1. Stage 2 found that some visitors had prior understanding of either one, two or all three concepts of waves, reflection and focusing before their exhibit experience. Prior knowledge was highest for reflection, with 78% of visitors knowing it, followed by waves and focusing with 70% and 21% of visitors knowing the respective concepts. Some visitors did learn concepts about sound from their exhibit experience. Approximately 50% of visitors who were identified on entry to the gallery as not knowing a concept, learnt about the concept through their exhibit experience (Table 4). The results show that the visitors' learning was highest for learning the concept focusing, with 51% of visitors gaining this knowledge through their exhibit experience. For waves and reflection, 50% and 45% of visitors gained these concepts respectively (Table 4).

A few visitors demonstrated an understanding of concepts in the pretest but did not demonstrate or transfer this understanding in the posttest. These visitors understood the concept in the context presented by the pretest, but failed to transfer their previous understanding to the posttest's context of parabolic dishes (Table 4).

CONCLUSION

Stage 1 provided a way to identify the scientific concepts being presented by the exhibit and were identified as waves, reflection and focusing. Stage 2 used a pretest and posttest format to investigate visitors' learning and the tests required visitors to annotate diagrams and provide some written comments to indicate their understanding of the scientific concepts. Two methods to analyse and investigate visitors' understanding were used in the Study 1. Firstly, in Study 1, developing a knowledge hierarchy (Perry, 1993) is an effective way to describe visitors' understanding of the concepts presented by the exhibit. Secondly, in Study 2, the use of diagrams which visitors could annotate to indicate their understanding of the exhibit's operation provided a way to determine their understanding of the concepts of waves, reflection and focusing. As White and Gunstone (1992) state, drawings provide an effective probe of understanding and reveal different attributes and qualities of the understanding that are unseen using other procedures, for example, written or verbal questioning. Clearly, the use of diagrams that visitors annotate provides an easier way to show or indicate their understanding. Few visitors could articulate the operation of the exhibit as being "your voice produces sound waves that are reflected by the parabolic reflector across the room to the other reflector where they reflected and focused for the other person to hear". For many visitors it was considerably easier to indicate this process by drawing sound waves being reflected and focused, as shown on Figure 13. The study found that sound exhibits that used parabolic reflectors are an effective way to teach visitors about waves, reflection and focusing. Stage 2 found that approximately half the visitors learnt a concept that they did not know through their experience of the *Parabolic Reflectors*, prior knowledge about the concepts was higher for male visitors, and for older visitors, and that females and younger visitors learned more.

The use of diagrams that require visitors to annotate was an effective way to determine their understanding of the three concepts and, more importantly, how the exhibit operated. Diagrams provide a way for the researcher to move away from the "heavy reliance on words in most commonly-used tests of understanding" (White & Gunstone, 1992, p. 98) and provide an elegant method of focusing the visitors' response to the concepts being investigated.

REFERENCES

Feher, E. (1990). Interactive museum exhibits as tools for learning: Explorations with light. *International Journal of Science Education, 12*(1), 35–39.
Krampen, M. (1991). *Children's drawings: Iconic coding of the environment*. New York, NY: Plenum Press.
Perry, D. L. (1993). Measuring knowledge with a learning hierarchy. *Visitor Studies: Theory, Research and Practice, 6*, 73–77.
White, R., & Gunstone, R. (1992). *Probing understanding*. London: Falmer Press.

Terence McClafferty
Charles Darwin University, Australia

Léonie Rennie, Emeritus
Curtin University, Australia

SECTION THREE

DRAWINGS THAT ILLUSTRATE THE PERCEIVED CULTURE OF SCIENCE (WHO AND WHAT)

DONNA FARLAND-SMITH

15. THE EVOLUTION OF THE ANALYSIS OF THE DRAW-A-SCIENTIST TEST

What Children's Illustrations of Scientists Tell Us and Why Educators Should Listen

INTRODUCTION

Asking students to "draw a picture of a scientist" has been a popular method for those wishing to engage in Draw-A-Scientist Test research (Chambers, 1983; Chiang & Guo, 1996; Fung, 2002; Maoldomhnaigh & Hunt, 1988; Newton & Newton, 1992, 1998; Song, Pak, & Jang; 1992; She, 1998). While the majority of DAST research concentrated on students' stereotypical images and their perceptions of scientists, the manner in which data derived from these studies have been analyzed has often been limited to such things as the reporting of frequencies and the computation of simple t-tests. This level of analysis has provided a starting point for the investigation of students' perceptions of scientists and interesting discussion regarding potential interventions that might be utilized to help students modify their perceptions. This may be why science education researchers have speculated about where these images derive without having further investigated this issue much beyond basic general observations for the better part of the last sixty years.

Analyzing images of scientists and labeling them stereotypical, rather than investigating where these images originate in students' schema, has left a gap in the existing DAST research. This may be due to the multifaceted complexity involved with such investigations. Even so, some notable questions regarding conceptions of scientists have arisen through DAST research: "When are concepts initiated?" (e.g. see Chambers, 1983), "When are concepts most likely to impact conceptual formation?", "Which concepts are central to students' personal science identities?", and "What are the influences that impact formation of such concepts?" In this chapter, the focus will be on (1) how pictures have been analyzed and contemporary approaches to analyzing pictures of scientists (2) what the pictures of scientists tell us, (3) to what extent does culture and science identity impact student perceptions, and student illustrations of scientists?

HOW CHILDREN'S PICTURES OF SCIENTISTS HAVE BEEN ANALYZED

A number of studies which asked students to "draw a picture of a scientist" contributed to what is commonly referred to as the stereotypical image of scientists (Chambers, 1983; Chiang & Guo, 1996; Fung, 2002; Maoldomhnaigh & Hunt, 1988; Newton & Newton, 1992, 1998; Song, Pak, & Jang; 1992; She, 1998). The issue of validity of the instrument is a difficult one, because it is not known whether the images children draw accurately reflect the scientist in one's imagination. This question, "does the DAST truly reveal the images held by children?" remains difficult to answer at best. Because the validity and sometimes reliability of the DAST was questionable, some skepticism and lower acceptance in the field of science education resulted. It wasn't until a scoring mechanism called the Draw-A-Scientist-Checklist (DAST-C) by Finson, Beaver and Crammond in 1995 that researchers were able to focus on something else besides the initial 'stereotypical image of the scientist' as expectations portrayed in students' drawings. The checklist was created from the common aspects or features found in illustrations from previous studies and was based initially on the scientists, but not explicitly on what the scientists looked like, where they worked and what they did for work. The DAST-C was an initial attempt to address more of what children were telling us. The Checklist was designed to allow researchers to check off those items that had appeared most commonly (hence more stereotypical) in prior research while notations were made for other items such as the magnifying glasses, etc. so that later analysis could account for those drawing components. This attempt to catalog and categorize children's pictures of scientists knowingly had a limited function of what a child might be trying to convey concerning their ideas about scientists.

Farland (2003) modified the DAST directions to explicitly include the three aspects of appearance, location and activity. After reviewing hundreds of sets of Draw-A Scientists Tests, it was evident students were providing much more information about perceptions of scientists than what was reflected in the previously established one-dimensional assessment (DAST-C). For example, when students were asked to "draw a scientist", they often included much more than the appearance of the scientist. Oftentimes, there was evidence that students were drawing scientists in particular places doing particular activities. It also was obvious students were able to illustrate the appearance (what scientists look like), location (where scientists work), and activity (what scientists do) of scientists in their drawings.

Several modifications to the "draw a scientist" directions were necessary as it was determined that when students were specifically directed to draw all three aspects, they were capable of including all three in the context of their drawings. As a result, a prompt was added directing students to include these three aspects and the modified DAST (Author, 2003) was developed. The directions were as

P. Katz (Ed.), Drawing for Science Education, 171–178.
© *2017 Sense Publishers. All rights reserved.*

follows: *Imagine that tomorrow you are going on a trip (anywhere) to visit a scientist in a place where the scientist is working right now. Draw the scientist busy with the work this scientist does. Add a caption, which tells what this scientist might be saying to you about the work you are watching the scientist do. Do not draw yourself or your teacher.*

A space was provided enabling students to illustrate their perceptions. This modified DAST also consisted of a second page of four questions asking for specific information about the drawing, in the event the illustration was unclear. The children were asked: 1) I am a boy/girl. 2) Was the scientist you drew a man or woman? 3) Was the scientist you drew working outdoors or indoors? 4) What was the scientist doing in your picture?

Based on the Draw-A-Scientist Test (DAST) developed by Chambers (1983), this test was also designed to capture students' images of scientists regardless of writing ability. The instructions for the original DAST were limited to "draw a scientist". The directions were expanded and improved to provide students with more detail. Students responded by incorporating aspects of appearance, location and activity into their drawings. The researcher understood that the expanded version of the directions could cause some researchers to question the specificity of the directions. The directions can be regarded as leading the students into illustrations. Rather, the specific directions were intended to collect those data and obtain a refinement that would be less likely to appear with the use of the more general DAST direction.

Farland (2003) used information collected from these more specific directions to create a rubric based on the variations collected, observed and analyzed to create a more comprehensive picture of students' perceptions of scientists. Hundreds of drawings revealed, for instance, 1) who is doing science, (white male, female, minority) and the overall appearance of scientists (crazy, mad scientist, normal-looking); 2) what location the scientist was in (basement, laboratory, etc); 3) what activity is being done (mixing chemicals, studying rocks, finding fossils), and what tools are being used (from explosives to more commonly used tools like magnifying glasses).

Using a rubric to analyze children's illustrations of scientists is a contemporary approach. I believe it is appropriate because it allows for individual creativity as there is no right or wrong answer for illustrations. I found, that after reviewing hundreds of students' illustrations of scientists students tended to draw images that included activity of scientists that could be separated into three different categories: Sensationalized, Traditional, or Broader than Traditional. Here is the distinct difference between the DAST-C and the mDAST/DAST Rubric combination. The DAST-C limited scoring to whether or not a particular drawing element was present in the drawing. The mDAST/DAST Rubric takes the assessment further, on a continuum, as the drawings are labeled as "Sensationalized," "Traditional," "Broader than Traditional".

mDAST Rubric

Appearance.   Illustrations that score a "0" in appearance can be referred to as "can't be categorized". These drawings may contain a stick figure, a historical figure, no scientist, or a teacher or student. Illustrations that score a "1" in appearance can be referred to as "Sensationalized." These drawings contain a man or a woman who may resemble a monster or who has a clearly odd or comic book appearance. Illustrations that score a "2" in appearance can be referred to as "Traditional". These drawings contain an ordinary-looking white male. Illustrations that score a "3" in appearance can be referred to as "Broader than Traditional". These drawings include a woman or minority scientist.

Location.   Illustrations that score a "0" in location can be referred to as "cannot be categorized". The scene of these drawings may be difficult to determine or that of a classroom. Illustrations that score a "1" in location can be referred to as "Sensationalized". These drawings contain a location that resembles a basement, cave or setting of secrecy, scariness or horror, often with elaborate equipment not normally found in a laboratory. Illustrations that score a "2" in location can be referred to as "Traditional". The setting of these drawing is a traditional laboratory with a table and equipment (and possibly a computer) in a normal-looking room. Illustrations that score a "3" in location can be referred to as "Broader than Traditional". These drawings include a scene that is not a basement laboratory and different from a traditional laboratory setting.

Activity.   Illustrations that score a "0" for activity can be referred to as "difficult/unable to determine". Illustrations that score a "1" in activity can be referred to as "Sensationalized". These drawings reveal an activity that may include scariness or horror, often with elaborate equipment not normally found in a typical laboratory. Drawings that include fire, explosives or dangerous work also are included in this category. Illustrations that score a "2" in activity can be referred to as "naïve or Traditional". These drawings reveal an activity that the student believes may happen, but in truth the activity is highly unlikely to occur. This category also includes drawings where the student writes, "this scientist is studying . . . or trying to. . .", but does not show how this is being done. Illustrations that score a "3" in activity can be referred to as "Broader than Traditional". These drawings portray realistic activities that reflect the work a scientist might actually do with the appropriate tools needed to perform these activities. A student may write, "this scientist is studying… or trying to…" and shows how this is being done.

These three categories, appearance, location and activity along with their scoring mechanism for Sensationalized, Traditional, and Broader than Traditional features is the nucleus of the DAST Rubric for understanding what children illustrate in a single picture of a scientist (Appendix A).

Classroom Applications

Previously, the interpretation of the results of the DAST were limited by the narrow range of data it provided. In order for educators to accurately evaluate and analyze perceptions of scientists and their work to drive future instruction they must have a multi-dimensional in-depth tool to analyze how children may be thinking about scientists. Helping students develop positive perceptions of scientists can only be preceded by a comprehensive assessment of the perceptions they harbor. In the classroom, the DAST Rubric is useful in assessing students' initial perceptions about scientists and science, thereby helping teachers to understand and broaden those perceptions. The DAST Rubric allows teachers to see similarities and differences in whole class perceptions of scientists, enabling teachers to target instruction as necessary. For example, if a teacher (at any level beyond grade 2) administers the modified DAST directions and assesses the illustrations with the DAST RUBRIC he/she is able to quantify which students harbor misconceptions about scientists and in which specific area; appearance, location, or activity. This is a powerful pedagogical tool because if the teacher notices that the majority of my class hold negative perceptions about the appearance of scientists then she can focus her instruction on exposing the students to non-stereotypical representations of scientists and re-test with the protocol after a significant period of time. Utilizing the mDAST Rubric as a tool versus a Checklist allows for different conversations to occur concerning children's illustrations of scientists. This contemporary perspective is able to extract more information from drawings and more effectively measure changes in students' perceptions about scientists and science.

Interpretations of the results of the DAST were previously limited by the narrow range of data it provided. In order for educators to accurately evaluate and analyze perceptions of scientists and their work to drive future instruction they must have a multi-dimensional in-depth tool to analyze how children may be thinking about scientists. Helping students develop positive perceptions of scientists can only be preceded by a comprehensive assessment of the perceptions they harbor. In the classroom, the mDAST/DAST Rubric is useful in assessing students' initial perceptions about scientists and science, thereby helping teachers to understand and broaden those perceptions. The mDAST/DAST Rubric allows teachers to see similarities and differences in whole class perceptions of scientists, enabling teachers to target instruction as necessary.

CONTEMPORARY APPROACHES

In spite of the need for such an instrument and the widespread use of DAST, criticisms of it, and its ability to capture what and how students think about scientists remain. For example, teachers and researchers alike have relied on these single drawings to make inferences about what students think about scientists and their work. Farland and McComas (2007) addressed one nagging criticism of the method of collecting students' illustrations of scientists through a singular piece of data. One problem with the traditional DAST is that students are asked to draw only one image and that may not be reflective of the range of views they possess. Farland and McComas (2007) suggested modifications to DAST that greatly enhanced the information that can be derived from the instrument without making it more difficult to administer. These modifications have resulted in the development of a new version of this classic instrument, the E-DAST or *Enhanced Draw-A-Scientist-Test*.

Many students view scientists as quite different from those in other jobs and, at the same time, often hold highly stereotypical and inaccurate views of scientists and the work they do. As a result of their school science experience students must understand not only the key concepts and principles of science and how scientific knowledge is applied, but also hold an appropriate view of the cultural and social contexts within which science functions (Kafai & Gilliland-Swetland, 2000). This includes student understanding of the variety of contributions of different people. With any learning goal, teachers and researchers must be able to assess students' knowledge of that concept; the same is true with knowledge of the human side of science.

Improving the validity and reliability of the DAST by having students make multiple rather than single drawings is the modification. The lack of precision afforded by the single-drawing version of DAST was first considered in 1989 when Maoldomhnaigh and Hunt demonstrated that students may possess more than one definition of the word scientist. Their study inspired the question, "how fair is it to offer students only one opportunity at drawing their perception?" For that matter, how many well informed adults would draw a stereotypical view of anything if given only a single opportunity to present their views?

Classroom Applications

Teachers can apply and evaluate E-DAST in their classroom to gather a clearer picture of how their students may be thinking about the human endeavor of science. Here are the steps:

1. Give students a piece of legal sized white paper and ask them to fold it into three equal parts.
2. Instruct students to place the paper with only one box showing.
3. Read the following directions to students: *Imagine that tomorrow you are going on a trip (anywhere) to visit a scientist in a place where the scientist is working right now. Draw the scientist busy with the work this scientist does. Add a caption which tells what this scientist might be saying to you about the work you are watching the scientist do.* Instruct them to draw a picture of a scientist in the one box in front of them.

D. FARLAND-SMITH

4. Monitor the class to ensure students draw in only one box and are working independently.
5. When the students are finished, instruct them to unfold the paper and draw two more scientists using the directions previously described. It is important that students do not know in advance that they will be asked to make multiple drawings.

With E-DAST, if a student draws scientists of differing ethnicities, of both genders doing work in a variety of settings it is reasonable to assume that they have a sufficiently robust view of the work of science and the true nature of who can be a scientist. On the other hand, if a student draws the same image three times, there is good reason to believe that it is the only view they possess.

Data from a preliminary study evaluating E-DAST have shown that if we were to make assumptions about what students' think of scientists with respect to *activity* from a single drawing, we would be correct only 24% of the time. In 76% of cases, the students' first drawing is *not* their only perception of a scientist.

Analyzing appearance. If a category is labeled Limited, it means the child illustrated a narrow representation of the category. For example, if a child's cumulative appearance category is labeled *Limited* it means that the cumulative score of all three pictures was between a 3 and a 4.5 in this category and suggests the child drew very similar appearances of all three scientists. Most likely, the child drew very stereotypical appearances of scientists on each opportunity. If a child's cumulative appearance category is labeled *Competing* it means that the cumulative score of all three pictures was between 4.5 and 7.5 and suggests that the child holds very different perceptions of scientists which compete within their understanding of what scientists look like. Most likely, the set of three pictures include a stereotypical representation of the appearance of a scientist and a non-stereotypical representation of the appearance of a scientist. If a child's cumulative appearance category is labeled *Expansive* it means that the cumulative score of all three pictures was between 7.5 and 9 and suggests the child holds very robust ideas about the appearance of scientists. Most likely, they included women in their pictures, or multiple scientists in more than one picture.

Analyzing location. If a category is labeled *Limited*, it means the child illustrated a narrow representation of the category. For example, if a child's cumulative location category is labeled *Limited* it means that the cumulative score of all three pictures was between a 3 and a 4.5 in this category and suggests the child drew very similar location in all three pictures. Most likely, the child drew very stereotypical location, like basements, of scientists on each opportunity. If a child's cumulative location category is labeled *Competing* it means that the cumulative score of all three pictures was between 4.5 and 7.5 and suggests that the child drew very different perceptions of the places where scientists work. Most likely, the set of three pictures include a stereotypical representation of the location (basement) of a scientist and a non-stereotypical representation of the location (outdoors) of a scientist, or just had three traditional pictures of a scientist working in a laboratory setting. If a child's cumulative location category is labeled *Expansive* it means that the cumulative score of all three pictures was between 7.5 and 9 and suggests the child holds very robust ideas about the location of scientists. Most likely, they included the possibilities of outdoors into their perception of where scientists work, and carried this through to more than one picture.

Analyzing activities. If a category is labeled *Limited*, it means the child illustrated a narrow representation of the category. For example, if a child's cumulative activity category is labeled *Limited* it means that the cumulative score of all three pictures was between a 3 and a 4.5 in this category and suggests the child drew very similar activities of all three scientists. Most likely, the child drew stereotypical representations of the activities done by scientists on each opportunity. If a child's cumulative activity category is labeled *Competing* it means that the cumulative score of all three pictures was between 4.5 and 7.5 and suggests the child drew very different perceptions of the activities done by scientists, which compete within their understanding of what they do. Most likely, the set of three pictures includes a stereotypical representation of the activity of a scientist and a non-stereotypical representation of the activity of a scientist. If a child's cumulative activity category is labeled *Expansive* it means that the cumulative score of all three pictures was between 7.5 and 9 and suggests the child holds very robust ideas about the activity of scientists.

By having students create multiple drawings of scientists, it is reasonable to assume that those students have a sufficient opportunity to represent their ideas beyond the stereotypical. For example, if they hold a robust view of the work of science and the nature of who can be a scientist, it will be evident across multiple pictures. On the other hand, if a student draws the same image three times, there is good reason to believe it is the student's only view (Farland-Smith & McComas, 2009). (See Table 1.)

WHAT DO CHILDREN'S PICTURES TELL US WHEN WE COMPARE CULTURES?

Children's illustrations have long been accepted as their representation of how they view the world. Children's pictures are filled with information they are trying to convey. We have learned from past research (Barman, 1996, 1997; Chambers, 1983) that when prompted, children will draw a picture of a scientist, but they will also be able to verbalize a lot of information about the context of their illustration. Farland-Smith (2009) contends that students undergo a specific process when developing perceptions of scientists and that process is intimately related to one's culture. A child's development and capacity for learning is related directly to the symbolism and the culture of the country in which the child lives.

Table 1. Draw-a-scientist rubric

Attribute	Sensationalized	Traditional	Broader than traditional	Can't be categorized
APPEARANCE (also refers to question #2)	Male or female who resembles a monster, or who has clearly geeky appearance (crazy hair, odd appearance, cape).	Standard looking white male or standard looking scientist unable to determine gender. This scientist clearly lacks any references that are bizarre (humpback).	Female, person of different ethnicity, or two or more scientists.	No Scientist Historical Figure Reflects teacher or student Difficult to discern
Student's Score	1	2	3	0
LOCATION (also refers to question #3)	Resembles a basement, cave or setting of secrecy and/or horror. Often elaborate, with equipment not normally found in a laboratory.	Traditional lab setting-a table with equipment in a normal looking room.	Anywhere other than a traditional lab setting.	Difficult to discern
Student's Score	1	2	3	0
ACTIVITY (from question #4 & support from caption)	Indicates that the student believes that the scientist's work is either magical or destructive, or embellishes the drawing with a storyline that is about spying, stealing, killing or scaring. Limited explanation of experiment. Often science done unrealistically under hazardous conditions. If I add some powder to this potion…I will rule the world. I can cause an explosion by…. Any indication of mixing chemicals (toxic or not) may include intention to harm others.	Indicates that the student sees the scientist involved in work that is miraculous in nature (naïve on the part of the student), not destructive. This activity lacks scientific sense. (Scientists could find a cure everyday if they wanted to) I have invented a cure for……. I have invented a time machine…… OR the student writes, "The scientist is studying or is trying to…." But does not show how the scientist is studying or researching.	Indicates that the student is portraying the type of work that a scientist might actually do with the tools needed. Trying to find a cure for…(words and pictures are indicators, possibly microscope) Testing a new drug Observing a rock Mixing chemicals, with an explanation of why, even if they are 'school type' OR the student writes "The scientist is studying…" and the caption or drawing shows HOW the scientist is doing this.	No answer to question #4 Difficult to discern
Student's Score	1	2	3	0

Bruner (1996) labeled this effect *culturalism*. It is a process that begins with children viewing scientists with positive or negative associations from within their culture. Students typically look to culture and people within their immediate environment to help reinforce or redefine their perceptions while synthesizing their own ideas. As children mature, they begin constructing personal perceptions of scientists, which are unlikely to change until they have personal contact with a scientist or experience a situation that causes a change in perceptions. For these reasons, students in different cultures are best examined in a cross-cultural comparative study in order to isolate cultural factors that help shape perceptions of scientists, and that do not, while being used to illustrate this point.

As a result, I did a Chinese-American comparative study. When comparing the two sample groups, Farland-Smith (2009) discovered that a higher percentage of Chinese students (32%) drew their scientists in places that resembled caves or settings of secrecy, scariness or horror, often with elaborate equipment not normally found in a real laboratory compared to American students (9%). Fifty-nine percent of American students drew their scientists in a traditional laboratory with a table and equipment, and possibly a computer, in a normal-looking room, compared to Chinese students (31%). When comparing the two populations, a higher number of American students (29%) included a scene or setting that was not a basement laboratory, and was different from a traditional laboratory setting, compared to 12% of Chinese students.

When examining these pictures closely it was found that Chinese students included themes in their settings or locations that appear to be related or unique to their culture. Many Chinese students included a bed or "resting place" in their pictures. In China, it is very common to nap mid-day in order to improve one's creativity. Thus the bed featured in the illustration is a very real part of the Chinese culture. It is important to note that not one bed or resting place was included in any of the 675 pictures drawn by American students.

Comparing settings among the two groups, another feature related to cultures was uncovered involving basements. Basements were often portrayed in pictures drawn by American students, while not one basement was represented in the 675 pictures drawn by Chinese students. One logical explanation is that Chinese students in this study lived in high-rise apartments and did not have personal experiences with basements. This setting was common among previous studies in the U. S. (Barman, 1997).

Upon further examination, many more Chinese students identified robots and inventions (a combined 29% of the drawings) as activities done by scientists. American students, on the other hand, tended to draw more pictures with chemicals or the process skills associated with science, i.e. observing, measuring, predicting with the appropriate tools. Chinese students tended to focus on the making of robots and the creation of monsters, instead of the use of chemicals. This stereotype is present in the Chinese culture and serves as an influence about how scientists are perceived. It is important to mention that this researcher would have been hard pressed to find a drawing from a Chinese student that included beakers and chemicals. Likewise, few American students participating in this study included robots in their pictures (Farland-Smith & McComas, 2009).

This research demonstrates a clearer understanding regarding the impact of cultures on American and Chinese students, and the resulting perceptions about scientists. Contrary to earlier research, this study found that a cultural influence is present among students that contributes to their understanding of who does science, where science is done, and what scientists do. This view, as opposed to the stereotypic notion developed decades ago, is important when looking at how perceptions can be influenced in the classroom. Students are influenced not only by the personal images they hold of scientists, but by their culture and the content of the science courses they experience in schools. A child's sense of who can be a scientist, where scientists work, and what scientists do is closely related to their cultural experiences. As a result, learning about, or perceiving, the role of scientists can be directly influenced by the classroom since each classroom is a culture of its own. While educational researchers often discuss the significance of one's culture in relation to children and education, before Farland-Smith (2009) culture had not previously been linked in terms of how children perceive scientists. By understanding how cultures influence young students' perceptions about scientists, educators will be better able to create classrooms and curriculum that will help inspire student interest in the sciences and scientists, at a time when those interests are waning in the United States. If we can examine what factors contribute to students' perceptions, then perhaps we can understand how cultures influence students' perceptions of scientists.

Why is it important for teachers to be aware of the role of culture in the classroom? If science educators can assume that humans construct their own knowledge, we can agree that knowledge takes place within the context of social interaction and culture. In learning about scientists, students may have to give up, replace or exchange their previous ideas for new understanding about the work scientists do. Traditionally, the overwhelming culture of science education has centered on mastering a designated body of knowledge. Consequently, students have obtained a narrow and somewhat erroneous impression of science and scientists. Today, teachers are challenged to provide a culture that fosters and broadens students' understanding of who does science, where scientists work, and what scientists do.

PERSONAL SCIENCE IDENTITY

Finson and Farland-Smith (2013) adhere to their belief that the significance of DAST illustrations was lost as the relationship between children's illustrations and their personal science identities remained poorly connected or un-established in the research. The idea behind asking a child to create a picture of a scientist (i.e. the Draw-A-Scientist Test) is so others can externally see how they may be making sense of the conception of the term "scientist". The visual data we classify as children's drawings are meaningless unless one tries to view them in context and as expressions of the child's view of his or her world (Di Leo, 1970) and as a reflection of his/her attitudes, experiences, and perceptions that relate to his/her science identity. A child's frame of reference is not the same as an adult's. The meanings of these illustrations are clear if we keep in mind that a child does not copy what he or she sees. Rather, the drawings are expressions of inner realism; the relationship between object and expression is not a direct one as appears to be the case for adults (Di Leo, 1970). Once we can begin to understand the language of a child's graphic expression, we are impressed by how much the child is telling about himself/herself through his/her drawings. The child's drawings are not imitation, but are personal projection as the child emphasizes what is important to him/her and omits or minimizes what he/she considers undesirable (Wolff, 1946).

Carlone (1994) defined one who has a science identity as someone who demonstrates competent performance in relevant scientific practices with deep meaningful knowledge and understanding of science, and recognizes oneself and gets recognized as "a science person" by others. The construction of this identity requires the participation of others as it is constructed socially within communities of practice (Tan & Calabrese Barton, 2007). Lave and Wenger (1991) concurred that students develop identities through engaging with the practices and tasks of the science class upon entering a community of practice such as the science classroom. Learning science in this community then becomes "a process of becoming to be, of forging identities in activity" (Lave & Wenger, 1991, p. 3). The community of practice is dependent on environmental factors inherent within that community as it is accepted that these identities are fluid and subject to change. According to Brickhouse and Potter (2001), having a science or technology-related identity does not mean that one will necessarily succeed in school, if that science-related identity does not also reflect the values of the school-mediated engagement or if the students do not have access to the resources they need to do well in science. However, successful participation in school science, despite the lack of resources in a home environment, can be better facilitated when students have a personal science identity upon which they can draw (Farland-Smith, 2012).

CONCLUSION

Chambers (1983) conducted one of the most influential studies to determine students' perceptions of scientists and shifted the science community from interviews, scales and surveys to the use of drawings through what has been called the "Draw-A-Scientist Test," (DAST). The purpose was simply to determine at what age children first developed distinctive images of scientists. However, the DAST became an area of research in science education by others who took the simple task of asking children to draw a scientist and quickly became fascinated with the results for a variety of reasons. The "tool" was relatively simple to replicate, easy to administer, and it never failed to produce "fun" amusing results. With an absence of thought-provoking results and deeper meaningful connections, the DAST became less and less a tool for science educators to conduct well designed investigations, failing to gain credibility amongst many science education researchers.

Farland (2003) discovered that the DAST Rubric was able to extract more information from drawings and more effectively measure changes in students' perceptions about scientists and science. This study demonstrated that much more information could be gleaned from the standard DAST than had previously been available, but this required the development of a modified protocol, and a rubric to standardize data collection in a variety of sub domains (the appearance, location, and activity) of the scientist. The separation of the categories of appearance, location and activity allow children's perceptions to be viewed in three different lenses creating a kaleidoscope of children's perceptions versus a checklist.

Finson & Farland (2013) demonstrated a way to improve the validity and reliability of the DAST by having students make multiple rather than single drawings as the modification. The lack of precision afforded by the single-drawing version of DAST was first considered in 1989 when Maoldomhnaigh and Hunt showed that students may possess more than one definition of the word "scientist". Their study inspired the question, how fair is it offer students only one opportunity at drawing their perception? For that matter, how many well informed adults would draw a stereotypical view of anything if given only a single opportunity to present their views?

First and foremost, these picture tell us about students' cultural experiences. Making students aware of real scientists can be a huge benefit in exciting students about science and the possibility of pursuing careers in science – careers that are experiencing a dramatic loss of interest in the United States today. These messages must be incorporated with traditional science content in the classroom and must be systematically and deliberately taught to young children (Roach & Wandersee, 1993). If aware that children come to school with a variety of scientist perceptions, teachers can use this knowledge to help young children to accurately understand what scientists look like, where they work and what they do. On the other hand, children need opportunities to voice the perceptions they have about the world in which they live. Allowing children in all cultures an opportunity to voice those perceptions provides educators with an opportunity to correct misunderstanding and hopefully influence children to consider scientists and science differently.

Secondly, these illustration provide insight into an individual's personal science identity. Some critics are dismissive of the significance of draw a scientist tests because they believe they yield meaningless representations of the concept of scientist. Boylan, Hill, Wallace and Wheeler (1992) add the intriguing consideration that even the act of asking students to draw a scientist may inadvertently indicate to students that a typical scientist exists. Doubts such as these regarding the reliability and validity of the DAST have caused some to disregard it as useful in spite of the desire by many to investigate students' perceptions of the nature of scientists. However, Finson & Farland-Smith (2013) concur there is something to be gained by considering children's illustrations since they have long been accepted as *representations* of how they view the world. Such pictures or illustrations can convey information about a child's personal science identity. Formerly, children's science identities, as well as teacher responses to these identities, have been considered as being shaped by gender, race, and class relations (Brickhouse, Lowery, & Schultz, 2000, Flicker, 2008). Teachers should be aware and pay close attention to the significance of DAST illustrations because the contemporary approach offers much more than a label of stereotypical or non-stereotypical. Rather, students' pictures of scientists expose cultural clues within a community of practice, and insight into students' personal science identity.

REFERENCES

Boylan, C., Hill, D., Wallace, A., & Wheeler, A. (1992). Beyond stereotypes. *Science Education, 76*(5), 465–476.

Brickhouse, N. W., Lowery, P., & Schultz, K., (2000). What kind of a girl does science? The construction of school identities. *Journal of Research in Science Teaching, 37*, 441–458.

Brickhouse, N. W., & Potter, J. T. (2001). Young women's science identity formation in an urban context. *Journal of Research in Science Teaching, 38*(8), 965–980.

Bruner, J. (1996). *The culture of education.* Cambridge, MA: Harvard University Press.

Carlone, H. B. (1994). The cultural production of science in reform-based physics: Girls' access, participation, and resistance. *Journal of Research in Science Teaching, 37*(8), 871–889.

Chambers, D. (1983). Stereotypic images of the scientist: The draw-a-scientist test. *Science Education, 67*(2), 255–265.

Chiang, C., & Guo, C. (1996). *A study of the images of the scientist for elementary school children.* Paper presented at the National Association for Research in Science Teaching, St. Louis, Missouri, MI.

DiLeo, J. H. (1970). *Young children and their drawings.* New York, NY: Brunner/Mazel Publishers.

Farland, D. (2003). *The effect of historical, non-fiction, trade books on third grade students' perceptions of scientists* (Unpublished doctoral dissertation). University of Massachusetts, Lowell, MA.

Farland, D. (2006). The effect of historical, nonfiction trade books on elementary students' perceptions of scientists. *Journal of Elementary Science Education, 18*(2), 31–48.

Farland, D., & McComas, W. F. (2007). *The enhanced (DAST): A more valid, efficient, reliable & complete method of identifying students' perceptions of scientists.* Paper presented at the meeting of the National Association of Research in Science Teaching Conference, New Orleans, LA.

Farland-Smith, D. (2009). Exploring middle school girls' science identities: Examining attitudes, and perceptions of scientists when working 'side-by side' with scientists. *School Science and Mathematics, 109*(7), 412–421.

Farland-Smith, D. (2009). How does culture shape students' perceptions of scientists? Cross-national comparative study of American and Chinese elementary students. *Journal of Elementary Science Education, 21*(4), 23–37.

Farland-Smith, D. (2012). Development and field test of a rubric for assessing the draw-a-scientist test. *School Science Mathematics, 112*(2), 109–116.

Farland-Smith, D. (2012). Examining the personal & social interactions between young girls & scientists: Critical aspects for identity construction. *Journal of Science Teacher Education, 23*, 1–18.

Farland-Smith, D., & McComas, W. F. (2009). Teaching the human dimension of science. *Science and Children, 46*(9), 32–35.

Finson, K. D. (2003). Applicability of the DAST-C to the images of scientists drawn by students of different racial groups. *Journal of Elementary Science Education, 15*(1), 15–26.

Finson, K. D., & Farland-Smith, D. (2013). *Applying Vosniadou's conceptual change model to visualizations on conceptions of scientists.* Charlotte, NC: Information Age Publisher.

Finson, K. D., Beaver, J. B., & Cramond, B. L. (1995). Development and field test of a checklist for the Draw-A-Scientist Test. *School Science and Mathematics, 95*(4), 195–205.

Flicker, E. (2008). Women scientists in mainstream film. In B. Huppauf & P. Weingarat (Eds.), *Science images and popular images of the sciences* (pp. 241–256). New York, NY: Routledge.

Fung, Y. (2002). A comparative study of primary and secondary school students' images of scientists. *Research in Science & Technological Education, 20*(2), 199–213.

Lave, J., & Wenger, E. (1991). *Situated learning: Legitimate peripheral participation.* Cambridge, England: Cambridge University Press.

Maoldomhnaigh, M., & Hunt, A. (1988). Some factors affecting the image of the scientist drawn by older primary school pupils. *Research in Science & Technological Education, 6*, 159–166.

Mead, M., & Metraux, R. (1957). The image of the scientist amongst high school students. In B. Barbar & W. Hirsch (Eds.), *The sociology of science* (pp. 38–61). Lewes, England: Falmer Press.

Newton, D., & Newton, L. (1992). Young children's perceptions of science and the scientist. *International Journal of Science Education, 14*(3), 331–348.

Newton, D., & Newton, D. (1998). Primary children's perceptions of science and the scientist: Is the impact of a national curriculum breaking down the stereotype? *International Journal of Science Education, 20*, 1137–1149.

Roach, L. E., & Wandersee, J. H. (1993). Short story science: Using historical vignettes as a teaching tool. *Science Teacher, 60*(6), 18–21.

She, H. (1998). Gender and grade level differences in Taiwan students' stereotypes of science and scientists. *Research in Science & Technological Education, 16*(2), 125–135.

Song, J., Pak, S., & Jang, K. (1992). Attitudes of boys and girls in elementary and secondary schools towards science lessons and scientists. *Journal of the Koran Association for Research in Science Education, 12*, 109–118.

Tan, E., & Calabrese-Barton, A. (2007). From peripheral to central, the story of Melanie's metamorphosis in an urban middle school science class. *Science Education, 92*(4), 567–590.

Wolff, W. (1946). *The personality of the preschool child* (pp. 134–148). New York, NY: Grune & Stratton.

Donna Farland-Smith
Ohio State Unviersity, USA

SULAIMAN AL-BALUSHI AND ABDULLAH AMBUSAIDI

16. USING DRAWING TO REVEAL SCIENCE TEACHERS' BELIEFS ABOUT SCIENCE TEACHING

INTRODUCTION: THE IMPORTANCE OF BELIEFS IN SCIENCE TEACHING

The twenty-first century has brought many challenges in economic, social, and political aspects of life. These challenges put great pressure on educational systems across the world to review the knowledge, skills, and values presented to students, and how they may create a skillful and educated person able to cope with the challenges of the new century (Ambusaidi, 2014). This educated person has to know more and acquire the skills to enable him/her to better understand and use his/her imagination and intelligence to work and interact with others. In order to fulfil this objective within education, the teacher is a key factor in preparing students to cope with and confront the challenges of the twenty-first century (Shishavan, 2010; Ng, Nicholas, & Williams, 2010). The type of teacher needed is one who possesses the knowledge and skills to enable him/her to teach their subject effectively. In addition, the teachers we need are those who have strong beliefs about the importance of their subject and their teaching of it. The literature has shown that teachers' beliefs are one of the indicators and predicators for good teaching inside the classroom (Rosenfeld & Rosenfeld, 2007).

Studying teachers' beliefs, for pre-service or in-service, is very important and has become the focus of educational research in recent years because of the role that these beliefs play in the identification of teachers' behavior and knowledge regulation. In addition, beliefs have a major role in teachers' perception and judgment on the various teaching and learning issues (Al-Harthi, 2014). It is also important to study beliefs because they have a significant impact on teachers' decisions regarding the instructional methods and teaching techniques that they implement in their classrooms, their utilization of new technology in teaching and, finally, their continuous professional development (Donaphue, 2003).

Beliefs are a valuable factor not only in decisions made about the curriculum and instructions, but also in the context of daily life (Ambusaidi & Al-Balushi, 2012). Pajares (1992) asserts that beliefs are the best indicators of the decisions individuals make throughout their lives. Nespor (1987) argues that teachers rely on their belief system rather than academic knowledge when determining classroom actions. Pajares (1992) indicated that beliefs are far more influential than knowledge in determining how individuals organize and define tasks and problems and are stronger predicators of behavior. Beliefs are made up of episodic knowledge, characterized by remembered stories and events, affective elements, such as feelings about students, and existential presumptions (Wallace & Kang, 2004). The remembered events, feelings, and presumptions are likely to play a large part in teachers' decisions about the steps taken in the teaching and learning processes.

Several studies have been conducted to explore science teachers' beliefs. The findings of these studies have indicated that beliefs have a strong impact on their behavior inside the classroom. Rosenfeld and Rosenfeld (2007) argue that effective teaching is built through teachers' beliefs about themselves as well as their beliefs about their students. If teachers believe in their abilities and the capabilities of their students and their desire to learn, this will positively impact science teaching and learning in the classroom. This is supported by Trowbridge, Bybee and Powell (2000), who pointed out that the ideas that science teachers hold about (1) themselves as science teachers, (2) their students, (3) science, and finally (4) teaching of science, contribute greatly in shaping effective science teachers. Wallace and Kang (2004) assert that teacher' beliefs about students, learning, teaching, and the nature of science influence teaching practices and might form barriers to the implementation of reform-oriented curricula.

In conclusion, there is an essential need to explore and identify pre- and in-service science teachers' beliefs about science teaching in order to develop and guide them to better teaching. The literature has documented several methods for identifying teachers' beliefs, such as conventional methods of questionnaires, a questionnaire based on Azjen's Theory of Planning Behavior (Ajzen & Fishbein, 1980), interviews, and drawings. The current chapter focuses on drawing as an effective tool to uncover science teachers' beliefs.

DRAWING AS A POWERFUL TOOL TO REVEAL TEACHERS' BELIEFS

Drawing is a very important component in science textbooks and is considered to be fundamental to visual learning in science lessons (Cook, 2008). It helps students to understand the content, especially those who face difficulty with textual narrations. In addition, visual representations encourage students to participate actively in the classroom when they are asked to observe and reflect. Pike (2008) points out, that children who read stories that include drawings remember details of these stories better compared to those who read them without these drawings. In addition, and according to Asoko and de Böo (2001) and Nalyor and Keogh (2000), representation including drawings helps children to develop thinking skills such as reasoning, prediction, analysis, and evaluation. Drawing makes thinking tangible or concrete, especially among children. Children usually understand things that are presented to them visually more than verbally. If such things happen, then children's thinking will be enhanced. Khamis (1999) asserts that offering students' scientific

P. Katz (Ed.), Drawing for Science Education, 179–189.
© *2017 Sense Publishers. All rights reserved.*

content accompanied by drawings, helps teachers to transfer the knowledge more effectively and helps students to understand this content. As it is known that about 29% of people have a visual preference (Smith, 1996), so if the knowledge is offered to this type of students via drawings, then we can expect that they will more easily understand the content presented to them. Also, drawings make natural phenomena become less abstract to students and help them understand scientific concepts much better. Cook (2008) argues that, in science, visual images, including drawings, are preferred by curriculum designers and teachers for displaying multiple relationships and processes that are difficult to describe verbally. Furthermore, Duchastel (1980) reported that drawing stimulates students' reading of difficult texts and learning of new words by facilitating their verbal responses to these words. Asoko and DeBöo (2001, 4) list several advantages for using representations in teaching, including drawing, such as:

- Capture and focus attention.
- Provide a stimulus for discussion.
- Provide a stimulus which requires effort to interpret and so aids thinking.
- Stimulate creative thinking.
- Provide something memorable and understandable which can be drawn upon later to support thinking.
- Require the identification of similarities and differences which aids understanding.

DRAW-A-SCIENCE-TEACHER-TEST CHECKLIST (DASTT-C) INSTRUMENT

In our method, to explore prospective science teachers' beliefs at Sultan Qaboos University, we used the Draw-A-Science-Teacher-Test Checklist (DASTT-C). This checklist was developed by Thomas, Pedersen and Finson (2001) from the Draw-A-Scientist Test (DAST) instrument. DAST was proposed by Chambers (1983) to identify students' mental images about scientists. Then, Finson et al. (1995) further developed the DAST instrument to make it easier to assess and judge its validity and reliability (Ambusaidi & Al-Balushi, 2012). A further development was made to the instrument by Thomas et al. (2001) who designed the DASTT-C to assess student teachers' mental images about teaching science.

The DASTT-C instrument consists of two parts (Ambusaidi & Al-Balushi, 2012):

1. Drawing part: participants are asked to draw themselves teaching.
2. Survey part: participants' beliefs are evaluated about three themes of teaching styles: exploratory, conceptual, and explicit.

The drawing part asks teachers to draw themselves while teaching their science subject matter and then elaborate more about their drawing by answering two questions about what both the teacher and students do (Figure 1).

Draw a picture of yourself as a science teacher at work.

What is the teacher doing? What are the students doing?

Figure 1. DASTT-C sample

The scoring sheet of the drawing consists of three components: teacher, students, and the learning environment. In the teacher and students components, two main criteria are considered while assessing a teachers' drawing: the activity that the teacher and students do and the position of both in the classroom (Ambusaidi & Al-Balushi, 2012). In each of the three components, a couple of statements describe them. Each statement is scored either 1 or 0 (Table 1). The total score ranges between 0 and 13. The closer the score is to 0 the more that teachers' mental images reflect student-centered learning; whereas, when the score is closer to 13, this means that teachers' mental images reflect teacher-centered learning (Thomas & Pedersen, 2003).

USING DRAWING TO REVEAL SCIENCE TEACHERS' BELIEFS ABOUT SCIENCE TEACHING

Table 1. The three components of scoring criteria

Component	Sub-component	Statements	
Teacher	Activity	1.	Demonstrating Experiment/Activity
		2.	Lecturing/Giving Directions (teacher talking)
		3.	Using Visual Aids (chalkboard, overhead, and charts).
	Position	4.	Centrally located (head of class)
		5.	Erect Posture (not sitting or bending down)
Students	Activity	6.	Watching and Listening (or so suggested by teacher behavior)
		7.	Responding to Teacher/Text Questions
	Position	8.	Seated (or so suggested by classroom furniture)
Environment		9.	Desks are arranged in rows (more than one row)
		10.	Teacher desk/table is located at the front of the room
		11.	Laboratory organization (equipment on teacher desk or table)
		12.	Symbols of Teaching (ABC's, chalkboard, bulletin boards, etc.)
		13.	Symbols of Science knowledge (science equipment, lab instruments, wall charts, etc.)

THE STUDY

We used the DASTT-C instrument with prospective science teachers who were at Sultan Qaboos University, Oman. We used a longitudinal approach to conduct the study. Thus, we administered the instrument three times: (1) at the beginning of their Science Methods I course, (2) at the end of their Science Method I course, and (3) at the end of their Science Methods II course and Practicum. The study was published elsewhere (Ambusaidi & Al-Balushi, 2012). The original study reported the results of both parts of the DASTT-C instrument: drawing and survey. Here, in this book chapter, we report on the drawing part of the instrument only.

Purpose

The purpose of the study was to evaluate prospective science teachers' beliefs of themselves as science teachers and to measure the progress of these beliefs across their preparation program. The beliefs focused on whether science teachers were student-centered or teacher-centered. The two main research questions that the drawing part of the DASTT-C instrument helped to answer were:

1. What were the beliefs (student- or teacher-centered) of prospective science teachers about themselves as science teachers?
2. What were the changes in prospective science teachers' beliefs (student- or teacher-centered) that occurred as a result of their enrollment in science methods and the practicum courses?

Sample and Context

The sample included 45 pre-service science teachers who were studying at the College of Education at Sultan Qaboos University in the Sultanate of Oman. They were 15 males and 30 females. The program prepares science teachers for grades 5–12. It has two courses that deal with teaching methods: the Science Methods I and Science Methods II. Towards the end of the program, teachers are enrolled in a training experience: the Practicum where they go to schools to practice science teaching. The program focuses on different teaching methods that are student-centered such as inquiry-based learning, problem-based learning, projects-based learning, cooperative learning, science learning stations, role playing, and scientific argumentation. It also trains candidates on different science teaching methods that could be used as teacher-centered or student-centered methods, such as graphic organizers (i.e. concept mapping, mind mapping, Vee diagrams), simulations and animations, round house, guided imagery, and using concept cartoons. During both science methods courses candidates were required to attend two sections per week: a theoretical section and a practical (microteaching) section. The duration of each section was two hours. During the microteaching section they were given the opportunities to peer-teach, reflect on their own teaching, and reflect on their peers' teaching. During the Practicum experience, they were placed in public schools to practice teaching. Also, they were required to submit an e-portfolio where they documented and reflected on their teaching activities.

Method and Procedure

The DASTT-C instrument was administered three times: (1) at the beginning of the Science Methods I course (Spring semester), (2) at the end of the same course, and (3) at the end of the Practicum experience and Science Methods II course (Fall semester).

Data Analysis

Participants' drawings were analyzed using Table 1 guidelines. Both drawing and written parts (Figure 1) were used in the analysis. The written part clarified what teachers and students were doing. Thus, it was used to score items 1, 2, 3, 6, and 7. If the item in Table 1 was observed, then 1 point was given. If not, then 0 was given. Since the total items were 13, the possible maximum score was 13. The score of each drawing was classified into three categories: student-centered (0–4), intermediate (5–6), and teacher-centered (7–13) (Thomas et al., 2001). Figure 2 illustrates the components of the drawing that are taken into consideration when analyzing science teachers' drawings in the DASTT-C instrument according to Table 1. Figures 3, 4, 5, and 6 are response examples.

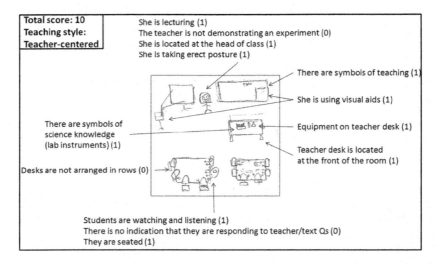

Figure 2. An example of teacher-centered instruction

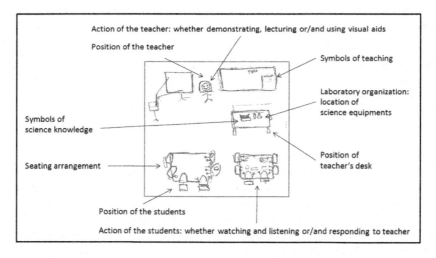

Figure 3. The analyzing components of science teachers' drawings

Validity and Reliability

The validity and reliability procedures for the Arabic version of the DASTT-C instrument are fully described in Ambusaidi and Al-Balushi (2012). The instrument underwent English-to-Arabic validity checking by two linguistic professors who were fluent in both Arabic and English. Then it was reviewed by seven science educators to check its content and language. The reliability procedure included calculation of the Pearson product moment correlation coefficient (r) between two raters who used the scoring checklist (Table 1) to score each drawing. The inter-rater reliability coefficient was 0.89.

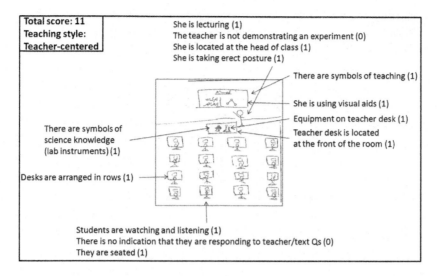

Figure 4. An example of teacher-centered instruction

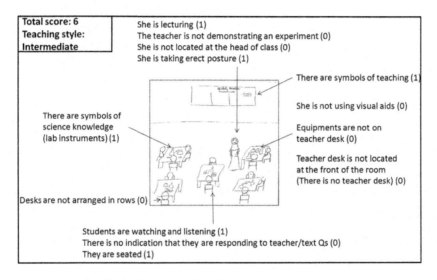

Figure 5. An example of intermediate instruction

MAIN FINDINGS: REVEALING SCIENCE TEACHERS' BELIEFS THROUGH THE DASTT-C

The DASTT-C instrument appears to be an effective tool to reveal science teachers' beliefs regarding their teaching. The following subsections illustrate the main outcomes of the analysis of prospective science teachers' drawings of themselves teaching science. The main themes that emerged from teachers' drawings are described below.

Styles of Teaching

Figure 7 demonstrates the mean score and standard deviations for the three administrations of the DASTT-C instrument. It could be seen that at the end of the Science Methods I course participants moved from the teacher-centered teaching style to the intermediate state between teacher-centered and student-centered teaching styles. However, at the end of the Science Methods II and Practicum courses, there was a slight change towards the student-centered teaching style. Participants remained in the intermediate stage. Similar observations were reported by El-Deghaidy (2006) who used the DASTT-C instrument on pre-service Egyptian science teachers. Also, Yilmaz et al. (2007) used the DASTT-C instrument on pre-service Turkish elementary science teachers. Only 20% of participants demonstrated a student-centered teaching approach. On the other hand, 40% of the teachers demonstrated the teacher-centered approach.

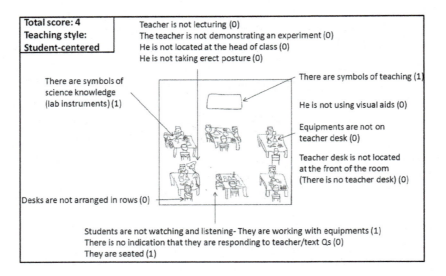

Figure 6. An example of student-centered instruction

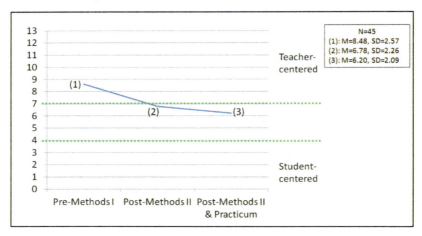

Figure 7. Prospective science teachers' performance in the three administrations of the DASTT-C instrument

The rest were at the intermediate stage. In addition, Simmons et al. (1999) reported that there was a small percentage (20%) of science and mathematics beginning teachers who believed in a student-centered teaching approach. There were even fewer teachers who actually used a student-centered teaching approach (10%).

Figures 3 through 6 clearly demonstrate distinct teaching styles. Figures 3 and 4 are teacher-centered, Figure 5 shows an intermediate stage between teacher-centered and student-centered, and Figure 6 is student-centered. Because of the seating arrangement, the first glimpse of some of the drawings might deceive the viewers. Being seated in groups does not mean that students are engaged in student-centered instruction. The DASTT-C instrument checklist (Table 1) incorporates different elements in order to decide whether a drawing is teacher-centered or student-centered. Also, what participants write underneath their drawings about what the teacher and students are doing is consulted.

Monitoring Progress: Types of Changing Beliefs

The DASTT-C instrument helps monitor progress throughout the teacher education program. As participants went through Science Methods I, Science Methods II and the Practicum, we observed changes in their drawings. These changes were in four main categories: (1) no significant change, (2) towards more student-centered, (3) fluctuation, and (4) towards more teacher-centered. Below are examples of these categories.

1. *No significant change.* In some drawings, there was no significant change. Participants either remained teacher-centered or student-centered. Figure 8 illustrates an example of a female science prospective teacher who maintained her teacher-centered style throughout the three administrations of the DASTT-C instrument.

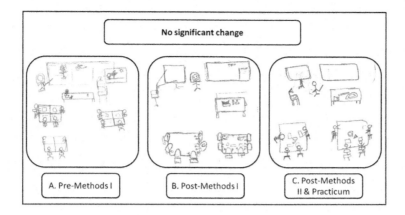

Figure 8. An example of a participant with no significant change in teaching style

2. *Towards more student-centered.* Some participants changed towards more student-centered by the end of their Practicum. Figure 9 shows that a female science prospective teacher shifted to a student-centered approach. More group-work and hands-on teaching could be observed.

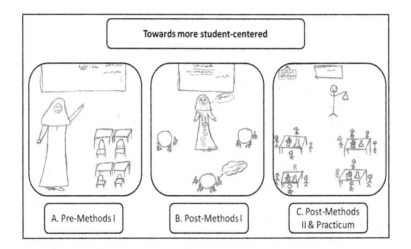

Figure 9. An example of a participant who changed to a more student-centered teaching style

3. *Fluctuation.* We noticed in some rare cases that participants flipped from teacher-centered to student-centered and then back to teacher-centered. Figure 10 demonstrates a male science prospective teacher whose approach changed after Science Methods I from teacher-centered to student-centered. However, after going to schools and practicing teaching in real situations, he flipped back to teacher-centered. There were no cases when a teacher started with student-centered, flipped to teacher-centered, then went back to student-centered. In rare cases we observed that some prospective teachers started as student-centered and ended up as teacher-centered. Figure 11 shows a female participant who was leaning towards a more student-centered approach. However, at the end of the Practicum she drew herself as a teacher-centered teacher.

Visual Representations

It was noticed in participants' drawings that they put some visual representations on the whiteboard. Figure 12 illustrates four types of these representations: tables, sketches, concept maps, and cyclic graphic organizers.

Instructional Methods

The drawings reflect some of the instructional methods used by the participants. Examples are lecturing (e.g. Figures 4, 7, 8A, 10, and 11C), classroom discussion (e.g. Figure 8B), laboratory demonstration (e.g. Figure 8C), inquiry-based and experimentation (e.g. Figure 6), and concept mapping (e.g. Figure 12C).

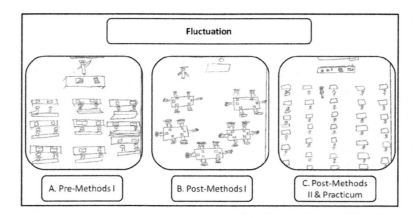

Figure 10. An example of a participant who kept changing his style

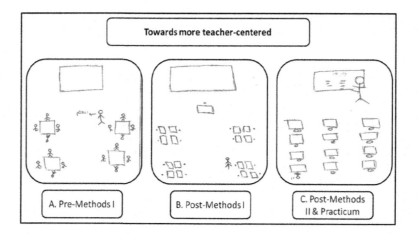

Figure 11. An example of a participant who changed to a more teacher-centered teaching style

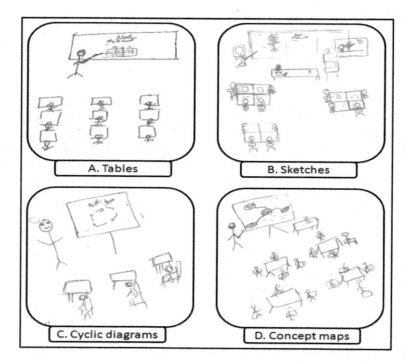

Figure 12. Different types of visual representations illustrated by participants

Teacher as the Dominant Figure

It could be noticed that some drawings present the teacher as the dominant figure. Clear cases are shown in the two leftmost drawings in Figure 8. The participant exaggerated the size of herself as a teacher compared to her students who appeared as tiny figures. This dominant position of the teacher was also observed by other researchers (Calderhead & Robson, 1991; Simmons et al., 1999; Yilmaz-Tuzun, 2008). In addition, it is obvious from other drawings presented above that the teacher is the active person in the classroom, while students are passive.

Classroom Environment

The drawings varied in terms of inclusion of elements of a classroom environment. All drawings had students' seats. Most had a whiteboard and a teacher's desk. Some of them had laboratory equipment, books, and a projector. Very few had wall or flip charts. The drawings also reflect the seating arrangements. Some of the drawings had a traditional row seating arrangement while others had a group seating arrangement. One drawing had a U-shape seating arrangement. These elements of classroom environment reflect different beliefs of how the classroom environment should be arranged.

Class size

Class size varied in participants' drawings. It ranged from four (e.g. Figure 8) to 30 (e.g. Figure 10) students. From the authors' experience with the participants as field training supervisors during the discussions held within the Practicum program, class size plays a significant role in some prospective science teachers' decisions regarding what type of teaching approach to adopt. Some hesitated to use student-centered methods with a large class size, mostly for fear of managing and controlling the students.

Facial Expression

Some DASTT-C drawings illustrate facial expressions. These expressions could reflect certain types of beliefs about teaching. For instance, some teachers in Figures 5, 7, 8, and 12 are smiling. Could these facial expressions reflect positive attitudes? Further investigation is needed.

DISCUSSIONS AND CONCLUSIONS

The above findings reveal different potentials for the DASTT-C instrument in revealing science teachers' beliefs. Tendency towards student-centered or teacher-centered approaches seems to be the main potential of this drawing instrument. Some participants in the study reported here had changed their beliefs towards more a student-centered approach. This significant change happened after their Science Methods I course. Prospective science teachers did not have real exposure to different teaching methodologies and different teaching styles before this course. Besides the knowledge they receive during this course, they also practice peer-teaching in the microteaching session, which is an essential part of this course. Thus, many started with naïve views about science teaching and then they were empowered with different types of information, discussion, practice, and reflection on different types of teaching methods. Their implementation of some of these methods during microteaching assisted them in grasping and adopting these methods. The DASTT-C instrument managed to capture and document the changes in these teachers' beliefs about science teaching.

Afterwards, the DASTT-C instrument was also able to capture the "*reality shock*" which some teachers had when they practiced science teaching in schools. The mean average of the participants in Figure 7 reflected a dramatic change from strongly teacher-centered beliefs to student-centered after Science Methods I, during which time participants were practicing teaching in the microteaching classrooms with 8–12 of their peers. However, this progress slowed down and minor changes took place after the Practicum course. Most probably, the reality shock played its role here. Although some participants managed to preserve their progress towards a student-centered style after they concluded their Practicum course, others changed back to a teacher-centered style. This reality shock has been observed by other researchers (Hudson, Beutel, & Hudson, 2008; Kallery, 2004; Mccormack & Thomas, 2005; Nahal, 2010). This phenomenon of reality shock is a characteristic of many novice teachers (Hudson, Beutel, & Hudson, 2008) who have an immature realization of the complexity of the teaching profession. One of the major aspects of teaching that frustrates novice teachers is classroom management (Nahal, 2010). It seems that the participants in the current study were after more control of their classrooms by preserving their teaching style as teacher-centered. This justification is stressed by Simmons et al. (1999) who also observed greater tendencies towards a teacher-centered approach by second and third year teachers than first year teachers. Simmons et al. explained that fresh graduates had more concerns about students' needs; their passions were confounded by the complexity of the actual teaching-learning environment.

Besides direct lecturing, the DASTT-C instrument was able to give indications of the types of instruction sought by prospective science teachers in terms of teaching methods and visual representations. The appearance of these instructional techniques might reflect the frequently used teaching approaches by teachers. If so, then the use of the DASTT-C instrument could be extended to include not only the beliefs but the practice of science teachers. Thus, further research is needed.

The DASTT-C instrument drawings reflected a view of the teacher as dominant. The teacher as the dominant figure in the classroom has been reported by other researchers (Calderhead & Robson, 1991; Simmons et al., 1999; Yilmaz-Tuzun, 2008). Was this a result of the wording of the instructions in the DASTT-C instrument which asked participants to "Draw a picture of *yourself* as a science teacher at work?" Would this phenomenon of dominance in teachers be less prominent if the wording was changed into, for instance, "Draw a picture of one of your science lessons" or "Draw a picture of your science classroom at work?" Again, more investigation is required.

In the findings we report here, the DASTT-C instrument proved to be a powerful tool to reflect the class size, a big problem for education in developing countries. The class size varies in Omani schools. On average, it is 30 in large cities. However, it is 40 in some cities. With such a large class size, it becomes difficult to give each student proper attention and respond to their needs.

LIMITATIONS AND FURTHER RESEARCH

Our use of the DASTT-C reflects a set of limitations in the instrument. First, since the participants are given one spot to draw, they could draw one scene only. Thus, different teaching practices could not be captured. For instance, although different types of instructional methods were included in the Science Methods courses, not all of them found their way into the drawings of science teachers in the DASTT-C instrument. This did not reflect the real practice by prospective science teachers. For instance, from our observations in their microteaching classrooms and in the schools during the Practicum program, they used guided imagery, role play, science learning stations, and brainstorming, yet none of these techniques were reflected in their drawings. There are three possible reasons for that: 1) some of these teaching methods might be difficult to draw; 2) they might be less practiced than the methods appear in the drawings; and 3) the DASTT-C instrument may not accommodate real teaching practice. Further research is needed to verify these reasons.

Second, the DASTT-C instrument does not tell the whole story by itself. For instance, inferences about attitudes towards teaching based on facial expressions are not accurate unless verified by another research tool such as a follow-up interview. Further research is needed to evaluate the combination of drawing and interviewing in revealing science teachers' beliefs. How much could both research tools offer to science education researchers?

Third, although drawing ability does not seem to be a critical factor in deciding on participants' beliefs when responding to the DASTT-C instrument, this assumption should be further investigated. Teachers with low drawing ability used stick-man symbols to represent teachers and students. When we were analyzing the drawings, this approach did not seem to affect our decision regarding participants' beliefs. However, would limited drawing ability prevent some participants from drawing this element or that? Further investigation is needed.

Fourth, small changes in the wording given to the participants in the DASTT-C instrument could affect their drawing. In this matter, Maoldomhnaigh and Mhaolain (1990) pointed out that changing the wording of the directions given to students in the DASTT-C instrument altered the type of drawings produced.

In conclusion, the DASTT-C instrument is a powerful tool in revealing science teachers' beliefs with regard to student/teacher-centered science teaching, following the progress of science teachers over a certain period of time, and capturing different elements of the teaching and learning environment in science classrooms. Furthermore, we believe that it has the potential to provide data on other aspects such as attitudes towards teaching, misconceptions about different approaches to teaching, and insights into a teacher's philosophy of teaching. Further research could be conducted to focus on extending the uses of the DASTT-C instrument.

REFERENCES

Ajzen, I., & Fishbein, M. (1980). *Understanding attitudes and predicting social behavior.* Englewood Cliffs, NJ: Prentice-Hall.
Al-Harthi, A. (2014). *Beliefs of female science teachers in cycle two basic education schools regarding the scientific arguments in their relationship with classroom practices* (Unpublished Master's Dissertation). Sultan Qaboos University, Muscat, Sultanate of Oman.
Ambusaidi, A. (2014, October 22–23). *Some good practices and innovations in teaching and assessment at higher education.* International Conference on Quality of Higher Education Curriculum, Isfahan, Iran.
Ambusaidi, A., & Al-Balushi, S. (2012). A longitudinal study to identify prospective science teachers' beliefs about science teaching using the Draw-A-Science-Teacher-Test Checklist. *International Journal of Environmental and Science Education, 7*(2), 291–311.
Asoko, H., & de Böo, M. (2001). *Analogies and illustrations: Representing ideas in primary science.* Herts: Association for Science Education.
Calderhead, J., & Robson, M. (1991). Images of teaching: Student teachers' early conceptions of classroom practice. *Teaching and Teacher Education, 7,* 1–8.
Chambers, D. W. (1983). Stereotypic images of the scientist: The draw – A- scientist test. *Science Education, 67*(2), 225–265.
Cook, M. (2008). Students' comprehension of science concepts depicted in textbook illustrations. *Electronic Journal of Science Education, 12*(1), 2–14.
Donaphue, H (2003). An instrument to elicit teachers' beliefs and assumptions. *English Language Teaching Journal, 57*(4), 344–350.
Duchastel, P. (1980). *Research on illustrations in instructional text* (ERIC ED No. 215324).
El-Deghaidy, H. (2006). An investigation of pre-service teacher's self-efficacy and self-image as a science teacher in Egypt. *Asia Pacific Forum on Science Learning and Teaching, 7*(2), 1–22.
Finson, K. D., Beaver, J. B., & Cramond, B. L. (1995). Development and field tests of a checklist for the draw-a-scientist test. *School Science and Mathematics, 95*(4), 195–205.
Hudson, S., Beutel, D., & Hudson, P. (2008). *Beginning teachers' perceptions of their induction into teaching.* Practical Experiences in Professional Education (PEPE) International Conference 2008, Edinburgh, UK. Retrieved from QUT Digital Repository: http://eprints.qut.edu.au

Kallery, M. (2004). Early years teachers' late concerns and perceived needs in science: An exploratory study. *European Journal of Teacher Education, 27*(2), 147–165. doi:110.1080/026197604200023024

Khamis, M. (1992). The effect of some variables of fixed photos that are integrated to verbal presentation in students' retention of given information. *Educational Technology Research and Studies, 2*(2), 115–138 (in Arabic).

Maoldomhnaigh, M. O., & Mhaolain, V. N. (1990). The perceived expectation of the administrator as a factor affecting the sex of scientists drawn by early adolescent girls. *Research in Science and Technological Education, 8*(1), 69–74.

Mccormack, A., & Thomas, K. (2005). The reality of uncertainty: The plight of casual beginning teachers. *Change: Transformations in Education, 8*(1), 17–31.

Nahal, S. (2010). *Exploring disparities between teachers' expectations and the realities of the education profession.* Paper presented at the Academic and Business Research Institute Conference, Las Vegas, NV. Retrieved September 11, 2011, from http://www.aabri.com/EIP.html

Nalyor, S., & Keogh, B (2000). *Concept cartoons in science education.* Sandbach, Millgate: House Publishers.

Nespor, J. (1987). The role of beliefs in the practice of teaching. *Journal of Curriculum Studies, 19*(4), 317–328.

Ng, W., Nicholas, H., & William, A. (2010). School experience influences on pre-service teachers' evolving beliefs about effective teaching. *Teaching and Teacher Education, 26,* 278–289.

Pajares, M. (1992). Teachers' beliefs and education research: Cleaning up a messy construct. *Review of Education Research, 62*(3), 307–332.

Pike, M. (2008). *The role of illustration in children's inferential comprehension* (Unpublished Master's Dissertation). University of Guelph, Canada.

Rosenfeld, M., & Rosenfeld S. (2007). Developing effective teacher beliefs about learners: The role of sensitizing teachers to individual learning differences. *International Journal of Experimental Educational Psychology, 28*(3), 245–272.

Shishavan, H. (2010). The relationship between Iranian English language teachers' and learners' gender and their perceptions of an effective English language teacher. *English Language Teaching, 3*(3), 3–10.

Simmons, P., Emory, A., Carter, T., Coker, T., Finnegan, B, Crockett, D., Richardson, L., Yager, R., Craven, J., Tillotson, J., Brunkhorst, H., Twiest, M., Hossain, K., Gallagher, J., Duggan-Haas, D., Parker, J., Cajas, F., Alshannag, Q., McGlamery, S., Krockover, J., Adams, P., Spector, B., LaPorta, T., James, B., Rearden, K., & Labuda, K. (1999). Beginning teachers: Beliefs and classroom actions. *Journal of Research in Science Teaching, 36*(8), 930–954.

Smith, A. (1996). *Accelerated learning in the classroom.* Stafford: Network Educational Press.

Thomas, J. A., Pederson, J. E., & Finson, K. (2001). Validating the Draw-A-Science-Test- Checklist (DASTT-C): Exploring mental models and teacher beliefs. *Journal of Science Teacher Education, 12*(3), 295–310.

Trowbridge, L., Bybee, R., & Powell, J. (2000). *Teaching secondary school science: Strategies for developing scientific literacy.* Lahman, NJ: Merrill.

Thomas, J. A., & Pederson, J. E. (2003). Reforming elementary science teacher preparation: What about extant teaching beliefs? *School Science and Mathematics, 103*(7), 319–330.

Wallace, C., & Kang, N-H. (2004). An investigation of experienced secondary science teachers' beliefs about inquiry: An examination of competing belief sets. *Journal of Research in Science Teaching, 41*(9), 936–960.

Yilmaz, H., Turkmen, H., Pedersen, J., & Cavas, P. H. (2007). Evaluation of pre-service teachers' images of science teaching in Turkey. *Asia Pacific Forum on Science Learning and Teaching,* **8**(1), 1–20.

Yilmaz-Tuzun, O. (2008). Pre-service elementary teachers' beliefs about science teaching. *Journal of Science Teacher Education, 19,* 183–204.

Sulaiman Al-Balushi
Sultan Qaboos University, Oman

Abdullah Ambusaidi
Sultan Qaboos University, Oman

SINAN ÖZGELEN

17. PRIMARY SCHOOL STUDENTS' VIEWS ON SCIENCE AND SCIENTISTS[1]

INTRODUCTION

In science education literature, there are many studies that investigated students' stereotypical images of scientists at all levels (e.g. Cakmakci, Tosun, Turgut, Orenler, Sengul, & Top, 2011; Kaya, Dogan, & Ocal, 2008; McCarthy, 2014; Narayan, Park, Peker, & Suh, 2013; Song & Kim, 1999; Yvonne, 2002; Turkmen, 2008). Why are students' images about science and scientists important for the science education community? Because, students' attitudes toward science are essential during their educational life and choice of occupation after school (She, 1998; Boylan, Hill, Walace, & Wheeler, 1992). Researchers found that boys and girls can have different attitudes about science and scientists (Jones, Howe, & Rua, 2000). Generally, primary students have stereotypical images for science and scientist (e.g. Yvonne, 2002; Barman, Ostlund, Gatto, & Halferty, 1997; Finson, Beaver, & Cramond, 1995; Huber & Burton, 1995; She, 1995). One of the reasons, I believe, is that they do not have first-hand experiences and knowledge about science (Talsma, 2007).

Some researchers suggest a direct relation between students' stereotypical images of scientists and their attitudes toward science (Bodzin & Gehringer, 2001; Flick, 1990; Mason, Kahle, & Gardner, 1991). In addition, students' attitudes about science and scientists can affect positively or negatively their choice of future careers (Boylan et al., 1992). Moreover, some studies showed that students' views about scientists influenced their motivation to become scientists (Finson et al., 1995).

Attitudes are affected by learning from role models. Observations affect students' views about science and scientists. Studies show that children start to construct images of scientists at early ages, in kindergarten and elementary school (Losh, Wilke, & Pop, 2008; Matkins, 1996). Elementary students observe their parents, teachers, and people on TV and in newspapers. Primary students come into schools with their own previous knowledge and ideas. During instruction students may refine their existing views, or change them entirely, depending on classroom activities.

LITERATURE REVIEW

One of the first studies about this topic was conducted by Mead and Metraux (1957), who asked American high school students to write about their views of scientists. The study revealed the stereotypical images of scientists for high school students, a famous description in the literature:

> The scientist is a man who wears a white coat and works in a laboratory. He is elderly or middle aged and wears glasses …he may wear a beard…he is surrounded by equipment: test tubes, bunsen burners, flasks and bottles, a jungle gym of blown glass tubes and weird machines with dials …, he writes neatly in black notebooks …One day he may straighten up and shout: "I've found it! I've found it!" …Through his work people will have new and better products…he has to keep dangerous secrets …his work may be dangerous …he is always reading a book. (p. 386)

Because there are difficulties in writing for younger students, Chambers (1983) developed the Draw-A-Scientist Test (DAST). Chambers aimed to discover students' image of a scientist and to establish the age in which characteristics first develop. This test gives students a chance to draw their views about scientists. Chambers (1983) collected data from 4807 children in 186 classes from kindergarten to grade five (the majority were from grades two and three). Based on the literature, Chambers determined seven characteristics as indicators of the standard image of scientists. There are; (1) Lab coat; (2) Eyeglasses; (3) Facial growth of hair; (4) Symbols of research; (5) Symbols of knowledge; (6) Technology; and (7) Relevant captions. Comparing students' grade levels, Chambers concluded that "the standard image has begun to appear in the child's consciousness in the second and third year of schooling; by the fourth and fifth year the image, as a rule, has fully emerged" (1983, p. 260). After Chambers, Finson et al. (1995) developed a useful checklist (DAST-C) for researchers. Finson (2003) conducted a study to seek validity for this list.

Past studies about this topic revealed that, overwhelmingly, children have a stereotypical image of scientists as being male, wearing eyeglasses, working in laboratories, bald, old, and so forth (Barman, 1999; Buldu, 2006; Chambers, 1983; Chiang & Guo, 1996; Fung, 2002; Hill & Wheeler, 1991; Jones & Bangert, 2006; Leblebicioglu, Metin, Yardımcı, & Cetin, 2011). Stereotypical images of scientists may demonstrate negative attitudes toward science and scientists (Mason et al., 1991). Previous studies showed that negative perceptions, especially girls' images of science and scientists, can negatively affect their future careers (Finson, 2003). Since students think that scientists must work hard all the time, they develop concern that they would not have time for themselves and their families, and that they would have a limited social life. Therefore, many students do not choose science as a career after school (Mason et al., 1991).

P. Katz (Ed.), Drawing for Science Education, 191–203.
© 2017 Sense Publishers. All rights reserved.

In point of fact, most students do not have a chance to meet a scientist during their school years; therefore, they can easily imagine some stereotypical images of scientists (Rampal, 1992). A review of students' attitudes toward science in elementary school was conducted by Koballa (1993). It revealed that negative views started at an early age. But the ages between 8 and 13 are accepted as the most important time of influence. In this regard, there are some studies from different countries (USA, Turkey). Generally, researchers used Chambers' (1983) DAST (Barman, 1997; Song, Darling, Dixon, Koonce, McReynolds, Meier, & Stafsholt, 2011; Turkmen, 2008). From then until now, there have been numerous studies in western countries. Parallel with these studies, in recent years some studies were conducted in Turkey (Akcay, 2011; Buldu, 2006; Cakmakci et al., 2011; Kaya et al., 2008; Korkmaz & Kavak, 2010; Leblebicioglu et al., 2011; Ozel, 2012; Togrol Yontar, 2000; Turkmen, 2008).

Many studies were conducted in early school, primary school, high school, and preservice teachers in universities. However, the present study's sample consisted of primary students. The sample consisted of third grade students. Therefore, their drawings are an important indicator to show this age group' views about science and scientists.

In the DAST literature there are some studies, which specifically concerned primary students as samples (Barman, 1997; Song et al, 2011; Turkmen, 2008). These studies were reviewed and their results are compared to the present study in the discussion. The first study was conducted by Barman (1997). Barman asked three questions to students: Will you draw a picture of a scientist doing science? Will you draw a picture of yourself doing science in school? Can you think of some ways you use what you learn in science outside of school? After students' drawings, interviews were conducted to fully understand the meaning or intent of drawings. During the analysis of the drawings and students' interviews, the Draw-a-Scientists Checklist (DAST-C) (Finson, Beaver, & Cramond, 1995) was used. Students' stereotypes of scientists were exposed. In his study, Barman (1997) had three levels for students, K–2, 3–5, and 6–8. These groups provided comparisons among different aged students' views. For the present study, results of the 3–5 level were taken, since the present study's sample is also in that grade level. Barman's sampl consisted of 649 primary students from 3–5 grades.

The second study was performed by Song et al. (2011). In their study, the researchers focused on the changes in primary students' views of scientists compared with Barman's (1997) study. They applied DAST for data collection and DAST-C for data analysis. Their samples consisted of 52 third graders from two different classes in two different schools. During the analysis some stereotypical characteristics were identified according to the DAST-C characteristics of scientists. The researchers compared 3rd grade students' drawings with Barman's (1997) to show whether there were any changes in 3rd graders' views of scientists over the last decade.

The third study was done by Turkmen (2008). He concentrated on 5th grade students. In total, 287 students were in the sample (120 boys and 167 girls). In that study, DAST was used, and each student was asked questions: Please draw a picture of a scientist? When you are finished, please explain what the scientist is doing? In his study, the researcher used a second questionnaire regarding the source of the scientist image. This was adapted by Turkmen and Pedersen (2005). During the data analysis the DAST-C was applied. Students' drawings were rated for specific stereotypic images. The researcher used some additional information obtained from the student narratives. These three studies were compared and discussed with the present study in the discussion part.

Purpose of the Study and Research Questions

The purpose of the study was to investigate 3rd grade primary students' views on science and scientists. Science educators, elementary school teachers, and also pre-service teachers should be responsible for helping primary students develop modern views of science and scientists. In this study, 3rd grade primary students' perspectives about science and scientists were sought. One of the purposes of this study was to investigate what kinds of images of scientists primary students hold in their minds. The second one was to determine whether the findings were similar to previous national and international earlier studies.

The process of analyzing students' stereotypes of images has some uncertainties, because researchers or teachers identify and interpret students' drawings. Sometimes, this can cause a misleading or oversimplified opinion about students' drawings. Jarvis and Rennie (1995) suggested that in order to prevent misunderstanding, students should be required to add some sentences related to their images of science and scientists. Therefore, in this study primary students were asked to answer three basic questions; (1) What is science? (2) Who does science? (3) How is science done? Primary students were asked to respond in writing or by drawing pictures about these questions.

METHOD

This study is exploratory in nature. Qualitative data collection methods were applied. These methods were open-ended survey questionnaires and students' drawings (Marshall & Rossman, 2006).

Sampling

The sample of this study was composed of 254 primary school students. All of the students were from 3rd grade, and they were from 11 classes from three different public schools in a province of Turkey's southern coast. Schools and classrooms were purposely determined, and convenience sampling was applied for students (Marshall & Rossman, 2006).

Instrumentation

The researcher prepared a sheet, which included three open-ended questions from the literature. These questions are; 1) What is science? 2) Who does science? 3) How is science done? This open-ended questionnaire was used with a similar sample and and tested before the study for bias, sequence, clarity, and face-validity. As a pilot study, gave 15 primary students the questions and then asked them, How do you understand the questions? The questions were reviewed in terms of whether there were any incomprehensible parts for primary students.

Primary students were asked these questions and the answers were written. They were then given a choice of whether they wanted to draw a picture for these questions. Drawing a picture was optional; therefore, some of the students answered the questions in both writing and drawing. Some others only answered the questions in writing, while still others chose only to draw pictures.

Data Collection

In the main study, the researcher selected three primary public schools in the center of the province. The researcher explained the study's aim to eleven classroom teachers individually and asked them to provide the survey to their students. Teachers were asked to administer the survey without any orientation or help to the students. Completion of the survey took approximately 30 minutes. In order not to disturb the classroom environments, the researcher did not enter the classrooms.

The researcher relied on the honesty and accuracy of primary students' responses. In this study, some of the answer for the first question (What is science?) were clearly answered by using a dictionary; thus, the researcher deleted these answers during the analysis.

Primary School Students & Textbooks

For the present study, the data collected from the eleven third grade classes totaled 254 primary students from three different public schools. All of the third-grade primary students textbooks were prepared and distributed by the government, and the same program is provided to all of the national schools.

Science and scientists topics are placed in the "social science" course textbooks. The textbook includes three related topics for the present study. The first one is about scientists and contains life stories of four famous Turkish scientists (only two pages). The second one is related to occupations, including scientists (only two pages). Lastly, there is a section about original designs, technology etc. (only three pages).

Data Analysis

In this study, the analyses of documents were separated into two main parts. The first one is written responses for the three questions. The second is the students' drawings. In order to analyze primary students' written responses for the three questions, a qualitative approach was used and some key words were chosen from students' sentences. The frequencies of these words were than counted and percentages calculated. During the analysis process, the unit was a statement. Palmquist and Finley (1997) defined a statement as "a paragraph, group of sentences, sentence or phrase that contained a single unambiguous theme" (p. 600).

In addition, the physical appearance was chosen as one of the major indication of a stereotypical image of a scientist. For the analysis of features of students' drawings, those about science and scientists were coded using an extension of Chambers' (1983) DAST score

Table 1. Coding categories for Scientist Images (from Talsma, 2007)

Personal Characteristics	Contextual features
1. Lab Coat (Usually but not necessarily white);	4. Symbols of research: instruments and equipment of any kind;
2. Eyewear, (glasses, goggles)	5. Symbols of knowledge: e.g. books and file cabinets
3. Facial growth of hair (including beards, mustaches, or abnormally long sideburns);	6. Technology: the "products" of science'
	7. Relevant captions: formulae, classification, the "eureka! syndrome, etc. (Chambers, 1983)
8. Gender	12. Work Day (greater or less than 12 hours)
9. Race	13. Professional Collaboration / Isolation (assistants, colleagues)
10. Grooming (crazy hair)	14. Living arrangements (alone, with others "family")
11. Personality- positive (nice, normal, caring) or negative (crazy, mad, grump,).	

S. ÖZGELEN

card. Scientists' characteristics were identified as contextual and personal characteristics (Talsma, 2007). The following table was transformed from Talsma (2007), and it brings together coding categories about images described for scientists in Chambers' (1983) and Talsma's (2007) coding categories. During the analysis process, the researcher and one expert (an elementary class teacher) coded separately. Then, they compared their codes for the all of the data. When there was inconsistent between them, they discussed and agreed on categories.

FINDINGS

All of the data, written responses and drawings were analyzed respectively. Before the data analyses, primary school students' answers and drawings were separated for the three questions in the survey. Since the primary students could answer the questions in two different ways as writing and drawings. Moreover, if they wished they could answer the questions by both writing and drawing. Table 2 shows the distribution of primary students' answers according to their response as writing, drawing, or both writing and drawing. According to the results, more than half of the students (n = 130; 51.19%) preferred to answer the questions both by writing and by drawing pictures. On the other hand, fewer than half of the students (n = 119; 46.85 %) responded to the three questions only in writing. Just 5 primary school students (1.96%) only drew pictures for the three questions and did not write anything.

Table 2. Distribution of 3rd grade students' responses

Kinds of students' responses	f (254)	% (100)
Written responses	119	46.85
Drawing responses	5	1.96
Written and drawing responses	130	51.19

Analyses of Written Responses

Before starting the data analysis, the numbers of students who answered each question were determined. As seen from Table 3, the first question (What is science?) was answered by 149 primary school students. On the other hand, 105 students did not answer this question. For the second question (Who does science?), 234 students responded while 20 students did not. The third question (How is science done?) was answered by 188 students while it was not by 66 students.

Table 3. Distribution of students' answered and unanswered questions

Written questions	Number of students answering	Number of students not answering
What is science?	149 (58.66%)	105 (41.34%)
Who does science?	234 (92.12%)	20 (7.88%)
How science is done?	188 (74.01%)	66 (25.99%)

What is Science?

Primary school students' answers for the first question were analyzed through content analysis (or the open coding method), and their frequencies and percentages were noted. As a result of analysis of the students' responses, codes emerged. Table 4 shows these codes and their frequencies. Since I viewed some codes as related to others, they were combined under "KIDS" abbreviation. Many primary students (80.67%) responded to the question with the concepts related to science as knowledge, search, discovery, and invention. Some of the students (16.67%) expressed "technology" to define science. Only two students defined science as "curiosity" and one as "creativity". Lastly, one student used "entertainment" as a concept while defining the science.

Table 4. Distribution of first question's answers

What is science?	f (150)	% (100)
Knowledge, Invention, Discovery & Search (KIDS)	121	80.67
Technology	25	16.67
Curiosity	2	1.34
Creativity	1	0.67
Entertainment	1	0.67

Who Does Science?

The answers to the second question' were analyzed and also their frequencies and percentages were determined. More than half of the students (64.12%) said "scientists" as an answer for the question. However, because of the structure of the Turkish language, students used this word to mean "man". Many of the students (12.21%) answered this question by saying that "people" do science. As in the previous question, some of the students (11.06%) mentioned that "curious persons" do science. Some of the students (5.72%) pointed to "scientists" as an answer. Some of the primary students (3.44%) responded "professors". Six students' answers were "hardworking people," while 3 students said "women scientists".

Table 5. Distribution of second question's answers

Who does science?	f (262)	% (100)
Scientists (Men)	168	64.12
People	32	12.21
Curious Persons	29	11.06
Scientists	15	5.72
Professors	9	3.44
Hardworking Persons	6	2.30
Women Scientists	3	1.15

How Science is Done?

Primary school students' responses about the third question were analyzed and their frequencies and percentages determined. Many of the students (28.27%) emphasized that science were done through "experiment". The second highest response to this question (22.94%) was that science was done by "hardworking". Some of the primary school students (16.80%) noted "research" while some (6.97%) said "reading books" as an answer for the third question. "Chemistry" was given as an answer by a similar percentage (6.56%) of the students. Some of the primary students (6.15%) responded with "discovery & invention" to the question of how science was done. Three different answers have the same percentage (2.87%): "thinking", "tools", and "creativity". A few students (2.05%) said "technology", while four students (1.64%) said "intelligence".

Table 6. Distribution of third question's answers

How is science done?	f (244)	% (100)
By experiment	69	28.27
By hardworking	56	22.94
By research	41	16.80
By reading books	17	6.97
By chemistry	16	6.56
By discovery & invention	15	6.15
By thinking	7	2.87
By tools	7	2.87
By creativity	7	2.87
By technology	5	2.05
By intelligence	4	1.64

Analyses of Drawing Pictures

A total of 135 drawings for the three questions were analyzed, since some of the primary school students preferred to answer the question in writing, not by drawing. Some of the characteristics about science and scientists were obtained from the 135 drawings in line with the related literature. Table 7 was constructed to show their frequencies and percentages.

During the data analyzes process, some characteristics were defined and analyzed together. For instance, there were images of; scientists wearing a lab coat or not, male or female, and young or elderly. The first two characteristics were related to clothing. It

Table 7. 3rd grade students' views about science and scientists

Characteristics of science and scientists	f (135)	%	Characteristics of science and scientists	f	%
1. Lab coat (usually but not necessarily white)	19	14.07	13. Female	35	25.92
2. Casual clothing	58	42.96	14. Male	89	65.92
3. Eyewear (glasses, goggles)	11	8.14	15. Caucasian	103	76.29
4. Not wearing glasses	92	68.14	16. Symbols of research: instruments and equipment of any kind	71	52.59
5. Facial hair (including beards, mustaches, etc.)	13	9.62	17. Symbols of knowledge: books, file cabinets	16	11.85
6. Normally trimmed hair (shaven beard, smooth face)	62	45.92	18. Technology: the "products" of science	30	22.22
7. Young people or teenager	90	66.67	19. Space-related: astronaut, space, planets, etc.	18	13.34
8. Middle aged or elderly	11	8.14	20. Relevant captions: formulas, classification, the "eureka!"	7	5.18
9. Personality – positive (nice, normal, caring)	86	63.70	21. Working indoors: laboratory, class, etc.	74	54.81
10. Personality – negative (crazy, mad, grumpy)	6	4.45	22. Working outdoors: garden, etc.	42	31.12
11. Professional collaboration (assistants, colleagues	47	34.81	23. Indication of danger	4	2.96
12. Professional isolation (working alone)	59	43.70	24. Scientist has mythic stereotypes (e.g. Frankenstein creatures, etc.)	1	0.75

is important to note that, during the analysis of the drawings, I was concerned about what the primary students' emphasized in their drawings. For instance, in some of the drawings, it was clear that the scientist was wearing a lab coat or wearing casual clothing. However, in some of the drawings it was not possible to tell, because primary students' drawings did not show any clothing. Some of the primary students (14.07%) depicted scientists wearing a lab coat in their drawings. However, many of the students (42.96%) drew scientists wearing casual clothing (e.g. Figure 1).

Another characteristic of scientists was their facial traits. Some of the primary students (9.62%) indicated hair or beards etc (e.g. Figure 2). However, many of the students (45.92%) drew scientists with trimmed hair, shaven beard, and smooth-faces in their drawings. There were similar results about eye glasses. Only 11 (8.14%) students drew scientists wearing glasses. On the other hand, many students (68.14%) pictured scientists as not wearing glasses. As noted in Table 7, some of the students (8.14%) defined scientists as middle aged or elderly. On the other hand, many of them (66.67%) drew scientist as young people or teenagers (e.g. Figure 3). The data analysis showed that, in approximately half of the pictures the primary students (43.70%) depicted scientists as "working alone". On the contrary, some of the students (34.81%) showed scientists as "working together with their colleagues" in their drawings (e.g. Figure 4). Another characteristic of scientists related to their personalities. Some of the students (4.45%) drew scientists as negative, crazy, or

Figure 1. Scientists in casual clothing

Figure 2. Scientists with abundant hair

Figure 3. Scientists as young people

Figure 4. Scientists working with colleagues

mad people. However, many of the primary students (63.70%) drew scientists as positive, nice, or caring people. We also found from the students' drawings their ideas about scientists' genders. Some of the students (25.92%) depicted scientists as female, while more primary students (65.92%) drew scientists as male.

Many of the drawings (52.59%) included symbols of research; instruments and equipment. Some of the primary students (11.85%) illustrated symbols of knowledge, such as books and file cabinets in their drawings (e.g. Figure 5). Some of the primary students (22.23%) showed items related to technology; the products of science. Other students (13.34%) drew indicators related to space, such as astronauts, planets etc. (e.g. Figure 6).

Another category was related to scientists' work situation. Some of the students (31.12%) depicted scientists working in the outdoors (e.g. Figure 7). Other primary students (54.81%) drew scientists working indoors, in a laboratory or class, etc. From Table 7, four primary students (2.96%) drew images of danger. There was one student who drew Einstein's very famous picture (e.g. Figure 8). This may be related to exposure to stereotypes of scientists.

Only 7 primary students (5.18%) used relevant captions, formulae, classification, or "eureka" in their drawings. Lastly, all of the drawings which included scientists (76.29%) showed them as Caucasian.

Figure 5. Working with symbols of knowledge

Figure 6. Science depicted with symbols of space exploration

Figure 7. Scientists working outdoors

Figure 8. Scientist drawn as Einstein

DISCUSSION

Primary students' writings and drawings are discussed in two separate parts. The first part focuses on students' written responses for the three questions.

Discussion of Students' Written Responses

According to the results, more than half of the students (58.66%) answered these questions. While defining science, primary students (80.67%) generally related their answers to knowledge, invention, discovery, and experiment. Science is a kind of knowledge. However, science is not equal to knowledge. According to dictionaries, science is "a branch of knowledge or study dealing with a body of facts or truths systematically arranged and showing the operation of general laws" (dictionary.reference.com). This definition can be acceptable for the natural and mathematical sciences. However, this is not suitable for social and philosophical sciences. Another definition of science is "systematic knowledge of the physical or material world gained through observation and experimentation" (dictionary.reference.com). Primary students also defined science as discovery and/or invention as a result of search/experiments.

According to these findings, primary students used "science" terms only for the natural sciences. Recently, similar research was conducted by Ozel (2012), who aimed to investigate kindergarten and 3rd and 5th grade Turkish students' perceptions of science and scientists through their images. Related to natural-social science findings, Ozel's students' drawings and writings indicated that scientists were inventing and designing new materials. Only a small percentage of students depicted scientists who were working in the field of social sciences. Similar results showed that the social dimension of science is missed in students' perceptions. Therefore, students have limited images of scientists and scientific research (Buldu, 2006; Finson, 2002; Rubin, Bar, & Cohen, 2003; Ozel, 2012).

The second highest answer to our first question, "What is science?" was "technology". There is no one definition everyone agreed on, but one of the most common is a body of knowledge used to make tools, extend skills, and extract or gather materials. Another definition for technology is "applied science". These meanings intersect. While the aim of the technology is the creation of artifacts and systems to meet people's needs, the goal of science is the pursuit of knowledge and understanding for its own sake (Sparkes, 1992).

Results showed that more than half of the primary students stated "scientists" – "bilim adamı" (in the Turkish language "bilim" means "science" and "adam" means "man") as an answer of the second question, "Who does science". However, this word was used as meaning "men" in the Turkish language. This is misused not only for this study, but also generally for Turkish students. These results show that stereotypes of images are mostly related to popular culture. A similar result was reported by Akcay (2011). Unquestionably, this cultural effect is evidenced by male characters in students' drawings. It can be concluded that primary students perceived science as "a special work" only done by a professional person. Some of the primary students used "people". This answer cannot be accepted as significant. Some of them stated "curious persons" as an interesting answer, because students think of "curiosity" for science. Just three students mentioned "women" while answering the question.

When asked how science is done, more than half of the students answered "experiment", "research", "chemistry", and "discovery and invention". These answers show that primary students perceived science as only "experimental science". One of the interesting answers was "creativity" for doing science, but this answer was very rare.

Discussion about Students' Drawings

In this section, this present study is compared to three other studies dealing with primary students (Barman, 1997; Song et al., 2011; Turkmen, 2008). Table 8 is a comparison of the three studies. Barman (1997) and Song et al. (2011) are studies from the USA. The second study showed the development/differences after a decade for USA primary students' views. Turkmen (2008) conducted his study in Turkey after the new science and technology curriculum was implemented. Therefore, the present study's results are very important for national and international similarities and differences among students' views about science and scientists. In this study, twenty-four characteristics were detected, many of them from the literature. However, some of them were new, and they were added into the table according to students' drawings. Before the discussion and comparison, one subject should be clarified as it related to the analysis of drawings. In the three earlier studies, researchers asked students to draw a scientist. However, in the present study the difference is that primary students were asked to draw about science, scientists, and doing science. For that reason, some of the percentages were different. For example, all of the students drew scientists as Caucasian, but some of the drawings did not include any person (only laboratory equipment, etc.). Therefore, the percentage of Caucasian scientists was reported at only 76.29% instead of 100%.

During the discussion, the results are compared according to the 3rd grade primary students' text book about science and scientists. In looking at drawings related to scientist's clothing, the three earlier studies have approximately the same percentages wearing a lab coat. In a decade, there was no change in USA primary students' views. Interestingly, a similar percentage was found by Turkmen (2008). This result is similar to other studies in the literature (Bodzin & Gehringer, 2001; Finson, Pedersen, & Thomas, 2006; Fung, 2002; Ozel, 2012; Thomas, Pedersen, & Finson, 2001). Nevertheless, in the present study, the percentage showing a lab coat was reduced. It can be concluded that only some of the Turkish 3rd grade students thought scientists wore a lab coat. However, a large percentage of students

Table 8. Comparison of the results with national and international studies

Studies about primary students' views on science and scientists	Present study (2012)	Turkmen's study (2008)	Song et al.'s study (2010)	Barman's study (1997)
Primary students' perceptions of science and scientists	Level 3rd % (N = 135)	Level 5th % (N = 287)	Level 3rd % (N = 52)	Level 3rd-5th % (N = 649)
1. Scientists wearing a lab coat	14.07	46.70	46.00	41.00
2. Casual clothing	42.96	53.30	—	—
3. Eyewear, (glasses, goggles)	8.14	30.70	23.00	28.00
4. Not wearing glasses	68.14	—	—	—
5. Facial growth of hair	9.62	17.40	7.00	9.00
6. Normally trimmed hair	45.92	—	–	–
7. Young person or teenager	66.67	–	–	–
8. Middle aged or elderly	8.14	69.70	32.00	32.00
9. Personality- positive	63.70	61.00	—	—
10. Personality- negative	4.45	—	—	—
11. Professional Collaboration	34.81	—	—	—
12. Professional Isolation	43.70	—	—	—
13. Female	25.92	—	—	—
14. Male	65.92	94.10	55.00	73.00
15. Caucasian	76.29	100.00	71.00	80.00
16. Symbols of research	52.59	86.10	85.00	94.00
17. Symbols of knowledge	11.85	51.20	21.00	35.00
18. Technology; "products" of science	22.22	40.00	15.00	15.00
19. Space-related ; astronaut, or planets	13.34	—	—	—
20. Relevant captions, "eureka"	5.18	33.50	27.00	13.00
21. Working indoor: laboratory etc.	54.81	79.80	83.00	88.00
22. Working outdoor: garden etc.	31.12	—	—	—
23. Indication of danger	2.96	1.70	21.00	18.00
24. Mythic stereotypes	0.75	2.50	25.00	11.00

illustrated scientists wearing casual clothing. One of the possible reasons can be related to students' text books. Monhardt (2003) stated that how scientists are presented in textbooks greatly influences what students believe about scientists. In their life sciences book (MoNE, 2011), there are two pages in which famous scientists are introduced with their pictures. In these pictures, scientists do not wear lab coats, but have casual clothing. This showed a shift in primary students' views of scientists from the earlier research.

As shown in Table 8, another stereotype is of scientists wearing glasses. In the present study, the frequency of 3rd grade students' drawings with glasses decreased in relation to the earlier studies. As before, in the students' text book, there are four famous scientists' pictures with only one of them wearing glasses. This may be one of the possible explanations of this result.

Another stereotype of scientists is facial hair. While the result of the present study is similar to USA primary students (Barman, 1997; Song et al., 2011), it is different from Turkish 5th grade students (Turkmen, 2008). Another specific scientists' feature in drawings is related to the ages of scientists. Interestingly, the rate of middle-aged or elderly scientists' drawings is very low compared to the previous studies in the USA. The striking difference, too, from Turkmen's (2008) results is very important, since at national schools Turkish primary students get the same curricula. This difference could be explained by teacher or parental factors. According to Turkmen (2008) primary students obtained their information about scientists from their teachers and parents. Another important feature is the personality of scientists in the drawings. Barman (1997) and Song et al. (2011) did not investigate this feature, but Turkmen's (2008) result is slightly lower than the present study. Science educators assert that students' perceptions affect their attitudes toward science (Bodzin & Gehringer, 2001; Flick, 1990; MacCorquodale, 1984; Rosenthal, 1993; Turkmen, 2008).

Another important feature drawn about scientists is professional collaboration / isolation. The other three studies did not mention this subject. The present study showed that many of students drew scientists working with other colleagues. However, more than that drew scientists working alone. Since the students' textbook pictured scientists alone, we can conclude that the textbooks had an effect on students' views about scientists.

Scientists' gender is another feature from students' drawings. Males dominate both the Turkish and USA culture. However, the present study showed that there is decline for the Turkish students. This can be explained again by examples given in the school textbook. In fact, in the 3rd grade students' textbook, three of four scientists are female. This result is noteworthy, especially for female students' attitudes toward science and scientists. Previous researches showed the same result of majority of students drawing scientists as males (Buldu, 2006; Chambers, 1983; Finson, 2002; Losh et al., 2008; Quita, 2003; She, 1998). This result can be related to the roles of females in the culture. It might also be that males dominate scientific knowledge presented in textbooks and school programs, such as examples of Newton and Einstein (Ozel, 2012). In order to encourage female students to be interested in science, teachers should introduce more examples of female scientists as role models (Ozel, 2012). If not, girls mostly accept that scientific careers are only suitable for men. This wrong message implicitly affects students when choosing their future career.

Another stereotype of science are the symbols of research. The results of this study indicate that this trend has changed. The present study showed that Turkish primary students have a tendency to exclude images of working indoors with research equipment in laboratories. Similar results were found by Narayan, Park, and Deniz (2007). These researchers showed that the mean of Turkish students on "symbols of research" was significantly lower than in other countries (India, Korea, and USA). The researchers interpreted this as a result of science not being taught at the third grade level as a separate course in Turkey.

Moreover, the present study analyzed students' drawings for outdoor work, whereas past studies did not consider this setting in analysis (Barman, 1997; Song et al., 2011; Turkmen, 2008). Technology as a product of science is one of the images of science. Turkish primary students have higher rates than USA students (Barman, 1997; Song et al., 2011). This can be explained by recent reforms in the Turkish elementary education program. This reform affected all the courses in elementary school that relate to science by changing the "science" course's name to "science and technology", along with the contents (MoNE, 2004). One of the new features of science that differ from earlier research is space-related drawings. In the current study, this image came forward, but not in the others. Images of danger in stereotypes were very low for the USA students. Lastly, we note that the sole mythic stereotype is a drawing that represent Einstein' famous picture of sticking out his tongue; this is not a stereotype, but it is very interesting for a 3rd grade primary student's image.

CONCLUSION AND RECOMMENDATIONS

According to the recent reform movements, developing students' views about science are important in order to grow scientifically literate people. Certainly, students' images of scientists are part of science. Therefore, broadening students' perceptions and their images are crucial responsibilities for curriculum developers, science educators, and classroom teachers.

In recent studies, researchers tried to determine which factors affect students' perceptions about science and scientists (She, 1995; Talsma, 2007; Turkmen, 2008). One of the influential factors was the content of science textbooks and classroom activities (Talsma, 2007). Moreover, McDuffie (2001) investigated teachers' stereotyped images of scientists. His research revealed that teachers' images of scientists are similar to their students on most significant characteristics. In addition, TV programs shape children's views toward science and scientists during primary school years (Britner & Pajares, 2001; Jones & Bargert, 2006).

In the science education literature, researchers provide evidence that students build images of scientists and science using their emotional and cognitive domains. Cultural environment, school culture, and classroom experiences affect students' images (Talsma,

2007). In related Turkish literature, a study was conducted by Akcay (2011) in which he found some results that differed from previous studies. Although many students drew scientists as males, there were drawings showing younger ages and scientists smiling while working. There were images with facial hair and lab coats; however, these images were less present in drawings by secondary level students than elementary students. Akcay suggested that when students get older, they come across many different and more accurate images of modern scientists.

In the Turkish context, results of some studies showed that students' drawings included stereotypical images of scientists (Cakmakci et al., 2011; Korkmaz & Kavak, 2010; Kaya et al., 2008; Togrol Yontar, 2000). These results are similar to western studies. On the other hand, some studies showed different results (Akcay, 2011; Buldu, 2006; Turkmen, 2008), which asserted that Turkish students have fewer stereotypical images than western students. Turkmen (2008) stressed that smiling scientists and the number of images using technology increased in the Turkish context. With respect to developed and undeveloped countries similar results were found by Sjoberg (2000) and Song and Kim (1999). They asserted that students in undeveloped and developing countries had fewer stereotypical images of scientists. This difference may be explained by observing that in western culture (developed countries) students encounter more stereotypical images through electronic and printed media.

The current study has some different results from past studies about primary students in Turkey (Korkmaz & Kavak, 2010; Narayan et al., 2007; Ozel, 2012; Turkmen, 2008). The present results showed that primary students had fewer stereotypic images for scientists and science from others. This difference may be explained by primary students' grade levels. In this study, students were in 3rd grade, while others were in 4th grade or higher. Similar results were found by Ozel (2012), who focused on determining elementary school students' stereotypical perceptions of scientists and whether these views significantly differed among grade level in Turkey. Ozel (2012) found that, 5th grade students' drawings included more stereotypical elements than kindergarten and 3rd grade students. Moreover, Ozel (2012) reported that while there is a significant effect of grade level on students' drawings of stereotypical appearance scores, there is no significant effect of grade level on students' scientific knowledge scores. It is possible for teachers to bring more books or magazines that discuss relevant scientists' life and works. These give a chance for students to see more concrete examples in daily life as they shape their views on science and scientists.

In order to develop primary students' perceptions about science and scientists, teachers can do some specific activities together with the school administration. They could visit scientists, who are studying social and/or pure science related topics. They might facilitate scientists' visits to the school with primary students. In addition, teachers might plan field trips, which include scientists' work areas and give general information about their specific topics.

In a specific study, Leblebicioglu et al. (2011) and a team of scientists planned a science camp for 6th and 7th grade students. Participants worked with scientists about the nature of science and interacted with them in formal and informal ways during the ten days. The researchers concluded that after the science camp students stereotypical images were decreased.

The present study did not focus on the reasons for stereotypical views, but it is crucial to mention here that one of the possible effects on students' perceptions on science and scientists is printed and visual media (TV, internet, newspaper, etc.). Some scientist characters in cartoons and TV programs may affect students negatively from choosing science as a future career (e. g., Finson, 2003; Finson et al., 1995).

Future studies should investigate possible reasons for students' negative perceptions. Teachers can test proposed activities in class or out of school. Researchers may design experimental or mixed methods research, which includes interviews and observations beside the DAST.

Finally, in many countries' primary educational systems, "science" courses are started as a separate course beginning with the 3rd or 4th grade level. As science educators, curriculum developers, and teachers we should think reflectively about this subject and consider why our upper grade students draw more stereotypic images of scientists compared to lower grades.

NOTE

[1] An earlier version of the study appeared as: Özgelen, S. (2012). Turkish young children's views on science and scientists. *Educational Sciences; Theory & Practice, 12*(4), 3211–3225.

REFERENCES

Akcay, B. (2011). Turkish elementary and secondary students' views about science and scientist. *Asia-Pacific Forum on Science Learning and Teaching, 12*(1), Art. 5.

American Association for the Advancement of Science (AAAS). (1993). *Benchmarks for science literacy: A Project 2061 report.* New York, NY: Oxford University Press.

Barman, C. R. (1997). Students' views of scientists and science: Results from a national study. *Science and Children, 35*, 18–35.

Barman, C. R. (1999). Students' views about scientists and school science: Engaging K-8 teachers in a national study. *Journal of Science Teacher Education, 10*(1), 43–54.

Barman, C. R., Ostlund, K. L., Gatto, C. C., & Halferty, M. (1997). *Fifth grade students' perceptions about scientists and how they study and use science.* AETC conf, U.S.

Bodzin, A., & Gehringer, M. (2001). Can meeting actual scientists change students' perceptions of scientists? *Science and Children, 39*(1), 36–41.

Boylan, C. R., Hill, D. M., Wallace, A. R., & Wheeler, A. E. (1992). Beyond stereotypes. *Science Education, 76*, 465–476.

Britner, S. L., & Pajares, F. (2001). Self- efficacy beliefs, motivation, race, and gender in middle school science. *Journal of Women and Minorities in Science and Engineering, 7*, 271–285.

Buldu, M. (2006). Young children's perceptions of scientists: A preliminary study. *Educational Research, 48*(1), 121–132.

Cakmakci, G., Tosun, O., Turgut, S., Orenler, S., Sengul, K., & Top, G. (2011). Promoting an inclusive image of scientists among students: Towards research evidence-based practice. *International Journal of Science and Mathematics Education, 9*, 627–655.

Chambers, D. W. (1983). Stereotypic images of the scientist: The Draw-Scientist Test. *Science Education, 67*(2), 255–265.

Chiang, C. L., & Guo, C. J. (1996). *A study of the image of the scientist for elementary school children.* A paper presented at the National Association for Research in Science Teaching Annual Meeting, St. Louis, MO.

Finson, K. D. (2002). Drawing a scientist: What we do and do not know after fifty years of drawings. *School Science and Mathematics, 102*, 335–345

Finson, K. D. (2003). Applicability of the DAST-C to the images of scientists drawn by students of different racial groups. *Journal of Elementary Science Education, 15*(1), 15–26.

Finson, K. D., Beaver, J. B., & Cramond, B. L. (1995). Development and field test of a checklist for the Draw-A-Scientist Test. *School Science and Mathematics, 95*(4), 195–205.

Finson, K. D., Pedersen, J., & Thomas, J. (2006). Comparing science teaching styles to students' perceptions of scientists. *School Science and Mathematics, 106*(1), 8–15.

Flick, L. (1990). Scientist in residence program improving children's image of science and scientists. *School Science and Mathematics, 90*, 205–214.

Fung, Y. Y. H. (2002). A comparative study of primary and secondary school students' images of scientists. *Research in Science and Technological Education, 20*(2), 199–213.

Hill, D., & Wheeler, A. (1991). Towards a clearer understanding of students' ideas about science and technology: An exploratory study. *Research in Science and Technological Education, 9*(2), 125–138.

Huber, R. A., & Burton, C. M. (1995). What the students think scientist look like? *School Science and Mathematics, 95*, 371–376.

Jarvis, T., & Rennie, L. J. (1995). Children's choice of drawings to communicate their ideas about technology. *Research in Science Education, 25*(3), 239–252.

Jones, R., & Bangert, A. (2006). The CSI effect: Changing the face of science. *Science Scope, 30*(3), 38–42.

Jones, M. G., Howe, A., & Rua, M. J. (2000). Gender differences in students' experiences, interests, and attitudes toward science and scientists. *Science Education, 84*(2), 180–192.

Kaya, O. N., Dogan, A., & Ocal, E. (2008). Turkish elementary school students' images of scientists. *Eurasian Journal of Educational Research, 32*, 83–100.

Koballa, T. R., Jr. (1993). *Synthesis of science attitude research of elementary grades.* Paper presented at the annual meeting of the National Association for Research in Science Teaching, Atlanta, GA.

Korkmaz, H., & Kavak, G. (2010). Primary school students' images of science and scientists. *Elementary Education Online, 9*(3), 1055–1079.

Leblebicioglu, G., Metin, D., Yardimci, E., & Cetin, P. S. (2011). The effect of informal and formal interaction between scientists and children at a science camp on their images of scientists. *Science Education International, 22*(3), 158–174.

Losh, S. C., Wilke, R., & Pop, M. (2008). Some methodological issues with "draw a scientist test" among young children. *International Journal of Science Education, 30*, 773–792.

MacCorquodale, P. (1984). *Self image, science and math: Does the image of the "scientist" keep girls and minorities from pursuing science and math?* Paper presented at the 79th annual meeting of the American Sociological Association, San Antonio, TX.

Marshall, C., & Rossman, G. B. (2006). *Designing qualitative research* (4th ed.). Thousand Oaks, CA: Sage.

Mason, C., Kahle, J., & Gardner, A. (1991). Draw-A-Scientist test: Future implications. *School Science and Mathematics, 91*(5), 193–198.

Matkins, J. J. (1996). *Customizing the draw-a-scientist test to analyze the effect that teachers have on their students' perceptions and attitudes toward science.* Paper presented at the Association for the Education of Teachers of Science Conference.

McCarthy, D. (2014). Teacher candidates' perceptions of scientists: 30 years after DAST. Presented at LERA, Lafayette, LA.

McDuffie Jr, T. E. (2001). Scientists – Geeks & nerds? Dispelling teachers' stereotypes of scientists. *Science and Children, 38*(8), 16–19.

Mead, M., & Metraux, R. (1957). Images of the scientists among high-school students. *Science, 126*, 384–390.

Ministry of National Education. (2004). *Elementary science and technology course curriculum.* Ankara, Turkey: Ministry of Education.

Ministry of National Education (MoNE). (2011). *Social sciences textbook.* Ankara, Turkey: National Education Press.

Monhardt, R. M. (2003). The image of the scientist through the eyes of Navajo children. *Journal of American Indian Education, 42*, 25–39.

Narayan, R., Park, S., & Peker, D. (2007). Sculpted by culture: Students' embodied images of scientists. *Proceedings of epiSTEME 3.*

Narayan, R., Park, S., Peker, D., & Suh, J. (2013). Students' images of scientists and doing science: An international comparison study. *Eurasia Journal of Mathematics, Science & Technology Education, 9*(2), 115–129.

National Research Council. (2000). *Inquiry and the national science education standards.* Washington, DC: National Academy Press.

Next Generation Science Standards. (2013). *Next generation science standards: For states, by states* Washington, DC: The National Academies Press.

Ozel, M. (2012). Children's images of scientists: Does grade level make a difference? *Educational Sciences: Theory & Practice, 12*(4), 3187–3198.

Palmquist, B. C., & Finley, F. N. (1997). Preservice teachers' views of the nature of science during a postbaccalaurate science teaching program. *Journal of Research in Science Teaching, 34*(6), 595–615.

Quita, I. N. (2003). What is a scientist? Perspectives of teachers of color. *Multicultural Education, 11*, 29–31.

Rampal, A. (1992). Images of science and scientists: A study of school teachers' views. I. Characteristics of scientists. *Science Education, 76*(4), 415–436.

Rosenthal, D. B. (1993). Images of scientists: A comparison of biology and liberal studies majors. *School Science and Mathematics, 93*, 212–216.

Rubin, E., & Bar, V., & Cohen, A. (2003). The images of scientists and science among Hebrew and Arabic-speaking pre service teachers in Israel. *International Journal of Science Education, 25*, 821–846.

She, H. C. (1995). Elementary and middle school students' image of science and scientists related to current science textbooks in Taiwan. *Journal of Science Education and Technology, 4*(4), 283–294.

She, H. C. (1998). Gender and grade level differences in Taiwan students' stereotypes of science and scientists. *Research in Science and Technological Education, 16*(2), 125–135.

Sjoberg, S. (2000). *Science and scientists: The SAS study.* Retrieved November 10, 2014, from http://www.uio.no/~sveinsj/

Song, Y., Darling, M. F., Dixon, J. W., Koonce, S. L., McReynolds, M. L., Meier, J. C., & Stafsholt, E. R. (2011). Pre-service teachers as researchers: 3rd grade students' views of scientists. *Teaching Science, 1*(2). Retrieved May 21, 2012, from http://www.cpet. ufl.edu/teachingscience/PDFs/Youngjin%20Song%20manuscript.pdf

Song, J., & Kim, K. S. (1999). How Korean students see scientists: The images of the scientist. *International Journal of Science Education, 21*(9), 957–977.

Sparkes, J. (1992). Some differences between science and technology. In R. McCormack, C. Newey, & J. Sparkes (Eds.), *Technology for technology education* (pp. 75–87). Wokingham: Addison-Wesley Publishing.

Talsma, V. L. (2007, April 16) *Scientist as 'Self' and 'Other': Using Self-Schema Theory as a Heuristic for the DAST.* A paper accepted for presentation at the annual meeting of the National Association for Research in Science Teaching, New Orleans, LA.

Thomas, J. A., Pedersen, J. E., & Finson, K.D. (2001). Validating the Draw-A-Science-Teacher-Test checklist: Exploring mental models and teacher beliefs. *Journal of Science Teacher Education, 12*(3), 295–310.

Togrol Yontar, A. (2000). Öğrencilerin Bilim İnsanı ile İlgili İmgeleri. *Education and Science, 25*(118), 49–57.

Turkmen, H. (2008). Turkish primary students' perceptions about scientist and what factors affecting the image of the scientists. *Eurasia Journal of Mathematics, Science and Technology Education, 4*(1), 55–61.

Turkmen, H., & Pedersen, J. E. (2005). Examining the technological history of Turkey impacts on teaching science. *Science Education International, 17*(2), 115–123.

Yvonne, Y. H. F. (2002). A comparative study of primary and secondary school students' images of scientists. *Research in Science and Technological Education, 20*(2), 199–213.

Sinan Özgelen
Mersin University, Turkey

JEREMY F. PRICE

18. UNDERSTANDING THE MEANINGS SECONDARY BIOLOGY STUDENTS CONSTRUCT AROUND SCIENCE THROUGH DRAWINGS

Learning science, more now than ever, has become a critical part of becoming a fully educated person: engaging in science has become an ever more necessary component for engaged citizenship and career success (Carson, 1997; Feinstein, 2011; Osborne & Dillon, 2008). Yet students often see science as an endeavor for someone else, contributing to a lack of access to necessary knowledge and practices (Aikenhead, 1996; Costa, 1995); in other words, science often lacks meaning for these students. Understanding and recognizing the meanings of science that students construct and the ways that they relate to science are an important task for educational research to encourage authentic and useful engagements with science learning (Archer et al., 2010; Calabrese Barton et al., 2012).

An assumption of this research is that as students engage in the negotiation of meaning around science, they are able to see themselves as a part of the scientific endeavor even if they do not necessarily become scientists themselves. They become a valuable part of an extended community of practice (Wenger, 1998) that allows the understandings and insights afforded by scientific inquiry to contribute to the greater social and ecological good. Through this negotiation of meaning, students are afforded the opportunity to view themselves as *competent outsiders* (Feinstein, 2011), a core aim for a *scientifically literate public* (Mooney & Kirshenbaum, 2009). As such, this research seeks to explore and interpret the meanings that students construct around the practices of science.

Much effort among educators and researchers has been dedicated to telling the story of learners often left out of the conversation around science and providing these learners and their communities a voice and providing the opportunity to participate in the discourses of science (Erickson, 2012; Jenkins, 2006; Lemke, 1990). This research seeks out a different path with similar ends in mind. Following the anthropologist James Spradley, who has written that when a researcher is interested in finding out what an idea or concept *means* to a research participant the researcher should ask what the idea or concept *looks* like (Spradley, 1979), the research that undergirds this chapter provided the space for learners to provide a *visual* interpretation of their understandings and perspectives around science. In doing so, these learners communicated a great deal of meaning and power that would have been more difficult to convey otherwise.

In addition, the research that went into this chapter follows a contextualized approach (Archer et al., 2010) to understanding the meanings that learners construct around science. There have been studies that examined how students have drawn *a scientist* (Chambers, 1983; Finson, 2002). Asking students to draw a scientist focuses on science as a singular unchanging identity; asking students to draw what doing—or practicing—science looks like focuses on science as a set of practices (Archer et al., 2010), which is more congruent with a meanings-based approach. Through the collection and analysis of illustrations and interviews with students, I seek to explore the question, *what are the meanings that students construct around doing science?*

By exploring this question, I have come to understand the importance of using meaning-centered drawings as a way to *inquire with* rather than *inquire about* (Ingold, 2013) students. I, as a researcher, was able to inquire deeply into students' understandings of and engagement with science as a broad approach to science. At the same time, the students were able to grapple with the purposes of science education, contribute to the cultivation of a public-oriented science literacy, and negotiate their place in science. With this shift in focus, I found that drawings are powerful tools for promoting student voice in educational change efforts (Haney, Russell, & Bebell, 2004).

In order to make this case, I describe the context and methods of the research followed by my research findings in two parts. The first part provides an overview of the meanings that the students in a 10th grade (students aged 15–16 years old) biology class at an American public high school illustrated in response to the prompt, "What does doing science look like?" The second part looks more closely at the drawings of one particular student. Taken together, the general and then specific cases show us how drawings, coupled with interviews and observations, can provide a fuller and more complete understandings of the meanings that learners construct around science.

RESEARCH CONTEXT AND METHODS

My research was oriented around the framing question, *what are the meanings that students construct around doing science?* To explore this question, the research in this chapter draws upon ethnographic traditions allowing for the examination of experiences, meanings, and identities in context (Brandt & Carlone, 2012; Calabrese Barton et al., 2012; Hammond & Brandt, 2004). I will provide some of this contextual information about the participating high school biology class before describing the research methods and data analysis procedures.

P. Katz (Ed.), Drawing for Science Education, 205–215.
© *2017 Sense Publishers. All rights reserved.*

Cotstead High School and the C-Block Biology Class

I worked with one middle-track high school biology classroom comprised of a range of students in terms of prior achievement, home languages and cultures, and socioeconomic class. The district is located in Cotstead,[1] an inner-suburb of a large New England city. Cotstead hosts many technology and biotechnology companies in expansive office parks along a stretch of an interstate highway, although residents of the city are greatly diverse with a large number of immigrant and blue collar families compared to its more affluent neighboring towns and cities. A school of about 1,400 students, about 12% of students at Cotstead High are African-American, 25% Hispanic, 5% Asian, and 0.4% Native American, while the remaining students are of White European background.

The teacher, Ms. Stoneham, is a second career veteran teacher who previously worked as a histologist at a local hospital. At the time of this research, she had been teaching high school science for 7 years and science at the middle school level for 9 years. She was completing coursework for a graduate degree through a local public university.

Ms. Stoneham's C-block biology class, like the district, was a very diverse set of students. Students in the class came from a broad range of economic backgrounds and over half of the class spoke a language other than English at home. Most of these students spoke Spanish at home (with families largely originally from Guatemala and Puerto Rico), but there were also students who spoke Brazilian Portuguese and Armenian at home as well. As a "middle-track" science class, there was an emphasis on study skills for academic success as well as the content of biology. Ms. Stoneham once remarked that these students were "kids who probably won't go to college but probably should." However, the tracking of students at the subject level masked some of the diversity of achievement and the expectations these students held for themselves. Most students in the class held college attendance as an important goal, and several were in honors-level classes for students at the highest achievement levels in subjects such as Mathematics, History, and English Language Arts.

I engaged in ethnographic observations and interviews with the teacher and the students for three full units of study, which translates to about eight weeks. During this time, the class covered their protein synthesis, Mendelian genetics and evolution units. In addition, the students engaged in activities co-designed by Ms. Stoneham and me. These activities, not reported here, were designed with the intent of facilitating the exploration of a broad range of uses of and perspectives on science. Some of these experiences included a role play centered on a socioscientific issue and the collaborative construction of a science-based public service announcement.

Activity Structure and Data Collection

Students were provided with the opportunity to reflect on what "doing science" looks like twice, once at the beginning of my time with Ms. Stoneham's C-Block class and once at the end. Based on a contextualized approach to identity in science (Archer et al., 2010) and recognizing the use of student generated illustrations as evidence of students' constructed meanings (Freeman & Mathison, 2009), students were first asked to draw a picture of what doing science looks like, and were provided with a pre-existing worksheet for these purposes as well as full sets of colored pencils. They were then encouraged to reflect on and report in words on what they included in their drawings. The illustrations were then passed around to groups in the class, and the students were asked to analyze the pictures for similarities, differences, and patterns.

It should be noted from a practical perspective that there was some general resistance to this activity the first time around. Several students indicated that they did not know how to draw well. One student, Gabriel, forcefully resisted the activity and complained quite vocally. Ms. Stoneham noted that Gabriel served as an intellectual leader in the class and other students often took their cues from him. She decided to assign other work for him to do outside of the classroom so that his attitude did not influence the rest of the class.

Data Analysis

All artifacts from the activities, both the reflections and the storyboards, were analyzed first over several rounds using the Atlas.ti qualitative data analysis software in a recursive and comparative manner utilizing qualitative content analysis (QCA; Mayring, 2000). QCA provided a detailed and holistic approach to highlight the meanings that are expressed in these artifacts through the similarities and differences in the artifacts. While it is understood that uncovering meaning requires both rigorous data collection and interpretation, only low- to mid-inference features of the drawings (Freeman & Mathison, 2009) were analyzed. These low- to mid-inference features are those elements that are clearly exhibited in the drawings themselves, although they may be related to other sources of data such as interviews to further understand the illustrator's sense of identity. Therefore, I engaged in a low-inference analysis of the illustrations (Freeman & Mathison, 2009, p. 161), looking for what was represented in the drawings. The analysis was accomplished through recursive and comparative coding (Charmaz, 1994). Class observations and teacher and student interviews provided supporting data.

I drew upon qualitative and ethnographic constructs for adhering to standards of quality and rigor (Anfara et al., 2002; Howe & Eisenhart, 1990). As part of this process, I utilized multiple data sources to provide a framework for trustworthiness (Freeman, deMarrais, Preissle, Roulston, & St. Pierre, 2007). In addition, I drew upon the voices of both the teacher and the students as a way of providing multiple perspectives and to reinforce the trustworthiness of this research (Anfara et al., 2002). Over the course of the research and analysis, I also consulted with the participants as a form of member check. Ms. Stoneham and several of the students were asked to review the memos and early drafts of this manuscript to build the credibility of this study (Anfara et al., 2002).

EXPLORING MEANINGS THROUGH DRAWINGS

I will first describe the characteristics students attributed to the doing of science that the drawings revealed, providing some broader categories I was able to place students' illustrations into. I will then discuss how these categories generally persisted across a set of activities designed to stretch these categories. I will describe how two students in particularly drew illustrations that demonstrated an entirely new category qualitatively different than the original categories. Their drawings provided a view of science being used to explore and solve social problems. Lastly, I will discuss one student—Debra—in depth, to demonstrate how drawing upon both visual and oral data (particularly ethnographic interviews) can provide an in-depth and powerful perspective on the meanings that learners bring to science and science education.

Holistically, the student pictures of doing science fell into four general categories: Gaining Knowledge; Science as Collection; Science as Activity; and Science as Nature, which will be described in more detail below. These categories provided a range of characteristics that students attributed to doing science, such as *where* science is done; *what equipment, knowledge, and concepts* are involved; *who* does science; and *how* science is done.

Before embarking on this analysis of the visual data, however, it is important to bring in some context from a particular discussion in class that occurred several days before the students engaged in their first drawings. This exchange became a very strong influence on the first round of drawings in particular.

The Power of Words on Pictures: Science as "Gaining Knowledge"

Several days before the students engaged in the drawing activity for the first time, Ms. Stoneham led the class on a discussion of what the word science meant:

Ms. Stoneham:	What does the word science mean?
Eduardo:	This class.
Ms. Stoneham:	Does anyone remember way, way, way at the beginning of class. Does anyone remember what science [means]? We cleaned out our binders, so this is going to be a tough one. Science, the word, means to gain knowledge. Remember? Gain knowledge. Yep [pointing to Margarid].
Margarid:	Yeah, but you gain knowledge in every class.
Gabriel:	The science of…
Ms. Stoneham:	Yup, the science of, what? The science of history. Yup, everything is kind of like a science. Right?

Through this dialogue, Ms. Stoneham set up the parameters and possibilities of the domain of science. She positioned science for her students as a process to "gain knowledge," and set the stage for them to take on the label and practices of a scientist. She further positioned the process of gaining knowledge—science—in a disciplinary-autonomous manner. In response to Margarid's point that "…you gain knowledge in every class," Ms. Stoneham replied that there is "[t]he science of history. Yup, everything is kind of like a science." Ms. Stoneham is presenting a universally-applicable mode of gaining knowledge, irrespective of discipline and content. It is important to understand that the students in Ms. Stoneham's C-Block class did listen to what she was saying; the influence of this exchange was evident in the students' drawings.

Categories of Science from Round 1

The analysis of the first set of student drawings revealed the core four categories of drawings which largely persisted over the course of the eight weeks. These categories will be presented in turn.

Gaining Knowledge. Drawings which tended to fall in the Gaining Knowledge category (Figure 1) were interpretations of Ms. Stoneham's own description of science revealed in the classroom discussion described above. Ms. Stoneham tended to describe the gaining of knowledge as an active process throughout the class discussions and in interviews with me. She discussed active modes of learning, asking questions, interpreting patterns, gathering evidence and engaging in reasoning as necessary components of learning science—of gaining knowledge.

Yet the students interpreted the process of "science as gaining knowledge" as passive. Things were drawn around heads or brains with arrows indicating that they were being put inside. The things which represented "knowledge" tended to involve a "typical" sense of science content (illustrations of viruses, cells, DNA strands), although at times included a broader and more general sense of "knowledge" to include other subject areas as well. One student drew a picture which depicted the Earth floating in space connected with arrows to a disembodied brain also floating in space. In large measure, these illustrations lacked context, an important part of both learning about

Figure 1. Representative drawings in the gaining knowledge category

and doing science. And while they may have not captured the *spirit* of Ms. Stoneham's idea of science as "gaining knowledge," they were strongly tied to the *idea* of "gaining knowledge."

Science as Collection. The second group, Science as Collection (Figure 2), tended to represent doing science as a collection of ideas, concepts, and paraphernalia. These collections did not tend to be tied to a particular place, nor did they typically involve human activity (with one exception, in the drawing in Figure 2 on the right with a person holding what appears to be a light or microscope). For the most part, these illustrations lacked context, although there may have been a fair amount of content. One student drew science as a book to depict knowledge across a range of subject areas collected in one place. The knowledge collected in this book included topics such as biology and the other school sciences topics (e.g., math, English, and business), and even child care. This student's representation is an interpretation of Ms. Stoneham's general description of science as representing all subject areas. Other students drew other objects and ideas, such as plants, test tubes, DNA strands, and the recycling symbol. It is also interesting to note that the lab bench depicted in the middle drawing of Figure 2—with a black top and a brown wooden bottom—reflects the form of the lab benches in the classroom. This is not entirely surprising, as much of the formal context for science occurs at school.

Figure 2. Representative darawings in the science as collection category

Science as Activity. Drawings of Science as Activity (Figure 3) were typically tied to particular places and included people in these places, providing more context than the prior two categories. Places were often represented in the drawings in this category, and were either outdoors in a natural setting or in a laboratory setting (or both, as in the left drawing in Figure 3). The laboratory-like settings reflected fairly closely the classroom's lab area, including the black-and-brown lab benches as can be seen in the rightmost illustration. The people in the drawings were usually doing things—such as investigating and examining or working with test tubes—that represented a fairly "typical" understanding of scientific activity. While the left drawing in Figure 2 tied back to Ms. Stoneham's knowledge statement with the word "Knowledge" tying both contexts and sets of activities together, the drawings in this category tended to be active rather than passive, and places and people were represented.

Figure 3. Representative drawings in the science as activity category

The middle picture in Figure 3 was a little different than the other illustrations in the Science as Activity category because it was not tied to a particular place. It was included in this category, however, because of the strong presence of the person in the drawing. This person, wearing what looks like a lab coat and glasses, was engaging in a number of different activities, mostly involving observations. This was the only illustration in this first round that included a person with a lab coat, and ultimately fed into the question of "who does science" and what people who do science look like. They were visited by a scientist from the nearby natural history museum several days after they engaged in the drawing activity. Discussing the visit the next day, Ms. Stoneham brought up the illustrations and asked her students to reflect on the people they drew in their pictures and how that connected to the idea of a scientist as a person:

Teacher: So, your impression of a scientist, then, does it change at all, are you adding to it at all? Because remember we did our drawings about what does it mean to do science.
Gabriel: Well, he seemed pretty normal to me.
Teacher: Isn't that nice, that science people are normal. Scientists are normal.
Beryl: I wanted him to be like wearing a lab coat.
Teacher: That's a very interesting point, that you wanted him to wear a lab coat. And a lot of you in your pictures, when you said doing science had lab coats on.
Beryl: Oh, when you said we're having a speaker, I said, oh, he's going to be wearing a lab coat.
Margarid: I thought it was going to be more chemistry stuff.

Ms. Stoneham brought attention to Beryl's prediction that the visitor would be wearing a lab coat, by pointing out that many of the students drew lab coats in their pictures (even though, as noted above, only one student drew a lab coat). This was a misconception on Ms. Stoneham's part, but I do not bring this up to discredit Ms. Stoneham or how she views her students. Instead, I introduced this dialogic exchange to highlight the deeply ingrained categories and assumptions that even the teacher holds of her students' representations of science. Ms. Stoneham concluded the conversation with the following:

So, those are the things that you're conjuring up when you think science. Kind of like a lot of you in your pictures you did lab stuff. You wear a lab coat. So as a scientist, you wear a certain set of clothes, and you work with certain equipment?

Ms. Stoneham reinforced the clothes and the equipment in order to call them into question and cast doubt on their certainty. These deeply ingrained categories of who does science were not easily displaced; the combination of the students' illustrations, the visit by the scientist, and the class discussion allowed these tacit underlying meanings to be brought to the surface.

The illustrations in the Science as Activity category demonstrated a cohesiveness to the paraphernalia and props represented in the drawings and they were oriented to doing a particular task. This cohesiveness and orientation is unlike the drawings in the Science as Collection category, where there was no clear or explicit sense of purpose to the scientific materials and ideas represented.

Science as Nature. The drawings in the Science as Nature category (Figure 4) ranged from the general to the specific. These drawings tended to depict "doing science" as nature itself, with scenes of grass, trees, animals, water, and suns. They also brought in specific content from the curricular unit being studied at the time, and tended to depict people with particular sex chromosomes (XX and XY). These drawings tended to reflect the notion that doing science is connected to nature, and that "science is everywhere," a theme which was often invoked in interviews as well as classroom discourse.

Figure 4. Representative drawings in the science as nature category

The "science is everywhere" theme was a topic of discussion in the small groups looking over each other's drawings. I sat down to observe one group consisting of Margarid, Henry, and Rosa. While the students were categorizing the drawings and answering some reflection questions, Margarid asked me a question which invoked a deeper discussion:

Margarid: Just like everything has to do with science!
Researcher: …[D]oes a painting of a fish [pointing to the fish tank on a nearby counter] have to do with science?
Margarid: A painting?

Researcher:	Yeah. I'm asking…	
	{two students talking at once}	
Henry:	It could be the actual, looking at the actual fish…	
Margarid:	…Looking at the actual fish, and it's a fish, and the fish is an organism, and the characteristics of the organism we're looking at science.	
Researcher:	OK, so… so, when you sit down in history class, is that science?	
Margarid:	No.	
Researcher:	No? How come?	
Margarid:	Yeah, it kind of is…	
Henry:	It's science history!	
Rosa:	It's not really science, they're not talking about science.	
Henry:	Well, it could involve it, it's just not mentioning it, because that's not what the subject's about, so they could involve it.	

I interpreted this discussion in part as a reaction to the classroom discourse several days beforehand when Ms. Stoneham introduced science as "gaining knowledge" and asserted that there is a "science of history." When asked about a painting of a fish—meant as an artistic representation—Margarid and Henry both pulled it under the umbrella of science. This move not only brought artistic representations and interpretation into the domain of science, but nature as well with Margarid's comment that "…it's a fish, and the fish is an organism, and the characteristics of the organism we're looking at science." They also dealt with the concept of subject matter when I asked them if history class was science. Rosa was willing to distinguish history from science, while Margarid was more tentative, and Henry was ready to classify history class as science because history "could involve" science. These categories of drawings and this conversation point to some difficulty by students in developing firm categories in defining what is and what is not "science." Grappling with these uncertainties is an important part of a science education, although this process was given some boundaries by Ms. Stoneham's explicit definition of science as gaining knowledge and insistence that science applies to any academic pursuit. In the interest of disclosure, I confided in these students that their questions were being debated by scientists and philosophers, and that I did not have a definitive answer for them.

Redrawing Science: A Reprisal of Meaning and Activity

When the students engaged in the Drawing Science activity a second time, some of the challenges to the activity, particularly Gabriel's public protests, did not occur. While a number of themes from the first activity did recur, there were some subtle yet striking differences between drawings for some individuals, namely Kimberly and Debra. In addition, an entirely new category of drawings by Juana and Rosa emerged, highlighting the ways that science can be leveraged for the public good.

A number of themes carried over from when the students originally engaged in the activity the first time. For example, there were representations of Science as Collection, Science as Activity, and Science as Nature (see Figure 5). There was an updating of the content that students drew in their representations (such as the Punnett Square in the drawing on the left of Figure 5, and the expansion of hereditary characteristics such as eye- and hair-color in the drawing on the right). For the most part, however, the drawings did not exhibit a great deal of change in terms of demarcating the field of science.

Figure 5. Representative drawings of themes in the second activity carried over from the first

Some subtle changes, however, did manifest themselves leading to some interesting differences between the beginning of the research period and the end. Kimberly, for example, drew the picture on the left of Figure 6 the first time around and the picture on the right about a month later. Both representations can be categorized as Science as Activity. Both drawings display a dual context: outside in nature and inside presumably in a laboratory. In the outside half of the context, grass, clouds and a tree can be seen, and even a squirrel makes an appearance in both drawings. In the laboratory half of the context, Kimberly drew in a lab bench and at least a graduated beaker. In the second drawing, there is no person outside like she drew in the first drawing. The word "Knowledge," which unified the two contexts in the first drawing, is also missing in the second drawing, as well as the proclamations by the people in the first drawing of "LIFE!" and "Chemicals." Lastly, the person inside the laboratory in the later drawing (presumably female) is wearing a lab coat and protective gloves while the person inside the laboratory in earlier drawing (presumably male) is wearing neither.

Figure 6. Kimberly's first (left) and second (right) drawings of science in action

These differences highlight a number of important interpretive distinctions between the two drawings. First of all, as time progressed from Ms. Stoneham's insistence that science is "gaining knowledge," the idea of knowledge as a unifying theme apparently became less important to Kimberly—or at least it played a less significant role in her meanings around doing science. Relatedly, she felt it important to describe the materials and objects of study in the first drawing, but not in the second. Of course, there are a number of factors which may have influenced Kimberly's decision on this particular omission (she may have felt pressed for time the second time while she did not the first), but these are important distinctions nonetheless. Lastly, despite Ms. Stoneham's best efforts to stem the idea that science requires a lab coat, Kimberly added one in the second drawing whereas there were no lab coats in the first drawing. This is a significant and unexpected consequence where, rather than depicting "normal" people doing science, a "typical" perspective on the field of science became more entrenched. This is counterbalanced, however, by the retention of the female figure. While there is research to suggest that the "typical" scientist is male (Matthews, 1996), Kimberly's "typical" scientist is female, moving the female figure from the outside world of nature to the inside world of the lab.

Scientists Helping and Improving Communities and the World

Despite the consistency of themes—with subtle changes—a new theme did emerge in students' drawings. Rosa's and Juana's drawings, on the left and right of Figure 7 respectively, depicted the idea that science can be used to improve society and make for a better life.

Rosa's drawing, on the left of Figure 7, included the label, "Scientists will help their community so the world will improve!!" She drew a schematic diagram with three figures labeled "Scientists" connected by an arrow labeled "Help" pointing to a group of six figures labeled "Community." A number of details deserve highlighting. First of all, Rosa positions scientists as members of a larger community. Not everyone is a scientist, but they are members of a larger population, and are oriented towards helping this larger community. Secondly, by helping their community, their work also not only has a positive impact on the community itself but the world at large.

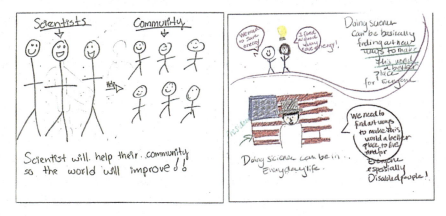

Figure 7. Rosa's and Juana's drawing of sceintists helping and improving communities and the world

J. F. PRICE

Juana drew similar themes to depict science in action. She wrote two explanatory sentences: "Doing science can be basically *finding out new ways to make this world a better* place for Everyone" and "Doing Science can be in Everyday life." Juana drew in two vignettes to illustrate her point. In the first vignette, two people, a male and a female, are in conversation. The male figure says, "We need to save energy," while the female character responds, "I found a good way to save energy!" Juana drew a light bulb above the female character's head. In the second vignette, a figure labeled "President" with a Lincoln-esque stovepipe hat in front of an American flag says, "We need to find out ways to make this world a better place to live for Everyone espessially [sic] Disabled people." The reference to people with disabilities is a connection to the subject of the public service announcement that she recently completed.

Juana brought in references to specific social issues that have roots for understanding through—and potential solutions in—science, that of energy conservation and the life of people with disabilities. In doing so, she brings in a political dimension as well. Energy conservation is a politically-charged economic and environmental issue which is at the forefront of the global climate change debate. She also attributes a charitable personality to a political figure, the President of the United States, in his speech in favor of using science to improve the lives of everyone, especially people with disabilities.

These two pictures represented a new category of science in action for these students, that science can be utilized to improve communities and the world at large. Rosa positioned scientists as members of a larger community of people and Juana introduced a political aspect to science in action. These illustrations are qualitatively different than the other categories of illustrations and bring science into a broader social and political context. These illustrations served as an indication that these two girls' sense of science was expanded.

In the next section, I will look more closely at the illustrations drawn by Debra. I will also bring in complementary passages from discussions and interviews I conducted with Debra. By doing so, I will demonstrate both the power and utility of combining visual data (illustrations) with oral data (interviews).

From the Aggregate to the Personal: Looking at the Case of Debra

Debra was an atypical student in Ms. Stoneham's C-Block class. She had spent most of her life in Brazil and had just started school in the United States) 20 months prior to my meeting her. While she had studied English in school in Brazil, Debra had been placed in an English Language Learners track in Cotstead. Ms. Stoneham and I discussed that based on Debra's interest and effort in science class, she would probably have been placed in a more academically rigorous track for science if her English language ability had been stronger.

Debra was one of the few students in the class who expressed that she enjoyed learning science and participating in science class on a regular basis. When asked what she enjoys about science class, she responded, "'Cause I want to be a doctor, so, or a biologist, so I have to know those stuff, and I find it really interesting." In her response, Debra utilized the same language that Ms. Stoneham had used in her teaching in terms of understanding how life works and gaining knowledge. However, Debra also brought in her own goals, to pursue a career in medicine or biology. She said that she had wanted to go into the sciences as a career since childhood, "'Cause I grew up, like, my grandma has a farm so I used to go to her farm every weekend, so I grew up with the nature kinda, with the environment." Her past experiences of spending time on her grandmother's farm helped her to appreciate nature and to propel her towards a career in the sciences.

While her visits to her grandmother's farm exposed her generally to nature and the environment, Debra brought up another experience which reinforced her interest in science and her choice to pursue a career in biology or medicine. She recalled her experience in helping with and seeing the events leading up to her step-sister's birth:

[My step-mother] had a baby so I followed her pregnancy and I got to watch the, like the labor. And it was really amazing. 'Cause I wanted to, when I say I want to be a doctor, I want to be a midwife, so, it was like a great experience

Not only was she granted access to see her step-mother's labor process, she was also asked to help out. At this point she clarified her career goals to becoming a midwife and Debra saw this experience as an opportunity to practice this role.

Even though she counted a career in the sciences (midwifery) as her goal, she faced a number of challenges, the first being support from her family. Debra's familial relationships are both complex—spanning a divorce, two re-marriages, a close-knit extended family, and two continents—and very influential. In discussing her relationship with her family, Debra implied that wanted to share her interest in and knowledge of science with her family and to make it a part of who she was in relation to them. When asked if she discussed science or biology class with her family, Debra replied:

Not really, because they are not really interested in that stuff, and when I start talking about that, they say, oh, my gosh, here she comes again! [Debra] with her biology stuff! … [T]hey find it very annoying.

While Debra felt unsupported and didn't feel like she could share her interest in the sciences with her family, she did have a friend outside of the class, Constança, with whom she felt she could relate. According to Debra, Constança shared her interest in the sciences:

No, but with my friends, I have just one friend, Constança, she loves biology too. And then we just talk about it, how, evolution works and stuff. And we share, I share with her what I learn in this class, and then she shares with me what she learns in chemistry class.

212

We can assume that Debra and Constança have a number of experiences in common, but experiences from the classroom—and the science classroom specifically—are included in their dialogue and the structure of their friendship. As Brickhouse and Potter (2001) pointed out, if engagement in science is deemed a marginalized activity and not valued as a form of identity-formation within one's social sphere, continued participation is made much more difficult. This friendship and common interest is a way that Debra and Constança are able to stem these other influences and build value for each other's interest in science.

Language was another barrier brought up by Debra. She discussed another of her influences, Richard Rasmussen, a role model from the Brazilian nature and science television program *Selvagem ao Extremo* ("Wildness to the Extreme"). One of the ways that Debra aspired to be like him was the way Richard Rasmussen talked and expressed himself:

I want to be able to talk about science and pronounce the words. Even in Portuguese, it's kind of hard, there are many big words, he [Rasmussen] talks about it without a problem.

She noted that Richard Rasmussen was able to "talk about science and pronounce the words… without a problem." Presenting Richard Rasmussen as a model, Debra described success in terms of being able to communicate clearly about science. This desire to be able to talk about science clearly, using "big words," was reflected in other instances as well. During a group activity, Debra blurted out, "I hate my stupid accent." I asked her to explain how her accent connected to learning science, to which she replied: "'Cause there are some words that I find it difficult to pronounce and then people make fun of you, like a lot."

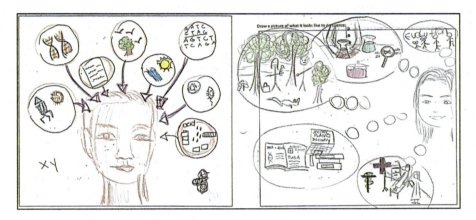

Figure 8. Debra's first (left) and second (right) drawings of science in action

Debra saw science as a domain needing both a particular vocabulary and a particular way of pronouncing this vocabulary. As a student learning English, she was unable to utilize and pronounce the specialized vocabulary with the same ease and facility that her peers seemed to already possess. While Debra said that she was no longer being made fun of, but those kinds of feelings and inadequacy despite her strong interest and desire to succeed in the sciences.

While at first glance the changes between her first and second drawings (Figure 8) may not seem significant, with the challenges she discussed in mind these changes in Debra's drawings became a study in her attempts to reconcile these challenges and build a place for her in science. Her first drawing was an example of the Gaining Knowledge category, with bubbles of science content and concepts entering a person's head through inward-facing arrows. Her second drawing was much more complex, and difficult to categorize using the themes developed through the first enactment of the activity. The main figure in her second drawing was herself, unlike her first. Illustrated through the conventional comic strip thought-bubbles, she is thinking about five different aspects of science.

Moving in a counter-clockwise direction from the top, the content of the first of Debra's thought-bubbles is the concept of evolution. Debra had earlier highlighted evolution as one of the main organizing principles of biology. The second aspect is a laboratory investigation, replete with different colored substances in beakers and containers. A faceless person is holding one of the beakers and a magnifying glass is centered on some letters. The third aspect Debra drew was two people experiencing nature, with trees, flowers, and animals. There is a bucket or container with a handle, which may indicate that the people are collecting something from the outdoors. The fourth aspect is a depiction of a pile of books, one of them propped up displaying its contents (DNA and RNA), as well as a laptop computer presumably displaying the Animal Planet and Discovery channel websites. Lastly, Debra drew a person in a bed being attended to by a health care worker, as well as a range of medical paraphernalia. She also drew a red cross and a caduceus, both symbolic of the medical profession.

While at first glance, one might assume that Debra's second drawing could be considered an example of Science as Collections, it is actually much more complex, exhibiting a great deal of depth that the typical Science as Collections illustration did not. With the exception of the representation of evolution—which she identified as a core tenant of biology—and the pile of books and the laptop, Debra went beyond drawing a collection of things and ideas to depicting a number of activities and practices of science. She also

J. F. PRICE

included a medical scene; medicine was important to her as a career goal to become a midwife, but it was also a representation of science being used in a way with which many people can connect and identify. Similarly, her depiction of the books and the laptop showcased not only the specific scientific content knowledge canonized in the books, but also the more publicly-accessible and public-oriented scientific content of Animal Planet and Discovery. Her second drawing not only demonstrated a range of scientific activities but also highlighted a number of functions of science, including understanding the natural world, serving as a repository of these understandings, sharing these understandings publicly, and using these understandings to improve human life.

In a sense, she was able to express meanings of science in her illustration that included her in the picture. While she expressed these same ideas orally through interviews, she was able to create a projection of what science looks like through her drawing.

CONCLUSIONS

Many of the illustrations in this chapter demonstrate that with these students—Ms. Stoneham's C-Block students—the meanings constructed around the idea of doing science were often decontextualized, illustrative of "typical" science as often portrayed in popular media, or tied solely to the classroom. There are unresolved tasks in science teaching, science curricula and, just as importantly, representations of science in the public sphere to provide experiences and models that allow learners to see the full range of science as a human activity in context and connecting with their own lives. Some students, such as Juana, Rosa, and Debra, were able to find and express these meanings. These students' illustrations provided rich evidence of the meanings around doing science.

By focusing on the meanings that students construct around and the relationships students indicate they hold with *doing* science—rather than *being* a scientist—this research provides a more nuanced view of how students relate to science and perceptions of how it connects with and adds value to their lives, even if they do not become scientists themselves (Archer et al., 2010). Drawings are particularly well suited for allowing participants to express meanings (Freeman & Mathison, 2009), and Juana and Rosa in particular were able to express these meanings through free-form drawing that other opportunities did not afford. Focusing on the meanings and the representations of these meanings also allowed the students, the teacher and the researcher to discuss and negotiate the meanings and purposes that science held for them, allowing the students to develop an identity with science and to recognize its importance in personal and public life even if they themselves do not go on to becoming scientists themselves. As such, the rigorous analysis of student drawings to elicit and understand the meanings that learners construct around science becomes an important tool for researchers seeking to understand science education holistically and not just instrumentally.

Yet another dimension beyond documentation and understanding emerges, and that is the notion of participant (and researcher) transformation (Brandt & Carlone, 2012; Fielding, 2004; Mertens, 2010). As noted previously, Ingold (2013) distinguishes between *inquiring with*—which is a transformative mode—rather than *inquiring about*. Through this research I have found that providing students with the opportunity to express meanings through drawing gives them the space to make connections and transform their core understandings about the place and meaning of science as well as their own relationships to it. It was also an important experience for Ms. Stoneham, who was able to gain insight into what her students bring to science and what they hope to get out of it. The illustrations served as a platform for discourse in the classroom, in particular when Ms. Stoneham engaged the class in a discussion on the question of what a person who does science looks like.

The most striking and powerful example, however, was that of Debra. As she gained confidence of expression through drawing, she was able to place herself in the picture of what it looks like to do science. Debra was able to portray a future that matched her goals of becoming a midwife, and she was able to see herself transcending some of the challenges that she discussed in her interviews with me. This was a prime example, in line with the notion of *inquiring with*, of transformation. Similar to Haney et al. (2004), who found that student drawings are a powerful tool to promote student voice in educational change efforts, I found that student drawings are a powerful tool to promote a public-oriented science literacy. These insights can provide impetus for educators and researchers to develop the appropriate educational structures, materials, and experiences for students to further engage and negotiate the meanings they construct around science.

NOTE

[1]   The name of the city and all names of participants are pseudonyms.

REFERENCES

Aikenhead, G. S. (1996). Science education: Border crossing into the subculture of science. *Studies in Science Education, 27*(1), 1–52.

Ainsworth, S., Prain, V., & Tytler, R. (2011). Drawing to learn science. *Science, 333*(6046), 1096–1097.

Archer, L., DeWitt, J., Osborne, J., Dillon, J., Willis, B., & Wong, B. (2010). "Doing" science versus "being" a scientist: Examining 10/11-year-old schoolchildren's constructions of science through the lens of identity. *Science Education, 94*(4), 617–639.

Brandt, C., & Carlone, H. (2012). Ethnographies of science education: Situated practices of science learning for social/political transformation. *Ethnography and Education, 7*(2), 143–150.

Brickhouse, N. W., & Potter, J. T. (2001). Young women's scientific identity formation in an urban context. *Journal of Research in Science Teaching, 38*(8), 965–980.

Calabrese Barton, A., Kang, H., Tan, E., O'Neill, T. B., Bautista-Guerra, J., & Brecklin, C. (2012). Crafting a future in science tracing middle school girls' identity work over time and space. *American Educational Research Journal, 50*(1), 37–75.

Carr, M., & Riesco, M. L. G. (2007). Rekindling of nurse-midwifery in Brazil: Public policy and childbirth trends. *Journal of Midwifery & Women's Health, 52*(4), 406–411.

Carson, R. N. (1997). Science and the ideals of liberal education. *Science and Education, 6*(3), 225–238.

Chambers, D. W. (1983). Stereotypic images of the scientist: The draw-a-scientist test. *Science Education, 67*(2), 255–265.

Charmaz, K. (1994). Grounded theory: Objectivist and constructivist methods. In N. K. Denzin & Y. S. Lincoln (Eds.), *Handbook of qualitative research* (pp. 509–535). Thousand Oaks, CA: Sage.

Costa, V. (1995). When science is "Another World": Relationships between worlds of family, friends, school, and science. *Science Education, 79*(3), 313–333.

Erickson, F. (2012). Qualitative research methods in science education. In B. J. Fraser, K. Tobin, & C. J. McRobbie (Eds.), *Second international handbook of science education* (pp. 1451–1469). Dordrecht, The Netherlands: Springer.

Feinstein, N. (2011). Salvaging science literacy. *Science Education, 95*(1), 168–185.

Fielding, M. (2004). Transformative approaches to student voice: Theoretical underpinnings, recalcitrant realities. *British Educational Research Journal, 30*(2), 295–311.

Finson, K. D. (2002). Drawing a scientist: What we do and do not know after fifty years of drawings. *School Science and Mathematics, 102*(7), 335–345.

Freeman, M., & Mathison, S. (2009). *Researching children's experiences.* New York, NY: Guilford.

Hammond, L., & Brandt, C. (2004). Science and cultural process: Defining an anthropological approach to science education. *Studies in Science Education, 40*(1), 1.

Haney, W., Russell, M., & Bebell, D. (2004). Drawing on education: Using drawings to document schooling and support change. *Harvard Educational Review, 74*(3), 241–272.

Ingold, J. (2013). *Making: Anthropology, archaeology, art and architecture.* New York, NY: Routledge.

Jenkins, E. W. (2006). The student voice and school science education. *Studies in Science Education, 42*(1), 49–88.

Lemke, J. L. (1990). *Talking science: Language, learning, and values.* Norwood, NJ: Ablex.

Matthews, B. (1996). Drawing scientists. *Gender and Education, 8*(2), 231.

Mertens, D. M. (2010). Transformative mixed methods research. *Qualitative Inquiry, 16*(6), 469–474.

Mooney, C., & Kirshenbaum, S. (2009). *Unscientific America.* New York, NY: Basic Books.

Osborne, J., & Dillon, J. (2008). *Science education in Europe: Critical reflections.* London: Nuffield.

Jeremy F. Price
Indiana University School of Education
Indianapolis, USA

SECTION FOUR

DRAWINGS TO CONSIDER THE ILLUSTRATOR'S IDENTITY DEVELOPMENT AS A SCIENCE TEACHER

19. DRAWINGS AS IDENTITY DATA IN ELEMENTARY SCIENCE TEACHER EDUCATION

Gaining insight and understanding of identity through drawings in science teacher education began with looking at pre and post drawings of the ideal elementary science teacher in the development of the DESTIN, or "Drawing-the-Elementary-Science-Teacher-Ideal Not" procedure (Mensah, 2011). From those drawings, meaning was made about elementary preservice teachers' past experiences in science education. In so many ways the images revealed stereotypes of science and science teachers, and the images of such were carried into their teacher education program. Over the course of the semester, the images drawn at the end of the course were drastically different from the initial drawings. These final drawings reflected who they wanted to become as science teachers. From the DESTIN procedure, identity became a central element and a basis for looking more deeply at the use of drawings for elementary science teacher education and identity work. Much of that initial research of the DESTIN procedure was developing theoretical possibilities and practical knowledge that can be helpful in understanding elementary preservice teachers' thoughts about science education, diversity, and identity and the kinds of experiences that will support their emerging science teaching practices and teacher identity. Using a similar method previously done with the DESTIN procedure, this chapter considers the usefulness of drawings when drawings become identity data in science teacher education.

DRAWING FROM THE PAST

The Drawing-Elementary-Science-Teacher-Ideal-Not (DESTIN) is one drawing strategy that was developed and used to explore elementary preservice teachers' images of science, science teachers, and science teaching. The procedure also looks at identity and diversity issues from analysis of the drawings that preservice teachers complete during a science methods course with comparative analysis and discussions. The DESTIN drawing procedure was derived from reviews of literature relating the image of the scientist and the school teacher, and reviews of literature on multicultural education and identity development (Table 1). The DESTIN procedure uses pre-and post-drawings with a narrative component in order to learn how views of science teaching change over time. It also uses an analysis around identity and diversity, which are not explored in other drawing tests, such as of Draw-A-Scientist-Test (DAST) by Thomas, Pedersen, and Finson (2001). We collect the pre-drawings and narrative that accompanied the DESTIN procedure, descriptive qualities the preservice elementary science teachers characterize as *the ideal science teacher not* or the teacher that they would not want to become, and the post-drawings completed at the end of the semester which is the *ideal science teacher* or the teacher that they would like to become. The drawings are analysed and provide insights into preservice teachers' prior thinking, emerging identities, and practices as elementary science teachers (Mensah, 2011).

Table 1. Review of literature

Image of scientist and teacher	Multicultural education
Barman (1996, 1999)	Gee (2002)
Beardslee and O'Dowd (1961)	Banks (2001)
Chambers (1983)	Gay (2000)
Finson, Beaver, and Cramond (1995)	Ladson-Billings (1995)
Goodman (1988)	Villegas and Lucas (2002)
Krajkovich and Smith (1982)	
Mason, Kahl, and Gardner (1991)	
Mead and Metraux (1957)	
Schibeci and Sorensen (1983)	
Thomas, Pedersen, and Finson (2001)	
Weber and Mitchell (1996)	

P. Katz (Ed.), Drawing for Science Education, 219–225.
© 2017 Sense Publishers. All rights reserved.

Negative images and stereotypes of scientists, science, and teachers are very prevalent in the minds of children and adults (Miele, 2014). The negative images and stereotypes of the scientist and the teacher draw much concern for preparing elementary science teachers. Many of their past experiences in school science, especially in high school and college, have shaped their current views of science teaching, and these images are the precursors of their developing teaching identities (Mensah, 2011). Therefore, science educators have a significant role in addressing the stereotypical perceptions and negative images that preservice teachers have about scientists, science, and science teachers. A focus on identity in the DESTIN procedure is critical for helping elementary teachers to develop positive images of science education, with a focus on their developing a positive image or identity as science teachers. From this gallery of DESTIN drawings we present and discuss some of them in this chapter. These images are divided into two major sections that relate science teaching and identity issues, where the drawings serve as data to be read and interpreted as text (Kress & Van Leeuwen, 1996).

Who Is The Science Teacher?

In previous work (Mensah, 2011) composite profiles of the *ideal elementary science teacher not* (pre-drawing) and the *ideal elementary science teacher* (post-drawing) were shared. Descriptive words were taken from the narrative component of the DESTIN procedure and two profiles were written. Using the same profiles, yet with different images, they reveal a great deal of text to be read as data from the drawings. For example, Figure 1 shows a representative image of the *ideal elementary science teacher not*:

Figure 1. Image of the ideal elementary science teacher not (pre-drawing)

The image of the *ideal science teacher not* was a female, middle-aged teacher; she was "boring" and "mean"; she assigned "too much work"; she was "standing and lecturing" to the class, and was "not student-centered"; she was "impatient" with her students, and she has low expectations for their success; the *ideal teacher not* was an "authoritative" person who disciplines by always "yelling" such things as "Sit down!" and "Shut up!"; her students were not happy because the class was "boring"; she would speak, "blah, blah, blah" but her students did not get anything out of the science instruction, or they would use class time to sleep; overall, the *ideal elementary science teacher not* was "uncreative" and "does not enjoy her job." (Mensah, 2011, p. 383)

In Figure 1, the science teacher is teaching; yet, the students are not learning. One student is asleep, and the other student is playing with paper airplanes and not listening to the teacher lecture about science.

What Does Science Teaching Look Like?

Similarly, in Figure 2, there is a drawing of the science teacher at the front of the classroom, and students are sitting in a "lecture-style" classroom. The teacher is teaching, just like the teacher in Figure 1. In both images, this data, supported by the narrative, depicts who the science teacher is and what science teaching looks like as memories of the preservice teachers they shared as science learners.

Figure 2. Image of the ideal elementary science teacher not (pre-drawing)

Weber and Mitchell (1995) stated, "images always maintain some connection to people, places, things, or events, their generative potential in a sense gives them a life of their own, so that we not only create images, but are also shaped by them" (p. 12). When we looked at the images the preservice teachers drew about the *ideal elementary science teacher not*, we see snapshots of how they are not able to connect to science in the classroom. Unfortunately, the connections are distant and no real relationship with science is made on a personal level, or with the science teacher. Thus, it is true that as science educators, we must find ways of re-shaping the past so that the generative potential that Weber and Mitchell speak of becomes new images of what science teaching should look like. In so many ways, it is the reshaping of the identity of the science teacher toward positive images and relationships of teaching and learning.

The images reveal identity. The dynamic nature of identity means that a person is a certain being within different contexts at different times. For instance, Britzman (1992) stated, "identity is a constant social negotiation that can never be permanently settled or fixed, occurring as it necessarily does, within the irreconcilable contradictions of situational and historical constraints" (p. 42). We have taken identity in this way to promote a change in what science teaching can look like for preservice teachers and for them to image themselves as the science teacher. For example, in the elementary science methods course, microteaching (Gunning & Mensah, 2010) is an assignment where the preservice teachers are given an opportunity to reshape images of science teaching while developing an image of the science teacher for themselves. They have to plan and teach science lessons, and assess their teaching by reflecting on student learning and their development as a science teacher.

In one image particularly, the science teacher and her students are outside the classroom doing science. From this drawing, science teaching is not confined to the straight-row seats of the classroom but is extended to teaching and learning science outside the classroom doors. In Figure 3, Gretal's image has the teacher asking questions rather than lecturing. In fact, in the narrative to the image, Gretal

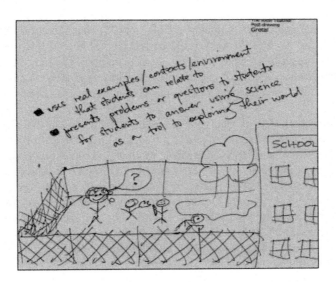

Figure 3. Image of the ideal elementary science teacher not (pre-drawing)

wrote that the science teacher "uses real examples" as she relates science to the "contexts/environment" in which children live. In her case, it is the urban school environment where she completed her microteaching. In addition, she writes that the teacher "presents problems or questions to students for students to answer" and that the students are able to use "science as a tool to exploring their world." This drawing speaks greatly to the practices of science where asking questions (for science) and defining problems (for engineering) are considered to be aspects of the scientific and engineering practices for science education described in the Framework for K-12 Science Education and development of the Next Generation Science Standards (National Research Council, 2011).

The *ideal science teacher* post-drawings display less traditional, stereotypical, and negative images of science teaching and the science teacher. For instance, these images are more child-centered, inquiry-focused, and collaborative. These approaches to science education are methods they experience as learners in the methods course and are encouraged to practice during microteaching. Their attention to these methods is drawn and evident in their drawings for analysis. Consequently, the science teacher and the science teaching displayed in these drawings (Figure 3, for example) are very different from the initial profiles drawn at the beginning of the semester (for example, Figures 1 and 2). Likewise, the teacher profile of the *ideal elementary science teacher* is described in the following way:

> The image of the *ideal science teacher* was "fun", "energetic", "enthusiastic", and "excited" about teaching science; she was "warm", "encouraging" and "welcoming" of her students; the *ideal teacher* could "connect to students" because she was "involved with the students" by forming "good relationships with her students"; her students saw her as "approachable" and "students trust her"; the *ideal science teacher* would "build on what students know by using students' experiences"; the teacher had a very "active", "hands-on", "student-centered" classroom; she was not limited to teaching just in the classroom but science teaching and learning could be conducted "outside the class", where science was "connected to the students' world"; the *ideal teacher* was "culturally aware and conscious of diverse students"; she was "understanding" and "tolerant of diverse students and learning styles"; overall, the *ideal science teacher* was "accepting", "respectful" and she "makes the classroom a safe place to learn." (Mensah, 2011, p. 384)

Teacher education programs are challenged to develop experiences that support the development of teacher identity with teacher candidates. An exploration of teacher identity and science teaching is captured in the drawings generated from the DESTIN procedure; in addition, identity of the teacher is explored further in the next section of this chapter. Drawing makes this aspect a usable approach for studying identity.

IDENTITY DATA IN DRAWINGS

Changes in preservice teachers' personal understanding about science teaching are unlikely to occur without a purposeful and systematic inquiry about their personal theories, beliefs, and practices of teaching. Moreover, as teacher educators who are interested in learning more about teacher identity and providing learning opportunities that support the development of teacher identity, we can use drawings to elicit important data for understanding identity.

Getting elementary preservice teachers to change their views of science is a major goal of ours as teacher educators. The change they undergo is a change in behavior that is shown in their teaching practices which ultimately means a transformation of their identities. This identity affects how they view science and teach science in their classrooms, and how they view themselves as science teachers. In addition, the change requires not only a particular understanding of science but a new understanding of how they see themselves and how they want others to see them. This idea relates to Gee's (2002) notion of identity; identity is "being recognized as a certain kind of person" (p. 99). It also relates to Holland, Lachicotte, Skinner, and Cain's (1998) idea of authoring, which is "the meaning that we make of ourselves" (p. 173) in particular spaces. Both of these ideas are conveyed with the DESTIN procedure and how drawings serve as valuable identity data. In the drawings, preservice teachers express identity and tell who they want to become, or how they would like to be seen by others, as an elementary science teacher. In other words, the drawings serve as one set of data for preservice teachers to tell a particular kind of personal story about who they are as elementary science teachers. The personal story is shown in their drawings and narratives.

For instance, the post-drawings represent identity data and show the transformation the preservice teachers undergo as science teachers, allowing for their identity to be constructed in a new way. Identity, as Gee (2002) explains, is the "kind of person one is recognized as being, at a given time and place" and "can change from moment to moment in the interaction, can change from context to context, and of course, can be ambiguous or unstable" (p. 99). For example, the change in content of the drawings at the beginning of the course to the conclusion of the course depicted a re-orientation to science and a detachment from negative science teacher identities that limited their relationship with science previously. They overcome an old conception of self as they develop a new conception of self as teacher, and this new conception of self is a person who can teach science. They replace their previous images of science and self with emergent science teacher identities (Mensah, 2012; Mensah, in press). In the process of transforming previous negative, stereotypical science images, the science teacher and science teaching align more with their present experiences and hope for the future. The images become who they are and how they want to be seen as science teachers.

In addition, Holland, Lachicotte, Skinner, and Cain (1998) describe "authoring the self" (p. 173), and Figure 4 represents this idea. Sonja's image is a self-portrait of a young, female, fashionably-dressed, elementary school science teacher. She draws herself with an up-swing haircut, V-neck blouse, mini-skirt, pointed-toe shoes, and make-up. Though she is neatly dressed, she is also "ready to get dirty." This young, modern, science teacher represents the culturally embedded assumptions of what an elementary school science teacher looks like as someone more aligned with who she is currently (Mensah, 2011). Sonja states the following in her narrative: "I am going to remain me—still act and dress the same but think differently about science now based on what I have learned" [during the semester]. Sonja is displaying a large smile, and she describes herself as "smiley and welcoming" to students. She wants to remain who she is, a warm and welcoming person, yet she authors herself as someone who will think differently about science.

Looking further at the image Sonja drew, she states that as the science teacher, she wants to be "respectful and understanding to my [her] students' questions, needs and concerns." These qualities are completely opposite from the composite profile of the *ideal elementary science teacher not* (pre-drawing) mentioned earlier. As a science teacher, she is "excited to be teaching and learning", which says a great deal about a positive outlook on teaching and her professional development as a science teacher. She is a "teacher learner" who is "always learning new things." She is a also "good listener" for her students and able to "observe more closely" the needs of her students. This image as data reveals strong notions of the role of the science teacher and Sonja's desire to build strong connections to her students.

Figure 4. Image of the ideal elementary science teacher (post-drawing)

DRAWINGS CONCLUSIONS

Fundamental issues of identity are not only invisible to others but also deeply invisible and personal to the person who authors himself or herself in science. We have to create ways of allowing the invisible to be seen, and drawing helps. Therefore, using drawings in science teacher education is a valuable approach to learn about past experiences and future hopes, particularly as these ways of reading the text of drawings reveal teaching, learning, and identity as well. As the Drawing-Elementary-Science-Teacher-Ideal-Not (DESTIN) procedure produces drawings and narratives of experience, it offers multiple viewpoints for engagement in teaching and learning and discussions of identity. From the profile descriptions generated from the narratives that accompany the post-drawings, we gain insights into preservice teachers' emerging identities as science teachers. These images may play a significant role in helping preservice teachers to imagine their practice and how they want to guide future science instruction in their classrooms. The preservice teachers draw who they are and who they want to become. This is extremely valuable data to note the kinds of experiences that may foster identity development and the kinds of learning that preservice teachers engage in during teacher education.

In these images of the *ideal elementary science teacher* some of the preservice teachers are constructing more "progressive" and "modern" images (Mensah, 2011; Weber & Mitchell, 1996) by choosing to draw themselves as the *ideal teacher*. These modern and contemporary images represent the kind of elementary science teacher who is more aligned with who they currently are and want to become, such as the case with Sonja. These images suggest that preservice teachers can develop a science teacher identity that is connected to who they are as individuals. With experiences in science teacher education that are less traditional, preservice teachers have the potential to break the stereotypical image, or at least challenge these notions. By being a representative contemporary image of the science teacher. They align themselves with practices that support new or reformed-based views of science teaching.

From previous research (Mensah, 2011, 2012) and looking at the collection of images in this chapter, it is evident that preservice teachers hold particular views and images of science, science teachers, and science teaching when asked to draw their past experiences in science. The negative images are strong and pervasive, and relate to other work done with drawings in teacher education, science education, and other fields that have used drawings (Dooley, 1998; Finson, 2002; Hancock & Gallard, 2004; Mead, 1951; Miele, 2014; Quita, 2003; Robinson, Kelsey, & Terry, 2013). In addition, Calderhead and Robson (1991) note that students had images of good teaching that were formed from one or more teachers they knew. Students took the positive attributes of these teachers to be their own. Seen in the DESTIN drawings, the positive images many of the preservice teachers are creating, such as student-centered learning environments and being sensitive to differences in the classroom, are seen on their drawings and described in their narratives. They imagine having learning environments that are supportive for students.

Studies have shown that children's perceptions of scientists are flexible, meaning they can change through certain interventions such as being exposed to female scientists as role models and guest speakers in the classroom, engaging in informal science experiences outside of school, or learning from hands-on inquiry activities in school (Finson, 2009; Minogue, 2010; Moseley & Norris, 1999). If this is the case for young children, interventions in teacher education can be useful as well, such as microteaching in elementary classrooms, participating in informal science experiences in the park, or museum, and Family Science Night (Johnston, Butler, Mensah, & Williams, 2011). In all of these experiences, drawing about them can be generative and meaningful data on science education and identity, particularly for the illustrator.

CONCLUSION

The preservice teachers and the images they draw offer meaningful data for analysis and discussion. When teachers hold negative images of science teaching, or have a bad experience in learning science, they are likely to maintain this image, and pass it on to their students, consequently affecting their teaching practice and the experiences of their students (Finson, 2002; Koch, 1990; Rosenthall, 1993). This makes the role of the science educator all the more critical in providing experiences that will assist preservice teachers in the development of alternate or positive images of science education. If alternative images are not discussed and fostered in science education, from elementary to secondary and higher education, the field and related areas suffer. It becomes much more of a challenge for recruitment and retention of people into the sciences and related fields, and science teaching.

Conversely, as preservice teachers are given opportunities to develop images of science education and science teaching where they re-draw positive experiences in teacher education, we can see the emergence of a positive identity. The preservice teachers who have positive science teacher education experiences may build images that also help to share their identity as science teachers.

We like using drawings because they are personal and collective reflections of experience. They are a rich source of evidence to promote discussions about education. With the DESTIN procedure it also informs us of the negative images found in science education and offers the possibility to change and replace them with positive images. Unlike the more traditional Draw-A-Scientist (DAST) or Draw-A-Science-Teacher (DASTT-C) tests, the DESTIN procedure looks at preservice elementary science teachers by providing insights into the kind of teacher they aspire to become. It also reveals how engrained negative and stereotypical images of the scientist or science teacher are and their influence on science teaching. Beardslee and O'Dowd (1961) state:

> To change an image as well developed and as widespread as the image of the scientist appears to be a most discouraging undertaking. This image is embedded in a system of other stereotypes with which people, even highly educated people, structure their social world. To eliminate the unfavorable connotations from *scientist* would require a brilliantly conceived long-term campaign of confrontation through mass media and of educational innovation that is not likely to be undertaken. (p. 1000)

We actually think that undertaking and overtaking the image of science and science teaching can be accomplished, within a limited amount of time and with a very limited amount of money (Huber & Burton, 1995), at least at the teacher education level. It requires science educators who see their work and themselves as not stereotypical, which is quite easy for both of us as African American female scientists and teacher educators. The ways in which we interact with preservice teachers invites an alternative view of science. Our presence dispels the stereotypical image of who can do science (Mensah, 2013; Mensah & Jackson, 2012), and offers a personal narrative to invite our preservice teachers to view themselves as science teachers. The DESTIN is a powerful approach to help preservice teachers to become aware of stereotypes of science teachers from their past, and begin the development of more positive images that include themselves as the science teacher.

REFERENCES

Gunning, A. M., & Mensah, F. M. (2010). One pre-service elementary teacher's development of self-efficacy and confidence to teach science: A case study. *Journal of Science Teacher Education, 22*(2), 171–185.

Holland, D., Lachicotte, W., Skinner, D., & Cain, C. (1998). *Identity and agency in cultural worlds.* Cambridge, MA: Harvard University Press.

Johnston, A., Butler, M. B., Mensah, F. M., & Williams, B. (2011). Playing with science: Models for engaging communities. Special issue on designing environments to promote play-based science learning. *Children, Youth and Environments, 21*(2), 312–324.

Ladson-Billings, G. (2001). *Crossing over to Canaan: The journey of new teachers in diverse classroom.* New York, NY: Wiley.

Mensah, F. M. (2011). The DESTIN: Preservice teachers' drawings of the ideal elementary science teacher. *School Science and Mathematics, 111*(8), 379–388.

Mensah, F. M. (2012). Positional identity as a lens for connecting elementary preservice teachers to science teaching in urban classrooms. In M. Varelas (Ed.), *Identity construction and science education research: Learning, teaching, and being in multiple contexts* (pp. 107–123). Rotterdam, The Netherlands: Sense Publishers.

Mensah, F. M., & Jackson, I. (2012, May). *(Re)visions of science and science teaching: Students of color transforming their ideas of teaching science in urban schools*. Critical Race Studies in Education Association Conference, New York, NY.

Miele, E. (2014). Using the draw-a-scientist test for inquiry and evaluation. *Journal of College Science Teaching, 43*(4), 36–40.

Minogue, J. (2010). What is the teacher doing? What are the students doing? An application of the draw-a-science-teacher test. *Journal for Science Teacher Education, 21*, 767–781. doi:10.1007/s10972-009-9170-7

Moore, F. (2006). Multicultural preservice teachers' views of diversity and science teaching. *Research and Practice in Social Sciences, 1*(2), 98–131.

Moseley, C., Desjean-Perrotta, B., & Utley, J. (2010). The draw-an-environment test rubric (DAET-R): Exploring preservice teachers' mental models of the environment. *Environmental Education Research, 16*(2), 189–208.

National Research Council. (2011). *A framework for K-12 science education: Practices, crosscutting concepts, and core ideas*. Washington, DC: National Academies Press.

Quita, I. N. (2003). What is a scientist? Perspectives of teachers of color. *Multicultural Education, 11*(1), 29–31.

Robinson, J. S., Kelsey, K. D., & Terry, R. (2013). What images show that words do not: Analysis of pre-service teachers' depictions of effective agricultural education teachers in the 21st century. *Journal of Agricultural Education, 54*(3), 126–139.

Villegas, A. M., & Irvine, J. J. (2010). Diversifying the teaching force: An examination of major arguments. *Urban Review, 42*(3), 175–192.

Zamudio, M., Russell, C., Rios, F., & Bridgeman, J. L. (2011). *Critical race theory matters: Education and ideology*. New York, NY: Routledge.

Felicia Moore Mensah
Teachers College, Columbia University, USA

Robin Fleshman
Teachers College, Columbia University, USA

SHIELLAH KELETSO

20. DRAWINGS TO IMPROVE INCLUSIVE SCIENCE TEACHING

A Teacher's Action Research Narrative

INTRODUCTION

I was in the seventh year of my science teaching in a Botswana Junior High School. The syllabus is an integration of Physics, Chemistry and Biology. I found myself frustrated. The national results on Mathematics and Science had declined. The Mathematics and Science results for my school had declined and continued to do so specifically in the classes I taught. This unfortunate waning was happening at a time when our nation was engaged in a crucial public conversation about education reform. There was a voice for rapid and radical reform. The conversation was pertinent following a nation-wide industrial action in which teachers had participated and whose aftermath was felt sharply in the lower learner performance. Renewed reconsiderations were hence necessary.

Our country, as is the case globally, explores the need for teachers to truly make a difference in all learners' social and academic lives. This is enshrined in the statutes that govern our education system that inform government's expectations in terms of professional development of teachers as lead agents (Botswana Inclusive Education Policy, 2011). Botswana is also cognisant of the evolving population of learner diversity and admits to having had a narrow approach to the concept of inclusion. Formerly, "all" had been limited to addressing the needs of an exclusive group of learners termed to have special educational needs, and mainly focused on disabilities. To broaden the view, the policy stated:

Action (will be) taken to change the education of children who are attending school, but not benefiting from what is currently provided, including children who are at a significant risk of failing to complete their basic education or of failing to succeed in maximising their potential. (Botswana Inclusive Education Policy Commitment Statement 3, 2011)

I did have children in my classes who were at significant risk of failing to maximise their potential, which will explain my thorough frustration. This was evident in their continued failure to pass, and thus my failure to perform as a teacher since my performance was measured by their grades. This, the performance of teachers measured by learners' grades and the reward thereafter attached to it, is the plight that teachers find themselves in. Palmer observes that "teacher bashing has become a popular sport and panic stricken by the demands of our day, we (public) need scapegoats for the problems that we cannot solve and the sins we cannot bear- (failure), and teachers make an easy target" (Palmer, 1997). Faced by such, I desperately needed to change my situation or risk losing my heart and maybe my job.

I thought of myself as a good teacher. I attended all my lessons on time. I planned for all my lessons or rather filled out the lesson plan template for all my lessons, but my students still did not show good results on the exams. This, my dilemma, had me at one point agreeing with Intrator (2002) when he asserts that "figuring out success and failure is a baffling experience". My effort did not translate to positive learner performance, and I felt vulnerable. I therefore needed intervention. I wasn't a solitary dreamer in wishing to change my situation. The newly approved policy further states that:

Action (will be) taken to ensure that teachers will be effective in enabling children to learn. (Botswana Inclusive Education Policy Commitment Statement 5, 2011)

The statement quoted above renewed my hope. In my search to find help I found an internet site designed by researchers at Project Nexus at the University of Maryland. This site featured an approach that used drawings to study and influence change in teaching and learning practice (http://www.drawntoscience.org/index.html). This approach also came in handy as a research tool. I engaged in action research using drawings in a bid to explore the policy's promise to ensure that teachers were effective in enabling learners to learn. As already asserted, Botswana intends to broaden her view on inclusive education by committing to effective and efficient teacher development and support, ensuring preparedness to handle an increasingly diverse learner population. An opportunity arose in a North-South collaboration among the countries of Sweden, Botswana, South Africa, Namibia and three of their Universities to explore appropriate approaches to implementation of inclusive education policies in those countries. One such approach was to engage teachers in action research or teacher research, as it is also known.

Action research seeks to have teachers reflect on their practice by studying their own teaching within their classrooms. In the case of my experience reported here, reflections were envisioned to assist in implementing the concept of inclusion as a cornerstone for a functional democracy. Introspection ensued to create an enabling environment where learners had a voice, were listened to, and

P. Katz (Ed.), Drawing for Science Education, 227–233.
© *2017 Sense Publishers. All rights reserved.*

classroom failure reduced. This chapter shares the findings of my action research which sought to assist me to become inclusive in my delivery of the integrated science curricula.

CLASSROOM DEMOCRACY IN CRISIS

The declining performance in my classes had eroded my self-worth as I grappled with both anger at the sources of resistance to learning and despair at the consequences that awaited me when the children failed. I was confronted with feelings of inadequacy and doubt. Figuring out success and failure was a baffling experience and not knowing whether I had succeeded left me vulnerable. I couldn't agree more with Palmer when he asserts:

> There are moments when the classroom is so lifeless or painful or confused – and the teacher is powerless to do anything about it – that my claim to be a teacher is a transparent sham. Then the enemy is everywhere: in those students from an alien planet, in that subject that I thought she knew, and in the personal pathology that keeps me earning my living this way. What a fool for I was to imagine that I had mastered this occult art – harder to divine than tea leaves and impossible for mortals to do even passably well! (Palmer, 2007)

Earlier in my teaching career, I, like Robert Kuzman in his story of the courage to teach, developed "strictness and distance that obscured my message of valuing the experiences and perspectives of my students and had thus hindered my efforts to engage authentically with them" (Intrator, 2002). It initially had been because of the narrow age gap at the beginning of my teaching engagement but later I believe it had become a habit. I now think that the strictness and distance I had cultivated drove fear into the hearts of my learners as was evident in their experiences represented in drawings. I believe that my fear of failure and what would happen to me were the children not to do what I wanted, simply reached out and infected them. The use of drawings enabled me to gain insights that would not have surfaced in a test or conversation.

THE BEGINNING OF CHANGE

"Inclusion is not a place, it's a shared value" (Bowers, 2004). Inclusion is further defined as intent to "look out for those individuals who, for whatever reason, may find themselves left out or overlooked, unable to participate in the activities – social and academic – that are usually associated with the school" (Evans 2007). To learn of the individuals who are overlooked, there is not a better way than to ask them, the marginalised. This truth was the anchor of the action research I engaged in. I sought to have learners participate in their learning through sharing their learning experiences, thus allowing me to form connections between what they knew and what I brought to class. I envisioned that approach to answer the need to be democratic, thus inclusive. I also wished to give learners a voice about what they were learning and how they felt about it. I thought that this approach would allow for better expression of thought and experience in contrast to the use of words which would have limited my learners – or so I thought!

Inclusion is about the quality of the learners' experiences: how they are helped to learn (versus how they are taught), achieve (versus pass), and participate (versus attend lessons). It also is the creation of a learning environment where barriers to learning are avoided whenever possible. Barriers to learning may stem from the individual learner, the learning environment or (most likely) the interface of both (Evans 2007). Since I was almost singly responsible for creating a learning environment that was conducive to learning, it therefore was appropriate to allow myself to be vulnerable in regard to my learners' assertion of their learning of science experiences.

METHOD

I adopted the method described on the Project Nexus website. The learners' experiences were captured in drawings where they were asked to draw themselves learning science. The drawings were then scored following four out of the six strands of science learning defined in *Learning in Informal Environments* (NRC, 2009), as described in the website below. These had evolved from the four strand model represented in the NRC report, *Taking Science to School* (NRC, 2007). There were 38 students. The rubric (0–4) reflected the degree to which each of these strands was present in a drawing (http://drawntoscience.org/researchers/scoring-rubric/rubric.html).

- Strand 1: Affective – Evidence of interest, excitement during learning and motivation to learn the science subject. Credit given for smiling mouths of the figures and specific indicators of excitement and motivation in thought bubbles
- Strand 2: Cognitive – Evidence of concepts – big science ideas, explanations of how things are happening, arguments to compare and look for alternatives and visual three dimensional models in the learning experiences.
- Strand 3: Implementation – Evidence of manipulating – access to materials, presence of testing tools, exploring – active involvement, predicting, questioning, and observing – looking intently as individuals or groups at an object or phenomena.
- Strand 4: Interaction – Evidence of participation in scientific and learning practices with others – groups for interaction and the use of scientific language and tools clearly drawn.

The learners further described what it was they had drawn in words to clarify what was actually happening in the drawings.

WHAT I FOUND

The initial collection of drawings revealed my plight to be much worse than I had anticipated. Table 1 summarizes the findings to the prompt, "Draw yourself learning science."

Table 1. Student drawing scores on first drawing

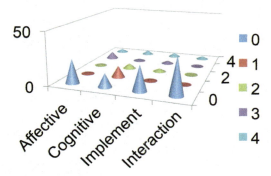

The findings from the drawings confirmed Holt's assertion that learners

fail to develop more than a tiny part of the tremendous capacity for learning, understanding and creativity. They fail because they are afraid, bored and confused. The learners are afraid above all else of failing and disappointing or displeasing the many anxious adults around them whose limitless hopes and expectations hang over their heads like clouds. They are bored because the things they are given and told to do in school were so trivial, so dull and make limited and narrow demands on the wide spectrum of their intelligence, capabilities and talents. They are confused because most of the torrents of words that pour over them in school make little or no sense. It often flatly contradicts other things they have been told, and hardly ever has any relation to what the already know. (Holt, 1990)

The drawings recorded a significant absence of fun – little or no evidence of excitement, smiles and motivation in learning. Minimal existence of any cognitive engagement was recorded. There was little or no evidence of reference to scientific concepts and principles and little or no evidence of interaction with the learning material, no manipulation of tools or experimentation. And finally my students represented their learning of science in isolation – no evidence of interaction with fellow learners, as is shown in Figure 1.

Figure 1. I am really too lazy to learn science because sometimes I think it is boring

I looked at this drawing of a boy sleeping during a science lesson. Conversations with this student revealed that he slept through much of the science lesson not because he had not slept well at night as had been presumed before, but because he was bored. The teacher had had several confrontations about the habit of sleeping during lessons and had sent the learner to the head of department for further assessment and/or reprimand. The examples below show other students who did not find my class a place where they were learning (Figures 2 and 3).

Figure 2. I will be just sitting down listening to the teacher and not hearing what she is saying at the same time, losing concentration again and again, disturbing others, Sometimes asking questions even though I am not listening. I don't know why, sometimes taking short notes

Figure 3. Student added text into drawing about lack of understanding as the teacher talks

MY CRISIS AS THE TEACHER

That my leaners were not learning was evident enough in the test scores. Nothing had prepared me for the honest feedback the drawings provided of why they were not learning. I had always known myself to be a strict teacher but never boring. I had convinced myself I was all uptight for the good of the learners. My class would be cowered to silence as I walked towards it from a mile off since none of the learners wanted to be on the offense list of the teacher, and I counted that for respect. I prided myself in the fact that I didn't mix languages – vernacular and English, and spoke fluent scientific English to learners whose reading levels were below grade as I later learned. And as it turned out from the drawings, to a significant number of my students, I spoke in monologue this whole time.

I realised soon enough that my quest for an inclusive classroom would be more complicated than I had thought and found myself agreeing much with Kurth, Sachai and Green when they argued that, "as we broaden the scope for participation to include diverse options, visions and voices we find ourselves confronted with many contradictions but little consensus; with many tangents but little time" (Kurth-Sachai & Green, 2006). I had very little time to make a difference since the national examinations were looming a short two months ahead.

I, as we must, shun ambiguity – "… to gather, to hold, to engage dynamically varied and valid truths, multiple meanings, dimensions, possibilities and plans" (Kurth-Sachai & Green, 2006). To have a group of 38 learners represent their experiences in unique ways that individually vied for my undivided attention, to connect to each learner and have them connect to the subject and to each other was unnerving to say the least. I sat through the scoring session of the drawings with trembling hands at one point where a learner had drawn a laboratory stool and nothing else. The learner was conspicuously absent from the drawing! I racked my brains to make meaning of the drawing. I was confronted with a variety of experiences which mirrored fear, anxiety, feelings of neglect, and self-pity.

I had to decide in the quickest possible way to simplify how I was going to solve my dilemma and avoid as much as I could the tendency to "limit forms of thought, expression and activity" as is the case for us humans when confronted with complexity. To achieve this, I had to be honest with myself, my own fears, limitations, weaknesses, prejudices and motives. I had to "weave a web of connectedness" as Palmer would have it, and make myself and my "subject vulnerable to indifference, judgement and ridicule" (Palmer, 2007).

A COMMUNITY FOR EFFECTIVE LEARNING

Establishing a kind of learning community where capacity for connectedness (among learners; to the subject, and between the teacher and the learners) was renewed and expressed became my new quest. The model of community which I had been functioning within promoted my services as a commodity to be critiqued and evaluated by strangers, hence, my feelings of being threatened. It also promoted teaching approaches that ascribed the role of the teacher as that of an expert and learners as amateurs. I had tried to be civil about it, practicing the classic democratic politics of negotiation, bargaining and compromise. In this process I lost all heart as I created fragmentation and competition instead of community and collaboration.

To create the ideal community for effective learning, I had to draw attention away from me (the teacher admitting that I was no expert) and from the students' achievement and/or failure (discarding both the teacher centred and student centred methodologies) and towards the science subject (making learning subject centred). Palmer, promoting this approach, states "the subject knows itself better than we (teacher and learners) can ever know it, and it forever evades our grasp by keeping its own secrets" (Palmer, 2007). In having the science subject at the centre of our learning attempts, we entered into complex patterns of communication where we shared observations and interpretations, correcting and complementing each other and in some unprecedented way evoked interest in the "secrets" of the subject.

We (it no longer was I or them) introduced the use of concept mapping, another graphic tool, as a way of spiking interest. We did this together with the learners creating the maps using computers. This move not only kept the learners interested as they created the maps the way they understood them but also shortened the very long monotonous lesson notes they hated so much to write. In concept mapping we had found an alternative to engage with the science subject, linking concepts and building on them to better understand relations within the subject and with real life situations. This allowed the learners to be creative, and, as we gathered around the subject, the teacher was seen in the light of an observation made of Barbara McClintock, to be "the one who knew where mysteries lay rather than someone who mystifies" (Palmer 2007).

The drawing feedback changed. Some students still drew themselves alone, probably because the prompt asked about themselves, but the interest and attention showed a different perspective as in Figures 4 and 5, below.

Figure 4. "Well, science I did not get it and understand anything at all, but since this science project thing I have performed well and did very well in my last exam getting a C (60%) from an E (38%) and not only getting better in science but in my school work, this days am able to like and read science and understand it and I will like to thank you my science teacher for what she have done and am optimistic about passing science"

Figure 5. "Wish you make me sit next to someone who understands more coz it's easy to learn when he explains rather than when the teacher is speaking"

I came to believe that good education is more a process than product. I was tasked with a duty to teach learners to become both producers of knowledge and intelligent consumers who could judge well for themselves that which others claimed to know. I was also tasked to challenge my learners' prejudices towards the subject and possibly leave them with some dissatisfaction that only they could answer in their quest for knowledge. In the marketing model of education in which customers are always right and the education is a product in the form of "good grades", my attempts may not be seen to have yielded satisfactory results. But in the truest comparison of the measure of fulfilment that both my students and I felt following this exercise, we learned a great deal, and we actually attained the highest pass rate in the department in the national examinations. This turned out not to be limited to the science subject as the class was rated best class in terms of transition to form 4 (senior high).

For effective practice I learned learners are not amateurs who I, as the expert, have to rid of their ignorance and bias. I assumed this position of humility in exchange for elevating my learners to their rightful place of being authentic diverse individuals who brought with them a richness of experiences which could affirm my quest to meaningfully teach them if indeed they needed to be taught. I often was tempted as we went along to fulfil my professional ethic – to do what I was trained to do, that of filling the space with factual information and covering the syllabus as expected. At times when I succumbed to that temptation I was sharply reminded that the space in which I taught and the informational demands of the subject I sought to teach were not mutually exclusive, and that I could meaningfully honour the discipline by teaching it at a deeper level instead of "marching armies of facts single-file through a lecture laden with information" (Palmer, 2007).

In opening up the learning space to be inclusive, there were days when I came out of class radiant with hope to have reached my goals and days where I was trapped in guilt. As we mapped concepts in our diverse community, I was the one adult tasked with listening and gathering the scattered pieces of our conversations and observations, to direct thoughts to where we were supposed to go. And in conclusion, in Palmer's words, "with that reframing, we accomplished three important things: we gathered up the elements of our dialogue and gave them coherence, we built a bridge to our next topic, and we did all that in a way that made students full participants." In Figure 6 below, you can see an example of students who see me as a teacher who offers them guidance when they ask for it as they draw their own science mind maps.

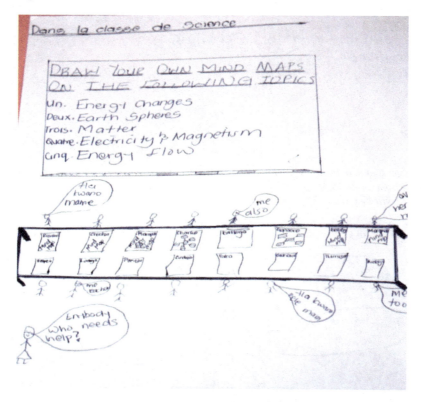

Figure 6. "Class cool, interesting, understanding everything, everyone enjoying, everyone busy"

REFERENCES

Andre, R., & Frost, P. J. (Eds.). (1997). *Researchers hooked on teaching: Noted scholars discuss the synergies of teaching and research* . Thousand Oaks, CA: Sage Publications, Inc,
Bowers, E. M. (2004). *Practical strategies for middle school inclusion*. Verona, WI: Attainment Company.
Evans, L. (2007). *Inclusion*. Oxford: Taylor and Francis.

Gore, M. C. (Ed.). (2010). *Successful inclusion for secondary and Middle school teachers: Keys to help struggling learners access the curriculum*. Thousand Oaks, CA: Corwin Press.

Holt, J. (1990). *How children fail*. London: Penguin.

Intrator, S. M. (Ed.). (2002). *Stories of the courage to teach: Honouring the teachers heart*. Hoboken, NJ: John Wiley and Sons.

Kurth-Sachai, R., & Green, C. R. (2006). *Re-envisioning education and democracy*. Charlotte, NC: Information Age Publishing.

Ministry of Education and Skills Development, Botswana. (2011). *Inclusive education policy*. Gabarone: Government Printers.

NRC. (2007). *Taking science to school*. Washington, DC: National Academies Press.

NRC. (2009). *Learning science in informal environments*. Washington, DC: National Academies Press.

Palmer, P. (1997). *The courage to teach*. San Francisco, CA: Jossey-Bass.

Petreson, J. M. (2003). *Inclusive teaching: Creating effective schools for all learners*. Upper Saddle River, NJ: Pearson Education.

Project Nexus website: http://drawntoscience.org/researchers/scoring-rubric/rubric.html

Shiellah Keletso
Junior Secondary School, Botswana

21. USING DRAWINGS TO EXAMINE PROSPECTIVE ELEMENTARY TEACHERS' MORAL REASONING ABOUT CLIMATE CHANGE

INTRODUCTION

For several decades, environmental and science education researchers have used drawings in diverse contexts to gain insight into learners' ideas about the environment and specific environmental topics. For example, researchers have engaged learners in drawing what they think about when they hear the word *environment* (Alerby, 2000), evaluated children's perceptions and concerns related to the environment by asking them to draw the Earth now and in the future (Barraza, 1999), and used drawings to analyze learners' mental models of the environment (Shepardson, Wee, Priddy, & Harbor, 2007). In our experience as researchers of science teacher education, we have likewise found drawings to be a productive tool for gaining insight into prospective teachers' ideas about environmental topics and about science teaching (Hestness, McGinnis, Riedinger, & Marbach-Ad, 2011; McGinnis, Hestness, & Riedinger, 2011; Katz, McGinnis, Hestness, Riedinger, Marbach-Ad, Dai, & Pease, 2011). For example, we have used drawings to examine prospective teachers' ideas regarding climate change and their roles in climate change education (Hestness et al., 2011; McGinnis et al., 2011). Drawings are nonthreatening data sources for investigation of prospective elementary teachers' thinking and do not take much time to generate in science methods courses. Combined with accompanying narrative summaries, they offer an exceptional method for investigators to gain new insight into prospective elementary teachers' thinking.

Currently, few would disagree that the environmental topic of climate change would benefit from additional educational research. Climate change is gaining attention in science education due, in part, to its inclusion in the Next Generation Science Standards (NGSS Lead States, 2013). As a topic that some consider sensitive, and that has direct societal implications, it fulfills the definitional criteria of being a socioscientific issue (SSI) (Zeidler & Keefer, 2003). At all points in their professional continuum—prospective to highly experienced—teachers of science need research-informed findings that apply to effectively teaching socioscientific issues, including environmental topics such as climate change.

In this chapter, we focus our attention on using drawings to investigate the relatively unexplored moral and ethical stances that teacher candidates may hold regarding the topic of climate change. Our research question was: *What potential insights might prospective elementary teachers' drawings of the causes and effects of climate change (and accompanying written explanations) provide regarding their developing environmental identities, specifically their moral and ethical stances related to the issue?* We believe that such fundamental research is needed to inform those in teacher education who are involved with preparing science teachers to address the topic of climate change. It is likely that for this new socioscientific issue in the NGSS, teacher candidates will need to grapple with their own moral and ethical stances. Only through in-depth research will teacher educators, curriculum developers, and policymakers begin to understand what moral and ethical stances teacher candidates may hold on the topic of climate change, and how those stances potentially impact their decisions concerning the implementation of climate change education as recommended in the NGSS.

LITERATURE REVIEW

Environment, Morality, and Identity in Science Education

Environmental issues such as climate change can be characterized as socioscientific issues (SSIs), or open-ended, ill-structured, and unresolved societal problems with linkages to science (Sadler & Zeidler, 2004, 2005; Sadler, 2011; Zeidler & Keefer, 2003). In outlining a framework for socioscientific issues education, Zeidler, Sadler, Simmons, and Howes (2005) emphasized that science teaching and learning must include consideration of the moral and ethical dimensions of socioscientific issues, arguing that any view of scientific literacy "falls short of the mark if it ignores the fundamental factors aimed at promoting the personal cognitive *and moral* development of students" (p. 362, emphasis added). This argument supports a view that teachers of science must be aware of, and prepared to address, the moral and ethical dimensions of socioscientific issues such as global climate change. However, Forbes and Davis (2008) suggested that even when science teachers view the moral and ethical dimensions of science as important, they "may not view them as an equally important dimension of their developing professional identity if not explicitly supported in teacher education programs" (p. 831). Here, Forbes and Davis appeared to suggest that moral and ethical development, particularly around socioscientific issues, may be an important element of identity development for teachers of science. Thus, the inclusion of socioscientific issues in science teacher education may be a promising practice.

Theorists outside of science education have likewise suggested connections between socioscientific issues (particularly environmental issues), morality, and identity. In the introduction to their edited volume, *Identity and the Natural Environment*, social psychologists

P. Katz (Ed.), Drawing for Science Education, 235–245.
© 2017 Sense Publishers. All rights reserved.

Susan Clayton and Susan Opotow (2003) argued, "Because environmental problems are increasingly important, and because environmental issues appear to engage moral reasoning and beliefs in a unique and powerful way, we need a better understanding of the connection between environmental issues and identity" (p. 19). Toward this end, Clayton (2003) proposed *environmental identity*, or one's connectedness with the natural environment, as a dimension of identity development worthy of investigation. In her research with adults, Clayton found a correlation between environmental identity and environmental attitudes. She suggested that stronger environmental identity typically accompanies more ecocentric worldview, or, a tendency to see nature as having value beyond its value to humankind. In espousing particular environmental attitudes (e.g., ecocentrism vs. anthropocentrism), Clayton argued, individuals are allowed to express fundamental values and ethical standards.

Other researchers have elaborated on the notion of environmental identity, including its connections to affect and behavior. In their work examining children's environmental identities, Gebhard et al. (2003) noted that participants had a tendency to express their environmental values by anthropomorphizing nonhuman objects, such as trees. In doing so, they "evoke[d] feelings of empathy for the object that permit[ted] it to be regarded as something worthy of moral consideration" (p. 92). Here, Gebhard et al. highlighted the connections between affect (e.g. empathetic feelings), morality, and environmental identity. Further, Kempton and Holland (2003) suggested that identity plays a considerable role in determining environmental behavior. As individuals' identities form within a cultural world (e.g., the world of environmental action), they argued, that world becomes more salient. As this occurs, individuals may become more knowledgeable about and accountable for their actions within that world.

Science education researchers have examined identity development among teachers and learners of science, focusing on such areas as science identity (Carlone & Johnson, 2007), professional identity (Katz et al., 2011, 2013), and cultural identity (Aikenhead & Jegede, 1999) in science education. However, few have examined environmental identity—including its connections to moral and ethical development—in formal science education settings. A notable exception is Blatt's work (2013, 2014) examining environmental identity development among high school students. Blatt (2013) described varying ways that students viewed themselves in relation to the environment (e.g., as a part of nature, as damaging to nature, as superior to nature, as separate from nature, as a protector of nature). She noted in particular the tensions between high school students' developing environmental identities and their simultaneously forming consumer-materialist identities (Richins, 2004) or "the significance an individual assigns 'to the ownership of material goods in achieving major life goals'" (Blatt, 2014, p. 472). The interaction of participants' varying identities, including their family (social) identity, student identity, consumer-materialist identity, and environmental identity, Blatt argued, could create internal conflict for participants and impact their actions. Here, she drew on Gee's (2005) notion of the individual having multiple, potentially conflicting, socially-situated identities.

While the concept of environmental identity has not yet been applied to the study of science educators, it is possible that like learners, teachers may experience tensions—with implications for their teaching practice—as they contend with the interactions between varying identities (e.g., professional identity and environmental identity). Katz et al. (2013) suggested that the "continuous tension in the evolving identities" (p. 1359) of beginning teachers may lead them toward pedagogical actions they see as ensuring their job security (e.g., focusing on information delivery) over actions they see as exemplifying effective, reform-minded science teaching.

This may be an inauspicious sign for the teaching of socioscientific topics with moral and ethical dimensions, such as global climate change. As researchers of socioscientific issues education have reported, teachers may avoid teaching topics they perceive as potentially controversial, even if they view them as worthwhile (Cross & Price, 1996; McGinnis & Simmons, 1999; Sadler et al., 2006). Such discrepancies between teachers' beliefs and actions may, to some degree, relate to the experienced tensions between their identities. Therefore, we believe that extending the body of research on teacher identity to include environmental identity may have the potential to provide new insights into teacher thinking and practice around the teaching of socioscientific topics with moral and ethical dimensions.

Using Drawings to Gain Insight into Environmental Perspectives

Studies that have engaged learners in drawing about the environment have frequently accompanied drawing tasks with written or verbal explanation tasks. In some cases, these combinations of approaches have helped researchers to interpret participants' intended meanings. For example, Shepardson et al. (2007) based their protocol on White and Gunstone's (1992) *draw and explain* approach. Here, learners were asked to draw a picture of the environment and then explain their drawing in their own words. Shepardson et al. argued that this approach helped to provide insight into "the interest and intent of the student at that time… [and] what the student views as crucial or salient" (p. 331). Similarly, Alerby (2000) asked learners to verbally comment on their drawn responses to the question, *What do you think about when you hear the word environment?*. These types of studies suggested that drawing provided one means for students to reflect upon and express their ideas about the environment, and the act of explaining (verbally or in writing) provided an opportunity to reflect more deeply on their thinking. Together, these methods also helped researchers to gain greater insight into the ideas that learners hoped to communicate about the environment through their drawings.

In addition to providing insight into learners' ideas and thought processes related to environmental topics, drawings have also helped researchers to better understand how learners see themselves in relation to the environment. Bonnett and Williams (1998) asked students to draw a picture of their favorite place, in order to examine participants' sense of connection to nature. In analyzing the drawings and accompanying interview responses, Bonnett and Williams were interested in how (or whether) students depicted natural places in their drawings. This approach suggested the potential efficacy of personally-relevant drawing prompts (e.g., "Draw your favorite...") for gaining insight into students' uniquely personal worldviews. In investigating learners' mental models of the environment through drawing, Shepardson et al. (2007) found that learners most often depicted the environment as a place where plants and animals live, but excluded evidence of humans (including themselves) or human activities. While to some degree, this may be related to the prompt given, it may also provide potential information about the ways in which learners see themselves, and humanity at large, as connected—or not connected—to the environment.

Research engaging learners in drawing has also provided insight into the affective dimensions of learners' thinking about the environment—particularly their worries or concerns about environmental problems. In analyzing children's drawings of the Earth now and in the future, Barraza (1999) found that more than one-third of the children depicted environmental problems, more than half depicted a future decline in environmental well-being, and very few depicted a positive outlook. Based on these interpretations, Barraza argued that drawings could be a useful means of accessing information about the development of students' environmental perceptions, and called for further research on children's depictions of environmental problems. Likewise, through conversations with learners regarding their drawings and other environmental images, researchers have noted the presence of concern and empathy, particularly regarding the welfare of animals (Alerby, 2000; Bonnett & Williams, 1998). In each of these studies, researchers also used drawings to interpret the extent to which learners appeared to hold either a point of view valuing all living things or only human interests.

Drawings have also provided researchers with insight into common themes or models that learners may share regarding the environment—particularly views that may be apparently positive or negative. In analyzing participants' drawings and comments about the environment, Alerby (2000) found that "the good world," or drawings depicting the environment as beautiful and clean (presumably positive characteristics), was the most common theme. In drawings categorized as representing "the bad world," learners expressed their ideas related to distant environmental problems, such as rainforest destruction. Within this category, Alerby noted variation in terms of learners' thoughts focused on "a 'now' perspective" (p. 217) versus more future-oriented thinking. Similarly, Shepardson et al. (2007) noted several common mental models of the environment that emerged in learners' drawings. In the most common model, students depicted the environment as a place where plants and animals live (similar to Alerby's "good world"). This suggests that human impacts on the environment may not have been salient features of students' thinking. Learners whose drawings fit into another model that depicted the environment as being impacted by human activity, may have viewed humans and human activities as more salient. Interestingly, this was most common with learners living in urban environments, where human impacts (presumably negative) on the natural world may be easily visible. These studies suggest that while learners are likely to have varied perspectives regarding environmental topics, drawings may provide a means of representing learners' ideas.

In applying what we learned from our review of the literature to our study, we sought to determine if the use of self-generated drawings would provide a method to elicit prospective elementary teachers' moral and ethical perspectives on the environmental issue of climate change in a creative and non-threatening way.

STUDY CONTEXT

The course in which this study was conducted was a required three-credit undergraduate science methods course in an elementary teacher education program at a major research university in the Mid-Atlantic. The enrolled teacher candidates were seniors. The course is one course of five different methods courses (language arts, mathematics, reading, science, and social studies) the teacher candidates take in the Fall semester, in addition to a 1-credit classroom management course. The course met one day a week for thirteen weeks for approximately two hours each class session, and the teacher candidates spent two full days a week in a professional development school. The authors of this study were the instructors of the course. The course has been the context of a series of investigations of pedagogical interventions (see McGinnis & Pearsall, 1998; McGinnis, 2003; Katz et al., 2011, 2013; McGinnis et al., 2011, Hestness et al., 2011; Hestness, McGinnis, & Breslyn, in press) with some recent investigations using drawing as a method to collect data.

METHODS

Climate Change Drawing Activity

As an introductory in-class creative activity for a lesson on teaching sensitive topics in science education, teacher candidates in the elementary science methods course were asked individually to draw on a blank sheet of paper their image of the causes and effects of climate change.[1] The prompt was, *"In the space below, draw all that you know about the causes and effects of climate change. On the back of the sheet, write what you intended to communicate in your drawings about the causes and effects of climate change."* An analysis was performed of the 59 drawings that we collected.

Analysis of the drawings. Procedurally, three members of the research team individually examined the drawings and their accompanying written explanations to identify what was salient in the drawings pertaining to the prompt. After this application of open coding, the research team convened and shared information on each drawing. Informed by the literature on drawings and how others had made sense of what was represented in the drawings, our team then found it fruitful to make sense of our salient observations of the drawings by subdividing our observations in two categorical dimensions: affective and behavioral. The affective dimension was operationally defined as evidence we detected in the drawings in which we concurred depicted the prospective elementary teachers' feelings of good or bad in regards to environment associated with the causes or consequences of climate change. We also included evidence in this category that we believed suggested insights into their feelings regarding optimism or pessimism or of an empathic disposition regarding life forms in the environment. The behavioral dimension was operationally defined as evidence we detected in the drawings in which we concurred depicted the prospective elementary teachers' or other peoples' actions that impacted the environment negatively or positively, particularly as to how they were associated with the causes and consequences of climate change.

Interviews with Two Focal Participants

We selected two focal participants to interview as a way to gain greater insight into the potential of drawings as a method for expressing the moral and ethical dimensions of prospective elementary teachers' environmental identities. Interviewees were selected based upon inferences we made during the initial coding process. We compiled a small subset of drawings that we interpreted as most clearly representing aspects of the illustrators' moral and ethical stances. From this subset, we selected two focal participants who we believed were expressing different kinds of environmental identities in their climate change drawings (i.e. one who we interpreted as potentially dismissive of climate change, and one who we interpreted as potentially concerned).

At the end of the class session in which they completed the drawings, one member of our research team conducted a one-on-one audiorecorded interview with each focal participant. Interviews lasted approximately 15 minutes each. During the interview, participants were asked to describe the causes and effects of climate change they chose to represent in their drawings. We then probed their thinking regarding how these causes and effects related to society, or the ways in which people contributed to or were affected by climate change. Finally, we asked explicitly whether the focal participants viewed these climate change causes and effects as moral or ethical issues, and to explain why they viewed (or did not view) them as such. We then transcribed the interviews and revisited each focal participant's drawing in light of the interview data, in order to develop assertions about the extent to which the drawings – and the process of discussing the drawings – allowed participants to express the moral and ethical dimensions of their environmental identities.

INSIGHTS

Climate Change Drawing Activity

The most salient representations in the prospective elementary teachers' drawings (supported by their accompanying explanations) were the following: images of the earth's temperature rising due to increased energy (primarily from the sun); greenhouse gases being released in the atmosphere (primarily CO2, natural and human related); melting ice (land and sea ice); the ozone hole; dying or endangered animals; pollution of the air and water (natural and human caused); sea level rising; habitat destruction; and over-population of humans. Figure 1 below shows two examples of how participants chose to represent these ideas in the drawings.

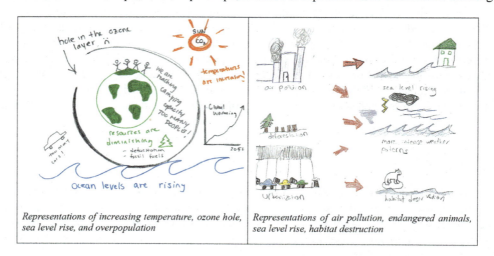

Figure 1. Examples of how two participants represented common features observed in the drawings

A secondary analysis of the drawings followed that focused on inferring the prospective elementary teachers' feelings—our affective dimension. We found evidence of this dimension in the drawings shown in Figure 2 (and accompanying explanations). Teacher candidates showed in the environment animals, primarily solitary, penguins and polar bears with sad faces on melting sea ice and fish in the ocean with x's in their eyes. One showed flowers that were dead. Another showed trees that were dead. One showed a human in the winter with sweat on a frowning face. Another showed humans with sad faces forced to leave their inundated homes. They also had humans exclaiming explanations such as "There's too many of us! AAAAAAAAH!" and, "Too much radiation!" One intern drew a large sand time clock under a large sun and in explanation stated, "There are many causes of global climate change, some we control, but most we do not."

These drawings suggested to us that the prospective elementary teachers' were expressing unhappy, pessimistic feelings along with empathy, at times, for life forms being harmed in the environment. In contrast, a few showed in their drawings timelines and cycles of change that the teacher candidates wanted to represent as depicting the natural cooling and warming cycles of the planet – an optimistic perspective from how they perceive the condition of the current state of change in the climate (but not one supported by scientific data). We present such an example in the next section, with focal participant Jill (Figure 4). Another intern showed multiple causes of climate change including erupting volcanoes—labeled as "natural causes"—along with overcrowding of people, smoke stakes in industrial sites, and cars on a road. He commented in a somewhat guarded optimistic manner that, "The earth naturally fluctuates in temperature over thousands/millions of years, but humans are not exactly blameless either."

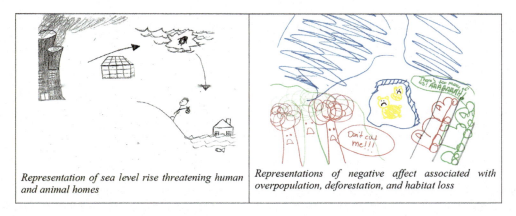

Figure 2. Examples of affective dimensions of two participants' drawings

Our secondary analysis of the drawings also focused on identifying depictions of human actions that impact the environment and contributed to climate change—our behavioral dimension. Many teacher candidates drew cars with emissions coming from the tailpipes, smoke stacks, or factories that were burning fossil fuels. A few drew depictions of deforestation and habitat destruction, overpopulation resulting in more pollution being released into the environment, and depictions of the ozone layer being diminished or an ozone hole growing larger. One explicitly made connection with urbanization, stating, "Urbanization also leads to the more CO2. The extra CO2 and other chemicals get trapped in the atmosphere and they trap heat in the atmosphere" as consequences of climate change (habitat destruction, more intense weather patterns, sea level rising, and economic issues). Others showed in their drawings money signs, and they explained that human actions related to climate change had negative economic effects. Figure 3 shows an example of a participant depicted human activities.

Figure 3. Example of human activities depicted in one participant's drawing
(e.g. agriculture, fossil fuel combustion from cars and factories)

Interviews and Analysis of Two Focal Cases

Focal participant: Jill. Jill was an Asian American teacher candidate in her early 20s, who had transferred into our university's Elementary Education program after completing a two-year community college program. Figure 4 shows Jill's response to the drawing prompt, *"Draw all that you know about the causes and effects of global climate change."*

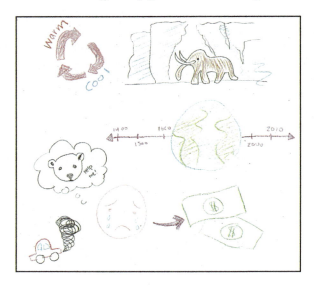

Figure 4. Focal participant Jill's drawing

Initial drawing analysis. In our initial analysis of the salient features of Jill's drawing, we noted a number of key elements. Jill drew three arrows moving in a circle, labeled "warm" and "cool", which we interpreted to potentially indicate a natural cycle of climate conditions. She also drew a mastodon or woolly mammoth in front of a glacier or iceberg, and an image of planet Earth on a timeline, with arrows pointing to before 1400 and after 2010. We interpreted this to indicate Jill's consideration of climate change as occurring over a long time span, and potentially, as occurring in the absence of human activity. We were unsure about why she chose to begin the timeline with the year 1400, but we suspected that she may be depicting the Little Ice Age (~1350–1850).[2]

Regarding the affective dimensions of her drawing, we were struck by Jill's image of a person crying. Coming from the person's head was a thought bubble with an image of a polar bear inside it, and the words "Help me!" We believed this image to show some indication that Jill saw climate change as a potential threat to wildlife, and that this could be upsetting to people. Also coming from the image of the person crying was an arrow pointing to an image of money. While we interpreted this as potential evidence of her awareness of the connection between climate change and economics, we were unsure exactly what she was seeking to communicate. However, we saw both of these elements – the possible inclusion of wildlife endangerment and economic concerns – as potentially connecting in Jill's mind to moral and ethical dimensions of climate change. We interpreted only a small portion of Jill's drawing as linked with behavior: in the lower corner of the drawing, Jill drew a car emitting a dark cloud of exhaust. We interpreted this as Jill connecting climate change with the use of vehicles, though we were unsure whether she saw this as a moral or ethical issue.

Illustrator's commentary on the drawing. Jill's written commentary of her drawing helped provide some additional insight. Jill wrote that she intended to communicate the idea that "Earth goes through cool and warm cycles" and that "there have been incidents of cooling and warming periods in the past (Ice Age, Little Ice Age, Medieval Warming Period)". This description helped to confirm our interpretation of Jill's possible view of global warming as being independent of human activity, and therefore probably not an issue of moral or ethical concern.

With regard to Jill's drawing of the crying person and surrounding images (polar bear in peril, dollar signs), Jill wrote that "Government/organizations take advantage of 'human-caused global warming' for $". This statement helped to clarify Jill's intention and suggested that she did, indeed, see moral and ethical dimensions of the issue. However, her concerns were not related to the negative effects of a changing climate on wildlife or the economy, but instead, to the problem of the public being misled to believe that climate change is a problem. This dishonesty, she appears to believe, is leading people to donate money to government or (presumably) environmental organizations, to deal with a problem that does not exist. Her use of quotation marks around "human-caused global warming" suggest a view that these groups are possible lying to or "tak[ing] advantage" of the public for their own financial gain. We infer that Jill sees these actions as unethical.

Finally, Jill wrote, "Humans have little impact on Earth's climate, but they still pollute and cause damage to the environment" (Jill, written description of drawing). We interpreted this explanation to her drawing of the car emitting a cloud of exhaust. This statement suggested to us that Jill does see some connection between human activities and the wellbeing of the environment, which potentially suggests that she views human activities as decisions having ethical ramifications in terms of their potential effects for the natural world. However, she does not believe this is the case for the specific issue of climate change, since she views anthropogenic climate change as untrue.

Interview. When we interviewed Jill, using her drawing as a starting place, we gained greater insight still into Jill's thinking regarding climate change and its moral and ethical dimensions. In describing her drawing, Jill reiterated many of the same points as in her written explanation, adding the clarifying information that: "I have a picture of someone thinking of a sad polar bear saying 'Help me!' and an arrow going to money to represent how they might give donations to help the polar bears." (Jill, interview). This statement suggested to us that Jill may specifically see environmental organizations' use of charismatic megafauna to prompt concern (and donations) as manipulative or unethical.

Jill also stated that she "included a drawing of greenhouse gases from car exhaust." This statement was particularly interesting to us, as we had not interpreted greenhouse gases (or the greenhouse effect) as something salient to Jill in her thinking about climate change. This suggested to us a potential disconnect with her explanation that humans did not contribute to climate change. However, it could be the case that Jill simply connects greenhouse gases with pollution in general (which is cited frequently in the literature), and not with the greenhouse effect per se.

Jill felt that she did not have "very concrete scientific knowledge" (Jill, interview) about climate change. She explained that most of her ideas about the topic came from an Earth Science course she had taken as a community college student, before transferring to the teacher education program at our four-year institution. Regarding this experience, Jill stated:

My teacher was big on how humans did not cause the global warming, that that was a propaganda… we have an impact on the environment and can have negative side effects from greenhouse gases but we don't have enough power to change the entire climate and she says how there are cycles the earth goes through and… sometimes organizations or the government may take advantage of that and kind of get people to make donations and use that money… just a theory. (Jill, interview)

We interpreted her statement "just a theory" to potentially indicate her uncertainty about this explanation. While she may have been uncertain, since this explanation appeared to be the most well-developed one that she had heard, and came from a trusted source, it was the explanation she chose to depict in her drawing. If this was the case, this insight suggests that drawings may not fully capture the nuance of uncertainty as well as some other data collections (e.g., interviews) might. When we asked Jill explicitly about whether she connected climate change – as she described the problem – with any moral or ethical issues. In response, Jill stated:

Yes definitely, if the government is realizing this and there isn't much human impact on the environment, then they are taking advantage of people's money and using people's sympathy for polar bears and basically lying to society, that is an ethical issue. (Jill, interview)

Here, Jill's use of an "If… then" construction suggested some uncertainty that was not as easily detected in her drawing or her written explanation. However, her drawing provided a concrete starting place and could serve as the basis of more elaborate explanations of her thinking – including regarding the moral and ethical aspects of the issue that she sought to communicate through drawing.

Focal participant: Melissa. Melissa was a White teacher candidate in her early 20s in her final year of our university's 4-year Elementary Education program. Figure 5 shows Melissa's response to the drawing prompt.

Figure 5. Focal participant Melissa's drawing

Initial drawing analysis.   In our initial analysis of Melissa's drawing, we interpreted that she drew varying causes of climate change on the upper half of the page, and primary and secondary effects on the lower half of the page. Salient causes of climate change for Melissa appeared to include emissions from factories and vehicles, meat consumption, deforestation, and political and economic issues. We interpreted that together, these led to global warming (represented by a melting Earth), which Melissa appeared to relate to increasing greenhouse gases. We further interpreted that Melissa saw global warming as leading to a variety of subsequent effects, including animal extinctions, food shortages, sea level rise, and extreme weather.

We noted several potential affective dimensions in Melissa's drawing, expressed through anthropomorphized elements of her illustration. She depicted the warming Earth with a frown, as well as a frowning polar bear—signifying that she saw these effects as undesirable, and potentially as moral and ethical issues, since human activities appeared to be involved in the causes. We were also interested in her inclusion of a donkey (symbol for the Democratic party in the U.S.) and an elephant (symbol for the Republican Party in the U.S), with the words "political/economic motivators". This suggested to us that Melissa saw climate change as a socioscientific issue—or as having a relationship to society, though it did not provide a clear depiction of her own stance on these political dimensions. In addition to these elements, we noted several of Melissa's ideas as being linked to human behavior. These included emissions from smoke stacks, a chainsaw cutting down a tree, a vehicle emitting gases, and production of beef. However, Melissa did not include any images of humans in her drawing, so it was unclear to us who she saw as responsible for these activities.

Illustrator's commentary on the drawing.   Melissa did not provide a written description of what she intended to communicate in her drawing, so we asked her to provide a verbal description. In doing so, Melissa confirmed that she saw air pollution from factories and vehicles as an important contributor to climate change, as well as deforestation and meat production. In elaborating, she described the role of methane emissions from beef production and the loss of forest as reducing the amount of carbon dioxide that could be stored on land—two ideas that were not evident to us in our initial interpretation of the drawing.

With regard to her inclusion of the political and economic dimensions of climate change, Melissa stated, "With a lot of the solutions to [climate change], …we know what the solutions could be, but there are political and economic reasons why we don't do those things" (Melissa, interview data). She also stated that she saw political and economic issues as both causes (e.g., inaction in mitigating the problem) of climate change and as effects of climate change (e.g., creation of political and economic tensions). We interpreted that inaction in the presence of known solutions might be an example of a moral and ethical concern for Melissa, but we would not have interpreted her idea about inaction on known solutions from her drawing alone.

Melissa's verbal commentary regarding the effects of climate change depicted in her drawing also added to our understanding of her thinking. In line with our initial interpretation, Melissa discussed her inclusion of animal extinction (especially polar bear habitat loss), sea level rise, extreme weather, and crop shortages. However, her commentary provided additional information about her thinking, including an awareness of some effects as locally relevant—including the impacts of sea level rise on nearby islands in the Chesapeake Bay. She also elaborated on her understanding of climate change and crop shortages (e.g., changing climate leading to increases in crop pests), though she did not appear to specifically frame food shortages as a moral (e.g., social justice) concern. Though she was highly conversant, and generally scientifically accurate, in her understanding of climate change causes and effects, her moral and ethical stances were somewhat difficult to clearly discern from her verbal description of her drawing.

Interview.   During Melissa's interview, we asked her to discuss her drawing in terms of the connections she saw between society and the dimensions of climate change she depicted. Unlike Jill, Melissa stated that all of the causes she drew were influenced by human activities. She talked about humans meeting their own needs by using resources, such as fossil fuels and forests, "in excess" (Melissa, interview). While she did not explicitly state that she saw these actions as wrong, she did frame them in terms of choices that people make at individual and institutional levels, stating:

> On an individual basis, you have to decide, am I going to buy this plastic thing, or am I going to use this reusable thing? For larger scale institutions like the beef industry or renewable energy, it's really a government issue, I think, and that goes back down to the individuals. Because if enough people are saying it, then the government is going to do it, but if not enough people are saying it, or there's not enough powerful people saying it, then nothing's going to happen, so it's very much a political issue, a government issue. (Melissa, interview)

Like Jill, Melissa appeared to believe that governments and organizations (or in Melissa's words, "special interest groups") played a role in climate change and decisions about climate change responses. However, Melissa appeared to take a more optimistic view that individual citizens could have influence with these institutions—with the caveat that powerful people must be involved, as opposed to Jill's view of institutions unethically taking advantage of or being dishonest with citizens. When we asked Melissa directly whether she saw climate change as a moral issue, she stated that she did see it as such, and brought up the notion of values. She stated,

> It's a matter of, I think, when it gets into the political and economic talk, it's a matter of what we value. Do we value, you know, transportation in our cars with gasoline, you know, over maybe not traveling as much and saving the Earth. Or do we value job creation, which goes a lot into the air pollution and factories... Do we value that higher than we value, again, the Earth? I think

it's all a balance of whether we value what product we're getting... versus the benefits that it's gonna give the Earth. (Melissa, interview)

Regarding personal actions to mitigate climate change, she spoke about her own decision to give up eating beef, both for environmental and health reasons.

While Melissa saw climate change as a major environmental problem, she did not appear to consider it highly urgent, since she generally viewed the effects as not yet impacting society. For example, she saw the disappearance of polar bears, as well as sea level rise, as mostly future concerns. She did reference extreme weather events, such as Hurricane Sandy, as a counterexample of climate change effects having an impact now. However, she did not bring up moral or ethical issues in particular here, such as climate change effects having a differential impact on under-resourced communities.

Like Jill, Melissa shared that some of her information about climate change had come from university-based classes, particularly a plant sciences professor who integrated climate change and sustainability heavily into his course. She also stated that she had learned about the topic in her day-to-day life as a college student on our "very green conscious" campus (Melissa, interview). Outside of school, Melissa stated that she had watched *An Inconvenient Truth* with her mother, which was her first introduction to the topic of climate change. She stated that much of her exposure to climate change, including its political dimensions, came from her family and her church, both of which she described as very politically liberal and engaged in environmental issues.

DISCUSSION

Having examined prospective elementary teachers' responses to the drawing activity, we return to our research question: *What potential insights might prospective elementary teachers' drawings of the causes and effects of climate change (and accompanying written explanations) provide regarding their developing environmental identities, specifically their moral and ethical stances related to the issue?* Overall, we found that the use of drawings provided an effective tool for helping our prospective teachers to reflect on their understandings regarding climate change as a socioscientific issue. Further, the drawings provided us with insight into what participants knew about the causes and effects of climate change, and how they saw humans as involved. However, from the drawings alone, we were unable to feel sufficiently confident in making inferences regarding the illustrators' moral and ethical stances on these matters. The illustrators' accompanying written explanations (and interview data when available) were essential for us to make such inferences.

Through the drawings, we saw much potential evidence of the affective dimensions of prospective teachers' views of climate change. As Gebhard et al. (2003) observed in their work with children, our participants often used anthropomorphization to convey emotion. In most cases, we interpreted that participants included anthropomorphic features in their drawings to convey negative emotions—which may have been linked to environmental values, such as a view of Arctic habitat loss as problematic or wrong. This was consistent with Barraza's (1999) finding that drawings about environmental issues often suggested a pessimistic outlook or worries on the part of the illustrator.

In a few instances, we found that participants' drawings of emotional features in the drawings was misleading when we considered the written descriptions of what they intended to convey. For example, one participant depicted a smiling fish in her drawing, but stated in the written description that aquatic life forms were dying as a result of climate change, not a case for showing happiness by smiling. This was one of various instances where we saw the inclusion of the written component as essential for interpreting the illustrator's meaning, in line with White & Gunstone's (1992) *draw and explain* approach. Similarly, when focal participant Jill depicted emotion in her drawing, (a person crying – see Figure 4) her written explanation and interview data revealed that she did not see the emotion she was conveying as genuine—that people might overdramatize climate change for personal or political gain. This level of nuance was not possible for us to interpret accurately from the drawing alone, though Jill's written explanation and interview were helpful in providing additional insight.

In examining the drawings, we were likewise challenged to interpret how our participants saw themselves in relation to climate change, or more broadly, in relation to the natural environment (Clayton, 2003). Strikingly, none of our participants included themselves in their drawings, and few included any images of people. It is possible that participants fell into the type of environmental identity category that Blatt (2013) described, i.e., as viewing themselves as separate from nature, and therefore not including themselves in the context of an environmental issue. Alternately, the absence of people—including oneself—may be an artifact of the drawing prompt, which did not explicitly ask participants to draw themselves in relation to the issue of climate change. As a result, we believe that to gain greater insight into how teacher candidates personally identified with the topic it would be beneficial to use a drawing prompt that explicitly asks illustrators to include themselves in the drawings (as modeled in Katz et al.'s, 2011, 2013, investigations of teacher identity development through drawings) or to draw a personally relevant aspect of the issue (as modeled by Bonnet & Williams, 1998).

Despite the challenges of interpreting how participants saw themselves in relation to the issue of climate change, we did note potential evidence of participants' awareness of the tension between environmental and consumer-materialist ideals (Blatt, 2013) or ecocentric and anthropocentric worldviews (Clayton, 2003). That is, in depicting the role of human activities as a dimension of climate change, we noted the frequent co-presence of damaging consumptive activities (air pollution from factories, vehicle emissions) and negative environmental consequences, similar to "the bad world" (degraded environment) that Alerby (2000) described. Whether participants saw these as moral problems was difficult to interpret in the absence of greater conversation about their intended messages. However, this finding did suggest that these tensions were salient to some or our participants.

Related to this, we feel confident that we were able to make interpretations regarding how participants saw human activities as related to climate change. A majority of participants included human actions such as fossil fuel combustion or deforestation as related to climate change. However, we were unable to interpret from the drawings alone how – or whether – participants saw their own activities as relevant. By interviewing focal participants about their drawings, we saw examples of how this information could emerge. For example, when Melissa discussed the inclusion of beef production in her drawing, she elaborated on her own decision not to eat beef. This example suggested to us that the illustrator's inclusion of certain features may have underlying connections to their environmental actions, and thus, their environmental identities. The process of discussing drawings, then, may provide a useful forum for understanding personal reasons for the illustrator's inclusion of certain features.

In summary, while the use of drawings as a tool for examining prospective teachers' moral and ethical stances related to climate change helped us gain insight into some dimensions of their thinking, it also raised new questions regarding the relationship between participants' moral and ethical perspectives and their personal environmental identities. Further, we wonder how and to what extent, if any, their emerging environmental identities might impact their future teaching practice.

LIMITATIONS

While the use of self-generated drawings was beneficial to us in our study, they also raised a validity concern related to the inferences we made. To address this concern, we asked all our participants to write out on the back of the sheets on which the drawings were made what they wished the viewer to see in the drawing. In addition, for our focal case study participants, we engaged in one-on-interviews in which we asked them to elaborate what they intended to convey in their drawings.

CONCLUSIONS

Oftentimes the teaching of science is portrayed to prospective teachers and others as a series of practices that project a view of teaching about nature that emphasizes rationality to the exclusion of a concern for morality and ethics. In our experience as teacher educators, considering prospective teachers' thinking about personal and societal responsibility regarding socioscientific issues such as climate change is necessary. We argue that by doing so it provides us a more holistic understanding of their developing identities. This is particularly true when the focus is the environment, and the topic is one that many teachers consider a sensitive topic due to how it is presented and perceived in their cultural context. As a result, we recommend highly the use of the drawing method to other researchers in science teacher education who are engaged in research on climate change education.

ACKNOWLEDGEMENTS

This research was supported in part by the National Science Foundation under Grant No. 1043262. Any opinions, findings, and conclusions or recommendations expressed in this material are those of the author(s) and do not necessarily reflect the views of the National Science Foundation.

We thank Katherine Wellington for her assistance in compiling and analyzing the drawing data used in this study.

NOTES

[1] The selection of *climate change* as an example of an acknowledged socioscientific issue for the lesson was explained due to its presence in the recently released Next Generation Science Standards.

[2] An argument sometimes posited by those who do not believe that humans activities are enhancing global warming is that Earth is still coming out of the Little Ice Age http://www.skepticalscience.com/coming-out-of-little-ice-age.htm

REFERENCES

Alerby, E. (2000). A way of visualising children's and young people's thoughts about the environment: A study of drawings. *Environmental Education Research, 6*(3), 205–222.

Aikenhead, G. S., & Jegede, O. J. (1999). Cross-cultural science education: A cognitive explanation of a cultural phenomenon. *Journal of Research in Science Teaching, 36*(3), 269–287.

Barraza, L. (1999). Children's drawings about the environment. *Environmental Education Research, 5*(1), 49–66.

Blatt, E. N. (2013). Exploring environmental identity and behavioral change in an Environmental Science course. *Cultural Studies of Science Education, 8*(2), 467–488.

Blatt, E. N. (2014). Uncovering students' environmental identity: An exploration of activities in an environmental science course. *The Journal of Environmental Education, 45*(3), 194–216.

Bonnett, M., & Williams, J. (1998). Environmental education and primary children's attitudes towards nature and the environment. *Cambridge Journal of Education, 28*(2), 159–174.

Carlone, H. B., & Johnson, A. (2007). Understanding the science experiences of successful women of color: Science identity as an analytic lens. *Journal of research in Science teaching, 44*(8), 1187–1218.

Clayton, S. (2003). Environmental identity: A conceptual and an operational definition. In Clayton, S. D., & Opotow, S. (Eds.). (2003). *Identity and the natural environment: The psychological significance of nature* (45–65). Cambridge: MIT Press.

Clayton, S. D., & Opotow, S. (Eds.). (2003). *Identity and the natural environment: The psychological significance of nature*. Cambridge: MIT Press.

Forbes, C. T., & Davis, E. A. (2008). Exploring preservice elementary teachers' critique and adaptation of science curriculum materials in respect to socioscientific issues. *Science & Education, 17*(8–9), 829–854.

Gebard, U., Nevers, P., & Billmann-Mahecha, E. (2003) Moralizing trees: Anthropomorphism and identity: Children's relationships to nature. In Clayton, S. D., & Opotow, S. (Eds.). *Identity and the natural environment: The psychological significance of nature* (pp. 91–112). Cambridge: MIT Press.

Gee, J. P. (2005). *An introduction to discourse analysis: Theory and method.* New York: Routledge.

Hestness, E., McGinnis, J.R., & Breslyn, W. (in press). Integrating sustainability into science teacher education through a focus on climate change. In Stratton, S., Hagevik, R., Feldman, A., & Bloom, M. (Eds) *Educating science teachers for sustainability. Association for Science Teacher Education* (ASTE).

Hestness, E., McGinnis, J.R., Riedinger, K., & Marbach-Ad, G. (2011). A study of teacher candidates' experiences investigating global climate change within an elementary science methods course. *Journal of Science Teacher Education, 22*(4), 351–369.

Katz, P., McGinnis, J. R., Hestness, E., Riedinger, K., Marbach-Ad, G., Dai, A., & Pease, R.(2011). Professional identity development of teacher candidates participating in an informal science education internship: A focus on drawings as evidence. *International Journal of Science Education, 33*(9), 1169–1197.

Katz, P., McGinnis, J. R., Riedinger, K., Marbach-Ad, G., & Dai, A. (2013). The Influence of informal Science Education Experiences on the Development of Two Beginning Teachers' Science Classroom Teaching Identity. *Journal of Science Teacher Education, 24*(8), 1357–1379.

Kempton, W. & Holland, D.C. (2003). Identity and sustained environmental practice. In Clayton, S. D., & Opotow, S. (Eds.). *Identity and the natural environment: The psychological significance of nature* (pp. 317–342). Cambridge: MIT Press.

McGinnis, J. R. (2003). The morality of inclusive verses exclusive settings: Preparing teachers to teach students with developmentaldisabilities in science. In D. Zeidler (Ed.), *The role of moral reasoning on socio-scientific issues and discourse in science education* (pp. 195–216). Netherlands: Kluwer.

McGinnis, J. R., Hestness, E., & Riedinger, K. (2011). Changing science teacher education in a changing global climate: Telling a new story. In J. Ling & R. Oxford (Eds.), *Transformative Eco-Education For Human Survival: Environmental Education In A New Era.* Charlotte, North Carolina: Information Age Publishing.

McGinnis, J. R., & Pearsall, M. (1998, October). Teaching elementary science methods to women: A male professor's experience from two perspectives. *Journal of Research in Science Teaching, 35*(8), 919–949.

NGSS Lead States (2013). *The Next Generation Science Standards: For States, By States.* Retrieved from http://www.nextgenscience.org/

Sadler, T.D. & Zeidler, D.L. (2004). The morality of socioscientific issues: Construal and resolution of genetic engineering dilemmas. *Science Education, 88*(1), 4–27.

Sadler, T.D. & Zeidler, D.L. (2005). Patterns of informal reasoning in the context of socioscientific decision making. *Journal of Research in Science Teaching, 42*(1), 112–138.

Sadler, T.D. (2011). Situating socio-scientific issues in classrooms as a means of achieving goals of science education. In T. D. Sadler (Ed.), *Socio-scientific Issues in the Classroom: Teaching, Learning, and Research* (pp. 1–9). Dordrecht: Springer.

Shepardson, D. P., Wee, B., Priddy, M., & Harbor, J. (2007). Students' mental models of the environment. *Journal of Research in Science Teaching, 44*(2), 327–348.

Turner, J. H., & Stets, J. E. (2005). *The sociology of emotions.* Cambridge University Press.

White, R., & Gunstone, R. (1992). *Probing understanding.* London, England: The Falme r Press.

Zeidler, D. L., & Keefer, M. (2003). The role of moral reasoning and the status of socioscientific issues in science education. In D. L. Zeidler (Ed.), *The role of moral reasoning on socioscientific issues and discourse in science education* (pp. 7–38). Springer Netherlands.

Zeidler, D.L., Sadler, T.D., Simmons, M.L., & Howes, E.V. (2005). Beyond STS: a research-based framework for socioscientific issues education. *Science Education, 89,* 357–377.

J. Randy McGinnis
University of Maryland, USA

Emily Hestness
University of Maryland, USA

DAVID WINTER AND CHRIS ASTALL

22. PRESERVICE HIGH SCHOOL SCIENCE TEACHER IDENTITY

Using Drawing Enhanced Learning Monographs

INTRODUCTION

The construct of teacher identity is complex and difficult to define. In addition to professional elements such as subject knowledge, teaching skills and understanding of pedagogical practices, it encompasses personal ideas about what teachers are and what they are expected to be. Sachs (2005) has described teacher identity quite succinctly as a framework for teachers to construct their own ideas of "how to be", "how to act" and "how to understand" their work and their place in society. In her review of teacher identity in science education, Avraamidou (2014, p. 164) summarised the nature and characteristics of teacher identity and identity development as *'(a) teacher identity is socially constructed and constituted; (b) teacher identity is dynamic and fluid and constantly being formed and reformed; and (c) teacher identity is complex and multifaceted, consisting of various sub-identities that are interrelated.'*

The process of teacher identity construction, for preservice teachers, is part of their learning and development and during their training identity is perhaps more readily influenced than at any other stage in their career. At this time there will be occasion for preservice teachers to explore and construct their identity through examining their prior experiences; practicing in safe contexts and supporting their understanding of a participatory role in varied learning communities (Luehmann, 2007).

The personal experiences that teachers themselves have of education are a powerful influence on their teacher identity, as is race, gender and personal history (Avraamidou, 2014). There is growing research evidence that also identifies the connection between an individual's emotions and the development of professional identity (Arvaamidou, 2014). We were aware that the most recent classroom experience for many of our graduate preservice teachers was the didactic lecture-style approach prevalent in their undergraduate university science courses. Several of the preservice teachers were career changers and we were also cognisant of the fact that these individuals may retain a professional identity encompassing particular conceptions associated with their past employment that competed with and framed their new and evolving teacher identity (Williams, 2010).

Our science methods course, as a component of a university-based teacher preparation programme, has been carefully designed to provide structured and safe opportunities for preservice teachers to engage in multiple experiences. We were interested in examining the changes and development of science teacher identity in our graduates as they progressed through the methods course. The principal features of drawings as an investigative tool to probe understanding have been considered earlier in this book. In this chapter we describe how drawings were used to explore developing science teacher identity in preservice teachers, specifically their existing and developing beliefs about science teaching and learning during this relatively short but pivotal time when they are learning their craft and making the transition from student to novice professional.

METHODOLOGY

Context and Participants

The participants in this study were preservice secondary school science teachers enrolled in a one year Graduate Diploma in Teaching and Learning programme. They had a minimum of a Bachelor of Science degree as part of the admission requirements for teaching. These prospective teachers were required to complete a one-semester science methods course designed to address the Science Learning Area of the New Zealand Curriculum for students in Year 9 (about age 13) to Year 13 (about age 18). The science methods course explores pedagogical content knowledge, teaching strategies, planning approaches, assessment practices and health and safety with an emphasis on practical work and student engagement. As part of the programme, this first semester course was divided into two 5-week teaching blocks, punctuated by a seven week teaching-practicum. This provided an opportunity to explore preservice teachers' developing beliefs of science teaching and learning as the course progressed. Of the 31 students enrolled, 13 agreed to participate in the study.

Limitations

The pre-service teachers self-selected to participate. It is acknowledged that self-selection can lead to bias in the resulting data as those who choose to take part may not well represent the entire target population (Olsen, 2008), In this study, prior to selection participants were informed that the research was to explore their ideas of teaching and learning science through drawings and interviews. We

P. Katz (Ed.), Drawing for Science Education, 247–261.
© *2017 Sense Publishers. All rights reserved.*

D. WINTER & C. ASTALL

attempted to minimise the respondents choice based on their propensity to engage, however the main factor that may have influenced engagement was the presumed time taken to participate. We acknowledge this possible limitation.

Data Collection

In this project we set out to explore how preservice teachers' identity and beliefs of science teaching and learning developed as they experienced new science teaching contexts, specifically a science methods course and associated programme practicum. We were interested in exploring the knowledge and beliefs constructed by the preservice teachers prior to and during engagement with the course, particularly as the focus on student-centred learning emphasises the role of the teacher as a guide or facilitator of activities and investigations, where student inquiry is promoted and teachers create a learning environment to support individual learning needs (Gluckman, 2011; Ministry of Education, 2007).

Drawings have been identified as providing rich sources of information (Weber & Mitchell, 1996; Hancock & Gallard, 2004; Katz et al., 2011; Katz et al., 2012; Ucar, 2012). The Draw a Scientist Teacher Test Checklist (DASTT-C), developed by Thomas, Pedersen, and Finson (2001), has been used to explore preservice teacher beliefs regarding teaching and learning science. The DASTT-C includes both a drawing and narrative component. The test initially requires the preservice teachers to *'Draw a picture of yourself as a science teacher at work'*, then it asks two questions *'What is the teacher doing?'* and *'What are the students doing?'* that provide a narrative to allow for additional description to help interpret and make sense of the drawing. This is especially important when metaphors, symbols or abstract imagery is presented for interpretation (Thomas et al., 2001).

Katz et al. (2011) adapted the 'Draw a Scientist Test' (DAST – Chambers, 1983) by asking subjects to draw a response to the prompt *'Draw yourself teaching science'* and *'Draw your students learning science.'* They were later able to analyse the drawings and code or score for particular attributes that were identified. Asking for these two images allowed for different perspectives on an individual's belief of teaching science as emphasis is placed specifically on the effect of the teacher's actions on learning and the role of the learner. Comparison of the resulting two images provided evidence of similar themes regarding beliefs of science teaching and learning (Katz et al., 2012).

In this study we also asked preservice teachers to complete two drawings at each sampling point. The sampling points were; T1, at the start of the course; T2, prior to teaching practicum; T3, following teaching practicum; and T4, at the conclusion of the course. There was no time limit to complete the drawings. In order to be able to identify their teaching beliefs the DASTT-C checklist was applied to each drawing (Thomas et al., 2001).

Drawing provides an alternative, supplementary data source that may reveal inadvertent glimpses of cognizance (Weber & Mitchell, 1996), however care must be taken to 'read' or interpret the drawings, particularly as the representations of teacher beliefs are individualised. Each image may contain a very personal story that would explain details about those aspects included in the drawing (Thomas & Pedersen, 2003). Since drawings are often deciphered through 'subjective prejudices and interpretations' they become most useful when combined with other forms of data collection (El-Deghaidy, 2006; Bennett, 2012). Often this supplementary data is gathered as written (Thomas et al., 2001; Markic & Ellis, 2008; Barak, 2014) and verbal explanations for drawings as well as interviews (Barak, 2014; Hancock & Gallard, 2004; Katz et al., 2011; Katz et al., 2012; Thomas et al., 2001) and student reflections (Rule & Harrell, 2006). In this study, we applied video narration as a method of supportive analysis. Once the drawings had been completed, the preservice teachers were then asked to complete a narrative video. This consisted of the preservice teachers talking to a fixed video camera about their picture, describing and explaining what they had drawn. This was repeated for both drawings.

Analysis

Each of the drawings was analysed using the DASTT-C (see Thomas et al., 2001 for further details), which provided an indication of the preservice teacher beliefs about science teaching. In summary, the checklist identified three general categories that each drawing was scored against: 'Teacher' that focused on the teacher's activity, position relative to the students and posture; 'Students' that focused on the actions of the students and their position in the classroom and 'Environment' that identified aspects of the classroom associated with the physical environment. The scoring rubric identified the presence of an element as representation of a teacher-centred approach to teaching. The final scores can range from 0–13, where a high score indicates a teacher-centred representation of teaching and learning and a low score depicts a student-centred approach. Thomas et al. (2001) assigned DASTT-C final scores to three models of teaching proposed by Simmons et al. (1999), which were the exploratory model (0–4), conceptual model (5–9) and explicit model (10–13).

The video narrations for each of the drawings were transcribed. Each transcription was then checked against the video and notes made when the preservice teacher made specific non-verbal cues such as facial expressions or hand gestures to emphasise a point. The transcriptions were then used to reanalyse the DASTT-C score for each of the drawings. The narrative component of the analysis frequently removed ambiguity in the interpretation of the drawing elements and also provided reasons or meaning for the images portrayed.

In addition to using the DASTT-C checklist, each of the drawings was analysed using a 'grounded theory' framework (Glaser & Strauss, 1967). Here, theory is derived and emerges from data systematically gathered and analysed using an inductive approach (Cohen,

Manion, & Morrison, 2007). The drawings were explored and themes regarding preservice teacher beliefs about science teaching and learning were identified and derived using a constant comparative method (Cohen et al., 2007).

RESULTS

Preservice Teacher's Beliefs of Science Teaching and Learning

Use of drawing prompts. Initial analysis of the drawings indicated that preservice teachers' drawings of themselves teaching science and drawings of students learning science had very similar contexts. Activities, subject-content and class layout reflected in those drawings showing preservice students teaching science were mirrored in the drawings of their students learning. We did identify, however, two distinct representations of science teaching and learning from the drawings.

In the first, the preservice teachers clearly identified a difference between their beliefs regarding themselves *teaching* science and how they saw their role in students *learning* science. These drawings indicated a schema of *teaching* science that involved imparting information, demonstrating practical work and providing instruction or clarification. They described it as delivering content. They often placed themselves at the 'centre' of the teaching process, as seen by their location at the front of the class, and they identified with clearly defined roles for the teacher that linked to behaviour management or control. The students, if drawn, were often shown seated as passive observers. Drawings were usually from an observer's perspective looking into the class at the teacher, who was often situated near the front of the room. These images typically had a high DASTT-C score indicating a teacher-centred approach to *teaching* science.

However, when drawing their students *learning* science, the drawings often depicted students working in groups, collaborating on tasks, completing independent work or engaged in inquiry, activities or experiments (Figures 1 and 2).

Figure 1. A preservice teacher response to 'Draw yourself teaching science' (DASTT-C score = 13) and 'Draw your students learning science' (DASTT-C score = 6) at the start of the course

Figure 2. A preservice teacher response to 'Draw yourself teaching science' (DASTT-C score = 12) and 'Draw your students learning science' (DASTT-C score = 4) prior to their teaching practicum

This appeared to be in contrast to the drawings showing them teaching. Drawings of students *learning* science showed the teacher positioned to the side or centrally and identified as a 'facilitator'. The DASTT-C scores were much lower and typically identified as a more student-centred inquiry based model of teaching. For this group of preservice teachers, where there appeared to be two different schema operating, it suggests that they perceive 'science teaching' and 'learning about science' as distinct pedagogical approaches. 'Science teaching' appears to be more of an active pursuit where the teacher maintains a dominant central role in imparting information and managing the learning environment, whereas 'learning about science' suggests the students are more actively engaged in understanding and the teacher assumes the role of facilitator. Preservice teachers who held these beliefs tended to retain them throughout the duration of the course and consistently showed very clear differences in their *'teaching'* and *'learning'* drawings (Figure 3).

Figure 3. A preservice teacher response to 'Draw yourself teaching science' (DASTT-C score = 8) and 'Draw your students learning science' (DASTT-C score = 4) at the conclusion of the course

In the second representation, preservice students identified a more complex belief of the process of teaching and learning. For this group of preservice teachers, their drawings identified multiple episodes of teaching and learning (Figure 4 and 5). Episodic teaching may involve teachers using a range of strategies that identify with student-centred and teacher-centred approaches.

These could be identified as teacher-centred (high DASTT-C score) where "teach episodes" are drawn characterised by the teacher explaining or demonstrating new content and linking this to the student's existing knowledge. Preservice teachers identified these teach episodes as connected to theory, practical demonstrations or teacher directed talk around a challenge or problem. The student-centred (low DASTT-C score) drawings often showed the students engaged in a "work episode". This is where students are able to work independently on written tasks, practical work and student inquiries often resulting in the practise of a new skill. These multiple teaching strategies became more difficult to code using the DASTT-C checklist as they often represented characteristics of both student-centred and teacher-centred approaches.

We encountered the portrayal of these multiple episodes in several drawings on each occasion that the DASTT-C instrument was administered.

Figure 4. A preservice teacher response to 'Draw yourself teaching science' (DAST-C score = 4) and 'Draw your students learning science' (DAST-C score = 2) showing episodic teaching. This example is prior to the start of the course

For a number of students this representation of teaching became very explicit in their drawings as the course progressed (Figure 5).

Figure 5. A preservice teacher response to 'Draw yourself teaching science' (DAST-C score = 4) and 'Draw your students learning science' (DAST-C score = 4) showing episodic teaching. This example is at the conclusion of the course

Changes in preservice teacher beliefs of science teaching and learning. Prior to the course, preservice teachers had high DASTT-C scores, suggesting teaching was initially perceived as more about giving information, lecturing and providing directions and demonstrating (an 'explicit' teaching model). In these images, students were typically seated in rows, watching and responding to the teacher. Drawings of students learning science, however, had much lower DASTT-C scores with students shown engaging in activities or with one another (an 'exploratory' teaching model). The changes over the duration of the course for the DASTT-C scores for both drawings are shown in Figure 6 and Figure 7. The drawings at T3 occurred following the practicum experience.

Drawings of preservice teachers *teaching* science showed a progressive shift from a teacher-centred, explicit model (DASTT-C score 10–13) to a student-centred, exploratory model (DASTT-C score 0–4), or a mixture of the two (identified as the 'conceptual teaching model') over the duration of the course (Figure 6).

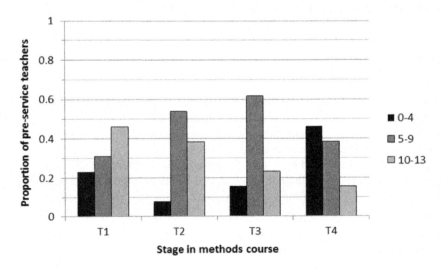

Figure 6. 'Draw yourself teaching science' DASTT-C score for secondary science preservice teachers (n=13) at four different stages throughout their course. DASTT-C scores indicate exploratory model (0–4), conceptual model (5–9) and explicit model (10–13)

Drawings of students *learning* science showed more of a student-centred approach, however following the practicum there seemed to be more of a shift towards a conceptual teaching model (Figure 7).

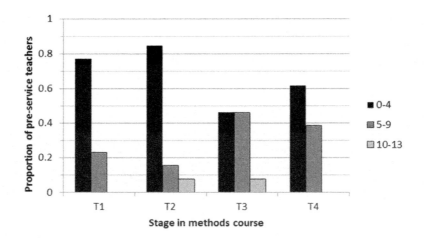

Figure 7. 'Draw your students learning science' DASTT-C score for secondary science preservice teachers (n=13) at four different stages throughout their course. DASTT-C scores indicate exploratory model (0–4), conceptual model (5–9) and explicit model (10–13)

The 'Hidden' Stories

The drawings made by the preservice teachers focused largely on the cognitive, psychomotor and social domains of learning and were supported by their accompanying video narrative. Explicit drawing elements that exhibited these characteristics included images of teachers transmitting information to attentive but passive students, students engaged in teacher-facilitated cooperative problem solving with their peers, teacher demonstrations, students performing practical work and the integration of computer-based technologies into inquiry learning tasks.

However, some of those influences that shape teacher identity are more abstract and these are difficult or impossible to identify and interpret through the images projected on paper. Even though the drawings allowed the preservice teachers to project attitudes and emotions, the interpretation or the explicit nature of those affective aspects were not revealed until we had examined the video narratives. It became clear that using the narration as a reflective tool allowed the preservice teacher to revisit the drawings and provide greater clarity regarding connections between their images and their experiences, something that as a viewer becomes very subjective and liable to misinterpretation. Indeed, the drawings provided a focus for thoughtful reflection with a number of preservice teachers pointing to elements within the drawings providing greater detail and even adding additional explanatory content to their drawings as they talked.

In terms of developing teacher identity, we defined three key themes to categorise these hidden elements presented within the drawings: the influence of experiences; affective expectations; and the developing comprehension of the complexity of teaching. All of these themes have the potential to drive particular behaviours, influence decision-making and shape outcomes.

(a) The influence of experiences. Personal and professional experiences act as a lens through which preservice teachers interpret their course content and begin to construct their developing teacher identity. Memories of their own educational experiences may be very strong and enduring, even though the most recent formal learning environment for most of our graduate trainees was the tertiary institution where they completed their undergraduate science qualification.

This influence of prior experiences was described by many of the preservice teachers in their drawings prior to the science methods course and some of these experiences endured throughout the programme. In her narration, Grace described how she drew her classroom as being set up

> the way my school laboratory was. I have always had a classroom where you do the work in the middle, like textbooks or drawings or any work on a desk. And then you go to the outsides and do practical work on the edges obviously to keep chemicals away from your work and books and everything.

Similarly, William explained

> I drew it like this because it's pretty much how all my high school classes were like. The teacher's at the front explaining stuff and the students were sitting and listening and doing activities.

For Kim the image of the physical environment of her high school persisted and she portrayed herself teaching and the students learning in this setting in her first drawings (Figure 8).

…I've drawn this because of, I think I've always been a student… portraying like someone teaching to me. So I've done it, I've drawn it exactly like my old school laboratory was like. So I've kind of drawn it from a student perspective, of me teaching in my old high school laboratory. I'm a chemistry major, so I've kind of taught it, like I'm teaching chemistry…

Kim then talked in detail about how she remembered her school classroom making connections to the layout of the whiteboard, skeleton display, position of benches and place for completing practical work. In her drawing of the students learning she was very clear about the classroom being set up with activities the way my school laboratory was…"

The memories of her own school environment persisted through the course and even following her practicum experience. She made clear reference to the the layout being influenced by her high school experiences, however the changes apparent in the drawings are around the activities of the teacher and students. For Kim, her high school experiences of science teaching spaces was reinforced by her practicum experience. As she stated;

…my drawing is very similar to the one I drew last time admittedly. I think that's because of the lab I was in on placement [practicum]. It was very similar to my old school lab and probably most labs.

Again for these drawings, even though the teaching space is predominantly the same, her use of that space and the interactions in her role as a teacher and those of her learners have developed considerably following the first set of drawings completed prior to the course. In her last set of drawings Kim identifies with her shift in thinking about her role as a teacher drawing on her previous experiences, not only as a high school student herself but also as a student within the programme;

[I've drawn] … footprints, handprints kind of just from the crime scene that we just did. And note the stars and the moon, how it's astronomy based, like there are lots of places where you can teach Science, it doesn't always have to be in a classroom. In the classroom I have drawn though, I've still got the same things. I've got Chemistry, but then I've also got Physics, so in the class we've been doing we've been looking at Physics circuits and everything like that. And I'm not very confident in it, but I think I…I need…I know I need to start incorporating other sciences into my classroom obviously because even though I'm just Chemistry [specialist subject] … so there's some Biology in here as well.

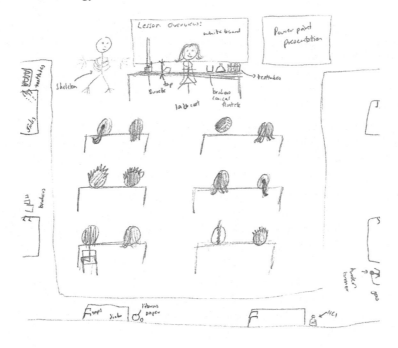

Figure 8. Kim portrays her experiences of teaching science in her drawing 'Draw yourself teaching science' at the start of the science methods course

Jasmine had a previous career in environmental conservation and significant personal experience working outdoors participating in field trips. This background and the type of learning that such activities support, explained why she portrayed herself in an outdoor setting for her first two drawings.

… my background is working in Fiordland and South Westland for quite a period of time. And so hence the trees. I did do a lot of sort of explaining and teaching when I was out there, if there were volunteers or if there were new people coming on board.

D. WINTER & C. ASTALL

Obviously they weren't at sort of Year 9 or Year 13 level, so there was a little bit more of a maturity and where we were most of the time was very isolated, so people were a bit more sort of self reliant about what they could do and looking after themselves. I had myself as teaching Science, laying out all the equipment in an area which would be considered the study site, and explaining to people the techniques involved in getting their data, their information. When I thought, when I was teaching Science that it would be as you can sort of see my hand pointing, that I would be in sort of a role of just giving out information. I'd be in kind of quite an authoritative role.

In her role as an outdoor educator, Jasmine refers to her drawing of students learning science and discusses what is not shown in the drawing:

…they're using their own equipment and they're carrying out their own experiments in groups…but then we would get back together after a certain period of time and from what I remember, and I remember this when I was drawing this, is that then we would go back to wherever we were staying. Because this is obviously more like a field trip. And then all the kids would collate their information and there would be quite sort of latish nights of getting information you know, ready for the next day or finishing what they needed to do.

Kate received her secondary education at a co-educational state high school in a small rural and remote town in South Australia. Teacher–student professional relationships were strong and several years after attaining a tertiary qualification and commencing her teacher training, Kate still recognised the enduring influence that her former school teachers had on her understanding of the world.

…A lot of my views of teaching come directly from how I was taught… I was influenced by my teachers, so I would have the same sort of influence on the students I teach. Because the teachers I had at school were probably the most influential…I found that the teachers I had in High School had a big impact on how I viewed the world and what opinions I had. So, my picture is pretty much directly how I remember my school being.

Following her practicum experience, Kate's reflections on her drawings of herself teaching science clearly shows the influence of experience on her developing teacher identity:

So on teaching practice, we've just got back from teaching practice, I've noticed that my first picture was very traditional, it was like you write on the board and the students write down your notes and kind of you teach and they learn. And then my second one [picture] was kind of the other extreme, where it was a lot more students teaching each other and interacting. And when I was on placement I kind of realised you need a balance of both. So, this kind of, is supposed to indicate that. So I'm still the teacher and I'm still the one passing on information but they, the students talk to each other and understand it to some degree, but at certain points in time they do actually just have to sit and listen.

John's narration of his initial drawing teaching science depends on memories of smells, colours and emotions. His drawing shows a typical high school laboratory layout, very similar to that described by Kim earlier. John models his drawing from his early high school and he describes the drawing as "almost replicating my school years as a science student." What is apparent from the narration is the clarity and depth of description and explanation that could not be interpreted from the drawing;\:

… and then there's a Bunsen burner and these benches sort of go across but they, they're the side benches where they can do experiments… then there's windows here… and that's the door, where the only entrance and exit into the classroom. I remember the classrooms, the roof was really high. It was a really old fashioned sort of classroom. Brown colours, and very dark and dingy. With old curtains. I'm remembering back to my Science class, but the way I kind of see it is, back in the day, the teachers would just stand there and just blah blah blah… no enthusiasm. So I want to capture the attention of the students.

In his narration, John reiterates a number of times about the importance of engaging the students, keeping them attentive and focused. Making reference to prior experiences of science teachers who did not engage him, he makes a number of comments about the need for the teacher to be enthusiastic. This concern regarding the desire to keep the students engaged and happy was also reflected in his drawing of the students learning science and as he describes in the narration:

…they're clearly quite attentive in what they're doing. They've got big smiles on their faces, they like what they're doing. So again I'm doing my very best here to make them have as much fun as they can…the main point of this is they're, they like what they're doing. They're happy about it. They're loving it. And I'm overseeing them.

It becomes clear in the narration from the drawings that John is starting to make connections between experiences of his own schooling, student engagement and behaviour and how this may be shaping his own teacher identity.

(b) Affective expectations. While attention is often focused on the cognitive domain in science education, it is known that affective constructs play an important role in the teaching-learning process. Birbeck and Andre (2009) have pointed out the difficulties of precisely defining the affective domain, although it has been described simply as an individual's beliefs, perceptions, attitudes, values and emotions (McCloud, 1992).

254

Examination of the drawings and interpretations using the DASTT-C provided one data source with respect to the teaching model. In some cases elements of the affective domain could be seen in the drawings, through the facial characteristics, body posture, annotations or speech bubbles, however the affective attributes were not always clearly identifiable and in some cases the drawings alone provided little information for interpretation (Figure 9). The narrations, however, provided an opportunity for the preservice teachers to explain their images and many made reference to the importance of the affective attributes in their teaching and student learning.

In narrating their drawings, preservice teachers discussed the importance of attitude, motivation and enthusiasm – both as a teacher and for the learner. There seemed to be a strong correlation between the affective attributes and the interaction between the teacher-student and student-student and the construction of a supportive learning environment. Preservice teachers identified the importance of using the affective attributes to engage and motivate students in science, often through fostering awe, wonder and challenge, and this was seen partly to facilitate learning and enthusiasm for science as a learning area as well as a means of managing the learning environment and controlling behaviour. There did not seem to be any pattern or correlation between the timing of the drawings and the presence of affective attributes within them.

Kate's image shows herself at a desk in front of the class (Figure 9). On the desk an assortment of science equipment suggests a practical demonstration. What really stands out is the smile Kate has drawn on her face. The difficulty arises when we try to interpret the smile. When asked to narrate the image, Kate starts to explain a developing philosophy for teaching based on affective attributes. She says:

> ...part of it's how enthusiastic you are, as you can see I've got a big smile on my face. If you care about what you teach about I think the students will care about what they're learning. If you care about it [what students are learning] and you can show them that it's an important learning aspect I think they'll appreciate it as well.

Kate explained she had drawn herself in the image of her Biology teacher from high school who she remembered had creative flair and enthusiasm for science that made the subject exciting. The role of affective attributes on Kate's developing philosophy is becoming apparent as she reflects on how the interactions between the students and teacher can lead to a developing relationship that will support her teaching. She says "I think one of my teachers once said, it's thirty percent content, seventy percent of how you pass the information on." In later drawings Kate refers to the need for the teacher to motivate students as she describes her role in "...getting involved, getting excited and being happy to answer questions and knowing the answers."

Figure 9. Kate's drawing to the prompt "Draw yourself teaching science' at the start of the science methods course

Similarly, John identifies this aspect in a number of his drawings. In his first drawing of students learning science, John has drawn smiles on the students' faces. He explains this in the narration as his role is ensuring the students are having fun and are engaged. John, in his drawing just prior to practicum, continues with the idea that his role as a teacher is to "encourage the kids and get them all excited and really enjoy coming to class and learning Science. And I'll try and be as enthusiastic as possible and make it fun." He sees his learners as being fully engaged and having "high energy, they're [full] of high energy, you can see with their mouths open and their eyes are wide."

In her reflections following practicum, another preservice teacher Karen, explained her belief that encouraging student interest and motivation was necessary in order to engage students in learning. Her drawing did not indicate the frustrations she had experienced on practicum nor her desire and aspirational goals for teaching science (Figure 10) and appeared symbolic. In her narration she explains her challenging practicum experience and her reflection identifies her growing desire to be able to use student interest in science as a means of keeping students purposefully engaged in learning.

> So what I've drawn here .... it's not just me, but it is what I represent as the topic or the concept or whatever it is that I'm trying to teach. The students are gathered around because they have genuine interest in the subject. I'm not saying that's what I did

in my placement, because I utterly, totally failed to do that. To be honest I don't know how I can create that kind of interest in students. How it can be done, or whether it really can be done. But that would be ideal in my mind and I would love to be able to teach that way.

Figure 10. Karen's drawing to the prompt 'Draw yourself teaching science' following her practicum

In her reflection on the drawing of her students learning, Karen makes further reference to her role as a teacher in encouraging students with learning. In particular, Karen is starting to think about her own attitudes and feelings in terms of her actions as a teacher.

It doesn't have to be with a PowerPoint presentation or the whiteboard, it doesn't need any tools, but just that…focus of everybody wanting to know more, interested and asking questions and being involved and being engaged in the topic. And you, yourself, being the one who is probably the most interested, the most enthusiastic on the topic of all, and the whole group working together to investigate and to discuss and to come up with the next step of the learning. Um, yes, I'd love to be able to teach that way. That would be my ideal.

At the conclusion of the science methods course, Karen reflects again back to her practicum and the need to excite, motivate and engage students in learning. She makes the connection between providing a "safe" learning environment in which students, and Karen, are prepared to take risks. She makes the connection between those affective attributes and her developing teacher identity when she states;

At least giving them or providing an environment in which they feel they would find out. They are engaged and they are excited about learning. And also they feel safe to try different things, even if they fail or make a mess or do something wrong that it doesn't matter. And so I think that's the kind of learning that I want my students to do. I don't know sitting here, having done my first placement I feel that that's almost an impossibility in real life. But one can only try. And I think that when I teach what I'm hoping to do is, I'm not expecting myself to be able to teach in this way all the time, but if I can start teaching in this way maybe for one project with one class, and then I'll do another, and one more, and if I can build it up that way, so that my lessons are more student oriented, it's inquiry based, and it is engaging and challenging and is investigative, rather than transfer of knowledge as such, then I guess I'd be happy.

(c) The complexity of teaching. Darling-Hammond and Bransford (2005) identify that successful teaching is a complex act requiring an understanding of how students learn, knowledge of the subject-matter taught, and the ability to organize and represent it to students in a way likely to best promote their learning within the specific context in which it takes place. Novice or experienced, to develop and improve classroom practice teachers need to develop the capacity for ongoing inquiry and reflective practice (Timperley, Wilson, Barrar, & Fung, 2007; Feiman-Nemser, 2001; Timperley, 2012).

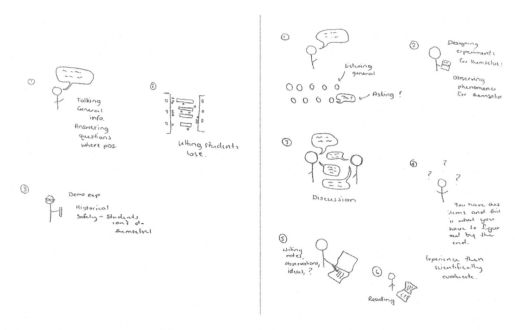

Figure 11. Sarah's drawings to the prompt 'Draw yourself teaching science' and 'Draw your students learning science' following her practicum

Following her practicum, Sarah, in both drawings, identifies some of the multiple roles of the teacher (Figure 11); facilitating interactions with students; demonstrating experiments for various reasons (safety, lack of resources, impracticality for whole class work); managing students as they engage with their own learning. Sarah explains her developing beliefs about science teaching as she states

> I think sometimes teaching students Science is not about telling them stuff and showing them stuff, it's about letting them loose to just experience it, and then decide for themselves what they actually needed to take out of it.

As Sarah talks she points to her drawings;

> To experience and then kind of scientifically evaluate maybe. It doesn't convey it, what I suppose I was trying to put in there, is… that there are no limitations, it doesn't really come across in the picture, but that's what I was intending.

Another student, Kate, recognised this complexity and tried to portray it in her drawings just prior to beginning her first practicum. She explains how her drawings have changed:

> You can see my drawing's changed compared to my first one. I don't have the blackboard or anything like that. [There is] more emphasis on inquiry teaching and learning… I've set out a task where they actually have to investigate, and they're working in groups, and actually bouncing ideas off one another and it teaches the students to, like it comes to them naturally as opposed to just rote learning content.

In her drawings following practicum, Kate reflects on the experiences and it is clear she is making adjustments to her beliefs about science teaching and learning.

> … when I was on placement I realised you need a balance of both. I'm still the teacher and I'm still the one passing on information but they, the students talk to each other and understand it to some degree, but at certain points in time they do actually just have to sit and listen. So it's kind of finding that balance where they are still processing information, and whether you're doing more, them teaching each other, and teaching themselves as opposed to just dictating.

In her reference to the drawing of students learning science, Kate's narration provides more indication of the role of practicum experience in developing understanding of the complexity of teaching. She is trying to understand how and when to implement different teaching models:

> …but there's a lot more teacher involvement compared to my last picture, because I'm pretty sure in my last one I kind of give them concepts and they go ahead and take initiative and do things on their own [student-centred exploratory model]. But with Science, because you're introducing so many new concepts, sometimes you need to be a bit more, I don't know, try to explain things a bit more. And not leave it for them to come to their own conclusions.

In her final set of drawings she explains the importance of developing teaching opportunities that allow students to gain a "better understanding of certain concepts…getting them to be more conscious of what Science is and how it's a part of our lives, and therefore how important it is." Kate then goes on to explain her beliefs about science teaching as she narrates her final drawing of students learning science:

> As you can see they're [students] actually teaching each other and it's less content based and more about them becoming objective learners and being critical about the information they receive and the information they gain. I want my students [to] be leaving their classroom with the view that whatever information is provided to them there can be more, what you're told isn't the be all and end all. They should be willing to explore that. I want my students to be more in-charge of their own learning…to be in control, control their own learning, to be able to impact how they want to learn and I think I want students to be more driven and be more responsible for themselves. It's not so much about the content [but] the Nature of Science and then understanding that they need to be better citizens in life. I think Science is a vital part of our education and they need to know more to better understand themselves, to better understand society, to be able to understand how life is. And why it is like it is instead of just accepting it for what it is.

At the end of the course, preservice teachers talked about the complexities of teacher-student interactions in terms of their teaching. They often identified a range of pedagogical strategies, such as hands-on activities, group investigative work, one-on-one tutorials, demonstrations, field trips, online tutorials and didactic teaching. Preservice teachers identified with the role of digital technology to support their teaching and student learning, through providing content knowledge, alternative modalities (videos, interactives) and opportunities to collaborate (shared learning spaces, online tutorial, collaborative documents). Comments from preservice teachers also mentioned the importance of a shifting role of the teacher towards being a facilitator of learning, encouraging students to be more responsible, independent learners. Figure 12 exemplifies this developing understanding of the complex nature of teaching and learning.

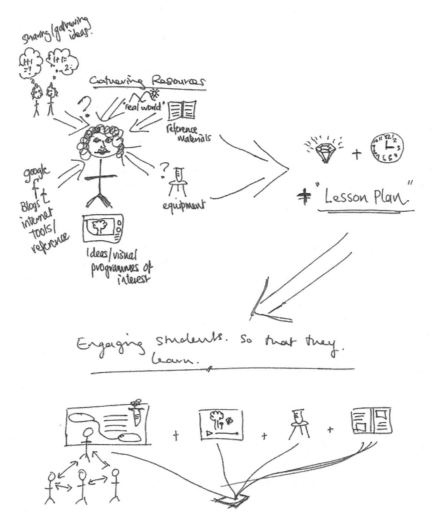

Figure 12. Jasmine's drawings to the prompt 'Draw yourself teaching science' following the science methods course

DISCUSSION

Our science methods course (indeed every course in our graduate diploma programme) was intended to equip the preservice teachers with the skills and knowledge to realise the aspirations of the New Zealand national curriculum. This outcomes-based statement of official policy, last revised in 2007, requires schools in New Zealand to promote and model articulated *principles, values* and *key competencies*[1] as they prepare students to live and work in a knowledge-based society (Ministry of Education, 2007). The *science learning area* of the curriculum encourages a social constructivist approach to learning and emphasises student-directed inquiry and understanding about the nature of science (Ministry of Education, 2007). These, and other characteristics of the curriculum, shift the responsibility and accountability for learning away from the teacher and onto the student and so fit well with a student-centred pedagogical model.

On entry into the science methods course, despite their diverse epistemological journeys, most of the participants saw themselves applying a teacher-centred and content orientated approach to science instruction that emphasised teacher authority and students acquiring teacher-transmitted knowledge. This contrasted markedly with participants conception of students learning science where they identified the focus as being on active learner engagement. This was often portrayed as students engaging and constructing knowledge through various practical tasks, often with other students, with the teacher providing support by acting as a facilitator and expert guide. The participants initially seemed unaware of the incongruence of these disparate views of science teaching and learning. As the science methods course progressed, we identified a gradual shift from a predominantly teacher-centred model to one that emphasised the importance of the learner. We suggest that this change occurred as the preservice teachers examined their beliefs about the respective roles of teacher and learner, developed their pedagogical content knowledge and understanding of the different modes of classroom interaction, and examined the tenets of a teacher-centred and student-centred pedagogy from both a theoretical and practical perspective.

Similar shifts in preservice teacher beliefs regarding teaching and learning science have been reported in other studies using the DASTT-C instrument (El-Deghaidy, 2006; Minogue, 2010; Thomas & Pederson, 2003; Ucar, 2012). In this study, the practicum (or field experience) provided opportunity for preservice teachers to explore their developing beliefs in context, their drawings and narrations clearly showing the influence of the classroom and their mentor teachers. As Hancock and Gallard (2004) identified, practicum provided opportunity to 'reinforce and challenge the beliefs held by preservice science teachers.' In studies that have explored preservice teacher beliefs about teaching and learning science, the influence of the practicum has been identified by few researchers (El-Dehghaidy, 2006; Hancock & Gallard, 2004; Katz et al., 2011; Mensah, 2011; Minogue, 2010; Thomas & Pederson, 2003; Ucar, 2012).

In our study, the use of drawings afforded our participants an efficient and unrestricted means to reveal their developing beliefs about science teaching and learning. We felt that aspects of these beliefs and the relationships between these aspects could be investigated more readily using drawings than by alternative probes. This aligns well with the views expressed by other researchers including White and Gunstone (1992) who assert that drawings provide participants with an opportunity for self-expression and a means for them to reveal qualities of understanding that are hidden from other procedures.

Our participants enjoyed completing the drawings and none expressed concern about a real or perceived lack of artistic ability or about the visual realism of their depictions.

Narration of the drawings revealed symbolism and meaning that were often abstract, individualised and personal to the participant. Once we were aware of these "hidden" aspects in our participants' drawings we were alerted to the potential for the drawings to be misinterpreted. There is always some subjectivity and ambiguity associated with the interpretation of images (Bennett, 2012; El-Deghaidy, 2006; Minogue, 2010). Minogue (2010) has already indicated that aspects of DASTT-C are difficult to apply or score. In our study, this subjectivity was reduced by both authors independently analysing the drawings and then meeting to reconcile differences. It would, however, be a simple matter to ignore or underrate elements of significant importance and make a less complex and less-than-adequate interpretation of what a drawing portrays. We suggest it is essential that drawings be accompanied by a comprehensive supporting data source, particularly when exploring complex phenomena, such as the multiple dimensions of science teacher identity and how these are constructed. We have no hesitation in recommending video narration for this purpose. We found recorded video to be a richer supporting data source than the more traditional written narrative that accompanies DASTT-C. The video recordings captured not only the linguistic content but additionally non-verbal cues such as hand gestures that participants used to emphasise important points and sometimes convey affective information. The video narration removed much of the ambiguity inherent in our interpretation of the images and provided insight into aspects of the participants beliefs that would have otherwise not been revealed to us.

The invitation to complete the video narration immediately after each set of drawings were completed provided the participants with the opportunity to make changes or add annotation, to think deeply about what they had portrayed on paper and to critically reflect on their evolving beliefs. Clearly the DASTT-C instrument allows preservice teachers to start constructing an image of themselves as a science teacher and to consider those influential aspects that shape their developing philosophies and beliefs. The ability to evaluate self and practice is an important and well-documented element of professional identity and one that we wished to cultivate in our preservice teachers. The video narration provided opportunity for our preservice teachers to reflect and consider their individual stories around the construction of their images. This characteristic of the data collection for our investigation complimented other strategies we use in our science methods course to develop inquiry into the teaching and learning relationship (Ministry of Education, 2007).

The relationship between beliefs about teaching and learning and practice was of special interest to us as the science methods course was punctuated by the seven-week practicum. The preservice teachers identified very clear connections to their beliefs of science teaching and learning and their experiences on practicum. For some, the experiences reinforced developing beliefs and our preservice teachers gained in confidence and were able to articulate a developing philosophy for teaching and learning. However, for others there were clear tensions between their notions of teaching and learning science as developed in the science methods course and the practice that they were exposed to whilst at schools. For some they were restricted in their opportunity to express their teaching and learning beliefs as this was not the established practice in their practicum school, even so the drawings and video narration provided an opportunity for critical reflection and reconsideration of their emerging beliefs.

We believe our study has implications for future iterations of our science methods course. At the next course occurrence we will at regular intervals during the course have our preservice teachers complete a drawing of themselves teaching science and a drawing of their students learning science. On each occasion that drawings are made the preservice teachers will explain their drawings to their peers, who will be invited to act as critical friends. By exploring individual preservice teacher narratives and by exposing discrepancies between the teaching and learning drawings we hope our preservice teachers will develop greater cognisance of their evolving beliefs about instruction and learning.

The complexity of science teaching and learning derived from a multitude of prior experiences can lead to tensions between the preservice teacher and their teacher educators and teacher mentors (Hancock & Gallard, 2004). As teacher educators, we are challenged by the emerging beliefs that the preservice teachers express, through drawing and narration as they move through their university science methods course, and the actual practice that they engage with on practicum. Are those preservice teacher beliefs enacted upon during practicum? Strauss (2001) identified that teachers held an espoused and an in-action model of teaching and learning. The espoused model being that identified by the teacher in interviews and the in-action model the one observed from practice. In the near future we aim to use drawings and narration to explore the beliefs of science teaching and learning and compare this to the enacted teaching and learning model of our preservice teachers.

NOTE

[1] Eight principles underpin school curriculum decision making. Values are those beliefs developed and expressed throughout the school community. Key competencies are five identified capabilities that are developed through the school curriculum. See http://nzcurriculum.tki.org.nz/

REFERENCES

Avraamidou, L. (2014). Studying science teacher identity: Current insights and future research directions. *Studies in Science Education, 50*(2), 145–179. doi:10.1080/0 3057267.2014.937171

Barak, M. (2014). Closing the gap between attitudes and perceptions about ICT-enhanced learning among pre-service STEM teachers. *Journal of Science Education and Technology, 23*(1), 1–14. doi:10.1007/s10956-013-9446-8

Bennett, D. (2012). The use of learner-generated drawings in the development of music students' teacher identities. *International Journal of Music Education, 31*(1), 53–67. doi:10.1177/0255761411434498

Birbeck, D., & Andre, K. (2009, November 19–20). *The affective domain: Beyond simply knowing* (pp. 40–47). ATN (Australian Technology Network) Assessment Conference 2009, RMIT University, Melbourne.

Chambers, D. W. (1983). Stereotypic images of the scientist: The draw-a-scientist test. *Science Education, 67*(2), 255–265. doi:10.1002/sce.3730670213

Cohen, M., Manion, L., & Morrison, K. (2007). *Research methods in education* (6th ed.). London: Routledge.

Darling-Hammond, L., Bransford, J., LePage, P., Hammerness, K., & Duffy, H. (2005). *Preparing teachers for a changing world: What teachers should learn and be able to do*. San Francisco, CA: Jossey-Bass.

El-Deghaidy, H. (2006). An investigation of pre-service teacher's self-efficacy and self-image as a science teacher in Egypt. *Asia-Pacific Forum on Science Learning and Teaching, 7*(2), 1–7.

Feiman-Nemser, S. (2001). From preparation to practice: Designing a continuum to strengthen and sustain teaching. *The Teachers College Record, 103*(6), 1013–1055.

Glaser, B., & Strauss, A. (1967). *The discovery of grounded theory*. Hawthorne, NY: Aldine Publishing Company.

Gluckman, P. (2011). *Looking ahead: Science education for the twenty-first century*. Auckland: Office of the Prime Minister's Science Advisory Committee

Hancock, E., & Gallard, A. (2004). Preservice science teachers' beliefs about teaching and learning: The influence of K-12 field experiences. *Journal of Science Teacher Education, 15*(4), 281–291. doi:10.1023/B:JSTE.0000048331.17407.f5

Katz, P., McGinnis, J. R., Hestness, E., Riedinger, K., Marbach-Ad, G., Dai, A., & Pease, R. (2011). Professional identity development of teacher candidates participating in an informal science education internship: A focus on drawings as evidence. *International Journal of Science Education, 33*(9), 1169–1197. doi:10.1080/0950069 3.2010.489928

Katz, P., McGinnis, J. R., Riedinger, K., Marbach-Ad, G., & Dai, A. (2013). The influence of informal science education experiences on the development of two beginning teachers' science classroom teaching identity. *Journal of Science Teacher Education, 24*(8), 1357–1379. doi:10.1007/s10972-012-9330-z

Luehmann, A. L. (2007). Identity development as a lens to science teacher preparation. *Science Education, 91*(5), 822–839. doi:10.1002/sce.20209

Markic, S., & Eilks, I. (2008). A case study on German first year chemistry student teachers beliefs about chemistry teaching, and their comparison with student teachers from other science teaching domains. *Chemistry Education Research and Practice, 9*(1), 25–34. doi:10.1039/B801288C

McLeod, D. B. (1992). Research on affect in mathematics education: A reconceptualization. In D. A. Grouws (Ed.), *Handbook of research on mathematics teaching and learning* (pp. 575–598). New York, NY: Macmillan.

Mensah, F. M. (2011). The DESTIN: Preservice teachers' drawings of the ideal elementary science teacher. *School Science and Mathematics, 111*(8), 379–388. doi:10.1111/j.1949-8594.2011.00103.x

Ministry of Education. (2007). *The New Zealand curriculum*. Wellington: Learning Media.

Minogue, J. (2010). What is the teacher doing? What are the students doing? An application of the draw-a-science-teacher-test. *Journal of Science Teacher Education, 21*(7), 767–781. doi:10.1007/s10972-009-9170-7

Olsen, R. (2008). Self-selection bias. In P J. Lavrakas (Ed.), *Encyclopedia of survey research methods* (pp. 809–811). Thousand Oaks, CA: Sage Publications, Inc. doi:http://dx.doi.org/10.4135/9781412963947.n526

Rule, A. C., & Harrell, M. H. (2006). Symbolic drawings reveal changes in preservice teacher mathematics attitudes after a mathematics methods course. *School Science and Mathematics, 106*(6), 241–258. doi:10.1111/j.1949-8594.2006.tb17913.x

Sachs, J. (2005). Teacher education and the development of professional identity: Learning to be a teacher. In P. Denicolo & M. Kompf (Eds.), *Connecting policy and practice: Challenges for teaching and learning in schools and universities* (pp. 5–21). Oxford: Routledge.

Simmons, P. E., Emory, A., Carter, T., Coker, T., Finnegan, B., Crockett, D., Richardson, L., Yager, R., Craven, J., Tillotson, J., Brunkhorst, H., Twiest, M., Hossain, K., Gallagher, J., Duggan-Haas, D., Parker, J., Cajas, F., Alshannag, Q., McGlamery, S., Krockover, J., Adams, P., Spector, B., LaPorta, T., James, B., Rearden, K., & Labuda, K. (1999). Beginning teachers: Beliefs and classroom actions. *Journal of Research in Science Teaching, 36*(8), 930–954. doi:10.1002/(SICI)1098-2736(199910)36:8<930::AID-TEA3>3.0.CO;2-N

Strauss, S. (2001). Folk psychology, folk pedagogy and their relations to subject matter knowledge. In B. Torff & R. J. Sternberg (Eds.), *Understanding and teaching the intuitive mind* (pp. 217–242). Mahwah, NJ: Erlbaum.

Thomas, J., Pedersen, J., & Finson, K. (2001). Validating the Draw-A-Science-Teacher-Test Checklist (DASTT-C): Exploring mental models and teacher beliefs. *Journal of Science Teacher Education, 12*(4), 295–310. doi:10.1023/A:1014216328867

Thomas, J. A., & Pedersen, J. E. (2003). Reforming elementary science teacher preparation: What about extant teaching beliefs? *School Science and Mathematics, 103*(7), 319–330. doi:10.1111/j.1949-8594.2003.tb18209.x

Timperley, H. (2011). *Realizing the power of professional learning.* Maidenhead: McGraw-Hill International.

Timperley, H., Wilson, A., Barrar, H., & Fung, I. (2007). *Best evidence synthesis: Teacher professional development.* Wellington: New Zealand Ministry of Education.

Ucar, S. (2012). How do pre-service science teachers' views on science, scientists, and science teaching change over time in a science teacher training program? *Journal of Science Education and Technology, 21*(2), 255–266. doi:10.1007/s10956-011-9311-6

Varelas, M. (2012). Introduction: Identity research as a tool for developing a feeling for the learner. In M. Varelas (Ed.), *Identity construction and science education research: Learning, teaching, and being in multiple contexts* (pp. 1–6). Rotterdam, The Netherlands: Sense Publishers.

Weber, S., & Mitchell, C. (1996). Drawing ourselves into teaching: Studying the images that shape and distort teacher education. *Teaching and Teacher Education, 12*(3), 303–313. doi:10.1016/0742-051X(95)00040-Q

White, R., & Gunstone, R. (1992). *Probing understanding.* London & New York, NY: The Falmer Press.

Wideen, M., Mayer-Smith, J., & Moon, B. (1998). A critical analysis of the research on learning to teach: making the case for an ecological perspective on inquiry. *Review of Educational Research, 68*(2), 130–178. doi:10.3102/00346543068002130

Williams, J. (2010). Constructing a new professional identity: Career change into teaching. *Teaching and Teacher Education, 26*(3), 639–647. doi:10.1016/j.tate.2009.09.016

David Winter
University of Canterbury, New Zealand

Chris Astall
University of Canterbury, New Zealand

ABOUT THE CONTRIBUTORS

Among the contexts of any work are the people who create it. The contributors to this book are listed below in alphabetical order by last name. While they have all come to use drawings as one method in their teaching or research, they are a widely diverse group from different cultures adding to the reader's ability to compare and perhaps identify with this work.

Sulaiman Al-Balushi is the Dean and an associate professor in science education at College of Education at Sultan Qaboos University (SQU) in Oman. He graduated from the University of Iowa in the USA in 2003. He has published several research papers in local, regional and international refereed academic journals. He has also co-authored different books, textbooks, training books and book chapters. Dr. Al-Balushi has participated in several international conferences around the globe. His research interests focus on science learners' cognitive abilities, mental models of natural entities and phenomena, imagination at the particulate level of matter and their beliefs and evaluation of the scientific models. He has reviewed different research manuscripts, book chapters, grant proposals and promotion applications. creative.electron@gmail.com

Abdullah Ambusaidi is a professor of science education at College of Education at Sultan Qaboos University in Oman. He had his Ph.D from the University of Glasgow in the United Kingdom in 2000. He worked as Assistant Dean for Undergraduate Studies and Head of Curriculum and Instruction Department at the College of Education at Sultan Qaboos University (SQU). Currently he is the Dean of Postgraduate Deanship at SQU. He has published more than 80 research papers in local, regional and international refereed academic journals. He co-authored of three science teaching methods book (in Arabic) and co-authored of seven books chapter in science, environmental and health education in Oman (in English). He has supervised more than 60 master theses and 4 doctoral dissertations. Dr. Ambusaidi has participated in several international conferences and seminars around the globe. His research interests focus on students' alternative conceptions, inquiry based learning, classroom environment, active learning of science and teachers and students beliefs about nature of science. ambusaidi40@hotmail.com

Chris Astall is a senior lecturer in the School of Teacher Education within the College of Education, Health and Human Development at the University of Canterbury. Chris is an experienced primary school teacher and has held leadership positions in schools including Head of Science and Deputy Principal. He has taught in schools in the United Kingdom and New Zealand. He has particular interests in the opportunities for ICT use in science and teacher education; developing sustainable approaches to science professional learning within Primary Schools and the development of attitudes and outcomes in teaching and learning of science with pre-service teachers. He is also part of the team at the Science and Technology Education Research Lab at the University of Canterbury. Chris was introduced to the use of drawings as an approach to exploring pre-service teacher perceptions of science teaching following an inspirational visit by Phyllis Katz to New Zealand in 2011. Email: chris.astall@canterbury.ac.nz

Miri Barak is an Asst. Professor at the Faculty of Education in Science and Technology, Technion- Israel Institute of Technology. She is a Cum Laude graduate of the Faculty of Biotechnology and Food Engineering, and worked in the past as an R&D Engineer. She received her MSc and PhD degrees at the Technion, and was a postdoctoral fellow at the Center for Educational Computing Initiatives (CECI) at MIT – Massachusetts Institute of Technology, US. Currently, she is the Head of the Science and Learning Technologies (SLT) group, promoting 21 century skills and the use of cloud applications in science and engineering education. Her studies examine sociocultural aspects of collaborative learning in large and small groups, self-regulated learning in distance learning, and the promotion of innovative and flexible thinking. She is an expert in the development and evaluation of educational programs and web-based projects. She is leading an international project on MOOCs- massive online open courses and a project on flipped classrooms. Her academic work is presented in peer-reviewed papers and book chapters in leading international and national publications. email: bmiriam@technion.ac.il URL: http://barakmiri.net.technion.ac.il

Amauri Betini Bartoszeck is an Associate Professor of Physiology and Neuroscience, the University of Paraná (Federal) Curitiba, PR Brazil. Mr. Bartoszeck received his Bachelor of Science in Natural History and Master of Science in Biological Sciences (Entomology) from the University of Paraná and fellowships from ECFMG, US, and Society of Biology, FSB UK. Currently he conducts research in the laboratory of Cellular Metabolisn, Educational Neuroscience and Emergent Science Education, especially in the early years as well as neurophysiology of invertebrates at the University of Paraná, Brazil. abbartoszeck@gmail.com.

Rob Bowker is the Director of the PGCE Primary Programme and a senior lecturer in science at the University of Exeter, Graduate School of Education. He is particularly interested in teaching and children's learning within informal learning environments. Email: r.bowker@exeter.ac.uk

ABOUT THE CONTRIBUTORS

Jill Cainey is a research scientist with over 20 years of experience in atmospheric science and climate change, in the UK, Australia and New Zealand. She works in the electricity industry and has a strong interest in technologies that mitigate climate change, especially in sustainable approaches to energy systems. She is particularly interested in communicating science and the teaching of science, and enjoys working with children and adults in informal settings and outside the classroom, to promote careers in science and engagement with the natural environment. Jill.cainey@csiro.au

Ni Chang is a full professor of early childhood education at Indiana University South Bend. Inspired by the research work of her advisor at Peabody College of Vanderbilt University and by the Reggio Emilia approach to early childhood education, she began her own journey of research in 1994 focusing on roles that children's drawings play in the teaching and learning of young children. Her research findings have consistently pointed to the importance of incorporating children's drawings in early curriculums. In the past 21 years, she has been devoting her time and effort to promoting research results via publications, conferences, and workshops. In addition, she has worked on increasing the awareness of the use of drawings with pre-service teachers. This book chapter represents some of her research work, in the hope of benefitting readers, but also stimulating promising conversations for the well-being of young children. nchang@iusb.edu

Amy Dai received her B.S. degree in plant pathology from National Taiwan University, Taipei, Taiwan in 1997. She received her M.S. from Ohio State University in 2001 and her Ph.D. from the University of Maryland (UMD), College Park in 2011. During her doctoral studies, she worked on Project Nexus with Dr. J. Randy McGinnis at UMD. The project adopted drawing as one of the means to understand teachers' thoughts about science teaching and learning. As a result, she applied drawing as a probe to understand children's conceptions of nature as in this chapter. After her studies, Dr. Dai worked in the Department of Education at the Taipei Zoo, Taiwan, to implement her ideas for informal science education. Animal conservation and children have been the two interest tat Dr. Dai is pursuing. As this book is published, she has been a full-time mother practicing her educational belief and theories with her own children. As her two girls grow, she has witnessed how young children express themselves and observe the world by drawing. She can be reached via email at amydai215@yahoo.com

Edith Dempster is currently a Senior Research Associate at the University of KwaZulu-Natal in Pietermaritzburg, South Africa, an independent education consultant, and a textbook author. She has a Ph D in Zoology, specialising in Animal Behaviour. Her research investigated mechanisms whereby closely-related rodent species maintain reproductive isolation. She started working in science teacher education in 1993, specialising in Biology teacher education. She has published several papers in science education, and been involved in curriculum policy developments in South Africa since 2001. One of her research interests focuses on language in science education in a multilingual environment, hence the use of drawings to elicit children's understandings without the barrier of language competence. Together with her postgraduate students, she has investigated the professional development of Biology teachers, the historical development of Biology school curriculum, and the impact of a Foundation year on students' progress into a degree in the sciences at university level. DempsterE@ukzn.ac.za

Michael W. Dentzau is science education faculty in the College of Education and Health Professions at Columbus State University, and the Executive Director of Oxbow Meadows Environmental Learning Center. Oxbow Meadows is an academic enrichment center that is jointly sponsored by the University and Columbus Water Works, the regional water and wastewater utility in Columbus, Georgia. Michael's research interests focus on ecological and environmental meaning making of individuals while experiencing informal science experiences. Drawings have been used in several contexts to gauge learners' alternative conceptions, mental model development, environmental interest and emerging association with the natural world. The importance of place to the individual learner figures prominently into the conceptual framework that supports these research interests. mwd09c@my.fsu.edu

Donna Farland-Smith is an Associate Professor of Science Education in The School of Teaching & Learning at The Ohio State University. She previously taught science all grades K-12. She was the Founder and Director of the Side-by-Side with Scientists Camp at OSU-M which served over 350 girls in the local community. Her research at the camp focused on middle school girls' attitudes and perceptions of scientists who as they work 'side-by-side' with scientists as well as the characteristics of scientists that most positively affect the girl's perception of scientists. Dr. Farland-Smith is also the Founder of The Little Buckeye Children's Museum which is a stimulating and fun place for families of all kinds to enjoy playing and learning together. It has reached out to all members of the community through educational programs for teachers and students and strives to serve children who might otherwise miss such important opportunities for constructive play. The museum was built in 2010 and currently has over 100 sponsors and over 30 exhibits. Farlandsmith@aol.com

Robin Fleshman is a doctoral candidate in the science education program at Teachers College, Columbia University in New York City, USA. Using a critical race theory lens, my dissertation research focuses on particular assessment practices in urban secondary science education and how that pertains to college readiness. In addition, I look at assessment practices, and using drawings as embedded

ABOUT THE CONTRIBUTORS

formative and/or summative assessments to measure students' scientific understanding and reasoning can furnish or support evidence of student growth. ref2134@tc.columbia.edu

Emily Hestness is a doctoral student in the Center for Science and Technology in Education at the University of Maryland. Her interests include climate change education, citizen science, curriculum design, and socioscientific issues education. As an environmental educator and science teacher educator, she has worked with learners of all ages in formal and informal science learning contexts. She was introduced to drawing as a research methodology during her work as a graduate research assistant on Project Nexus (www.drawntoscience.org), a National Science Foundation project that examined the preparation of elementary teacher candidates through the blending of formal and informal science education. She is currently using drawings in her dissertation work examining middle school students' identity development and agency in relation to the topic of climate change.

Martin Hopf studied mathematics and physics and worked for several years as a high school teacher. Afterwards he joined the physics education research group at the University of Munich and earned his PhD in 2007. In 2008 he was appointed as professor for physics education research at the Austrian Educational Competence Centre Physics at the University of Vienna. His main research interests are educational reconstruction of Physics, students' competencies and pedagogical content knowledge of student teachers. He is married and the father of two daughters. Martin.hopf@univie.ac.at

Lauren Humphrey is the Lead Evaluator and Project Manager for the National Marine Aquarium, Plymouth. She has developed, managed and delivered the Conservation through Tourism Award project, which combines elements of marine biology as well as evaluation. Email: lauren.humphrey@national-aquarium.co.uk

Phyllis Katz was the founding Executive Director of Hands On Science Outreach (HOSO), an afterschool science enrichment program that grew nationally with NSF awards. She earned a doctorate in science education from the University of Maryland. She has written science books for children and articles for adults on science teaching and learning. She worked on the Advisory Board for the Magic School Bus TV series. Dr. Katz is currently a Research Associate at the University of Maryland and was part of the Project Nexus team exploring the influence of an internship in the afterschool program on elementary teacher candidates, using drawings as one data source. She has been an active advocate for informal science education (which she prefers to call CSL—continual science learning) at NSTA and NARST. She has presented at many conferences and remains active in creating materials to promote science education. Since the 1990s, she has done research using both drawings and photographs to stimulate and interpret science learning. Contact: pkatz15@gmail.com

Shiellah Toro Keletso is a graduate of the University of Botswana with a Bachelor of Education (Special Education). Since beginning to teach science in 2007, she has met many students of different abilities; has participated in varied styles of school management practices; and has witnessed the plight of the education system. Having resolved to find answers to some of the challenges with the teaching and learning of science, she has tried unorthodox methods in the classroom. Mrs Keletso has exploited the old adage that a picture is worth a thousand words to inspire her students. A firm believer in clear communication between the teacher and students , Sheillah promotes inquiry and engages in reflective practice. This has led her and her students to explore the teaching and learning process together. Her essay bears witness to the challenges, pleasant and unpleasant 'discoveries', and unexplored learning and teaching methods that this work-in-progress has revealed. Mrs. Keletso believes that her passion for her work with children, teachers, and curriculum development supports her goal of sharing research-based and relevant information that will help teachers expand tools to deliver even better science. She practices at home with her three inquisitive children. angelface.shiellah9@gmail.com

Terence McClafferty began his career as a science teacher in outback Australia and later developed and delivered science programs to students with Australia's principal scientific organisation, CSIRO, and the Australian Science Teachers Association. He completed graduate studies at Curtin University and Florida State University, and in 1998 joined the Western Australian Museum to establish its Discovery Centre in Perth, Western Australia. Working with families and children visiting interactive galleries he developed an interest in what these groups were learning. The annotation of drawings provided a way to research visitors' learning, including young children and non-English speakers. Importantly, it provided evidence to science center management on the achievement of exhibits' learning outcomes. Currently he is delivering extension programs at Charles Darwin University targeting high school students as a way to improve students' attitude to undertake higher education. terry.mcclafferty@gmail.com

J. Randy McGinnis is Professor of Science Education and Director of the Center for Science and Technology in Education in the Department of Teaching and Learning, Policy, and Leadership at the University of Maryland, USA. His teaching practice as a science educator for 35 years includes elementary – Oregon and Georgia, middle level – Swaziland, Africa, and high school – Bronx, NYC, and higher education – University of Georgia and University of Maryland. Randy consistently has been an advocate and proponent of innovation and creativity in science education research, curriculum, instruction, and assessment. In his 2012 NARST Presidential

265

ABOUT THE CONTRIBUTORS

Address ("Re-imagining Research in Science Education for a Diverse Global Community") he used student generated drawing to support his argument for innovation. Randy's research interests include science teacher professional development across multiple disciplinary areas and topics including climate change education and exceptional learners in science. jmcginni@umd.edu

Felicia Moore Mensah, Ph.D. is professor of science education and the program coordinator of the science education program at Teachers College, Columbia University in New York City, USA. Since receiving my doctoral degree, I have published extensively in the area of science teacher education. My research interests are equity, diversity and social justice education with an emphasis on improving science experiences for PreK-16 teachers and students in urban classrooms. I have used drawings in my teacher education courses for access in thinking about science teaching and identity in a non-threatening way. Drawing reveals stories that can be shared for conversations about identity and science education. fm2140@tc.columbia.edu

Susanne Neumann studied physics and mathematics at the University of Vienna and earned her PhD in science education research at the Austrian Educational Competence Centre Physics (University of Vienna). Her PhD research focused on students' misconceptions in the field of radiation. Susanne Neumann has been teaching physics in an Austrian secondary school for 12 years. She also works in the field of teacher pre- and in-service training. She is married and has one daughter. susanne.neumann@univie.ac.at

Sinan Özgelen is currently an Associate Professor at the department of elementary science education at Mersin University in Turkey. He has many articles in indexed journals about science education and he serves as a reviewer as well. In addition, he participates in international science education conferences (NARST, AERA, and ESERA) as a member. He was one of the writers of the National Elementary Science book for 5th grade. His research interests include students' and teachers' views about nature of science, inquiry-based instructions, scientific literacy, and history-philosophy of science. Currently, he is the co-chair of the Institute of Educational Sciences at Mersin University. E-mail: sinanozgelen@mersin.edu.tr

Patricia Patrick is a professor of Informal Science Education at Texas Tech University. In cooperation with the Houston Zoo, I have developed a Masters of Education in Curriculum and Instruction for Informal Science Education. I began to utilize drawings in my research approximately 8 years ago. My sister, who is an artist and middle grades art teacher, wanted to integrate science into her art classes. We began with using photography and published a short article about our experiences. Later we incorporated drawings as a way to define students' knowledge of scientific concepts (digestion, water cycle, etc.) and science places (zoos, aquariums, etc.). Please contact me at trish.patrick.ise@gmail.com

Jeremy Price is an Assistant Professor of Technology, Innovation and Pedagogy in Urban Education at Indiana University School of Education in Indianapolis, Indiana. Dr. Price teaches undergraduate and graduate courses in educational technology, STEM and STEAM topics, curriculum design, and social-emotional approaches to teaching and learning. He engages in research on meaningful engagement by PK-12 students in STEM learning environments, supporting teacher reflection, and exploring teachers' intentional social networks. Dr. Price was introduced to the use of drawings in education through a qualitative research course he completed in graduate school, and he quickly appreciated the ability of hand-drawn pictures to provide research participants and students with the opportunity to express themselves in a direct and creative manner. He uses participant-drawn illustrations in most of his research efforts and many of his courses. jfprice@iupui.edu

Léonie Rennie is Emeritus Professor in Science and Technology Education at Curtin University. Her research interests include learning science and technology particularly in out-of-school settings and she authored the definitive chapter on learning science outside of school in the first and second editions of the Handbook of Research in Science Education. Her scholarly publications include over 200 refereed journal articles, book chapters and monographs, most recently co-author of Knowledge that Counts in a Global Community: Exploring the Contribution of Integrated Curriculum (Routledge) and co-edited Integrating science, technology, engineering, and mathematics: Issues, reflections and ways forward (Taylor & Francis). In 2009, she received the Distinguished Contributions to Science Education Through Research Award from the US-based National Association for Research in Science Teaching. L.Rennie@curtin.edu.au

Katrina Roseler taught 7th grade life science for 10 years and identifies herself as a middle school science teacher. Her interest in drawings developed as a result of her enthusiasm for free choice learning experiences and the impacts they have on the development of personal science knowledge and possible science identity. Her dissertation research used drawings as data to identify undergraduate experiences with science in and out of school environments. As a science educator, Katrina is focused on tapping into experiences that engage all learners to explore the natural world through the lens of science. She views free choice learning experiences, such as sports and cooking, as platforms for the development of scientific questions about the world. Using free choice learning opportunities utilizes personal investments to enhance student learning experiences and Katrina is dedicated in this outcome. Her research interests have also included investigating the impact of Research Experience for Teacher's (RET's) on the implementation of classroom inquiry practices

266

and STEM faculty professional development; specifically how to promote the adoption of engaging student-centered instructional practices at the post-secondary level. Contact Katrina at Chaminade University of Honolulu, katrinaroseler@gmail.com

Angshuman Sarker is a teacher in the school at Shishu Polli Plus, (Sreepur Village), Tengra, Gazipur in Bangladesh where he is also the CASTME project, Mothers Talking Everyday Science, facilitator. He completed honours and masters degrees in soil science from Khulna University in Bangladesh . Recently he completed two other masters degrees in public health from the American International University of Bangladesh. angshuman.bd@gmail.com

Michèle Stears is currently a Senior Research Associate at the University of KwaZulu-Natal in Durban, South Africa and involved in the professional practice of undergraduate students. She has a D.Ed in Science Education. Her research for this study investigated the meaning of relevant science in different contexts. She started working in teacher education in 1984 at a College of Education where her main focus was teaching. In 2002 she joined the University in KwaZulu-Natal as biology education specialist. She has published several papers in science education. Her research interests focus on curriculum, experiential education, environmental education and assessment strategies, hence my involvement in the use of drawings as a tool to assess learners' understanding of science. Her postgraduate students and she have investigated the implementation of new curricula in developing countries as well as formal environmental learning. Stearsm@ukzn.ac.za

Sue Dale Tunnicliffe, Ph.D., is at the Institute of Education, University College, London, in the UK. She has done research and writing on science education in zoos, museum dioramas, and classrooms. She has been interested in family talk around museum visits, and the development of children's anatomy knowledge. Her research has focused on young children and she was instrumental in the development of The Journal of Emergent Science, aimed at those who teach the youngest students. Dr. Tunnicliffe travels widely to share her research and participate in teacher education. She has a keen interest in the underserved and has worked in Bangladesh, Mauritius, and Brazil among other locations. Dr. Tunnicliffe received the National Science Teachers Association Faraday Award in science communication in 2016. lady.tunnicliffe@mac.com

Jatila van der Veen, Ph.D., is a Project Scientist in the Experimental Cosmology Group, Department of Physics, University of California, Santa Barbara. Her current research focuses on how people learn physics and astronomy through non-traditional methods of arts-based science and math teaching and immersive virtual reality simulations. She is currently the Project Manager for Education and Public Outreach for the NASA side of the joint ESA/NASA Planck Mission, and has led the efforts to develop educational materials for college level and museum displays. She is also a continuing Lecturer in the College of Creative Studies at UC Santa Barbara, and Adjunct Professor of Astronomy at Santa Barbara City College. Jatila has also been a professional dancer for most of her life, thus learning physics through the arts comes naturally for her. Currently, in her spare time she practices Afro-Brazilian, Middle Eastern, hip-hop, and International Latin ballroom styles, and in the summers teaches physics through dance at Notre Dame University's Art 2 Science camp. websites: www.web.physics.ucsb.edu/~jatila and www.planck.caltech.edu/epo/epo-team.html

Gary Wind is Professor of Surgery with a joint appointment in anatomy at the Uniformed Services University of the Health Sciences. He also is a staff surgeon at Walter Reed National Military Medical Center. He is director of an intensive postgraduate microvascular surgery course. He is a self-taught artist, sculptor and medical illustrator. Dr. Wind has written and illustrated five medical texts and has produced an award-winning surgical educational website. His medical texts have been translated into multiple languages and second and third editions have been published. Dr. Wind's non-medical art is concentrated on human and animal figurative sculpture. gwind@vesalius.com

David Winter lectures in Science Education in the College of Education, Health and Human Development at the University of Canterbury. He has a background in forensic science and teaching science to secondary school and tertiary level students. His research interests include the use of ICT to enhance science teaching and learning and laboratory safety practices and regulation. His most recent work focuses on the use of drawings as a tool to investigate student perceptions about teaching and learning processes. He is part of the team at the Science and Technology Education Research Lab at the University of Canterbury. Email: david.winter@canterbury.ac.nz

INDEX

A

Accessibility through drawing, 1, 6, 87, 106
Action research, viii, 227–232
Advantages of drawing, 1, 87, 112, 113, 147, 180
African rock art, 2
Analyses, drawings, 32, 90, 91, 240, 242
Anatomical drawings, 5
Aquarium drawings, 97–101, 103, 106
Assessments and drawing, 11–28, 44, 97–104, 108, 130, 144, 172
Australia, museum sound exhibit, 155
Australian rock art, 1
Austria, 6, 114, 115, 121n2, n5, n6

B

Bangladesh, anatomy concepts by mothers, 87–93
Botswana, teacher action research, viii, 7, 227–232
Brain research and drawing, 43, 46, 89, 150–153, 207, 230
Brazil, young children and anatomy, 55, 62

C

Climate change, 7, 42, 97, 212, 235–244, 244n1
Conservation and drawing, 97–108
Contextual model of learning, 6, 77, 123–133

D

Democracy and drawing, 1 ,8, 228
DESTIN, (Drawing-the-Elementary-Science-Teacher-Ideal-Not), 219–225
Draw-A-Scientist Test (DAST), 4–7, 32, 171–177, 191, 219, 224, 248
Drawing history, 5, 6
Drawing prompts, 4, 21, 32, 77, 79, 82, 125, 128, 132, 171, 229, 237, 240, 241, 243, 248–251, 255–258

E

Early childhood drawings, 73–85, 135–145
Efficiency of images, 5, 6, 131, 133, 220, 221, 223
Einstein, 12–25, 113, 198, 200
Elementary age students, 13, 39, 58, 59, 74–77, 83, 191, 192, 201
Evidence, vii, 1–6, 11, 32, 41, 55, 56, 83, 92, 104, 106, 107, 124–126, 130–132, 138, 171, 200, 206, 207, 214, 224, 228, 229, 237, 238, 240, 243, 247, 248

F

Fukushima, 6, 118, 120, 121

H

High school, 6, 7, 20, 21, 49, 71, 75, 191, 192, 205, 206, 220, 227, 236, 247–260

I

Identity and drawing, 7, 219–224, 247–260
Inference in drawing interpretations, 2, 4, 173, 188
Information and communication technologies (ICT's), 5, 31–36
Integrated curriculum, 6, 140, 143, 144
Israel, 5, 35

M

Mauritius, 6, 97, 104–107
Medical drawings, 51, 67–71
Memory and drawing, 3, 5, 32, 87, 98, 254
Mental models and drawing, 3, 6, 55, 58, 59, 87, 235, 237
Methods, drawings, 4, 82, 112, 115, 244
Mixed methodologies, 201
Moral reasoning, 7, 235–244
Museums and drawing research, 123, 128, 155

N

Nature, children's concepts, 6, 56, 73–85
New Zealand teacher education, 7

O

Ochre as early drawing pigment, 2
Oman, 181, 188

P

Parks, 2, 62, 75, 79, 80, 84, 85, 87, 105, 123, 133, 206, 224
Physics of sound, 6, 155–167
Preference for drawing, 14, 57, 180
Pre-service teachers, 5–7, 32, 41–45, 63, 135, 179, 181, 183, 192, 247
Prior knowledge, drawing evidence, 99, 103, 104, 125, 130
Prompts in drawing, 4, 21, 32, 77, 171, 237, 249–251
Prospective teachers, 7, 180, 181, 183–185, 187, 188, 235–244, 247

R

Radiation, 6, 112, 113, 115, 117–120, 121n5, 239
Rock art, 2, 56

S

Scientists, 2, 4, 7, 11–13, 17, 21, 23, 32, 33, 98, 105, 112, 115, 116, 144, 171–177, 180, 191–201, 205, 207, 209–212, 214, 219, 220, 224
Secondary school students, 55, 149
Sound, visitors learning from exhibit, 155–167
South Africa, 2, 6, 89, 147–149, 151, 153, 227

T

Taiwan, children and nature, 6, 73, 76, 84
Teacher education, viii, 32, 43, 149, 184, 219–224, 235, 237, 241, 244

INDEX

Teacher preparation and drawing, vii, 6, 7
Technology and drawing, 1, 99
Theory for drawing, 56, 57
Theory of mind, 3
Turkey, 7, 89, 192, 199–201

U
UK, 6, 84, 89, 97
United States, 11, 43, 70, 73, 74, 83, 124, 176, 177, 191, 205, 212
   California, 11–29, 205–215
   Florida, 6, 125, 126
   Indiana, 135–145

   Maryland, vii, 7, 27, 227, 235–245
   New York, 219–225
   North Carolina, 41–59

V
Video narratives to enhance drawing data, 7, 252
Visitors to museums, 49, 57, 129
Visual data, vii, 2, 176, 207, 212
Visual thinking, 5, 12, 13

Y
Young children, 1, 6, 39, 55, 56, 60, 61, 63, 73–76, 84, 87, 88, 135, 136, 139–144, 148, 177, 224

CPSIA information can be obtained
at www.ICGtesting.com
Printed in the USA
LVOW02s1453190117
521536LV00005B/29/P